GOVERNMENT ENTERPRISE

GOVERNMENT ENTERPRISE
A COMPARATIVE STUDY

Edited by

W. G. FRIEDMANN, DR. JUR., LL.D.,

Barrister-at-Law
Professor of International Law and Director of International
Legal Research, Columbia University

and

J. F. GARNER, LL.D.,

Solicitor of the Supreme Court
Professor of Public Law, University of Nottingham

Published under the auspices of

The British Institute of International and Comparative Law
The United Kingdom National Committee of Comparative Law
and
The International Legal Research Program
of Columbia University

NEW YORK
COLUMBIA UNIVERSITY PRESS
1970

Published in Great Britain in 1970 by Stevens & Sons Limited
Printed in Great Britain

FOREWORD

THE *causa causans* of the present volume may perhaps be found in the Colloquium on the theme of Public Corporations organised by the United Kingdom Committee on Comparative Law in Cambridge in 1968. It had, in any event, been hoped to publish the proceedings, and in the course of debate the suggestion emerged, with which happily Professor Friedmann agreed, that it might be possible to combine in some form the publication of these papers with a new edition of the book on the same theme which he had edited in 1954—inevitably there would be some overlap with that; hence the present volume. Thanks are due to all those, authors, editors, publishers, institutions, who have made the conjunction possible. In that conjunction the weight of new material is evident.

Underlying the proposal to hold a colloquium on this subject was a belief in the practical value of comparative study. Shared problems may sometimes find solutions more easily than those that are regarded as peculiar, and it was fortunate that the colloquium could be held so soon after the Select Committee had reported on Ministerial Control of Nationalised Industries. That report had, at least, brought into the light some of the realities of the British situation, even if it did not do much else. Among these practical purposes was the hope that attention might be drawn to movement since 1954, and that material would emerge which could be the starting-point for some fresh thought about government enterprise. There is the contrast between the use of public corporations in East Africa, and in the older "under-developed" areas in Italy or in Scotland. Even more important is the clear indication which has emerged that the problems are by no means exhausted by those of the classical form of nationalized industries. Rather the major questions arise in the context of governmental holding companies and of governmental shareholdings in "private" companies. When such mixed enterprises take on, as increasingly the major ones tend to do, an international character, the problems mount. Issues of different styles of control, issues of different systems of law are only two of the many complicating factors. It is evident that the form of public enterprise will become of increasing importance if the philosophy (which may in origin have been Italian) that it is the function of public enterprises not to prop up decaying industries but rather to promote those which are at the fringes of evolution, becomes generally accepted. There are signs that this is about to happen.

To these problems the colloquium could, on its time-scale and with its planning and organisational resources stretching the parent committee's

vi FOREWORD

traditional shoestring to its limit, offer no solution. It hoped to evoke new anxieties and to produce a few more insights into the way others were facing the modern problems of public enterprise. The full exploration remains to be done and is urgent as the following papers show.

J. D. B. MITCHELL*

* Salvesen Professor of European Institutions, University of Edinburgh, Scotland.

PREFACE

THE present volume, which is the fifth in the series of *British Institute Studies in International and Comparative Law*, is based on the work of a colloquium which was held at the University of Cambridge in September 1968 and organised by the United Kingdom National Committee of Comparative Law, with the assistance of the British Institute of International and Comparative Law. The colloquium was under the direction of Professors Wolfgang Friedmann and J. F. Garner, and the British Institute takes this opportunity of expressing its gratitude to them for their collaboration in preparing and revising the colloquium materials for publication.

The British Institute acknowledges its indebtedness to the work of all the contributors to the colloquium, to the officers and members of the United Kingdom National Committee and to the International Legal Research Project of the Columbia University who have each played a valuable part in this enterprise.

We also acknowledge with gratitude the kindness of Professor J. D. B. Mitchell, who was Chairman of the United Kingdom National Committee of Comparative Law at the time of the colloquium, in writing a Foreword.

K. R. SIMMONDS
Director

The British Institute of International
and Comparative Law,
32, Furnival Street,
London, E.C.4.

ACKNOWLEDGMENTS

THE Editors in presenting this book to the public wish to express their thanks to:

The British Institute of International and Comparative Law, the United Kingdom National Committee of Comparative Law and Columbia University, for sponsoring the book.

The University of Toronto for agreeing so readily to the use of some of the material (revised) that appeared in *Public Corporations*, published by Toronto in 1954 under the editorship of Professor W. Friedmann.

Professor J. D. B. Mitchell of the University of Edinburgh for writing the Foreword, and as Chairman of the Cambridge Colloquium that preceded the preparation of this book.

The Editors and publishers of *Political Quarterly* for agreeing to the inclusion of Professor Robson's materials. The contributors, for working against pressure but—we think—to such good effect.

W.F.
J.F.G.

CONTENTS

PART III. OTHER COUNTRIES

PART IV. CONCLUSIONS

Part I
The United Kingdom

CHAPTER I

PUBLIC CORPORATIONS
IN THE UNITED KINGDOM*

1. INTRODUCTION

UNTIL very recently Government enterprise in the United Kingdom has almost invariably taken the form of the public corporation, but at the present time expansion in the scale of Government capital investment in joint stock companies seems to be growing in popularity in Whitehall. As will appear from later chapters in this book, the pathway towards this new form of Governmental management over vital industrial and commercial undertakings has been blazed by several continental countries, in particular by Italy,[1] and more recently by France[2]; but the United Kingdom is now rapidly catching up in this process.[3] The idea of the "mixed enterprise," whereby the Government acquires a majority or a minority holding or even the whole of the shares, in an undertaking which remains juristically a "private" company,[4] will not be further discussed in this Introduction, as this topic is left for elaboration in the chapter by Mr. Daintith.[5]

Here it is proposed to discuss the chronologically older concept of the public corporation "properly so called," which has been a feature of the "nationalisation" statutes in this country of the 1940's—the Morrisonian concept described by Mr. Drake in Chapter 4.[6] The concept is, however, by no means moribund; the National Coal Board, the Gas and Electricity Boards, and British Railways are examples of the importance of the public corporation in the modern economy, and the recent measures converting the centuries-old Post Office into a new public corporation, and creating Passenger Transport Authorities by the Transport Act 1968, demonstrate that the device is still popular with the United Kingdom legislature. It must not be overlooked, however, that in Britain public corporations may be concerned with functions other than the operation of a nationalised industry. In addition there are many corporations which can only be described as having regulatory

---

* By Professor J. F. Garner, University of Nottingham.
1. See Chap. 8, *post*, p. 133.
2. Chap. 6, *post*, p. 107.
3. See Chap. 3, *post*, p. 53. That the U.K. has not been entirely devoid of the public law joint stock enterprise is to be seen in the Bank of England, chartered in 1694.
4. As contrasted with a public corporation, although in the sense of the English Companies Acts, it may well be a "public" company.
5. Chap. 3, *post*, p. 53.
6. *Post*, p. 26.

3

functions; in other instances it is difficult to distinguish them from specialised Departments of State. It is therefore proposed in this chapter to describe the different varieties of public corporations as they exist in the United Kingdom at the present time, then to explain the legal and administrative machinery, in so far as there is any common pattern; the subject of controls over these corporations is left for discussion in the chapter by Mr. Drake.[7]

2. A CLASSIFICATION OF PUBLIC CORPORATIONS

First it may be considered desirable within the context of the law of the United Kingdom[8] to attempt a definition of the expression "public corporation." Canada is perhaps the only common law jurisdiction that has classified public corporations in any authoritative manner by statute, for certain limited purposes;[9] but in the United Kingdom a statutory definition has never been found to be necessary, no doubt because no legal consequence would follow from such a definition. Britain knows no truly federal constitution,[10] and it has therefore never been necessary to allocate the creation or control of "public corporations" either to the federal or to a lesser legislature, and, unlike civil law countries, there is no clear cleavage between public law and private law, such as may make it necessary to allocate public corporations to one or other branch of the *corpus juris*.[11] In consequence there has never been any statutory interpretation of the expression, nor has it ever had to be considered by the courts, although closely related terms such as "public authority" or public body"[12] have had to be so considered.

Nevertheless, we should be able to recognise a public corporation when we see one; it has become an important "third arm" of Government in addition to the traditional instruments of the central executive and local authorities, and the public corporation should be clearly distinguishable from its older rivals in the bid for power in the State. It may therefore be appropriate to define a public corporation in this country as a legal entity established normally by Parliament[13] and always by legal authority (usually in the form of a special

7. *Ibid.*, especially at p. 30.
8. Technically the United Kingdom includes four distinct legal systems (England and Wales, Scotland, Northern Ireland and the Isle of Man), but there are only a few relevant differences between the four systems in so far as the subject-matter of this chapter is concerned.
9. See the chapter by Professor Friedmann, *post*, p. 303.
10. It can be argued that the separation of legislative powers as between the Parliaments of Great Britain and Northern Ireland constitutes a federal structure, but this is much less elaborate than the detailed provisions of the standard federations such as USA and the Commonwealth of Australia.
11. Chap. 6 shows how the French lawyers have been compelled to reach a compromise on this topic.
12. See Sect. 4, *post*, p. 10.
13. But sometimes by a Minister under statutory authority, or by the Royal Prerogative; see *post*, p. 9.

statute[14]) charged with the duty of carrying out specified Governmental functions (more or less precisely defined[15]) in the national interest,[16] those functions being confined to a comparatively restricted field,[17] and subjected to some degree of control by the executive,[18] while the corporation remains juristically an independent entity not directly responsible to Parliament. It is a "person" in law,[19] possessing but rarely any of the privileges of the Crown, and subject to the ordinary rules of the law in such matters as contractual and tortious liability, and being liable to State or local taxation[20]; as there is no separate system of administrative law in the United Kingdom and the courts regard Governmental "persons" (with the sole exception of the Crown itself[21]) in the same manner as they do any other person, public corporations are not in practice often given any special procedural or other legal privileges. On the other hand, owing to the doctrine of parliamentary sovereignty, the legislature in these islands may give to a particular corporation—or to corporations of a specified class—or classes—as many powers and privileges, and submit it to as many special rules, as Parliament sees fit[22]; the legislature is restricted neither by a written constitution on the pattern of the United States, nor will

14. But not always; the statute may authorise a Minister to establish such corporations as he may see fit, in certain specified circumstances (see, *e.g.* the joint planning boards that may be created under s. 3 of the Town and Country Planning Act 1962). The Location of Offices Bureau was created by statutory instrument (S.I. 1963 No. 792), made by the Privy Council under authority conferred by s. 8 (2) of the Minister of Town and Country Planning Act 1943.

15. Sometimes these will be expressed in the widest possible general terms.

16. Often exercisable over the whole country (*e.g.* the Atomic Energy Authority), but not necessarily so, as in the case of the gas, electricity and regional hospital boards.

17. For example gas or electricity distribution; this feature differentiates the *ad hoc* public corporations from local authorities which, apart from other characteristics, invariably possess a number of different functions, often unrelated to one another, except in that they are exercisable only over the authority's area.

18. This will vary considerably between different public corporations; see Sect. 5, below.

19. It therefore can sue and be sued in its own name in the courts, it is liable to criminal prosecution if it (as distinct from its servants, a point on which special statutory provision is often made) commits a crime, it can express its will by means of a common seal, it has perpetual succession, and, before the need for this was abolished by the Charities Act 1960, it was customary to provide in the enabling statute that a public corporation had power to hold land in mortmain without the need to obtain a licence from the Crown.

20. Only the Crown and emanations of the Crown are immune from liability to central taxation; the Independent Television Authority (for example) cannot claim such immunity (see Television Act 1954, s. 1 (12), nor can the British Broadcasting Corporation, although this body was created by Royal Charter (see *BBC* v. *Johns* [1965] Ch. 32). Electricity boards, gas boards, the British Railways Board, the Post Office and water undertakings are all exempted by statute from liability to pay rates in the ordinary sense, but they are required to make commensurate contributions to the rates as if their premises had been rateable (Rating and Valuation Act 1961; Post Office Act 1969, s. 51). Crown premises are exempt from rates, but the Treasury makes *ex gratia* contributions to local authorities in lieu of rates on the same basis.

21. The privileges of the Crown itself in litigation are not as great as they were, since the Crown Proceedings Act 1947; see also *Conway* v. *Rimmer* [1968] 2 All E.R. 304.

22. Originally the gas and electricity boards enjoyed a specially short period of limitation in respect of civil actions brought against them, but as Parliament can give, so it can take away, and these special periods were abolished by the Law Reform (Limitation of Actions, etc.) Act 1954.

the courts apply in the administrative sphere any "general principles of law," similar to those applied by the French administrative courts.

We turn now to our attempted classification of public corporations in the United Kingdom. This division of what is really a heterogeneous list is not of any precise legal significance, but it may help to describe the function of the public corporation in Britain; the groups are also unequal in size and perhaps not precisely arranged in content.

(1) Commercial undertakings

Commercial undertakings, or the nationalised industries, owing their origins, for the most part, to the "nationalisation" statutes of the years immediately after the Second World War. In this group are to be found the following:

(i) *Broadcasting and communications*
The British Broadcasting Corporation established by Royal Charter in 1927; the Independent Television Authority established by the Television Acts of 1954 and 1964; and the Post Office, which became a public corporation under the Post Office Act 1969.

(ii) *Fuel and power*
The National Coal Board (Coal Industry (Nationalisation) Act 1946); the Central Electricity Council and the twelve area electricity boards[23] (Electricity Acts 1947 and 1957); the Gas Council and the twelve area gas boards (Gas Act 1948); and the Atomic Energy Authority (Atomic Energy Authority Act 1954).

(iii) *Transport*
The British Railways Board,[24] the London Transport Board, the British Transport Docks Board, and the British Waterways Board, all constituted under the Transport Act 1962[25]; the British Airports Authority, established by the Airports Authority Act 1965 to manage the airports at Heathrow, Gatwick, Stansted and Prestwick; and the British Overseas Airways Corporation and the British European Airways Corporation, both established under the Air Corporations Act 1949. In this group also should be placed the Transport Holding Company[26] established by the Transport Act 1962 but dissolved by the Transport Act 1968, after having been given slightly extended powers in

---

23. Plus two boards in Scotland; see Electricity Acts 1947 and 1957.
24. Replacing the former British Transport Commission.
25. See s. 2 thereof.
26. This special corporation, expressly required to hold and manage these securities in public transport companies as if it were "a company engaged in a commercial enterprise" (see Transport Act 1962, s. 29) is the nearest parallel known in this country to the ENI and IRI of Italy (see Chap. 8, *post*, p. 133); powers are given by s. 53 of the Transport Act 1968 for its dissolution by Ministerial order. However, the Railways Executive, the National Freight Corporation (concerned with the carriage of goods by road) and the National Bus Company, will in future each be required to carry on their activities "as if they were a company engaged in a commercial enterprise": Transport Act 1968, s. 134.

1968.[27] This body was formed to hold Government shares in public transport companies, originally owned for the most part by the former railway companies and acquired by the State on nationalisation of the railways in 1947. The National Freight Corporation, the National Bus Company and the passenger transport executives and passenger transport authorities established under the Transport Act 1968 may also fall within this sub-group.

(2) Managerial bodies responsible for the administration of a public service

Here the profit motive is virtually non-existent, although the "consumer" may be required to pay for some services provided, such as private beds in national service hospitals. Some corporations in this group, although legally independent persons, may in practice be scarcely distinguishable from central government departments; this is particularly true of the regional hospital boards which are required to carry on their functions "for and on behalf of" the Minister of Health, and are subject to detailed directions from him.[28] In this group are to be found (amongst others) the following:

(i) the regional hospital boards and the hospital management committees[29];

(ii) the new town development corporations and the New Towns Commission, established by the New Towns Acts of 1945, 1949 and 1965;

(iii) the National Ports Council established under the Harbours Act 1964[30];

(iv) the Housing Corporation created by the Housing Act 1964 to assist housing societies and associations to provide new housing;

(v) the Water Resources Board, a research body established by the Water Resources Act 1963 and primarily concerned with matters of water conservation;

(vi) a number of public corporations that carry on specified functions over defined and restricted areas, such as the river authorities constituted by the Water Resources Act 1963 (replacing the former river boards), joint sewerage boards, port health authorities, joint planning boards, combined police authorities, and perhaps the passenger transport authorities established by the Transport Act 1968. These bodies are not local authorities, as their members are nominated or appointed by a Minister and are not elected, but many of them have statutory powers to precept for their finances on local rating authorities, and they operate over defined local areas.

This group of corporations is not expected to be financially self-supporting, and in consequence tends to be to a greater extent subject to Ministerial

27. Transport Holding Company Act 1968.
28. National Health Service Act 1946, s. 12.
29. The hospital management committees are themselves but creatures of the regional hospital boards, as they are required to carry on their functions "for and on behalf of" the relevant board.
30. Constituted to manage the ports and harbours round the coasts of this country.

control than are the so-called commercial undertakings. It also overlaps to some extent the next group, and indeed some corporations could perhaps be classified under either group.

(3) Regulatory and advisory bodies

This group of corporations includes those entrusted by statute with the regulation and furtherance of social policies defined (with a greater or lesser degree of particularity) in their constituent statutes or with the giving of advice to their "parent" government departments. Sometimes they are little more than a specialised branch of a Ministry; thus, the Prices and Incomes Board[31] is very "close" to the Department of Economic Affairs; the Location of Offices Bureau,[32] designed to encourage the moving of offices away from Central London, could have been constituted as a section of the Ministry of Housing and Local Government, and the Land Commission (which also has certain "managerial" functions[33]) has some obviously specialised planning functions which could have been entrusted to a central department; the Medicines Commission, established by the Medicines Act 1968 has principally advisory functions (see s. 3 of that Act). Other corporations of differing degrees of dependence on their appropriate Ministries, include the Hairdressers Council,[34] the White Fish Authority,[35] the Horserace Betting Levy Board,[36] and the Decimal Currency Board.[37] The Industrial Reorganisation Corporation, established by an Act of 1966 and discussed fully in Chapter 3, *post*, and the National Research Development Corporation established by the Development of Inventions Act 1967, would seem also to fall within this group. The Highlands and Islands Development Board (see Chap. 5) may also be regarded as primarily of a regulatory character, although of course it also performs substantial managerial functions. The Race Relations Board on the other hand, primarily a "regulatory" corporation, has some of the characteristics of an administrative tribunal.

3. ANOTHER METHOD OF CLASSIFICATION

Govermental bodies that are neither local authorities nor "emanations" of the Crown,[38] *i.e.* those that are clearly branches of the central executive, could

31. Originally constituted under the royal prerogative; see below.
32. Constituted by Order in Council; see note 14, above.
33. Principally, of acquiring, holding, managing and eventually disposing of land. Their other principal function is to assess and collect as the "betterment levy," a form of tax imposed on land values by the 1967 Act.
34. Hairdressers (Registration) Act 1964, providing for the registration of hairdressers and the maintenance of reasonable standards in the trade.
35. Sea Fish Industry Acts 1951 and 1962.
36. Betting, Gaming and Lotteries Act 1963.
37. Decimal Currency Act 1967. The Board's principal function is to facilitate the transition from the existing currency and coinage to the new decimal currency and coinage (s. 5), and presumably when this has been achieved the Board will be wound up, which the Treasury is given power to achieve by order made by them (s. 6 (1)).
38. See Diplock L.J. in *B.B.C.* v. *Johns* [1965] Ch. 32, 81–82. This is an expression which has been much criticised as having no precise meaning.

also be classified according to the mode of their formation; perhaps a little more practical system of classification than the purely functional one adopted in Section 2, above, as this method does at least indicate differences of some legal consequence.

(i) *Public corporations established directly by statute*

The great majority of all corporations fall into this class, the respective constituent statutes establishing them by name and endowing them with corporate personality.

(ii) *Public corporations established under statutory authority*

This class consists of those corporations that are brought into existence by some person or body empowered so to act by a constituent statute. Thus, the Location of Offices Bureau was created in 1963 by the Minister of Housing and Local Government under powers conferred on his predecessor in title[39] by the Ministry of Town and Country Planning Act 1943.[40] The Public Health Act 1936,[41] the Water Act 1945[42] and the Town and Country Planning Act 1962[43] all contain powers enabling the appropriate Minister to constitute joint sewerage and port health boards, joint water boards and joint planning boards for specified areas, while the Police Act 1964 provides that two or more county borough council and/or county council police forces may be amalgamated, and the new force will be administered by a public body to be called "the combined police authority" which will than have corporate personality.[44] Similar arrangements are made by the Transport Act 1968 for the "passenger transport authorities."

(iii) *Public corporations established by the Royal Prerogative*

The Crown has always had power at common law by virtue of the Royal Prerogative to create a new corporation, and many charitable foundations have been so incorporated. The British Broadcasting Corporation is one of the few executive bodies that have been so incorporated (in 1927), and the former Nature Conservancy was incorporated by Royal Charter in 1949. The Bank of England was incorporated by Royal Charter as long ago as 1694, but by the Bank of England Act 1946 all its capital stock is now vested in the Treasury Solicitor[45] and the Governor, Deputy Governor and the sixteen directors are appointed by the Sovereign. The National Board for Prices and Incomes was

39. The Minister of Town and Country Planning.
40. See the Location of Offices Bureau Order 1963 (S.I. 1963 No. 792), made under s. 8 (2) of the Act of 1943, and now amended by s. 88 of the Town and Country Planning Act 1968.
41. s. 6.
42. s. 8.
43. s. 2 (2).
44. Police Act 1964, s. 3 (1).

originally constituted by Royal Warrant in April 1965, but it was put on a statutory basis by the Prices and Incomes Act 1966. There are also in this class the Agricultural Research Council, the Medical Research Council, the Science Research Council, the Natural Environment Research Council, the Social Sciences Research Council and (possibly) other research councils established by Royal Charter under the Sciences and Technology Act 1965.

(iv) Other public bodies established by statute or by the Royal Prerogative,[46] which are strictly not public corporations in that they have not been given corporate personality, but which resemble public corporations by reason of the nature of their functions. This class includes such different "creatures" as the Law Commission,[47] formerly the Race Relations Board,[48] the Criminal Injuries Compensation Board[49] and the Council on Tribunals.[50] These bodies have been given defined specific tasks by the respective constituent statutes or by the Prerogative, and they are not subject to any detailed control by a Minister of the Crown in the performance of those tasks. They are perhaps advisory rather than regulatory in character,[51] but they are dependent for their finance on the central exchequer and they are required to report periodically to Parliament.

4. The Legal Status of Public Corporations

Many corporations have little in common with one another and most corporations have their own individual constituent statute; with the exception, however, of the bodies discussed in the last sub-paragraph, all have corporate personality and therefore can sue and be sued in the ordinary courts in their own name. In legal proceedings brought by them or against them they do not have any special privileges, there being no longer any special period of limitation applicable to them,[52] and of course there is no question of their being

45. Bank of England Act 1946, s. 1 (1); Bank of England (Transfer of Stock) Order 1946 (S.R. & O. 1946 No. 238).
46. See for example, the Criminal Injuries Compensation Board.
47. Law Commission Act 1965; the Commission is not given corporate personality by the Act.
48. Race Relations Act 1965; under the Act of the same title of 1968, the Board was converted into a public corporation: see Sched. 1, para. 1.
49. Established by the Royal Prerogative, without any statutory authority. The money paid out on the recommendation of the Board is carried on the Home Office vote. Even more than the Race Relations Board, this body is really a specialised administrative tribunal.
50. Tribunals and Inquiries Act 1958.
51. Perhaps the only exception here is the Race Relations Board, which, with the Criminal Injuries Compensation Board, has some of the characteristics of a tribunal. It should be noted that there are also a considerable number of bodies whose duties are purely advisory in character such as the Building Regulations Advisory Council and the Clean Air Council.
52. Law Reform (Limitation of Actions, etc.) Act 1954.

subject to the jurisdiction only of specialised courts, as Great Britain knows no separate *droit administratif* of the Continental pattern.[53] They are also subject to income tax and other revenue legislation[54] to the same extent and in accordance with the same regulations as others of Her Majesty's subjects. Such privileges as remain to the Crown in litigation[55] cannot be claimed by public corporations, except in a few cases (principally again the regional hospital boards and the hospital management committees established by the National Health Service Act 1946 and the Sugar Board when acting as agent for the Minister.[56]) These exceptions are all cases where the corporation is required by the statute to act for and on behalf of a Minister of the Crown; but in at least two cases it is expressly provided in the constituent statute that the corporation is not to be regarded as the servant or agent of the Crown.[57] Consequently, the maxim of statute law interpretation to the effect that a statute shall not be deemed to bind the Crown unless it is expressly so provided,[58] does not entitle the normal public corporations to any special position.[59] However, there are cases where statutes confer special privileges on particular corporations; thus the powers of a local authority to serve public health notices on the owners or occupiers of land do not apply fully to the British Railways Board or the National Ports Council[60]; the National Coal Board are given similar special statutory privileges[61] and so are the electricity and gas boards.[62] Most of these privileges are, however, designed merely so as to enable the corporations concerned to perform their statutory functions efficiently, and they are not true exceptions from the principle that public corporations are "ordinary" corporate persons in the eye of the law.

Public corporations are in a strange position so far as concerns the statutes

53. Continental countries have their own problems of jurisdiction here; as Professor Drago (*post*, p. 107) points out, *les établissements publiques* and *les entreprises publiques* have to be classified as being within the jurisdiction either of the *tribunaux administratifs* or the *cours judiciaires*.

54. Only the Crown, central departments, and corporations acting solely as agents of the Crown or a central department (*e.g.* the hospital boards and hospital management committees) are exempt; a body such as the BBC is certainly not exempt: *BBC* v. *Johns* [1965] Ch. 32. As to rates, see note 20, *supra*.

55. Privilege in respect of documents, modified since *Conway* v. *Rimmer* [1968] 2 All E.R. 304., choice of venue, freedom from liability to an injunction or a prerogative order, etc.

56. Sugar Act 1956, s. 3 (3).

57. The Independent Television Authority (Television Act 1954, s. 1 (12)) and the British Airports Authority (Airports Authority Act 1965, s. 1 (7)).

58. *Willion* v. *Berkley* (1561) 1 Plowd. 227.

59. Except in the case of those that act "for and on behalf of" the Crown; see, *e.g. Nottingham No. 1 Area Hospital Management Committee* v. *Owen* [1958] 1 Q.B. 50. See also *Tamlin* v. *Hannaford* [1949] 2 All E.R. 327 (British Railways).

60. Public Health Act 1936, s. 333.

61. See, for example, Town and Country Planning Act 1962, s. 14, and class XIX of Part I of Sched. 1 to the Town and Country Planning General Development Order 1963 (S.I. 1963 No. 709), made thereunder.

62. Class XVII of the General Development Order, above.

that make the soliciting or offering of bribes to servants or officers of certain agencies a crime (the Public Bodies Corrupt Practices Act 1899 and the Prevention of Corruption Act 1916). These statutes apply only to "public bodies," an expression which is defined[63] to include as well as local authorities, "public authorities of all descriptions." In *R.* v. *Newbould*,[64] it was held that this expression was to be construed *euisdem generis* with "local authorities," and therefore was not wide enough to include, in particular, the National Coal Board. Presumably it would therefore be held not to apply to other public corporations, except where a statute may have expressly so provided; thus a hospital board or an airways corporation is *not* a "public body" for this purpose, but a joint planning authority (being sufficiently "near" local government), or the British Railways Board, *is* a "public body," in the latter case because the parent statute, the Transport Act 1962, s. 1 (1), expressly declares it to be a "public authority."

Being creatures of statute, all public corporations are subject to the *ultra vires* doctrine. This may be described as a general principle of the common law to the effect that a legal person created by statute can execute only those functions that it is expressly or by necessary implication empowered to do by its constituent statute (or by any subsequent amending statute). Therefore, when the National Coal Board wished to participate in the search for and the extraction of oil and natural gas from the Continental Shelf, they had to obtain additional powers from Parliament[65]; diversification of function on the scale practised by the State Collieries in the Netherlands, would have been legally quite impossible for the Board. On the other hand, it must be appreciated that statutory powers conferred on the corporations (especially in the case of nationalised industries) are frequently so widely drawn as to make the *ultra vires* doctrine nugatory as a means of exercising judicial control over the activities of the cocporation.[67] On the other hand, a public corporation may in some instances be made subject to a specific statutory duty which it may find difficult to perform and the courts even more difficult to enforce. Thus, in section 31 of the Post Office Act 1969, it is made "the duty of the Post Office so to exercise its powers as to secure that its revenues are not less than sufficient to meet all charges properly chargeable to revenue account, taking one year with another." Duties expressed in such vague and hortatory terms

63. Public Bodies Corrupt Practices Act 1889, s. 7, as amended by s. 4 of the Prevention of Corruption Act 1916.
64. [1962] 2 Q.B. 102.
65. National Coal Board (Additional Powers) Act 1966.
67. Thus, the Atomic Energy Authority is empowered to produce, use and dispose of atomic energy, and "to do such things as may seem to them necessary and expedient for the exercise of the foregoing powers," and similar powers are conferred on the National Coal Board and the Post Office: see Atomic Energy Act 1946, s. 2 (1), read with s. 1 (1) of the Radio-Active Substances Act 1948, the Coal Industry Nationalisation Act 1946, s. 1 (2), and the Post office Act 1969, s. 7 (2). These words are not, however limitless, as was evidenced by the need felt by the National Coal Board to obtain additional powers in 1996 (see note 65, above).

look much more like "duties of imperfect obligation," rather than duties enforceable in a court of law.

5. STRUCTURE OF PUBLIC CORPORATIONS

In matters of detail, constitutions of particular corporations may vary greatly. The following are, however, the matters that are commonly dealt with in the constituent statute or regulations.

(i) *The governing body*

It is usual to specify that the superintending Minister shall appoint the members of the governing body; it will usually be provided that there are to be not less than a specified minimum number of members nor more than a specified maximum,[68] and rarely will the latter number be more than twenty.[69] Speaking generally, the Boards of United Kingdom public corporations are smaller than are many of their Continental counterparts; thus, there are sixty members of the French *Comité National de l'Eau,* but only eight members of the British Water Resources Board; and the tendency in Britain seems to be to reduce the numbers.[70] Express provision is usually made for a chairman and a deputy (or "vice") chairman, and often both or one of these is appointed on a full-time basis, to be paid such salary "as the Minister may with the consent of the Treasury determine"; other members of the governing body will more rarely be paid salaries,[71] but all will usually be paid expenses in accordance with scales approved by the Treasury (even if the finance is provided from the corporation's own funds). It is also customary for express provision to be made for pay and pensions for officers and servants of the corporation.

The question of the amount of the salary paid to the chairman of a nationalised industry has on occasion provoked public discussion. Clearly, sufficient must be offered to attract the best man available, and where the corporation is competing against private industry, much more may have to be paid than is customary in the public sector; thus, the Chairman of the National Coal Board, for instance, may have to be paid more than the Parliamentary

68. There is no maximum number of members specified for the Medicines Commission although there is a minimum of eight (Medicines Act 1968, s. 2 (2)).

69. An interesting situation arises if the membership of a corporation (as is understood to be the case at the time of writing with the National Coal Board) falls below the minimum specified in the constituent statute. Further provision for a quorum (which can be attained) is surely not adequate. For example, the Coal Industry Nationalisation Act 1946, s. 1, provides that there "shall be a National Coal Board," and by s. 2 (2) (as amended) it is provided that "The Board shall consist of a chariman and not less than eight nor more than eleven other members." If there are less than eight members at any one time, it would seem that the Board is invalidly constituted and therefore powerless.

70. Thus, s. 38 of the Transport Act 1968 reduces the size of the British Railways Board from a potential nineteen to sixteen members.

71. See, for example, para. 6 (1) of Sched. 1 to the Land Commission Act 1967.

Secretary in the Ministry of Power or than the Minister himself, and when Lord Beeching was chairman of the British Railways Board, he was paid considerably more (£24,000) than the Prime Minister or the Lord Chancellor of the day.

The terms of the appointment of a chairman or of an ordinary member are usually left by the statute to be determined by the Minister, and so will be dependent, presumably, on the contractual terms of the correspondence that passes between the Minister and the person appointed,[72] but it is also customary[73] for the statute or regulation to provide that the office of a member of the governing body may be declared by the Minister to be vacant if the member is absent from meetings for a specified period, if he is adjudged a bankrupt, or makes a composition or arrangement with his creditors, or if he is incapacitated by infirmity of mind or body, "or is otherwise unsuited to continue to discharge his duties."

The last-mentioned case amounts to the conferment on the Minister of a summary power of dismissal. The courts of this country have not yet had occasion to examine the effect of these words in the context of a public corporation, or in particular whether a member of a governing body could be dismissed without first being given a "hearing" by the Minister. As a general rule, following such cases as *Fisher* v. *Jackson*[74] and *Ridge* v. *Baldwin*[75], it seems that the basic principles of natural justice should be observed and a "fair hearing" allowed; perhaps the courts would also declare invalid a decision of a Minister dismissing a member if it could not be shown that there were any grounds at all for considering him to be "unsuitable."[76] It is not clear whether such a remedy should be sought on the basis of a breach of contract or as an administrative remedy on the grounds of a breach of the principles of natural justice,[77] the former seems preferable as the Minister would appear to be acting as agent for the public corporation in question in making what is virtually a contract of employment.

In practice the power of dismissal is rarely used; members of governing bodies are normally appointed for a limited period, and the appointing Minister who is not satisfied with the conduct of his appointees is normally content to wait for the term to run out, although it is normally provided that a member is to be eligible for re-appointment. In a difficult case, pressure

72. By the Post Office Act 1969 the Minister will be required to notify the terms of appointment of members of the Post Office to Parliament.
73. But this is not so in the case of the Public Health Laboratory Service Board; the constituent Act (Public Health Laboratory Service Act 1960) provides for the appointment of members of the Board by the Minister for periods of office of three years, but makes no provision for the dismissal of a member during the currency of his term of office (*see* Sched. to the Act).
74. [1891] 2 Ch. 84.
75. [1964] A.C. 40.
76. *Ross-Clunis* v. *Papadopoullos* [1958] 2 All E.R. 23.
77. See, for example, *Vidyodaya University of Ceylon* v. *Silva* [1964] 3 All E.R. 865.

may be used to persuade a member to resign before the expiration of his term of office.

In selecting nominees for membership of public corporations, Ministers are frequently given an unfettered discretion by the constituent statute,[78] but in some cases a Minister may be required to choose such persons as may to him appear to be qualified in certain specified respects,[79] or representatives of particular interests,[80] and the Minister may be required to consult with interested bodies or individuals in making his selection of appointees.[81] In practice the courts would find it difficult to supervise such statutory requirements, although they could of course ensure that in appropriate cases some proper consultation had been taken.[82] In most cases[83] the constituent statute creating a new public corporation will amend Schedule I of Part II to the House of Commons Disqualification Act 1957 so that members of the governing body, on taking up appointments as such, will be disqualified from being Members of the House of Commons.[84]

(ii) *Procedure*

Rules in the statute regulating the procedure to be observed by a public corporation, will probably be of the scantiest. They will usually provide for a quorum of members to constitute a valid meeting of the governing body (often fixed at one-third of the total number), and it is frequently provided that the corporation "shall have power to regulate its own procedure."[85] Express provision is customarily made for the case where a member of the governing body has an "interest"[86] in the subject-matter of some transaction within the corporation's sphere of activity; in such a case it is normal to provide, following

78. See, for example, para. 2 of Sched. 1 to the Land Commission Act 1967.
79. Para. 3 of the Sched. to the Public Health Laboratory Service Act 1960.
80. See, for example, s. 1 (4) of the Industrial Reorganisation Corporation Act 1966.
81. See para. 3 (*d*) and (*e*) of the Sched. to the Public Health Laboratory Service Act 1960.
82. "Consultation" was defined by the court in *Rollo* v. *Minister of Town and Country Planning* [1948] 1 All E.R. 13. In appointing members of the Post Office, the Minister is required to consult with his own appointee, the Chairman of the Post Office: Post Office Act 1969, s. 6 (3).
83. See, for example, Water Resources Act 1963, Sched. 6, para. 4. The Schedule to the 1957 Act itself lists as disqualified persons members of most of the more important then existing public corporations. For a more considerable amendment of the 1957 Act, see s. 155 of the Transport Act 1968.
84. The members of regional hospital boards and hospital management committees are not included in the disqualification list in the 1957 Act, and the Hairdressers (Registration) Act 1964 is an example of a constituent statute (relating to the Hairdressers Council) which does *not* add to that list.
85. See Land Commission Act 1967, Sched. 1, para. 8; the Decimal Currency Act 1967 gives to the Board thereby established a power to determine the arrangements as to meetings of the Board (Act of 1967, Sched., para. 13).
86. Such provision seems to be almost invariable; see, for example, Land Commission Act 1967, Sched. 1, para. 10; Decimal Currency Act 1967, Sched., para 14; the Post Office Act 1969 does not however quite follow precedent in this respect (see Sched. 1, para. 3 (2) thereof).

a corresponding rule applicable to local authorities generally,[87] that the member shall disclose the fact of such interest (either generally or specially in each particular instance) and thereupon refrain from taking part in any deliberation or discussion undertaken by the corporation concerning that matter. Unlike the local government precedent it is not customary to provide in relation to public corporations that a failure to observe this requirement should amount to a criminal offence, but presumably such failure could justify the Minister considering that an offending person was no longer "suitable" to continue to be a member.

Provision is usually made for the corporation to have a common seal, and for acts of the corporation to be made by use of the seal, to be authenticated by the corporation's secretary or some other specified officer. Other matters, such as the summoning and frequency of meetings of the governing body, are normally left to be determined by the corporation itself. Meetings are but rarely required to be open to the Press and public, as the Public Bodies (Admission to Meetings) Act 1960 does not normally apply.[88]

(iii) *Staff*

It is customary for the constituent statute to provide that a corporation shall be entitled to employ and remunerate staff, usually on such terms as may be approved by the Treasury. Persons so employed are not civil servants and their terms of service will be regulated by the ordinary law of contract as modified by general statutes, such as the Contracts of Employment Act 1963 and the Redundancy Payments Act 1964.

The staff of regional hospital boards and hospital management committees do not at once accord with this statement. The regional hospital boards are required to carry on their functions for and on behalf of the Minister of Health,[89] who in turn acts for and on behalf of the Crown[90]; the hospital management committees can act only as agents for their respective hospital boards. Therefore it was held in *Owen v. Nottingham No. 1 Hospital Management Committee*[91] that a hospital management committee was not subject to controls imposed by the Public Health Act 1936[92] in accordance with the general principle that the Crown is not bound by a statute unless it is expressly so provided. At first thought, therefore, it seems that officers and servants of hospital boards are servants of the Crown, but even if this is so it is also clear that the usual provision of the common law to the effect that a Crown servant may be liable to dismissal without notice, does not apply to such cases,

87. Local Government Act 1933, s. 76, as amended by the Local Authorities (Pecuniary Interests) Act 1964; the local government rule is in many respects more detailed and stringent than those provided for in the enabling statutes constituting public corporations.
88. But the 1960 Act is expressly applied to regional hospital boards.
89. National Health Service Act 1946, s. 12 (1).
90. *Ibid* s. 6.
91. [1957] 3 All E.R. 358.
92. See now Clean Air Act 1956.

as section 66 of the National Health Service Act 1946 empowers the Minister of Health to make regulations providing (*inter alia*) for conditions of service under which officers or servants may be employed for the purposes of that Act.[93] However, the Contracts of Employment Act 1963 seems not to apply to these employees, as this Act is not expressly declared to be binding on the Crown; moreover, it was held in *Pfizer Corporation* v. *Minister of Health*[94] that the hospital boards operating under the Act of 1946 were administering a "service of the Crown."

Paragraph 12 of the First Schedule to the Post Office Act 1969 makes special provision for employees of the Post Office, by requiring this new corporation to obtain the consent of the Minister of Posts and Telecommunications before determining the employment of such an employee "on security grounds" (an expression defined so as to preserve for Post Office employees the same rights as are enjoyed by civil servants).

(iv) *Reports*

The constituent statute usually provides that a public corporation shall submit an annual report on the conduct of its affairs to the responsible Minister, who is then directed to lay the report before Parliament. In the case of the nationalised industries these reports are customarily substantial documents documented with statistical detail. To some extent they provide publicity for the corporation, as they are normally put on sale to the public by Her Majesty's Stationery Office when they are placed before Parliament and they may give rise to news items appearing in the national Press. There may also be a debate in the House of Commons on the affairs of the corporation on a motion calling attention to the report.

(v) *Accounts*

The accounts of a corporation are normally required by the statute to be audited annually and to be submitted to the Minister with the annual report. Express provisions as to the method of audit are not customary and in practice most corporations employ private firms of qualified professional auditors for the purpose; it is regarded as the function of the Comptroller and Auditor-General to carry out audits only of the accounts of those corporations "close" to the central government, such as hospitals. A professional audit can be only a financial check and verification of accounts; it is not concerned with questions of legality[95] and still less is it concerned with efficiency or the business methods of the corporation.

93. The National Insurance and Redundancy Payments Acts are expressly made applicable to Crown employees: National Insurance Act 1965, s. 98; Redundancy Payments Act 1965, s. 36.
94. [1964] Ch. 614.
95. There is no provision corresponding to that in s. 228 (1) of the Local Government Act, to the effect that the auditor is required to ensure that all payments made by the corporation are "authorised by law."

6. Controls over Corporations

This is a subject to be considered in more detail in a subsequent chapter,[96] but it seems desirable to outline the nature of the various controls here, as they are dependent on the terms of the constituent statute. They may be summarised as follows:

(1) Membership

As above mentioned, the appropriate Minister is normally given power to appoint and dismiss the members of the governing body.

(2) Functions

Some powers of the corporation may require Ministerial approval before they can have legal effect. Many corporations are given powers to acquire ownership of land or possibly lesser rights in land,[97] against the wishes of the owners (compulsory purchase, "or expropriation"), but in any case where they wish to exercise this power the compulsory order will not take effect unless and until it has been confirmed by the appropriate Minister.[98] Planning permission may also have to be obtained if development of land is involved in any project.[99] More important than these, however, is the common requirement that the approval of a Minister and also (usually) the consent of the Treasury must be obtained before the corporation can raise a loan for capital expenditure.

(3) Finance

Where a corporation is not self-supporting, it will be dependent on the Government for the source of its revenue. Sometimes this may mean a capital grant; but more commonly it will mean that the corporation needs sanction to raise a major loan. In many instances the constituent statute may have made provision, and it will not normally be necessary for the corporation to prepare an annual budget, but often the sum set aside will prove not to have

96. *Post,* p. 30.
97. As in the case of the National Coal Board, under the Open-Cast Coal Mining Act 1958. S. 29 of the Town and Country Planning Act 1968 confers a general power of compulsory acquisition of land on the Minister of Public Building and Works, if it is "necessary for the public service," and this (presumably) includes the purposes of a public corporation. Specific powers of a similar extent are conferred on the Minister of Posts and Telecommunications for the purposes of the Post Office (1968 Act, s. 29 (2); Post Office Act 1969, s. 55).
98. Normally in accordance with the procedure of the Acquisition of Land (Authorisation Procedure) Act 1946.
99. There are exemptions in favour of certain statutory undertakers; see especially Town and Country Planning Act 1962, s. 170, as amended by the Town and Country Planning Act 1968, s. 71.

been adequate and the corporation will have to come back to Parliament for more; which it is not likely to obtain without the approval of the Government.

(4) Directions

The statute will often confer on the sponsoring Minister a power to give directions to a public corporation, which directions will be mandatory and of legal effect. In form the directions must presumably be in writing although there is rarely any express requirement for this,[1] but they will not normally be required to be made by statutory instrument. As will be seen from Chapter 2[2] the powers to make directions are not used frequently in practice[3]; rather similar in legal status are the powers of a Minister to make regulations under statutory authority which may appear to be of general effect, but which by reason of their content apply in practice only to one or a few of the public corporations.[4] Such regulations will, on the contrary, normally be required to be made by statutory instrument. The corporations will also be subject, as are other legal persons, to regulations of a more general effect, such as those implementing the economic policy of the Government for the time being. Controls over prices and incomes may apply to all industries, but they will be of particular relevance to the gas and electricity boards and to the National Coal Board. Some corporations are subjected to different "purpose built" controls. Thus, the charges made by the London Transport Board are subject to the approval of the Transport Tribunal,[5] and the Minister of Housing and Local Government has power to control the charges made for the supply of water by meter by a water board,[6] while fares charged by the passenger transport authorities are subject to the approval of the local traffic commissioners.[7]

(5) The courts

By reason of the doctrine of *ultra vires* applicable to all statutory persons, the courts may declare illegal any executive act of a corporation which is not expressly or by necessary implication within its statutory powers. As will be seen from Chapter 2 this control is not as effective as it might seem in theory.

1. An exception to this is to be found in s. 23 (3) of the Transport Act 1968, which provides that Ministerial directions must be in writing.
2. *Post*, p. 32. In the case of directions given to the Post Office, the Minister may require the Post Office to keep the directions secret: Post Office Act 1969, s. 11 (6).
3 Possibly the power to give directions of a very specific character conferred on the Minister of Posts and Telecommunications by s. 12 of the Post Office Act 1969 will prove to be an exception from this observation and will be used frequently.
4. *e.g.* regulations as to gas pressure made by the Minister of Power under s. 55 of the Gas Act 1948.
5. Transport Act 1962, s. 47.
6. Public Health Act 1936, s. 127.
7. Road Traffic Act 1960, s. 135. In administering this control, the Commissioners are expressly required to have regard to the "public interest."

(6) Parliament

The extent of control of Parliament over the affairs of a public corporation, depends basically on the contents of the constituent statute, but in practice this control will depend on the ingenuity of the Parliamentary draftsman as there will rarely be time for Members to discuss a Bill in detail. Once a corporation has been constituted there are even fewer opportunities for Parliament to investigate its detailed operations. However, debates in the House of Commons on the affairs of a corporation may be initiated on the following occasions:

(i) *Supply*

When the House is in Committee of Supply there may be a debate on the vote included in the estimates for the financing of the corporation.

(ii) *Adjournment debate*

A member of the House may be able to obtain an adjournment debate concerning the affairs of a public corporation, if he can show it is a definite matter of urgent public importance (House of Commons Standing Order No. 9), and provided it is a matter for which the Government had administrative responsibility (for example, the giving or failure to give statutory directions by the Minister to the corporation in question).

(iii) *Debates on reports of the House of Commons Select Committee on the Nationalised Industries*

This Committee is discussed further by Professor Robson in Chapter 4, *post*, p. 79, but this obviously can apply to a limited number only of public corporations.

(iv) *Questions*

Questions in the House addressed to a Minister about the affairs of a public corporation must be restricted to those matters "for which a Minister is made responsible"[8] by statute. These matters can be classified under the following headings—

(*a*) matters in respect of which the Minister may give directions under statutory powers,[9]

(*b*) responsibilities in specific matters, such as safety in mines, gas pressures, etc.,

(*c*) power to obtain information from the corporations concerned. Under this heading the Minister will sometimes accept a question, answering it by saying that he has been informed by the board to a certain effect.

The Speaker has also undertaken to allow certain questions on what might

8. See Erskine May's *Parliamentary Practice*, 17th ed., p. 355.
9. Above, p. 19.

be regarded as day-to-day administration of the corporation, where the matter raised is one of urgent public importance which could have been raised on a motion for an adjournment debate under Standing Order 9[10] (*supra*, sub-para (ii)).

(v) *Reports*

Reports of the corporations are, as mentioned above, customarily required by their constituent statutes to be prepared annually and laid before Parliament, in most cases accompanied by the audited accounts; these documents will then be delivered to the Votes and Proceedings Office, and it will be for the Government, if thought necessary, to include provision in the business of the day for a debate on the report, or for a private member to endeavour to raise a matter in the report by notice of motion. In some cases the superintending Minister may have specific powers to call for further reports or information.[11]

7. THE CORPORATIONS AND THE PUBLIC

In this paragraph it is proposed to examine the relationship between a public corporation and members of the public. The public corporation is unlike the other two main branches of modern government, the central executive and local authorities, in that it is not even in an indirect sense subject to control by any elected representatives, either Members of Parliament or locally elected councillors. Parliament has therefore sometimes seen fit to construct a special machinery whereby representatives of the public, or of the "consumers' interest," may make their views known to the corporation concerned. Consumer councils, as they have become to be known, have thus been established in the gas and electricity industries, for the National Coal Board, and for the "users" of railway and national air transport. These must be considered separately.

(1) The gas and electricity consumer councils

By the constituent statutes establishing the area gas and electricity boards, consumer councils also were established for the area of each board.[12] Membership of each consumer council is drawn from persons nominated by local authorities and other organisations in the area (such as Chambers of Trade, and Trade Union Federations), but the appointments are all made by the Minister, and there are no elected representatives. Each area consumer council is staffed by employees of its parent gas or electricity board, the chairman of the consumer council is a member of the area board, and although

10. Erskine May, *op. cit.* p. 356.
11. See *e.g.* Post Office Act 1969, s. 11 (9).
12. Gas Act 1948 and Electricity Act 1947; as the areas of the respective gas and electricity boards do not exactly coincide there are separate consumer councils for each gas and electricity board.

B

meetings of the councils are often held on "neutral" premises, their offices are always situated at the offices of the area boards concerned. Meetings of the consumer councils are commonly (but are not legally required to be) open to the Press and to the public, and many consumer councils have established divisional committees covering parts of the area, thereby associating more individuals in their functions.

The purpose of the consumer councils is to receive complaints from consumers or members of the public about the service provided by the boards; they are entitled to investigate these complaints and make representations thereon to the board concerned.

In practice the investigation is not always very deep; most councils are served by a very small staff and they have none of the facilities expected of an Ombudsman type of organisation. Their secretary, an officer of the board (and often rather a junior officer), has little incentive to drive home a particular complaint or to investigate one too deeply. The chairmen's status on the boards also may "foster a sense of confidence and co-operation between the councils and the boards,"[13] but does not really cause the consumer councils to behave like watchdogs over the affairs of the boards; indeed, their function may often more truly be described as one of spokesmen for and interpreters of the boards' policy.

Ineffectiveness as a complaints investigation machine has increased as time has progressed from the original constitution of the consumer councils in 1948–49. Because a consumer council's affairs are rarely effective or interesting, they do not get good coverage, and therefore their existence may well be unknown to many housewives or consumers, and consequently complaints are not made to them as often as could be the case. To add to this unsatisfactory state of affairs, in many areas it becomes difficult to find able persons who are willing to serve as members on the councils, and so the general standard of competence falls even lower.

(2) Coal

Two consumers' councils were established for the coal industry by the Coal Industry Nationalisation Act 1946, s. 4: the Industrial Coal Consumers Council and the Domestic Coal Consumers Council. These two bodies are very closely related, both having the same secretary, and offices at the Ministry of Power. The Industrial Council currently (1967) has twenty-eight members, two of whom are members of the National Coal Board, and the others are industrialists, trade unionists, and one representative each of British Railways, the Gas Council and the Central Electricity Generating Board.[14] The

13. Expressions used to describe the relationship between these two types of bodies in many reports of the (central) Gas and Electricity Councils.
14. It seems to be a feature of both Councils that persons appointed as members are often re-appointed when their term of three years elapses. There are several members of the Industrial Council who have served for 10 years or more.

Domestic Council has twenty-nine members and these are representative of women's organisations (the current chairman is a prominent member of the Women's Institutes), local government and coal merchants and distributors, and includes also the same two members of the National Coal Board.

The annual reports for 1967 of these two bodies, printed together, were both very short; the Industrial Council sees its primary function as being to protect the interests of industrialists, who in the light of their own commercial judgment, are consumers of solid fuel, "rather than to influence such judgment by investigations into cost." They therefore make representations from time to time about prices but also interpret aspects of NCB policy to industry and the public.

The functions of the Domestic Council are similar, but they seem to be somewhat more active. They receive complaints from time to time (for example, in 1967 about the quality of fuel supplied at West Drayton Depot, although as the Council "have no expertise in the matter" they could do no other than accept the explanation proferred by the Board[15]), and they make representations to the Ministry or to the Board on such matters as coal prices, the arrangements for distribution and the sale of bituminous coal in smoke control areas.

Very little publicity is given to the activities of these Councils and it is doubtful whether they really exercise much—if any—control over NCB policy. They may on occasion be used as a sounding board and interpreters of new policies.

(3) Transport

A number of area transport users consultative committees were established by section 56 of the Transport Act 1962; in spite of their name they are concerned only with rail transport. There is also a central transport users consultative committee which may make general observations on rail transport. Railway passengers may (and in practice often do) refer complaints about the operation of the railways to the area committee and they can make recommendations thereon to the British Railways Board. In particular, when the Board propose to close a length of railway line, representations may be made to the area committee, and they may then decide to hold a public sitting.[16] Proceedings on such an occasion often resemble an arbitration rather than a consultation, although the latter is the true nature of the proceedings, for the committee in the course thereof are charged with the duty of ascertaining the views of the travelling public, in order the better to advise the Minister, who may not proceed with the closure until he has received the committee's report. There are several occasions on record in recent years

15. Report for 1967, para. 13.
16. Such sittings are not, however, statutory inquiries, and therefore not subject to the supervision of the Council on Tribunals; see Hansard, March 9, 1964, at col. 4.

when the Minister has refused to make a railway line closure order after receiving a report from an area committee. A similar body is apparently not considered necessary for road passenger transport, as the new road passenger transport authorities set up under the Transport Act 1968 will have considerable representation from local authorities in their areas.

(4) Air Transport

There was formerly a single Air Transport Advisory Council, established by section 12 of the Civil Aviation Act 1949, which was required to consider any representations made with respect to the adequacy of the facilities provided by the British Overseas Airways Corporation, the British European Airways Corporation or the since defunct British South American Airways Corporation, but this Advisory Council was abolished by section 9 (*b*) of the Civil Aviation (Licensing) Act 1960. In place thereof, section 4 of the Act of 1960 requires the Air Transport Licensing Board (which is concerned with civil aviation generally, and not only the two public corporations, BOAC and BEAC) to consider any representation "from any person" relating to, or to facilities in connection with, air transport services by means of United Kingdom registered aircraft, or with respect to tariff or other charges in respect of any such service or facilities. Having considered any such representation, they must report thereon to the Minister of Aviation and make recommendations thereon. In addition, before granting, revoking, suspending or varying a licence for air services, they are required to consult with the appropriate regional advisory committee,[17] the Channel Islands Air Advisory Council or the Isle of Man Airports Board, whichever may be relevant to the particular case.[18] This consultation takes place regularly, and the Licensing Board in their annual reports customarily express their gratitude for the advice given them.[19]

(5) Post Office

The latest addition to the ranks of British public corporations, the Post Office, is to have a users' council for the whole of the United Kingdom, to be called the Post Office Users' National Council, and there are to be separate "country councils" for Scotland, Wales and Northern Ireland (but none for England).[20] The Post Office is required to consult with the National Council before it puts

17. There are regional committees for Scotland, Wales, Northern Ireland, Northern England, North West England and the West Midlands, established by the Civil Aviation (Licensing) (Second Amendment) Regulations 1966 (S.I. 1966 No. 241); the Regulations do not precisely delimit the English regions.
18. Civil Aviation (Licensing) Act 1960, s. 5 (2) (*h*); Civil Aviation (Licensing) Regulations 1964 (S.I. 1964 No. 1116), regs. 8 (1) and 20, as amended by S.I. 1966 No. 241.
19. See *e.g.* their report for the year ended March 31, 1968, para. 3.
20. Post Office Act 1969, s. 14.

into effect "any major proposals relating to any of its main services,"[21] and also the National Council must consider any matter relating to the services provided by the Post Office which is the subject of a "representation" (a word which is not defined) made by or on behalf of a user of the services; if the Council consider any action ought to be taken on that matter, they must inform the Minister and the Post Office accordingly.[22] The country councils have a similar duty in relation to matters arising in their respective parts of the United Kingdom; they may also refer a matter to the National Council.[23]

Conclusion

It may also be relevant to point out that the Parliamentary Commissioner for Administration[24] has no jurisdiction in matters concerning the public corporations in Britain,[25] with the solitary exception of the Decimal Currency Board.[26]

21. *Ibid.* s. 15.
22. *Ibid.* s. 15 (9).
23. *Ibid.* s. 15 (8).
24. Established by the Parliamentary Commissioner Act 1967.
25. In this respect Britain is not out of step with Sweden, the home of the "Ombudsman"; see *post,* p. 176.
26. S.I. 1968 No. 1859.

CHAPTER 2

THE PUBLIC CORPORATION
AS AN ORGAN OF GOVERNMENT POLICY*

ALTHOUGH the tide of nationalisation, which characterised the post-war years 1945–50 in Britain has receded appreciably, each year sees a number of Acts of Parliament relating to public enterprise added to the statute book. Some of these Acts merely re-organise existing corporations, whereas others either add new names to the list of "traditional" public corporations,[1] or experiment with new forms of public control. The line demarcating the "public" and "private" sectors is becoming increasingly difficult to draw with any precision. The mixed enterprise, straddling rather uneasily the line separating the public from the private sector, and the Trojan Horse of government participation in the private sector, formerly through the NRDC and the IRC but now extended by the Industrial Expansion Act 1968, combine to show that Government control is not confined to the conventional nationalised industries. Even the latter have not been averse to some mild flirtation with the wicked capitalists, *e.g.* the joint scheme to exploit central heating between the NCB and a "private" company, or the partnership between the Gas Council and commercial companies in exploiting North Sea gas. Some of the ancillary functions of the proposed passenger transport authorities in the Transport Act 1968 transgress the frontiers of private enterprise.[2]

Experimentation with other forms of public ownership has not, however, consigned the public corporation to history. Thus, in the industrial or commercial sphere (with which this chapter is concerned) the Airports Authority Act 1965, the Iron and Steel Act 1967 and the recent transfer of the postal and telecommunications services of the Post Office to a single corporation, demonstrate that the idea of the public corporation has not fallen into desuetude. According to the White Paper, "Reorganisation of the Post Office,"[3] the change from Government department to independent public corporation is aimed at securing "effective freedom of a kind appropriate to

---

* By C. D. Drake, M.A., Ll.B., University of Durham.

1. Fuller information is given in J. F. Garner, "New Public Corporations," [1966] *Public Law*, p. 324, and see Chap 1, *ante*, p. 3.

2. See now Transport Act 1968, permitting certain "fringe" activities (*e.g.* National Bus Company may let vehicles on hire and act as travel agents; Railways Board may operate hotels and camping sites; PTA's may operate car parks, repairing facilities, etc.) As regards such activities, the authorities are required to "act as if they were a company engaged in a commercial enterprise": s. 134; *cf.* s. 9 which imposes on PTAs the duty to secure a properly integrated and efficient system of public passenger transport to meet needs of the area with due regard to town planning and traffic policies of local councils and to economy and safety of operation.

3. Cmnd. 3233.

a nationalised industry" and to the scale of Post Office trading operations.[4] "The organisation and techniques common to Government departments have been developed over the years for quite a different purpose. They do not suit the Post Office any longer, so its status is being changed."[5]

Outside the industrial or commercial sphere, the heterogeneity of function which has characterised the post-war corporations is perpetuated in the creation of public corporations such as the Land Commission and the National Board for Prices and Incomes. The chairman of the latter has defined its purposes as educative, consultative and judicial; the constitutional lawyer is more likely to fall back on the magic label "regulatory."

Advocates of nationalisation have learned (like their nineteenth-century counterparts who urged universal education) that nationalisation is not an end in itself, but only a means to an end. The chairman of the British Railways Board, prior to his sudden departure, complained that there had been three fundamental changes in transport policy in the years 1947–67, and that a fourth was in the offing.[6] The latter point is a reference to what is now the Transport Act, in which there is a division of functions between the British Railways Board and a New National Freight Corporation whilst a form of "municipalisation" in the form of passenger transport authorities seeks to achieve the integration of rail and road services within particular areas. Local control with indirect democracy has been preferred to nationalised boards in local areas, but responsible to the Ministry of Transport.

What follows is an attempt to assess the nature and extent of (i) the independence, and (ii) the control and accountability of the commercial and industrial nationalised industries in Britain in 1968.[7] The main emphasis will be upon the question of Ministerial control, although parliamentary accountability and legal control will be discussed.

The "Morrisonian" concept

A typical description of the nationalised undertakings is that given by the Ministry of Transport in its Memorandum to the Select Committee on Nationalised Industries[8] according to which they: "operate within a statutory framework which is based on the 'Morrisonian' approach, the underlying

4. £700,000,000 is spent by customers on commercial services alone. If plans to invest £2,000,000,000 in the next five or six years in capital expenditure are carried out, the Post Office will, it is estimated, rank among the ten largest industrial concerns in the world. Management "on commercial lines" is required if Post Office trading operations "are to be efficient." (Post Office Report and Accounts, 1967.)

5. Post Office Report and Accounts, 1967. The view that the change would confer freedom "to take decisions boldly" contrasts with Professor Galbraith's scepticism concerning bold, risk-taking merchant adventurers in the private sector; boldness by the holders of exclusive monopolies (ignoring Kingston-upon-Hull) differs from boldness by firms in competition.

6. Select Committee on Nationalised Industries (hereafter SCNI), H.C. 1966, 440—III.

7. Excluding the NCB and "mixed enterprises."

8. H.C. 1966, 440—X.

concept being the vesting of nationally-owned industrial enterprises in purpose-built corporate bodies with a large measure of independence but with statutory general duties to provide services and, at the least, to 'break even' in doing so." That this, however, is not the whole story, at least in relation to transport, appears from the warning which follows to the effect that: "the Government must play an increasingly active role in initiating changes in policy when this seems desirable, and in ensuring that the nationalised undertakings function in harmony with the Government's plans for the development of transport as a whole." In short, the dilemma of the public corporation of the kind under consideration is that it is torn between the Scylla of commercial freedom and the Charybdis of public accountability. The Morrisonian concept arose out of the experience of the London Passenger Transport Board and is based on the idea of using the autonomous trading corporation by harnessing it, not to the search for profit, but to the service of the public. The arguments in favour of autonomy are familiar.

(1) Industrial and commercial operations conducted on a large scale are best entrusted to the new class of managers who possess the managerial skill and the enterprise considered to be lacking in a civil service in which the administrative cadre is dominated by the "generalist" tradition.[9] Such managers are able to take decisions "boldly." They lack the timidity and the "red tape" of the civil service.

(2) Within the broad mandate of their statutory duties and powers the nationalised undertakings are free to get on with the job of day-to-day administration. Too much parliamentary surveillance may prejudice the freedom to act boldly as well as smacking of *gouvernement d'assemblée* which constituted such a patent defect in the Fourth French Republic.[10]

(3) Freedom to manage is not inhibited by any formal provision for "worker control" in that the Acts reject syndicalist ideas of running the industries for the benefit of the workers engaged therein. Trade union leaders have been appointed to the boards but not as representatives of the workers engaged in the industries run by the boards. There are loosely worded duties to consult trade unions on terms and conditions of employment.[11] In view of the long trade union struggle for the

9. See now the Fulton Report (Cmnd. 3638) which considers that the cult of the generalist is obsolete at all levels and in all parts of the Civil Service. A single, unified grading structure covering the whole non-industrial part of the Service is recommended, together with a new breed of managerial civil servant having great professionalism. Greater mobility is also urged, *e.g.* between the Service and nationalised industry.

10. The chairman of the Electricity Council welcomes informed discussion in Parliament on the nationalised industries on major issues, but not "continual sniping" which would discourage people from entering the industries—H.C. 1966, 440—I (ev. 242).

11. See for example, Air Corporations Act 1967, s. 23.

socialisation of the basic means of production,[12] labour relations ought in theory to be a model for those in the private sector.

Provision is, however, made for some Ministerial powers in staff matters, *e.g.* for the training of managers, but broadly the boards are free within the scope left them by the prices and incomes legislation to negotiate terms and conditions of service of employees, provided that they send copies of any agreements to the relevant Minister and the Secretary of State for Employment and Productivity.[13]

(4) The analogue of the big public company in the private sector carries with it the correlative of independence, *viz.* legal accountability. The public corporation would be subject to the *vires* doctrine; it would be responsible for breach of contract, tort and crime and would, by reason of its independence, be unable to seek refuge in Crown immunities, *e.g.* from the application of statutes (which do not bind the Crown in the absence of express words or necessary intendment).

The *locus classicus* of the "autonomous" view is put by the Herbert Committee which, in its Report on the electricity industry, suggested "that the less the principle of commercial operation is invaded the better it will be for the efficiency of the industry." If the Minister requires the industry to act "on other than purely economic considerations," he should do so by clear authority and against the background of a clear demarcation between the commercial freedom of the corporation and the power of the Minister to impose non-commercial criteria.[14]

Control and accountability

Few would argue that the nationalised industries should be left entirely free of control (*i.e.* with freedom of action) and free from accountability (*i.e.* irresponsible for their actions). The size of their assets and the scale of their investments make large claims upon scarce national resources. "Basic" industries such as those providing fuel and transport have an importance in the economy which cannot be measured by totting up their assets and capital. In

12. "To work for the supersession of the capitalist system by a Socialistic order of society" is one of the objects of the National Union of Railwaymen. In its Memorandum to the Donovan Commission on Trade Unions and Employers' Associations, the British Railways Board pointed to a "remarkably good record" as regards stoppages due to industrial disputes. Against this should be set the frequent occasions upon which the threat of strike action or "go slow" tactics has produced wage increases. The London Transport Board has been affected to a much greater extent by unofficial stoppages, but many of these relate to its omnibus services. The chairman of the LTB felt constrained to say that "there is a difference, as my Board sees it, between a public service and, for example, an organisation which makes candy floss," adding that those who join a public service ought to accept "certain responsibilities, perhaps certain restraints." (Evidence of LTB to Donovan Commission.)

13. See s. 46 of the Coal Industry Nationalisation Act 1946; Electricity Act 1957, s. 12; Gas Act, 1948, s. 57.

14. The Herbert view is criticised in W. A. Robson, *Nationalised Industry and Public Ownership* (1960), p. 298.

the citizen's view, rightly or wrongly, the rise in subsidies from £5,000,000 in 1959 to £151,000,000 in 1966 on operating account, reinforces the need for control—there is a greater tendency for "back-seat driving" in a deficit industry than in one making profits. The argument is not about whether control is needed, but over the degree of control and the manner of its exercise.

MINISTERIAL CONTROL

The Minister–Board relationship rests on the distinction between general policy and superintendence on the one hand and day-to-day administration on the other.[15] This distinction has been transmuted into a distinction between commercial viability and social control, but this is a change of words and not of substance. The doctrine of Ministerial responsibility requires that the Minister shall be responsible to Parliament for the exercise or non-exercise of his powers. What is disquieting is the blurring of the line of demarcation between the Board's and the Minister's powers respectively.

This blurring may be attributed to (i) the vagueness inherent in those sections in the statutes laying down general duties, and (ii) the manner in which formal Ministerial powers may act as a force constraining the acceptance of the exercise of power informally. Regarding the former, the task of the draftsman commissioned to translate inchoate political ideology into legal norms has surely been an unenviable one. Thus, area gas boards are charged "to develop and maintain an efficient co-ordinated and economical" gas supply for their areas. The two airway corporations are obliged to develop air services "to the best advantage" provided that in doing so they exact "reasonable charges." Who is to decide what is efficient or economical or advantageous? With respect to the second point, that is to say, the Ministerial mailed fist in the velvet glove, it is possible that parliamentarians schooled in the distinction between law and convention hoped that some constitutional conventions would evolve for the nationalised industries. The hope has not been realised. Allowing for the increased legal powers of Ministers in post-war nationalising statutes, it seems clear that the scale and frequency of Ministerial intervention has grown without a corresponding increase in parliamentary accountability. A common criticism is voiced by a distinguished publicist when he states: "They (*i.e. the Ministers*) should not be permitted to remain in the twilight zone in which some of them love to dwell, flitting happily from one private meeting to another, talking things over with the chairman at lunch, in the club, in the House of Commons, in the department, without disclosing either to the public or to Parliament the real extent of their

15. A nationalised industry's board may have dealings with several industries; *e.g.* the Electricity Council deals directly with the Ministry of Power and indirectly through that Ministry with the Department of Economic Affairs, The Treasury, the Ministry of Technology, the Ministry of Housing and Local Government and the Board of Trade.

intervention." (Italics mine.)[16] Before we peer into the "twilight zone," something must be stated of the formal statutory powers of Ministers.

Formal Ministerial powers

The Acts cannot be likened to "Model Clauses Acts" but they do exhibit certain similar features.[17] Using, as far as one can, the Electricity Acts as a stereotype, the Minister of Power has powers relating to the appointment of members of councils and boards, capital development, research programmes, training and education, area board schemes for the generation of electricity, the transfer of property from one board to another, the form of accounts (with Treasury approval), the appointment of auditors, authorisation to borrow (with Treasury approval) and the raising within statutory limits of the permitted borrowing limit, the establishment and management of reserve funds, consumers' or consultative councils and general directions. The list is not exhaustive.

The extent of Ministerial power can be judged from an examination of statutory powers, relating to appointments, general directions, investment and borrowing.

Appointment of members

It is usual to confer upon the Minister the power to appoint the chairmen, deputy chairmen and members from broadly defined categories and to fix their remuneration (with Treasury approval). The Minister may further be empowered to make regulations concerning tenure of office, of which those for the gas industry are typical. These provide, *inter alia*, for the duration of the term of office "not exceeding five years" and for termination of office, *e.g.* for absence of six months without justification and, more significantly, the Minister's power to declare an office vacated should the member "in the opinion of the Minister" become "unfit to continue in office or incapable of performing his duties." It has been suggested that the member's dependence upon Ministerial goodwill may have an inhibiting effect on freedom of action.[18] Vicissitudes in the economy and changes in policy heighten the feeling of insecurity.

16. W. A. Robson, *op. cit.*, p. 162. Lord Reith's disclosures concerning Ministerial pressure show that a body such as the British Broadcasting Corporation, the independence of which is generally valued, is not immune.

17. It has been suggested that the statutes reveal a lack of accepted principles and should be replaced by a common legislative code, *e.g.* the Local Government Act 1933 (W. Thornhill, Memo. to SCNI, H.C. 1966, 440—XII). The corporations do however differ radically; some are statutory monopolies, whilst others compete with rivals (*e.g.* the airway corporations); some are monolithic in structure, whilst others are based upon geographical factors; some have a policy board whilst others have an executive board, etc.

18. The Minister of Transport did not agree that independence was being undermined when taxed with the following: "When we asked Sir Stanley why he was not more belligerent he said it was because you were not only his sponsoring Minister, but you were his banker and you also controlled his investment and most other details of his enterprise and he said 'How do you expect me to be belligerent under these circumstances?' " (Minutes of Evidence to SCNI, H.C. 1966, 440—X at 1562). The

The device of using "appointing trustees," as formerly employed in the London Passenger Transport Board, has evoked little support, as has the suggestion of Lord Simon of Wythenshawe that members should be appointed on the recommendation of existing boards, such appointment normally to last until retirement—that the latter might result in a self-perpetuating industrial oligarchy is one fear. A more modest and defensible idea is that put forward by Professor W. A. Robson to the effect that appointment should be for a limited number of years specified at the time of appointment and subject to termination on grounds of disability, insolvency, neglect, misconduct, or other grounds, if reasonable cause can be shown.

General directions

It is common to reserve to the Minister the power to give such directions of a general character as to the exercise and performance by that board of their functions as appear to the Minister to be in the national interest, provided that before doing so he consults with the board concerned.[19] The power can only be exercised in relation to the statutory functions of the board and where the national interest is implicated, although, predictably, there is no definition of the latter elusive concept. The power to issue general directions has been rarely used, e.g. it has never been in use in relation to any board for which the Minister of Power is responsible, nor by the Minister of Transport under the Transport Act 1962 (although it was used twice during the fifteen years during which the 1947 Act was on the statute book).

Nevertheless, the existence of such reserve powers cannot but play a major part in setting the psychological relationship of superior or inferior between Minister and Board.[20] The chairman of the Electricity Council, in his evidence to the Select Committee on Nationalised Industries, suggested that it would be proper, in what he stressed was a hypothetical situation, for a board to refuse to comply with an unconstitutional Ministerial direction. Such a situation is likely, under the present system, to remain hypothetical. Professor W. A. Robson points out that: " . . . it would be quite impracticable

---

chairman of the British Railways Board has since been replaced. The writer can think of one chairman with the aura of a powerful, public *persona* who is far from inhibited. It has been suggested that short-term contracts subject to premature determination may deter the emergence of career managers on to the boards.

19. The formula for gas and electricity; for coal, the power to issue general directions relates to functions in matters appearing to the Minister to affect the national interest. S. 4 (1) of the New Towns Act 1965 allows the Minister "to give directions for restricting the exercise by them of any of their powers under this Act or for requiring them to exercise those powers in any manner specified in the directions"— social-purpose corporations are closer to policy considerations.

20. The Select Committee on Nationalised Industries makes the interesting points in its first report that "it is undesirable that the use of this power should be thought to imply a 'public row' " and that the power should occasionally be used. The more open use of the power would, it is suggested, afford greater publicity *at the time* (and not after the event when the exercise of the power is referred to in the annual report of the board) and would also serve to clarify the Minister–Board relationship: H.C. 1967–68, 371—I, published after this chapter was written).

for a public corporation to challenge in the courts the legality of a Ministerial direction. In such a situation the Government would have the means at hand to exert overwhelming pressure in many different ways on the corporation."[21]

Investment control

Amongst the financial powers of Ministers, those relating to control of investment and borrowing have been chosen to illustrate the extent of control. The commercial public corporations are required to act in accordance with a general programme settled by them with the approval of the Minister when carrying out measures of re-organisation or development which involve substantial outlays on capital account. The long-term investment programmes of the boards[22] are reviewed annually by the boards and by the Minister. The latter gives approval to capital expenditure for the next financial year, together with a limit on commitments which can be entered into before the next annual review in respect of the following year. The feasibility of a capital programme depends upon its soundness within the industry affected and upon its conformity with broader national policy. The Minister of Power is charged "with the general duty of securing the effective and co-ordinated development of coal, petroleum and other . . . sources of fuel and power in Great Britain."[23] That there is competition between the fuel industries is clear; but it is also clear that the competition does not take the form of economic natural selection which produces the survival of the fittest as happens (or is supposed to happen) in the private sector. The White Paper on "Fuel Policy"[24] explains the need to move from a two-fuel economy (oil and coal) to a four-fuel economy (oil, coal, natural gas and nuclear energy). This must be accomplished "on considerations of national policy."

"Competition" against the background of an integrated policy, as in fuel and transport, is defended on the grounds that (i) it gives the boards concerned a clear indication of their place in the market a number of years ahead, and (ii) wasteful competition and the squandering of scarce resources are largely avoided.[25] In a limited sense an integrated policy is an agreed measure; e.g. the fuel policy was thrashed out through the Ministerial Co-ordinating Committee[26] and in other ways. Frequently, there are rumblings that the "competition" in the sense described is not working fairly, e.g. the electricity

21. *Op. cit.* p. 141.
22. Six years for electricity.
23. Ministry of Fuel and Power Act 1945, s. 1 (1).
24. Cmnd. 3438.
25. The discontinuance of competitive advertising agreed in the coal, gas and electricity industries' "Concordat" to apply in 1966–67 showed a degree of forbearance which it is hard to imagine in private enterprise. But the Monopolies Commission found that the expenditures of two firms manufacturing household detergents were "unnecessarily high" in relation to advertising and promotion and recommended a 40 per cent reduction in selling expenses to accompany a price reduction (Report of Monopolies Commission on Household Detergents, H.C. 1966, 105).
26. "There are violent arguments. It is not a finishing school for young ladies" (Minister of Power to SCNI, H.C. 1966–67, 440—IX).

industry has voiced its restiveness on certain matters, such as its lack of freedom to buy fuels "at prices which are economic and not tilted by social
consideration or by beliefs that certain fuels 'ought' to be used in one way
rather than another."[27]

That the "national interest" may transcend the interests of a particular
industry or group of industries is shown by the Treasury support for the
Board of Trade on the question of particular aircraft procurement programmes
which is based on the considerations that the ordering of foreign aircraft
might have repercussions on our own aircraft industry, on exports and on the
balance of payments problem.[28]

Another matter on which some restiveness is evident is the degree of
detailed surveillance over development programmes. It is customary, as we
have seen, to require Ministerial approval before a "substantial outlay" is
made on capital programmes; in practice the sponsoring Minister gives an
indication of an acceptable ceiling for capital expenditure without approval.[29]
Delays, in some cases of several months, in approving capital projects, perhaps acceptable by Civil Service standards, are felt to be inappropriate in
commercial affairs. Another fairly common criticism is that good working
relationships are established with a Ministry official who has built up considerable technical expertise only for the latter to be plucked out and sent to
some other department. It would appear that the Ministerial power to require
information may act as a constraint on ventures with some speculative
elements, although many requests originate with M.P.'s seeking the answer
to some query either through a question or more informally.[30] Lack of direct
access to the Treasury is sometimes resented because it is felt that something
may be lost in the translation when the sponsoring Ministry puts a particular
project to the Treasury.[31]

Since this was written, the First Report of the Select Committee on
Nationalised Industries has recognised that statutory powers of strategic con-

27. Other criticisms were differing financial objectives, remission of oil duty for gas
boards, investment grants to private firms for private electricity generation (H.C
1966–67, 440—I).
28. "The financial interests of the industry are not necessarily the same as the
national economic interest" (Treasury Memo. to SCNI, H.C. 1966–67, 440—VIII).
29. London Transport Board appear happy with the £250,000 limit on individual
capital projects; other Boards seem to hint that the distinction between substantial and
non-substantial is interpreted in a way favourable to the Minister.
30. That the latter course may be hazardous is shown by the Strauss Case in which
an M.P. who raised questions concerning the disposal of scrap by the London Electricity Board with the Minister by letter was threatened with a writ for libel by the
Board. The House of Commons ended the chequered history of this case by deciding
(with a narrow majority) that the threat was not a breach of privilege because the letter
did not constitute a "proceeding in Parliament." The Report from the Select Committee on Parliamentary Privilege states that had the House considered the question
whether there had been a contempt of Parliament, i.e. an improper obstruction likely
substantially to interfere with the parliamentary duty of the Member affected, it might
possibly have received an answer favourable to the Member (Select Committee on
Parliamentary Privilege (H.C. 1966–67, 34, para. 82)).
31. BOAC have the unusual right of direct access (but not BEA).

trol may easily be used to obtain detailed control. The White Paper of 1961[32] is criticised for giving inadequate guidance on investment policies (*e.g.* the emphasis upon a financial objective expressed as a return on total net assets could result in the inclusion of uneconomic projects where an industry looked like overshooting its target!) The 1967 White Paper[33] is welcomed to the extent that it places emphasis upon proper criteria for investment decisions (*e.g.* the use of discounted cash flow techniques using an 8 per cent. test rate of discount); the use of proper investment (and pricing) criteria allows proper decisions to "emerge." There is however some criticism of the Treasury's reluctance to abandon the third criterion, *viz.* the financial objective.[34]

External borrowing

To the extent that a nationalised industry cannot finance its investment programme from internal sources, it must borrow. Such borrowing is usually limited by: (*a*) Act of Parliament which sets an upper limit, and also (*b*) statutory instrument which, within (*a*), sets an effective limit.[35] Ministry and Treasury control are maintained by means of annual and short-term approvals (*e.g.* weekly or daily) at which the terms of borrowing are signified. Direct stock issues to the public became difficult in 1955 when the Issue Department of the Bank of England became alarmed that it might become cluttered up with a lot of unsaleable stock which the public did not want; since the Finance Act 1956, the Treasury has been empowered to make advances of long-term capital (as had been done for the NCB from the outset) and to borrow for that purpose. Roughly half of the capital of BOAC, however, is exchequer dividend capital on which a variable return, like a dividend, is paid to the Exchequer, although this device is only suitable for nationalised industries which, in the words of the Treasury, are "fully viable." Because of the amounts involved, direct resort to the capital market is ruled out, except for small sums; the chairman of the Electricity Council accepted that the Treasury could not envisage "a fish of our size flopping about in a bowl."[36] A useful reminder of the Minister's role is provided by the following: "The borrowing limit imposed by Parliament is therefore a limitation on the Minister's power to lend, not an authorisation to the corporation to spend."[37]

32. "Financial and Economic Obligations of the Nationalised industries," Cmnd. 1337.
33. "A Review of Economic and Financial Objectives", Cmnd. 3437.
34. H.C. 1967–68, 371—I.
35. Subject to affirmative procedure. For electricity the overall limit is £4,400,000,000, and the limit, at the time of writing, is £4,100,000,000 as set by statutory instrument. Deficits on revenue account may require additional statutory power for the Minister to make grants (*e.g.* Transport Finances Act 1966); the Coal Industry Act 1967 increases the borrowing limit of the NCB to £900,000,000 or such greater sum not exceeding £950,000,000 as the Minister may specify and also permits grants in connection with pit closures, and payments to redundant workers.
36. H.C. 1966–67, 440—I. Ministers prefer to exercise close control through investment rather than through borrowing by the industries.
37. Second Report, SCNI, H.C. 1967, 673.

Informal Ministerial control

When the Minister acts within his statutory authority (and is seen to so act) there is little difficulty. The same cannot be said of the "twilight zone" or the "grey area" in which Ministerial pressure may be applied *sub rosa* by means such as the "lunch-table directive." The Minister's statutory powers, including his power over the board member's tenure of office, reduce his need to use such powers—the request submitted *sotto voce* can be the royal command. The absence, in practice, of a clear division of responsibilities, cannot but inhibit freedom of action by the board and makes it difficult to envisage any useful form of court intervention. Doubts were expressed above concerning judicial intervention in the event of an "illegal" general direction. That such a possibility cannot entirely be dismissed as theoretical is shown by the letter addressed by the Minister of Labour in 1966 to the Confederation of British Industry urging employers to break their contracts with workers in deference to the wages "freeze." A Mr. Leonard Allen successfully claimed arrears of wages illegally withheld in deference to the Government's policy since the latter did not constitute law.[38] The distinction between policy and law is not always perceived by Ministers. Aircraft purchases, pit closures, rail closures, choice of fuel for power stations and other controversial issues exemplify the important role of the Minister—this role will now be examined in relation to two matters, namely, pricing and wages policies.

Pricing policy

The boards are given a vague mandate in the matter of financial responsibilities. Typical is section 18 of the Transport Act 1962, which provides that: "Each of the boards shall so conduct their business as to secure that their revenue is not less than sufficient for making provision for the meeting of charges properly chargeable to revenue, taking one year with another."[39] It is one thing to say that the nationalised industries are expected to meet the demand for their goods or services in an efficient and economical way whilst "breaking even" after a contribution to reserves; it is another thing to spell out what "efficient" and "economical" means. The chairman of the Electricity Council testified as follows: "In my judgment there was quite insufficient guidance to nationalised industries for ten years after nationalisation. . . . There were circumstances in which one would have one board chairman in the electricity industry who believed in making profits; he made profit. One would have another board chairman who believed that one should break even;

---

38. More surprisingly the Court of Appeal found for Allen in a later claim by the latter which he made despite the activation of Part IV of the Prices and Incomes Act 1966 and the making of an order specifically applicable to Allen's employers. (See *Allen* v. *Thorn Electrical Industries Ltd.* [1968] 1 Q.B. 487.)

39. Under the Transport Act 1968, the National Freight Corporation and the passenger transport authorities are subject to a similar duty.

and he broke even."[40] Since 1961, clarification of this state of affairs was achieved in that the industries concerned have been expected, at the least, to balance their books over a five-year period after providing for interest and depreciation.

It is true to say that in pricing policy the boards have "substantial freedom from statutory control." Sometimes a licensing tribunal may be used such as the Transport Tribunal[41] or the Air Licensing Transport Board.[42] Apparent legal freedom (and an independent tribunal) may belie the true state of affairs, at least in transport, electricity and gas.

Although the Minister of Transport has no statutory power to fix rail charges the then Minister revealed that she and the British Railways Board (harassed by debt and therefore vulnerable to "back-seat driving") "necessarily keep in close touch about pricing developments which have wide implications."[43] In 1965, the Minister of Transport was forthcoming in Parliament about an "exchange of views" with the London Transport Board, which culminated in the latter agreeing not to press for an increase in fares before the Transport Tribunal in return for an assurance that any deficit thereby resulting would be met. The London Transport Board's feeling that discretion is the better part of valour is shown by their statement that they considered it "proper to advise the Minister of their intention to apply for increases in fares." The Railways Board and the electricity and gas boards are similarly discreet.[44]

Ministerial interference with pricing decisions and indeed with other decisions such as investment and services is justified on the ground that a public enterprise, particularly one holding a statutory monopoly, cannot have complete freedom of action. Otherwise it might adopt a pricing policy which conceals inefficiency, or which is successful "in a straight narrow commercial sense" but which offends against broad policy or the interests of others.

Few would argue that *carte blanche* should be bestowed on public enterprises. What is felt is that certain changes may be required in the mode of controlling these enterprises. First, there ought perhaps to be greater definition of the area of permissible Ministerial intervention.[45] Second, admitting the need for national policy to prevail, such policy should be "objectified" in

40. Oral evidence to SCNI, H.C. 1966–67, 440—I.

41. The larger part of its jurisdiction was abolished in 1962.

42. BEA were free to fix charges on domestic flights until 1966, but complains that since then fares have been fixed too low by the ALTB—2nd Report of SCNI, H.C. 1967, 673. This Report recommends that the ALTB should be wound up since it has neither a licensing function nor a fare-fixing function.

43. The Minister admitted that she had no statutory power to defer increases but added that she could request a deferment: H.C. of 1966–67, 440—X.

44. The legality of a general direction on a specific matter, *e.g.* pricing, has not been tested in the courts.

45. See now H.C. 1967–68, 371—I, which recommends that Ministerial power should be (1) *formalised, e.g.* by giving power to issue specific directions in the national interest, and, (2) *publicised* when exercised in the form of White Papers and periodic statements of policy making plain standard pricing policy.

some coherent statement setting out the appropriate objectives—there is a feeling that the boards have often to change courses suddenly according to the shifts and stratagems of hard-pressed Ministers who themselves frequently change office. Third, there is a greater need of publicity in Minister–Board relationships so that Parliament and the public may be informed, and the same applies to problems of co-ordination, which are often left to the arcane and pragmatic Civil Service techniques for informal inter-departmental consultation.[46] Certain hopeful signs have however emerged.

First, the nationalised industries play a part in economic planning by participation on NEDC and other bodies, such as advisory councils or consultative committees.

Second, the revelation of concrete policies in the form of White Papers helps to give the boards some idea of their destination, *e.g.* those recently dealing with transport and fuel policy. Thus the broad parameters of control required to ensure that statutory obligations are met are provided in the White Paper on the Economic and Financial Objectives of Nationalised Industries.[47] According to the latter, pricing policy should ensure:

(*a*) that revenues normally cover accounting costs in full;

(*b*) that the consumer should pay the true costs of the goods and services he consumes subject to permissible cross-subsidies, *e.g.* where a statutory requirement, such as rural electrification, exists or where justified by "wider economic or social considerations"; and

(*c*) that prices should be reasonably related to costs at the margin—reflecting, perhaps, that in the post-war years average costing tended to provide goods and services too cheaply.

The White Paper states that: "Insofar as the industries observe the principles set out in the White Paper, the Government does not intend to interfere in the day-to-day responsibility of management to propose increases, and will endeavour to leave management the maximum discretion in adjusting their price structure to meet competition and to take advantage of commercial opportunities." There is here confirmation of the belief that commercial and national interests can be separated. By using cost-benefit analysis techniques, as is currently being done on the railways, it is possible to arrive at some distinction between commercial costs and "social" costs.[48]

One final, but important, sign of the move towards pricing policies arrived at on more objective lines is the decision to refer all major price increases in the nationalised industries to the National Board for Prices and Incomes which

46. See, for example, the decision of an electricity board to have 100,000 tons of coal delivered by road in the London area instead of by water. The preference for informal contact is shown by the Minister's statement that it would be a waste of time to have regular meetings of something with a title such as "The Co-ordination of All Possible Aspects of Transport Policy Committee."   47. (1967) Cmnd. 3437.

48. The Ministry of Nationalised Industries suggested in H.C. of 1967–68, 371—I would not be responsible for social obligations which would remain under the aegis of other departments. Efficiency versus national interest would be institutionalised in different Ministries.

will consider the justification for the increase, its timing and the extent to which costs can be reduced by increased efficiency against the industry's overall financial objective. The National Board for Prices and Incomes has already castigated the Central Electricity Generating Board for reaching its target "while prejudicing the ability of the Area Boards to reach theirs and throwing on them the entire burden of the shortfall in sales below estimates"; it recommends that the screening of the CEGB from market pressure is inimical to efficiency and recommends that the proposed increase in the bulk supply tariff should be somewhat less than the CEGB proposal.[49]

Wages policy

Worker control is conspicuously absent from the British nationalisation statutes, although syndicalist or guild socialist notions have not been completely abandoned in this country. Not least among the reasons for the absence of worker control is the attitude of trade unions themselves, which, in general, prefer to fulfil their role in improving the lot of workers within an "oppositional" frame of reference. In its Memorandum to the Donovan Commission, the Electrical Trades Union, a progressive and adaptable union, as is shown by the recent scheme for the grading of electricians, put the traditional trade union attitude: "At the risk of sounding banal, it must be said that management has a duty to manage. If it does not perform this duty it has no right to be in that position. It is not the duty of trade unionists to participate in management. Their duty, quite clearly, is to protect and advance the interests of their members." This union, with members serving in both the private and public sectors, was clear that "participative mangement" would blur traditional loyalties—trade union representatives on the boards would be likely to incur the odium of being "obstructionists" from their management colleagues and the odium of being "collaborators" from their trade union colleagues.

Nevertheless, the statutes reflect the general notion that the nationalised industries ought in some way to be model employers with industrial relations which would serve as exemplar to those in private industry. It is common for the statutes to include provision for machinery for joint consultation on terms and conditions of employment and on matters affecting the safety, health and welfare of workers. Both in the statutory duty to consult representative organisations and in the range of matters upon which consultation may, in theory, take place, the nationalised industries differ from their counterparts in private industry. In pursuance of their statutory obligations, the boards have, with trade union co-operation, set up national joint councils and other joint bodies together with arbitration machinery.[50] They are also

49. Report No. 59, Cmnd. 3575. Report No. 57, Cmnd. 3567, refers to tariff structures in relation to gas prices.
50. Full details are provided in the *Handbook of Industrial Relations* (1961) DEP, pp. 68–122.

subject to the Fair Wages Resolution of the House of Commons of 1946.

A common feature of the statutes is the absence of Ministerial power to fix wages and conditions of service, although it may be necessary to inform him of settlements reached. The Minister is, however, frequently given statutory functions in relation to training and education.[51]

Despite his exiguous statutory power the degree of Ministerial intervention in wages and conditions of service is remarkable. Nearly all of the industries giving evidence to the Select Committee on Nationalised Industries in 1966–67 testified that they informed the Minister of negotiations and their outcome and that there had occurred what the London Transport Board termed "a gradual but marked increase in the influence which successive Governments have sought to exercise over negotiations with trade unions on their claims for increased pay and major improvements in conditions of service. British Railways Board seem to have suffered more than most from governmental interference. Elaborate domestic machinery has been set up for the settlement of grievances at local, sectional and national level. The agreement of 1956, which makes this provision, stipulates that in no circumstances will a matter in dispute between the British Transport Commission (since dissolved) and a railway trade union or unions, which is within the ambit of the agreed machinery, be referred to any person or body outside the machinery until the matter has been considered at all stages of the machinery for which it is eligible. The British Railways Board states that—"Despite this provision, there is an increasing tendency on the part of the trade unions to by-pass the appropriate machinery and seek discussion with the Ministry of Transport or the Ministry of Labour and, on critical decisions, with the Prime Minister." The Board recognises that a trade union may approach a Minister in connection with a matter for which the latter has statutory responsibility, either in the Nationalisation Act, or in some other legislation, such as the Conciliation Act 1896 or the Industrial Courts Act 1919, or when the national economy is likely to be affected, but apart from these occasions it deprecates Ministerial intervention in the day-to-day relations of the board with their employees.

Fortunately there are signs that a more objective approach to wages policy is emerging as is happening with prices. The activation of Part II of the Prices and Incomes Act 1966 and the lengthened powers of delay in relation to pay settlements conferred by the 1967 Act allow a statutory "early warning" system to operate in which the National Board for Prices and Incomes will have its say on matters affecting salaries and wages referred to it.[52] The guidelines for productivity awards set out by this board provide an objective test whereby less labour-intensive methods may be used and Ministerial control

51. Since 1963 a fortnightly return has been made to the MOT of important negotiations.

52. The SCNI, mindful of the temptation to use incomes policy as a pretext for detailed control in staff matters, urge that the industries might report direct to the Department of Employment and Productivity.

(which has hitherto been exercised on the basis of productivity) diminished. The formation of training boards for the nationalised industries marks a welcome devolution of authority in training and education for which hitherto the Minister has assumed responsibility and for which he retains statutory responsibility.

PARLIAMENTARY ACCOUNTABILITY

The "Morrisonian" idea of the public corporation is, as we have seen, that there shall be managerial freedom in day-to-day matters with Ministerial control (and therefore Ministerial responsibility) in certain matters. To the cynical it might appear that this is an attempt to have the best of both worlds. Accountability to Parliament is provided for by questions, motions for the adjournment, Bills and delegated legislation, debates on the annual reports of the nationalised industries and the Select Committee on Nationalised Industries.[53]

Question Time provides the opportunity for the exercise of the M.P.'s historic right of interpellation as it has developed in this country, providing that the Minister is responsible for the matter raised.[54] He may be questioned concerning the exercise or non-exercise of a statutory power, *e.g.* one relating to training, research, finance or the power to issue a general direction. Thus, the Minister of Transport has been asked—"if she will give a general direction to the Railways Board to investigate the cause of the excessive noise on British railway trains in transit and make recommendations as to the best means of stopping the noise"—but a question concerning the late arrival of a train would not be in order. The Minister may refuse to answer a question concerning day-to-day management assuming that it has appeared on the Order Paper. Under the Speaker's Ruling in 1947–48 a question to which an answer has previously been given or refused has been held to be inadmissible, but the harshness of this has since been modified. In general Ministers have been reluctant to answer questions involving the exercise of their power to require information, although exceptions to this rule exist, *e.g.* statistical information on a national basis; even if an answer is given, it may use the formula "I am informed that . . . " thereby clearly indicating that no formal responsibility is accepted on the Minister's part.

Adjournment debates, which are excellent at unearthing detailed information, may be used, but the competition is intense. In 1966–67 (to June 19, 1967) there were fourteen adjournment debates on the nationalised industries; typically, twelve concerned the railways, which are everybody's business, one concerned BOAC and one related to coal mining.

53. There are other opportunities, such as the debate on the Queen's Speech, on supply, etc.
54. We have seen that letters to the Minister, not appearing on the Order Paper, may be hazardous for the M.P. concerned.

Bills, or statutory instruments subject to affirmative procedure, provide another opportunity of discussion, particularly when borrowing powers are involved. Private Bills provide another opportunity, especially if they are classified as "general purpose Bills" in which debate may range over the scope of the Bill, although, it must be added, the opportunity to debate this type of Bill is not always taken.

One of the most valuable forms of parliamentary discussion is that provided for in the Select Committee on Nationalised Industries[55] (set up in 1956 after much doubt) and on its reports, on which regular sessional debates take place on the floor of the House. There can be little doubt that the Select Committee has done much to publicise the affairs of the nationalised industries by showing where they have erred or by demonstrating an unhealthily close Minister–Board relationship. It also appears to have a cathartic effect for the boards themselves, who can secure a sympathetic ear for their hard lot. It is a tribute to this particular Committee that the device of the Select Committee charged with the oversight of a particular area has been extended to cover agriculture science and technology. On the debit side, the SCNI devotes much time to a particular industry and issues a full report which, however, does not always receive the attention it deserves, perhaps because the report lacks the topicality of instant news. Mindful of this, the idea of examining short-term issues has been toyed with. Another defect is that it might be ten years or more before a particular industry comes under the microscope. The Select Committee is conscious that it lacks professionally qualified staff to undertake specialist work, *e.g.* management audits and so forth; this would liberate the Select Committee to concentrate on political aspects. There is nothing comparable to the staff working under the Comptroller and Auditor-General who serve the Public Accounts Committee so well. Suggestions have been made that there ought to be some Audit or Efficiency Commission, not necessarily working under the SCNI, which could look at the nationalised industries as a whole. If there were such a body there are advantages in putting it to work under the SCNI.[56]

The problem of *de facto* Ministerial interference without parliamentary

55. The term "nationalised industries" is not defined by the Select Committee's terms of reference, which, however, show that the industry must (1) be established by statute (2) have its controlling board appointed by a Minister of the Crown and (3) not have annual receipts wholly or mainly derived from moneys provided by Parliament or advanced by the Exchequer. The Post Office has been added by name. In its Special Report (H.C. 1967–68, 298) a wider order of reference is suggested, *viz.* all bodies which are or could be subject to control by the Government where such body, by reason of the fact that it disposes of an income arising from its operation falls outside the purview of the Estimates Committee or the Public Accounts Committee. If implemented bodies such as the Bank of England, BP Co. Ltd., Cable & Wireless Ltd., etc. would be included.

56. But the SCNI has now urged the creation of a new Ministry of Nationalised Industries which would be responsible for efficiency (H.C. 1967–68, 371—I). On the question of an Audit Commission, see Professor G. Treves' chapter, *post*, p. 133.

accountability is generally acknowledged[57]; there is less unanimity about the solution. Professor A. H. Hanson puts what he recognises is a minority view when he suggests that the limitations on Ministerial power should be removed so that Parliament can operate with greater freedom as in Australia and New Zealand. He recommends that the Minister–Board relationship should be liberalised and not formalised; he doubts the efficacy of the latter because, as he says, no power on earth can prevent a Minister from consulting with a board on a particular matter.

As indicated above, there are signs that Ministerial intervention will be based more upon objective criteria made public in the form of White Papers and the like. Despite the criticisms of lack of a formal differentiation of functions between Minister and Board the reorganisation of the Post Office will apparently follow the well-trodden path. A study of the White Paper shows financial dependence for borrowing on the Minister, a considerable list of familiar Ministerial powers, freedom from parliamentary surveillance on day-to-day matters and a consumer council system, both national and subordinate, "neutered" by the provision for consultative rights only.

In its First Report concerning the Post Office, the Select Committee on Nationalised Industries, recommended a change in the direction of "formalisation." "In so far as Ministers require the corporation to act in a way that conflicts with its commercial responsibilities they should do so publicly and by means that ensure full Ministerial accountability to Parliament."[58] The need for consultation with the Ministers on tariffs, is granted, but it is also suggested that the process should be given statutory recognition. It is admitted that the existing parliamentary accountability of the Post Office, as at present constituted, is bad, since it tends to stifle initiative and enterprise. The changes to be made by the Bill provide a demonstration of faith in the continuing validity of the Morrisonian concept with a degree of increased formalisation; it remains to be seen whether the new corporation will be able to operate effectively within a frame of reference which includes commercial autonomy and public accountability.

JUDICIAL CONTROL OF THE NATIONALISED INDUSTRIES

Two seemingly contradictory themes are discernible in the subject of judicial control in its application to the nationalised industries. According to the first,

57. A gloomy view is taken by Professor G. W. Keeton in *The Passing of Parliament*— the title "public corporation" is a misnomer since its affairs are more private than an ordinary public company; departmental control is considerable and sometimes illusory, as *e.g.* in the groundnuts scheme, the Scarcroft Case; the public corporations are "dummy monopolies"; parliamentary control is not effective—"The nationalised industry has the appearance of some Frankenstein monster."

58. H.C. 1966–67, 340. There was discussion of the idea of giving the Chairman of the board the right to ask for a letter from the Minister setting forth the request; a further idea was to make such request subject to approval by the House of Commons.

the legal position of the public corporations of an industrial or commercial character is assimilated to that of an ordinary corporation in the private sector. The public corporation is endowed with no special immunity with regard to its contracts, its torts (including vicarious liability for the torts of its servants), its crimes[59] (whether they involve *mens rea* or are of strict prohibition) and its subjection to certain statutory duties.[60] According to the second theme, it is observed that such public corporations have a considerable freedom from legal regulation and appear to operate outside the constraints of the "administrative legality" which apply to other public authorities, *e.g.* local authorities. Each of these themes is valid because each operates in a different area.

Legal regulation

It is commonplace that, in the absence of a legal theory of State, English law has emphasised the distinction between Crown agencies with their still considerable immunities, substantive and adjectival, and other agencies whether discharging "public" or "private" functions. That a body has public functions and no "profit motive" does not *per se* suffice to attract immunity. The distinction between public authorities which attract the special immunities of the Crown and those which do not has been complicated by an historical distinction between (*a*) "primary and inalienable functions" of Government vested in the great officers of State who are "emanations from the Crown,"[61] and (*b*) public functions laid upon public bodies but lying outside "the province of government." Some difficulty has been experienced in exorcising this dichotomy of governmental and non-governmental public functions from our law, based as it is on the notion that certain functions "belong" to government. Thus, in *Tamlin* v. *Hannaford*, in which the former British Transport Commission was held to be bound by the Rent Restriction Acts, Denning L.J. (as he then was) admitted that—"It (the BTC) is, of course, a public authority, and its purposes, no doubt, are public purposes, but it is not a government department nor do its powers fall within the province of government."[62]

59. In the Scarcroft Case, an electricity board was fined for breach of building regulations: see, for example, *Evening Standard* (London), November 20, 1950.
60. The general principle is put by Blackburn J. in *Mersey Docks and Harbour Board* v. *Gibbs* (1866) L.R. 1 H.L. 93, at p. 110, "that, in the absence of something to show a contrary intention, the legislature intends that the body, the creature of statute, shall have the same duties, and that its funds shall be subject to the same liabilities, as the general law would impose on a private person doing the same thing."
61. *Gilbert* v. *Trinity House Corporation* (1886) 17 Q.B.D. 795, at p. 801—"All the great officers of State are, if I may say so, emanations from the Crown" *per* Day, J.; *Coomber* v. *Justices of Berkshire* (1883) 9 App. Cas. 61, based upon the notion that governmental functions rest upon some *a priori* division of functions; *Mackenzie-Kennedy* v. *Air Council* [1927] 2 K.B. 517.
62. [1950] 1 K.B. 18. His Lordship after deprecating the use of analogies from other bodies with different constitutions, controls and purposes, pointed out that the Territorial Forces Association "are not concerned with commercial matters, but with the defence of the realm, which is essentially the province of government." The Post Office was a (then) government department which was concerned with commercial matters, but this was "an anomaly due to its history."

However, in the *Pfizer* case,[63] Willmer L.J. in the Court of Appeal, had recognised that in mid-Victorian times the treatment of patients in hospitals would have been regarded as "something quite foreign to the functions of government" but added that since then there had been "a revolution in political thought, and a totally different conception prevails today as to what is and what is not within the functions of government." Whether or not part of the National Health Service was one of the services of the Crown could only be decided "by studying the provisions of the statute which brought it into operation." In the House of Lords, Lord Reid said: "It may seem anomalous that there should be this distinction depending on the nature of the organisation which Parliament has set up and not on its purposes; but I think that it is now well recognised that, by reason of the structure of their organisation, the nationalised industries, for example, are not services of the Crown." The structural forms by virtue of which a public service may be administered were discussed by Willmer L.J. in *British Broadcasting Corporation* v. *Johns*[64] (in which an examination of the BBC Charter led to the conclusion that the BBC could not claim Crown exemption from taxation). First, a government broadcasting service could be used, as in Nazi Germany. Secondly, a commercial corporation (like the British Transport Commission) might be used which would enter into contractual relations with those receiving the broadcasts. Thirdly, broadcasting might be entrusted to an independent legal *persona* licensed to carry on a broadcasting service without entering into contracts with those who would otherwise have been its customers. The BBC fell into the last category and, as such, could not shelter under the special privileges of the Crown. Diplock L.J. expressed the hope that no one would ever again in a court of law use so imprecise a metaphor as "emanation of the Crown."

In the words of one American judge, dealing with the immunity of State-owned agencies—"It is doubtful whether any activity of the State may properly be called private."[65] In *Baccus S.R.L.* v. *Servicio Nacional Del Trigo*,[66] the Court of Appeal (Singleton L.J. dissenting) declined to adopt a restrictive view of sovereign immunity and held that corporate status and trading activity were not incompatible with such immunity. The idea of "primary and inalienable" functions of government is patently obsolete.

63. *Pfizer* v. *Ministry of Health* [1964] 1 Ch. 614, at p. 641, affirmed [1965] A.C. 512. Held, that the Minister of Health could authorise a firm to make, use and exercise tetracycline of which the appellants were proprietors of the patent, since provision to the hospital service of the National Health Scheme was included in the phrase "services of the Crown" (Patents Act 1949, s. 46 (i), *i.e.* the Minister could "raid the patent register."
64. [1965] Ch. 32.
65. Judge Mack in the case of *The Pesaro*, 277 Fed. 473 (overruled by Supreme Court). *Cf.* the distinction between acts *jure imperii* and acts *jure gestionis* in the "Tate Letter" (*see* 26 Dept. State *Bull.* 984 (1952)).
66. [1957] 1 Q.B. 438.

Freedom from legal regulation

How is it that despite the legal accountability of the nationalised industries (as shown in the *Tamlin* case), it can be said "that in this country control by the courts is practically non-existent in practice"?[67] Various explanations can be given for this state of affairs.

(i) *Width of statutory powers*

The mandatory statutory duties and the permissive statutory powers incidental thereto (corresponding to the "objects clause" in the memorandum of association of a registered company) are drawn in wide terms. An example of a statutory duty is provided by section 24 (1) (c) of the Betting, Gaming and Lotteries Act 1963, charging the Horserace Betting Levy Board with the duty of applying contributions for purposes, one of which is "the improvement of horse racing," which purpose may be effectuated by the power given by section 25 of the same Act "to engage in any activity connected with" the statutory purposes and including in particular the power to lend or invest money.[68]

The width of statutory powers conferred may be significant for a number of reasons.

In the first place, although the public corporations are statutory creatures who cannot go outside the statutory powers accorded them, it is difficult to establish an *ultra vires* act when powers are so generously bestowed. This is shown by *Charles Roberts & Co. Ltd.* v. *British Railways Board*,[69] in which a declaration that the Railways Board were not empowered to manufacture railway tank wagons with a view to their sale to an oil company for use on the Board's railways was refused. The Board were obliged by the statute "to provide railway services in Great Britain and, in connexion with the provision of railway services, to provide such other services and facilities as appear to the Board to be expedient"[70] and the Board was empowered, subject to the Act, to "do all other things which in the opinion of the Board are necessary to facilitate the proper carrying on of their business."[71] The Board might also "construct, manufacture, produce, purchase, maintain and repair anything required for the purposes of the business."[72] Ungoed-Thomas J. held that the provision of wagons raised questions of expediency and of what was incidental to the Board's business and of these questions the Board were the best judge— it could not be said as a matter of law that the manufacture of tank wagons

67. *Cf.* Chap. 1, *ante*, p. 12.
68. For an example of the use of this power which resembles the powers given by s. 2 of the Industrial Expansion Act 1968, without, of course, the scope of the latter, see the £1·1 m. takeover bid by the Levy Board for United Racecourses (*The Times Business News*, April 30, 1969).
69. [1965] 1 W.L.R. 396.
70. Transport Act 1962, s. 3 (1).
71. *Ibid.* s. 14 (1).
72. *Ibid.*, s. 13 (1).

for sale could never be required for the purposes of the Board's business. The *ultra vires* doctrine, as in the case of companies registered under the Companies Acts, provides an unreliable tool in the hands of someone seeking to restrain certain activities in the absence of express statutory prohibition.[73]

In the second place, the vagueness inherent in the statutory obligation renders it virtually impossible for a private individual to secure its performance by mandamus, quite apart from the troublesome question of *locus standi.* Thus, the British Airports Authority is under a duty "to provide at its aerodromes such services and facilities as are in its opinion necessary or desirable for their operation"[74] and has power "to do anything which is calculated to facilitate the discharge of its duty under this Act."[75] It is difficult to envisage a court issuing a mandamus to compel the performance of this public duty at the suit of a private individual. This is borne out by the requirement that the Authority shall provide "adequate facilities for consultation in matters affecting their interest" in the management and administration of any aerodrome to users of the aerodrome, local authorities and "other organisations representing the interests of persons concerned with the locality in which the aerodrome is situated."[76] The argument that provision is made for consumer representation in the nationalisation statutes has carried little weight in view of the general weakness of such representation.

Thirdly, it is clear that according to the nature of its statutory authority a statutory undertaker may escape liability in tort. What is not clear is the principle upon which such exemption from liability rests.

Metropolitan Asylum District v. *Hill,*[77] in which statutory authority was held to be unavailing as a defence to an action for nuisance arising out of the erection of a smallpox hospital in a residential district, has been used to support the proposition that the defence of statutory authority is inapplicable where such authority is *permissive* as opposed to *mandatory.* It is true that the Act in question contained nothing of a mandatory or imperative nature, but what is more significant is that the court construed the Act in a manner which led it to three conclusions, *viz.*: (i) the Act did not necessarily require anything to be done which might not be done without causing a nuisance; (ii) there was no evidence in the Act that the legislature supposed it to be impossible for the acts authorised to be done without creating a nuisance; and (iii) no intention to interfere with private rights could be garnered.[78]

If any one of these three indications is missing, Lord Blackburn's famous

---

73. Similarly, neither of the two airways corporations may manufacture airframes, aero-engines or airscrews unless authorised by an order by the Board of Trade (Air Corporations Act 1967, s. 3 (3)).
74. Airports Authority Act 1965, s. 2 (1).
75. *Ibid.* s. 2 (3).
76. *Ibid.* s. 2 (7).
77. (1881) 6 App. Cas. 193.
78. See *Pride of Derby and Derbyshire Angling Association* v. *British Celanese Ltd.* [1953] Ch. 149.

dictum in *Geddis* v. *Proprietors of the Bann Reservoir*[79] may be invoked: " . . . it is now thoroughly well established that no action will lie for doing that which the legislature has authorised, if it be done without negligence, although it does occasion damage to anyone; but an action does lie for doing that which the legislature has authorised, if it be done negligently." *Dunne* v. *North Western Gas Board*[80] provides an example of the application of this principle. The plaintiff had been injured by an explosion of gas which had escaped from a gas main belonging to the defendants. The gas main had been fractured by the collapse of a sewer, itself caused by the escape of water from a water main, both the sewer and the water main belonging to Liverpool Corporation which had permissive statutory power to provide water. The Gas Board were held not to be liable because (i) the injuries had been caused by the escape of water and no negligence had been established against them, and (ii) outside negligence, there was no liability either under the rule in *Rylands* v. *Fletcher*, or in nuisance. "Gas, water and electricity are all capable of doing damage," stated Sellers L.J., "and a strict or absolute liability for any damage done by them would make the undertakers of these services insurers." His Lordship considered that it would be odd if facilities so much sought after by the community should, when they were brought to the places in which they were required, saddle those bringing them with liability even though no negligence were shown. Nor were the Gas Board liable for nuisance in the absence of negligence.

It will be seen, therefore, that section 1 (9) of the Gas Act 1948,[81] which for the avoidance of doubt, provides that "nothing in these provisions shall be construed as authorising the disregard by any such board of any enactment or rule of law," produces some "tail-chasing" where the rule of law itself provides for the exemption of statutory undertakers! That there is no magic in the label "permissive" is shown by the court's judgment in favour of Liverpool Corporation, the second defendants, who had provided water under powers that were clearly facultative.

Relief against the hardship inherent in the *Geddis* principle is provided to a limited extent by section 14 of the Gas Act 1965, which enacts that a gas authority shall be absolutely liable in civil proceedings for damage caused by gas in an underground gas storage or by gas in the boreholes connected with underground gas storage or any such boreholes. For the purpose of the law of tort, liability under this section is to be regarded as arising from a duty owed by the gas authority to the person suffering the damage and any

79. (1878) 3 App. Cas. 430.
80. [1964] 2 Q.B. 806.
81. Para. 33 of Sched. 3 provides for the imposition of a penalty on an area board which fails to prevent the escape of gas of which they have been notified; para. 42 provides that "Nothing in this Act shall exonerate an area board from any indictment, action, or other proceeding for any nuisance caused by them." Sellers L.J. was clear that whether there was a saving or nuisance clause or not, the principle that there was no liability outside negligence applied.

occurrences giving rise to such liability are to be included in the references to wrongful act, neglect or default in section 1 of the Fatal Accidents Act 1846.

(ii) *Ministerial control*

The courts are reluctant to be seen as trespassers in the Ministerial preserve. To some extent this reluctance is attributable to the fear of encroaching on the rights of Parliament to whom the Minister is, in theory, responsible, but another factor is the judicial distaste for some of the loosely drawn norms in the Acts.

The statutes contain penumbral references to criteria of efficiency, economy, reasonableness and the like, reinforced by power to act in a manner "calculated" to effectuate these desirable ends. It is no matter for surprise that the judiciary, known for its antipathy towards the idea of *laesio enormis* and, since *Faramus* v. *Film Artistes' Association*,[82] emphatic in its refusal to settle new canons of reasonableness in contract additional to the established principles of public policy, should be equally unenthusiastic in applying such vague criteria.

In the *Roberts* case, discussed above, Ungoed-Thomas J., dealing with the duty section of the Transport Act 1962, which obliged the Railways Board to "provide railway services" and "such other services and facilities as appear to the Board to be expedient," was clear that the Board alone was judge of what was expedient. Section 13 (1) permitted the Board to manufacture anything required for its business, subject to Ministerial approval under subsection (4). In so far as the Board were not competent to judge "business considerations" the decision rested with the Minister. Not only was his Lordship loth to enter into business matters (beyond holding that the manufacture of wagons for sale could not be said, as a matter of law, to be *ultra vires*), he was also opposed to argument based upon economic policy, *e.g.* that the Board might, by manufacturing for sale, have a home market as a basis for their export trade. "Economics and trade form no part of a judge's qualifications. In general, judges are not qualified to decide questions of economic policy, and such questions by their nature are not justiciable. In this case, in particular, Parliament has expressly provided by section 13 (4) that the Board's powers of manufacture are to be controlled by the Minister who, with the advice available to him, is the proper person qualified to weigh economic considerations."[83] *South of Scotland Electricity Board* v. *British Oxygen*[84] shows that even when justiciable issues are specifically raised in the

82. [1964] A.C. 925: *cf.* the views of Lord Denning M.R. in the Court of Appeal [1963] 2 Q.B. 527.

83. [1965] 1 W.L.R. 396, at p. 400: but that he may *have* to weigh them, even where he has a wide discretion, is demonstrated in *Padfield* v. *Ministry of Agriculture* [1968] A.C. 997.

84. [1959] 1 W.L.R. 587.

statute, in this case those of "undue preference" and "undue discrimination," some difficulty is experienced in deciding how far the court may probe into business matters despite a statutory obligation to publish tariffs. The majority of the House of Lords admitted costs as a relevant factor in determining the alleged discrimination between high voltage consumers of electricity and low voltage consumers, even though the former, which included the respondents, were charged less. Lord Reid dissented on this point since in his view an inquiry into costs would involve an "elaborate investigation," although he agreed that discrimination on a matter other than price might be proved.

The doctrine of Ministerial responsibility tends to have an inhibiting effect on the development of judicial control on the lines of a *Rechsstaat* system, since the judges are wary of trenching upon the ill-defined area of Parliamentary privilege. In *Harper* v. *Secretary of State for the Home Department*,[85] the Court of Appeal allowed an appeal against the granting of an *ex parte* injunction restraining the Home Secretary from submitting to Her Majesty in Council draft orders relating to constituency boundaries, which orders had been approved by both Houses of Parliament. Sir Raymond Evershed M.R. said: "My reading of these rules and of the whole Act is that it was quite clearly intended that, in so far as the matter was not within the discretion of the commission, it was certainly to be a matter for Parliament to determine. . . . If it were competent for the courts to pass judgments of that kind on the reports, I am at a loss to see where the process would end and what the function of Parliament would then turn out to be."[86]

CONCLUSIONS

On the assumption that the Morrisonian type of public corporation is with us for some time, in what ways may the desiderata of commercial autonomy and public accountability be more easily reconciled? The syndicalist solution of worker control is ruled out, as is consumer control.

1. Ministerial control cannot be dispensed with, but should be formalised and publicised. In particular, to the existing power to give general directions might be added power to give specific statutory directions on particular matters.[87] The right of a chairman to insist on a letter is a valuable safeguard since, by promoting publicity, it facilitates parliamentary accountability. The national interest should be objectified in the form of meaningful policies incorporated in published papers.

2. There would appear to be a need for a more closely regulated statutory framework within which the industries might, consistently with "administra-

85. [1955] Ch. 238.
86. At p. 251.
87. The SCNI make the same point in its report (H.C. 1967–68, 371—I) and also recommends greater use of general directions, enlargement of Ministerial power to give specific directions and the issue of periodic statements of policy by Ministers.

tive legality," have greater freedom of action. The law should not, as Lord Wilberfore says "limp painfully behind" economics as a normative science or art.[88] Much of the difficulty springs from the historical antithesis between law and policy in this country.

In the U.S.S.R. and the Peoples' Democracies, nationalisation is part of an economic order in which the legal concepts and mechanisms have been developed in varying degrees. The Plan as a "Super-Law" with its own peculiar sanctions, State arbitration and a refined concept of public property, far removed from the *ius utendi, fruendi et abutendi*, are characteristics of a developing jurisprudence for public enterprise.[89] In the U.S.A., and, to a large extent, in the social market economy of the Federal German Republic, nationalisation is seen as an exceptional departure from the legal and economic postulates of a liberal, free enterprise régime. This country, occupying an intermediate position between these extremes, still lacks a coherent economic and legal framework for public enterprise. At times, policy may vary with the length of the Minister's foot, and even if it does not, is often shrouded in that secrecy which Max Weber saw as the besetting sin of bureaucracy. The use of White Papers to explain policy in recent years has been welcomed above. One idea worth exploring is the possibility of incorporating criteria on pricing, investment and other "commercial" matters as schedules to the nationalisation statutes. This has recently been done in prices and incomes legislation, although it must be admitted that in *Allen* v. *Thorn Electrical Industries Ltd.*[90] the judiciary applied the telescope, in Nelsonian fashion, to its blind eye. Closer statutory definition of specific Ministerial powers, the use of objective pricing and investment criteria and enhanced independence for board members will not, of themselves, produce healthy, thriving industries. What it will do is give the industries themselves a clear idea of the area within which they can practise commercial freedom, whilst, at the same time allowing Parliament and the public to know the principles upon which the industries are supposed to operate.

The national interest, whether in the form of "social obligations" or otherwise, will still remain. If a public corporation is asked to depart from the path of commercial rectitude (and a start has tentatively been made in segregating social and commercial costs) it should only do so on a formal request and on the clear understanding that the taxpayer and not the consumer of the industry's service will foot the bill.[91]

3. The valuable work of the Select Committee on Nationalised Industries would be reinforced if it were provided with a body of persons with specialised knowledge of industrial and commercial problems. It is doubtful if such a

88. Presidential Address to Holdsworth Club, University of Birmingham.
89. Katzarov, *Nationalisation*.
90. *Supra*, p. 38.
91. See, for example, s. 39 of the Transport Act 1968, relating to unremunerative services kept open "for social or economic reasons."

body, whether known as an Audit Commission or as an Efficiency Commission, should be given independent status.[92]

4. The courts will never be competent to adjudge questions of business or economic expediency, but with this qualification it is hoped that in time the interest of the Law Commission in administrative law will produce more effective machinery for controlling public authorities than at present exists. There is no reason why local authorities, which now undertake trading activities on a large scale, should be subject to closer judicial surveillance than the nationalised industries. Perhaps the activities of the "Ombudsman" (the Parliamentary Commissioner for Administration) may eventually be extended to the nationalised industries.

92. As to the suggested Ministry for the Nationalised Industries, see Professor Robson, Chap. 4, *post*.

CHAPTER 3

THE MIXED ENTERPRISE
IN THE UNITED KINGDOM*

PREAMBLE: THE INDUSTRIAL EXPANSION ACT 1968[1]

THE Industrial Expansion Act has as its object, as its hopeful short title implies, the amelioration of both the quantity and the quality (in terms of profitability, efficiency, and technological advancement) of industrial production in the United Kingdom. Its chosen method is rationalisation and extension of Government financial support for private industry. Section 2 of the Act sets out in precise terms the projects for which, and indicates the methods by which, such support may be given. To be eligible, projects must be calculated to improve industrial efficiency or profitability, or to create, sustain, or expand productive capacity, or to promote or support technological improvement in processes or products; and must be incapable of being undertaken without Government assistance. Support may be given in any form, but six possible forms are set out in the Act: loans or grants; guaranteeing repayment of loans or interest; underwriting of losses; purchase of goods or services; taking up share holdings; and purchase of the undertaking (or a part of it) of any enterprise concerned.

None of these methods of support is new. In general terms also, the giving of financial assistance by the Government to particular firms or industries has long been accepted as legitimate by both major parties.[2] Support under the Act, however, may only be given under an industrial investment scheme, made in the form of a statutory instrument by the sponsoring Minister with the approval of the Treasury, laid before Parliament in draft and requiring an affirmative resolution of the House of Commons in order to become

* By T. C. Daintith, M.A., University of Edinburgh.
   1. c. 32. For a full account of the reasons for the Act, its main provisions and possible applications, and the arguments to which it has given rise, see Samuels, "Government Participation in Private Industry" [1968] J.B.L. 296. This article was presented, in slightly different form, as a paper at the Cambridge Colloquium on the Control of Public Corporations, and the writer is grateful to Mr. Samuels for permitting him to incorporate material from this paper into the brief account of the Act and the debates that follows. See also "Industrial Expansion," Cmnd. 3509 (1968), and for the Parliamentary Debates, 757 H.C. Deb., cols. 1571–1700 (February 1, 1968) (Second Reading); Standing Committee E, February 15 to March 21, 1968; 762 H.C. Deb., cols. 377–568 (April 3, 1968) (Report and Third Reading); 291 H.L. Deb., cols. 1205–1257 (May 2, 1968) (Second Reading); 292 H.L. Deb., cols. 388–444 (May 16, 1968) (Committee); 765 H.C. Deb., cols. 2176–2230 (May 30, 1968) (consideration of Lords' amendments).
   2. For an account of the activities of the Conservative Government in this sphere, see Henderson, "Government and Industry," in Worswick and Ady (eds) The British Economy in the Nineteen-Fifties (1962), pp. 326–377.

C

effective.[3] The Act can therefore be seen (and the Minister of Technology, who introduced it into Parliament, was at pains to present it in this light) as no more than the provision of a legal framework within which financial assistance may be given subject to determined conditions and fixed procedures which preserve Parliament's rights of scrutiny, rather than, as was formerly the case, *ad hoc* and often without adequate publicity or opportunities for Parliamentary control.[4] The Confederation of British Industry, however, and the Conservative Opposition in Parliament, preferred to see the Act as signalling the intention of the Government to intervene more often and more vigorously than before in the affairs of private industry, and hence attacked the measure before and during its passage through Parliament.

Their strongest condemnation was reserved for the provision which specifically empowers the Government, under an industrial investment scheme, to subscribe for or to purchase by agreement shares in a company specified or described in the scheme (with the consent of that company) or to be formed under the scheme.[5] This statutory power represents but one of several applications to date by the Labour Government of the principle articulated by the Labour Party when in Opposition in 1961 in its policy document, *Signposts for the Sixties*: "Where national assistance is required by manufacturing industry it should be made conditional upon public participation in the enterprise."[6] Three earlier examples may be cited. In 1965 the Government, in coming to the aid of the ailing Fairfield Shipyard on the Clyde in the best British tradition of *ad hoc* intervention, took a substantial share of the equity in the new company formed to operate the yard and a continuing power of control.[7] In 1966, the Government secured the passage of legislation[8] setting up an Industrial Reorganisation Corporation endowed with, *inter alia*, a general power to acquire and hold securities, and to form companies,[9] in the performance of its statutory task of promoting and assisting the reorganisation and development of industry[10]; and the Corporation has since utilised this power on a number of occasions.[11] In 1967, a Shipbuilding Industry Board was established with similar powers and functions in the field of shipbuilding.[12] Two important factors, however, distinguish the Government shareholdings envisaged in the Industrial Expansion Act from those authorised by the two above-mentioned statutes. First, shares will

3. Industrial Expansion Act 1968, ss. 1, 16.
4. See note 71, *infra*.
5. s. 2 (2) (e).
6. *Signposts for the Sixties* (1961), p. 16.
7. The participation in Fairfields is fully discussed later in this chapter.
8. Industrial Reorganisation Corporation Act 1966 (c. 50).
9. s. 2 (3) (a) and (b).   10. s. 2 (1).
11. See First Report and Accounts of the Industrial Re-organisation Corporation (1967–68) H.C. 252, Appendix 1; Report and Accounts for the year ended March 31, 1969 (1968–1969) H.C. 286, Appendices 1, 2 and 4.
12. Shipbuilding Industry Act 1967 (c. 40). The Act implements the proposals of the Shipbuilding Inquiry Committee (The Geddes Committee), Cmnd. 2937 (1966).

be held directly by the Government, in the person of the appropriate Minister, whereas under the Industrial Reorganisation Corporation Act and the Ship-building Industry Act shares are held by the Corporation and the Board[13] respectively, public corporations whose directing boards are composed of businessmen rather than politicians or civil servants.[14] Secondly, while the Board is a body with a life-span limited by statute[15] and the Corporation is expected (though is under no statutory duty) to provide temporary or "bridg-ing" rather than permanent financial assistance,[16] no suggestion has been made by the Government that participations under the Industrial Expansion Act will be of limited duration. Equity investment, by its very nature, implies a degree of permanence.

In the Parliamentary debates, Opposition speakers were quick to exploit these differences. They depicted the new power of share acquisition as a device whereby men without financial or business competence would be enabled to tie up indefinitely large sums of taxpayers' money in unremunera-tive investment in projects *ex hypothesi* uneconomic in that any viable project would obtain support from the private financial market. At the same time, they reiterated fears earlier expressed in relation to shareholdings under the Industrial Reorganisation Corporation and Shipbuilding Industry Acts: that the Government would be tempted, in the award of contracts, granting of loans, and giving of administrative permissions of various kinds, to dis-criminate unfairly in favour of enterprises in which it or its agencies had shares, or that these means might be used to induce companies to accept Government shareholdings against their best interests. The Government, by way of reply, asserted that it had good advice available, that there were worth-while projects in need of its assistance, that it was setting up an Advisory Committee which would help to ensure fairness,[17] and, significantly in view of the promise in *Signposts for the Sixties*, that loans or grants would be the normal method of assistance and shareholdings only taken where there were good reasons for so doing.

Whether the Government will in fact use the new powers it has secured frequently, successfully and fairly is a matter of economic and political pre-diction beyond the scope of this chapter. The basis of the discussion that

13. When the Board is dissolved (see note 15, *infra*) any shares it then holds will vest in the Minister of Technology: Shipbuilding Industry Act 1967, s. 9 (3). The Board may not take up a shareholding, nor sell any shares, without the Minister's consent: s. 6 (2) and (3).

14. Statutory qualifications for membership are laid down by the Industrial Re-organisation Corporation Act, s. 1 (4), but not by the Shipbuilding Industry Act. The Chairman of the Corporation is at present Sir Joseph Lockwood, Chairman of E.M.I. Ltd.; of the Board, Sir William Swallow, a former Chairman of Vauxhall Motors Ltd.

15. Under the Shipbuilding Industry Act, s. 9 (1) and (2), the Board must be dissolved not later than the end of 1971.

16. "Industrial Reorganisation Corporation," Cmnd. 2889 (1966), para. 6.

17. s. 5 of the Act empowers the Minister of Technology to appoint an advisory committee, which was in fact constituted in October 1968. Its functions are discussed *infra*, p. 77.

follows is the fact that by participating directly in industry by way of taking shareholdings in private companies, the Government will be creating a new and possibly large and economically significant group of mixed enterprises. Such a mixed sector, composed of enterprises in which private and public ownership and control are combined, is already of importance in the economic life of France and Italy,[18] and French experience of direct Government participations[19] shows that the determination of the proper legal attributes and the proper measure and methods of public control of the mixed enterprises thereby created poses difficult problems for courts and legislature alike.[20] It is these problems which will be explored in the light of British experience of the mixed enterprise which, while far less considerable in economic terms, is yet varied and affords useful precedents for the future.

The Definition of a Mixed Enterprise

The term "mixed enterprise" may be used to describe an enterprise, a substantial part of whose capital is privately subscribed, which is constituted as a company subject to the Companies Acts or is otherwise endowed with corporate status, in which the Government itself, a public corporation, or a local authority has a substantial financial interest of a permanent character, coupled with the ability to exercise a measure of internal control either by way of voting power conferred by the ownership of shares or by the possession of a right to nominate directors or both. While most shareholdings taken up under the Industrial Expansion Act will produce mixed enterprises within this definition, it should be noted that the required substantial and permanent Government financial interest need not necessarily be in the form of a shareholding. Provision by the Government of a permanent guarantee fund or of a permanent subsidy may be sufficient if coupled with the necessary powers of control. Conversely, not every Government shareholding is constitutive of a mixed enterprise. Insistence on a substantial private participation excludes from consideration such companies as Power Jets (R. and D.) Ltd., Remploy Ltd., Cable and Wireless Ltd., or Railway Sites Ltd., of which the Government or a public corporation is sole owner, and others like Associated Humber Lines Ltd., where the element of private participation is very small (9 per cent.). The need for permanence rules out companies to which the Government has given temporary financial assistance by way of loan, even in those few cases where, as a condition of providing assistance, the Treasury

18. See generally Chazel and Poyet, *L'économie mixte* (2nd ed., 1965); Posner and Woolf, *Italian Public Enterprise* (1967); Ducouloux, *Les sociétés d'économie mixte en France et en Italie* (1963): also Chaps. 6, 7 and 8, *post*.

19. Italian mixed enterprises are administered through State Holding Companies, the Instituto per la Ricostruzione Industriale (IRI) and the Ente Nazionale Idrocarburi (ENI) which are public corporations.

20. See, *e.g.* Vedel, "Le contrôle par les commissions parlementaires de la gestion des entreprises industrielles nationalisées et des sociétés d'économie mixte," *Droit Social*, 1955, p. 137; Fabre and Morin, "Quelques aspects actuels du contrôle des sociétés d'économie mixte," *Revue de Droit Public*, 1964, p. 767.

has secured and exercised a right to appoint a part-time director[21]; nor will account be taken here of the problems posed by such holdings as the Government's 500 6 per cent. Cumulative Preference £1 shares in the Parkend Saw Mills Co., by which the public purse obtains an income of £30 per annum. Application of these criteria to the lists published from time to time in Hansard [22] of companies in which the Government, the nationalised industries and other public corporations such as the National Research Development Corporation, hold shares and of companies to which the Government appoints directors will show that a great number do not qualify as mixed enterprises; but enough—mostly partly-owned subsidiaries of nationalised industries—will pass these tests to give the lie to any suggestion that mixed enterprise is an unknown or insignificant form of organisation in the United Kingdom.

THE MOTIVES FOR MIXED ENTERPRISE

The interposition of a public corporation between the politically responsible Minister and the mixed enterprise produces a different situation and different problems of control from those which will stem from the direct participations under the Industrial Expansion Act. So too do partnerships between private enterprise and local authorities, of which the Manchester Ship Canal Co. is the best known example in the United Kingdom. Attention will therefore be confined to the small group of mixed enterprises already established in which the Government, through its Ministers, participates directly. At first sight, it is hard to see what factor of public interest links these undertakings: the Government has a direct stake in the oil industry (through British Petroleum Ltd.); in the aircraft industry (Short Brothers and Harland Ltd.); in the ship-building industry (Upper Clyde Shipbuilders Ltd.); in shipping (David MacBrayne (1928) Ltd.)[22A]; in sugar (British Sugar Corporation Ltd.); in agricultural securities (Agricultural Mortgage Corporation Ltd., and Scottish Agricultural Securities Ltd.); in an international finance company (Suez Finance Co. Ltd.); and, since July 1965, in computers (International Computers (Holdings) Ltd.). A closer inspection reveals a number of different motives for these participations.

Strategic considerations dictated the purchase by the Government, in 1914, of 2,000,000 newly created £1 Ordinary and 7,500 existing £1 Preference shares in the then Anglo-Persian Oil Co., which from 1935 to 1954 went under the name of the Anglo-Iranian Oil Co. and is now the British Petroleum Co.

21. As may be done, for example, when loans are given under the Local Employment Acts 1960–66.
22. The latest lists appear at 736 H.C. Deb., cols. 241–42, 247–50, 277–321 (written answers; November 21, 1966; shareholdings of public corporations in the fuel and power, aviation and surface transport industries respectively) and 740 H.C. Deb., cols. 49–54 (written answer; January 31, 1967; direct Government shareholdings, holdings of other public corporations, Government-appointed directors). The list at 736 H.C. Deb., cols. 277–321 now needs revision in light of the redistribution of holdings as between public corporations effected under the Transport Act 1968, ss. 4, 28 and Scheds. 3 and 7.   22A. See note 44, *infra*.

Ltd. (BP). The Admiralty had decided to replace coal with oil as fuel for the fleet, and the purchase gave the Government voting control of Anglo-Persian, besides providing the company with sufficient fresh capital to construct necessary new port facilities. By this means a reliable and economical supply of fuel for the Navy was assured.[23] Demands of wartime production and supply likewise explain the Government's 69·5 per cent. share holding in Short Brothers and Harland of Belfast, which is administered through a wholly-owned holding company, S.B. (Realisations) Ltd. In 1943 the Minister of Aircraft Production took over the whole share capital of Short Brothers (Rochester and Bedford) Ltd. under Defence Regulation 78 because the firm's production performance was unsatisfactory.[24] Four years later the firm closed its English factories and merged with Short and Harland of Belfast, another aircraft constructor, in which it already held 60 per cent. of the shares, the remainder being in private hands. The merger, which gave the enterprise its mixed character, has proved expensive for the Government. Financial difficulties have led Shorts to depend upon it for working capital, yet the level of unemployment in Northern Ireland renders it politically impossible to close the firm down. BP and Shorts are now the only mixed enterprises which could be of strategic importance to the United Kingdom, but this was once not so. What is now the Suez Finance Co., in which the Government owns 44 per cent. of the equity, was until the nationalisation of the Suez Canal in 1956 its operating company. In 1875, when the Government acquired its shareholding, and for many years thereafter, the well-being and co-operation of the Suez Canal Co. were vital to British Empire communications both civil and military.[25] A similar desire to secure overseas communications runs through the history of the Government's interest in Cable and Wireless Ltd., in which from 1938 to 1946 it held 2,600,000 £1 shares, in addition to (from 1929 onwards) approving appointments to the post of chairman and to one other seat on the board[26]; and analogous arrangements of government-blessed monopoly in return for Government directors prevailed

23. For the purchase agreement and its background, see Agreement with the Anglo-Persian Oil Company Limited: Explanatory Memorandum, Cd. 7419 (1914), and for authorisation of the purchase, Anglo-Persian Oil Company (Acquisition of Capital) Act 1914 (4 & 5 Geo 5, c. 37).

24. For the announcement of the acquisition, see 388 H.C. Deb., cols. 157–160 (March 31, 1943), and for further details, 388 H.C. Deb., cols. 1193–1194, 1851–1852 (April 14 and 22, 1943). The Government only took the shares because the directors refused to co-operate with the controller it had earlier installed under Defence Regulation 55, and the affair ended in litigation between one of the proprietors and the Treasury as to the proper value to be put on the company's shares for purposes of compensation: *Short* v. *Treasury Commissioners* [1948] A.C. 534.

25. The purchase was authorised by the Suez Canal (Shares) Act 1876 (39 & 40 Vict. c. 67).

26. See Agreements made in Pursuance of the Recommendations of the Wireless and Cable Conference, Cmd. 3338 (1929); "Cable and Wireless Ltd: a Statement," Cmd. 5716 (1938); and Imperial Telegraphs Act 1938 (1 & 2 Geo. 6, c. 57). By virtue of the Cable and Wireless Act 1946 (9 & 10 Geo. 6, c. 82) the Government acquired the remaining 27,400,000 shares, but Cable and Wireless' status as a limited company was not by that Act and has not since been altered.

in the heavily subsidised air transport industry between 1925, when Imperial Airways was founded, and 1939, when the Government bought out its shareholders and created a public corporation, the British Overseas Airways Corporation, to run the service.[27]

While the strategic value of locally-owned air transport facilities was undoubtedly a weighty factor, it is unlikely that the then Government, given its political complexion, could have taken even the small powers of control it did had not the aviation companies been in need of a considerable and continuing programme of Government financial assistance in order to survive. Assistance to a struggling industry provided the occasion here for the creation of a mixed enterprise—Imperial Airways—as it did for several of the enterprises still existent today. The formation of the British Sugar Corporation Ltd. followed a pattern almost identical to that of Imperial Airways. British growers of sugar-beet were, in the nineteen-thirties, finding it impossible to compete with imports of cane-sugar.[28] Rather than take the economic, but politically inexpedient step of letting the domestic industry die, the Government mounted a complex and expensive rescue operation designed to provide a guaranteed market for the domestic product while permitting the importation of sugar at current world prices, in implementation of which it forced the amalgamation, into the British Sugar Corporation, of the fifteen British companies manufacturing sugar from home-grown beet.[29] This intrinsically unprofitable task the Corporation continues to perform, with the aid of public subsidies to meet revenue losses, and public loans to provide working capital, within the statutory framework of the Sugar Acts of 1936 and 1956.[30] These subsidies are provided by the Sugar Board, a public corporation, out of the proceeds of a surcharge which it is empowered by the latter Act to impose on the sugar sales. The Board which also has the function of buying and selling Commonwealth sugar at approved rates, holds 25 per cent. of the Corporation's issued share capital of £10 million, and the Government holds directly a further 11·25 per cent.

Another case-history of the same kind and from the same period is that of David MacBrayne (1928) Ltd. Since the latter part of the nineteenth century the depopulation of the Hebrides had been a cause of concern to the Government. In an attempt to stem the tide by keeping down living costs (in which costs of transportation played a large part) the Government had for many years before 1928 given to the family firm of MacBraynes, who carried

27. See Report of Civil Air Transport Subsidies Committee, Cmd. 1811 (1923); 329 H.C. Deb., cols. 417–479 (November 17, 1937) (debate on a motion for a public inquiry into civil aviation); Report of Committee of Inquiry into Civil Aviation, Cmd. 5685 (1938); British Overseas Airways Act 1939 (2 & 3 Geo. 6, c. 61).
28. Report of the Greene Committee on the Sugar Industry, Cmd. 4871 (1935).
29. See "Sugar Policy: Government Proposals," Cmd. 4964 (1935), and "Amalgamation of the Beet-Sugar Manufacturing Companies," Cmd. 5139 (1936).
30. Sugar Industry (Re-organisation) Act 1936 (26 Geo. 5 & 1 Edw. 8, c. 18); Sugar Act 1956 (4 & 5 Eliz. 2, c. 48).

passengers, goods, cattle and mails among the Western Isles and to and from the Scottish mainland in their small steamers, a subsidy in the form of lucrative mail contracts to offset their regular losses. In 1928, however, after a disagreement on the terms of a new mail contract, the MacBrayne family withdrew from this trade, and the new company was formed under Governmental and Parliamentary pressure to take over their assets and operate their services with similar public assistance.[31] Half of its capital was subscribed by the London, Midland and Scottish Railway Co.,[32] half by a shipping firm, Coast Lines Ltd. A somewhat similar story lies behind the Government's 17·5 per cent. share in Upper Clyde Shipbuilders, brought about by the amalgamation into that group in February 1968 of the Fairfield yard, which the Government had rescued from imminent closure in 1965 by arranging for the formation of a new company, with 50 per cent. Government participation, Fairfields was saved not only to keep its modern equipment in use and its labour force in employment, but also because the situation offered the opportunity to use the yard as a "national proving ground" for the new techniques in industrial relations associated with Mr. Iain Sewart, and in order to involve the trade unions concerned in ownership and management, a role which, but for Government participation in the equity capital, they might have been unwilling to play.[33] The absorption of Fairfields into a larger group without these special characteristics has thus deprived the investment of a part of its purpose.[34] At the same time the amalgamation, which was arranged by the Shipbuilding Industry Board under the provisions of the Shipbuilding Industry Act 1967, has, it is hoped, greatly strengthened the ability of Fairfields and the other yards in the group to meet and conquer fierce foreign competition.

It is this economic strategy of strength through concentration, this time pursued by the Minister of Technology, that has now produced a single British manufacturer of commercial and scientific computers, in order that the domestic industry might maintain and improve its position in the world market in face of American dominance and increasing European competition. The Minister has persuaded the two major British computer companies, International Computers and Tabulators Ltd. and the English Electric Co. Ltd., to merge their interests in this field, and under the first industrial investment scheme, the Computers Merger Scheme 1968[35] has agreed, both to

31. See Report of a Select Committee on the Western Highlands and Islands of Scotland (1928) H.C. 117. The proposed contract which provoked the disagreement was printed as (1928) H.C. 61.

32. For this, but not for the scheme itself, statutory authorisation was needed: Western Highlands and Islands (Transport Services) Act 1929 (19 Geo. 5, c. 6); as to the Highlands and Islands generally, see Chap. 5, *post*, p. 91.

33. See 722 H.C. Deb., cols. 2102–07 (December 22, 1965) (statement of Mr. George Brown).

34. Stewart, "What did we prove at Fairfield?" *The Times*, April 23, 1968.

35. S.I. 1968 No. 990. Further information about the project is given in "Industrial Investment: The Computers Merger Project 1968," Cmnd. 3660 (1968). The House of Commons debate on the scheme is reported at 766 H.C. Deb., cols. 1495–1540 (June 21, 1968).

provide up to £13,500,000 by way of grants to defray a part of the new group's research and development expenditure until 1971, and to take up a 10·49 per cent. shareholding in the company formed to effect the merger, International Computers (Holdings) Ltd. The size of this shareholding, whose nominal value is £3,500,000 of which £3,150,000 is not due to be paid up until 1972, is just sufficient to prevent the Government's being compulsorily bought out following a successful takeover bid for the remainder of the company's shares[36] and it may therefore be calculated to render such bids (by American interests, for example) much less attractive.[37]

The Government's financial interest in the two agricultural securities corporations, the Agricultural Mortgage Corporation Ltd. and the Scottish Agricultural Securities Corporation Ltd. (both of which are companies limited by shares and subject to the Companies Acts) is of a special kind. The corporations were formed at the instigation of the Government in accordance with the terms of the Agricultural Credits Act 1928[38] and the Agricultural Credits (Scotland) Act 1929,[39] their share capital being subscribed by clearing banks of London and Edinburgh respectively. To enable them to carry out their statutory functions of providing credit for the purchase and improvement of agricultural land, the Government provides a guarantee fund to secure the borrowing of each corporation, which is effected by way of issues of debentures. In other countries, Government intervention in agricultural finance has commonly been effected through the agency of public corporations, or even as part of the functions of central Government departments.[40]

THE MECHANISMS OF CONTROL

It is essential to the concept of mixed enterprise here adopted that the Government should have the ability to exercise a measure of internal control over the affairs of the company. In each of the cases discussed so far, the Government

36. By virtue of s. 209 of the Companies Act 1948 (11 & 12 Geo. 6, c. 38). The writer is indebted for this observation to Mr. Douglas Lawton. So long as the Minister is providing the agreed support for the research and development programme (this is to say, until 1971), such a successful bid, if effected without the consent of the Government, would also involve a breach by the other major shareholders in International Computers (Holdings) Ltd. of the terms of a Memorandum of Understanding to which the Minister was a party. See "Industrial Investment: The Computers Merger Project 1968," Cmnd. 3660 (1968), para. 13.
37. With a similar purpose, the Government in 1903 acquired £66 of Ordinary Stock in the Cunard Steamship Co., including a £20 "Government Share" carrying voting rights equal to 25 per cent. of all votes—thus enabling it to block any proposal to amend the company's articles of association so as to allow shares to be held by foreigners: Davis, "Government as a Shareholder," The Guardian, March 13, 1967.
38. 18 & 19 Geo. 5, c. 43.
39. 19 Geo. 5, c. 13.
40. As, for example, the Agricultural Refinance Corporation of India, and the Federal Farm Mortgage Corporation of the USA, now incorporated into the US Department of Agriculture.

possesses, or possessed, a right to nominate directors, in addition to any voting power conferred by the ownership of shares. Further controls, usually statutory in origin, have, however, also been imposed in several cases. The Sugar Act 1956, which amended in part and re-enacted in part the Sugar Industry (Reorganisation) Act 1936, gives substantial powers over the activities of the British Sugar Corporation both to the Minister of Agriculture, Fisheries and Food (in Scotland the Secretary of State) and to the Sugar Board. Under section 17 of the Act, the Minister may fix the price of the home-grown beet to be purchased by the Corporation and approve the conditions of sale of beet, and may set the quantities to be purchased by the Corporation area by area; under section 23, he may direct the Corporation to place sums to reserve, and, if the Corporation fails in its obligations, may direct the withholding of payments by the Sugar Board, such as payments to meet the Corporation's losses on revenue account under section 20. Section 23 also requires the approval of the Minister and the consent of the Treasury for any alteration of the Corporation's memorandum or articles of association. The articles themselves confer considerable further powers on the Government, in addition to those which their direct shareholding would secure to them. Three of the directors are appointed jointly by the Minister of Agriculture, Fisheries and Food and the Secretary of State for Scotland, including the chairman, who enjoys, in relation to any proposal coming before the board which in his opinion involves a matter of public interest, a suspensory veto, which can be made absolute by the Government. The articles also set a limit on the size of the annual dividend which can be exceeded only with the permission of the Ministers. These provisions were inserted in pursuance of an agreement between the Government and the amalgamating companies.[41] The rather similar provisions to be found in the articles of the Agricultural Mortgage Corporation and the Scottish Agricultural Securities Corporation were, however, required to be inserted by section 2 of the Agricultural Credits Act 1928 and the Agricultural Credits (Scotland) Act 1929 respectively.

A less obvious statutory source of powers of control is the Highlands and Islands Shipping Services Act 1960,[42] section 2 of which empowers the Secretary of State for Scotland to make grants or loans to firms providing shipping services in the Highlands and Islands. MacBraynes' subsidy is at present given by virtue of an exercise of this power, in return for which the company, under the terms of an undertaking entered into on December 21, 1961, ceded considerable powers of control over fares and services to the Government, in addition to a right to appoint two directors. This was, however, simply a continuation, with minor modifications, of non-statutory arrangements which had been in force since 1928 under the mail contracts

41. "Amalgamation of the Beet-Sugar Manufacturing Companies," Cmd. 5139 (1936), para. 5.
42. 8 & 9 Eliz. 2, c. 31.

through which the subsidy was formerly administered.[43] At no time has the Government had a direct shareholding in MacBraynes, but the Transport Act 1947, by nationalising the railway companies, operated to transfer the half-interest of the London, Midland and Scottish Railway to the British Transport Commission. The Transport Act 1962 vested the shares in the newly-created Transport Holding Company, but under the Transport Act 1968, section 28 (2)(a), they were passed on to yet another new public corporation, the Scottish Transport Group.[44] One public corporation or another has thus since 1947 been an equal partner in management with Coast Lines Ltd. The Computers Merger Scheme of 1968 suggests that arrangements under the Industrial Expansion Act 1968 will be similar to those under which MacBraynes now operates: the financial assistance which the Minister is authorised by statute to give provides the *quid pro quo* for the powers of control contractually ceded to him by the enterprise. In the case of International Computers, the position is complicated by the fact that the Minister has obtained one set of powers for a limited period in return for his grants towards research and development expenditure, and a second, different set (including the right to nominate a director) by virtue of his shareholding. Under clause 12 of the support agreement between the Minister of Technology and International Computers,[45] so long as the Minister holds not less than 5 per cent. of the company's shares, he can veto any association (other than of a routine trading character, with foreign companies, any major change in the nature of the business and any disposal of important assets; he must be consulted before the appointment or dismissal of the chairman or chief executive of the company; and (a fine example of "government by contract") the company's dividend policy must be consistent with the Government's recommendations to industrial companies generally.[46]

So far as its interests in other companies are concerned, the Government has relied entirely on internal controls provided for in the companies' articles of association. In the case of BP (Anglo-Persian), part of the agreement between the Government and the company was that revised articles would be drafted. These provided for the representation of the Treasury on the board by two *ex officio* directors, who are empowered to call extraordinary general meetings and to veto any resolution of the board or of an executive

43. Published as (1928–29) H.C. 4; (1938–39) H.C. 16; (1946–47) H.C. 108; (1948–49) H.C. 82; (1951–52) H.C. 151. The 1961 undertaking has not been so published.

44. Since this chapter was written, in July 1969, the Group bought out Coast Lines Ltd. MacBraynes is thus no longer a mixed enterprise, but still has a Government subsidy and a Government director.

45. For which see the Computers Merger Scheme 1968 (S.I. 1968 No. 990), Sched., Pt. 2. The Minister's powers of control relating to his research and development grants are set out in cl. 10.

46. The right to nominate a director is contained in the articles of the company: see "Industrial Investment: The Computers Merger Project 1968," Cmnd. 3660 (1968), paras. 14, 15.

committee thereof. These powers look sweeping, but are hardly exorbitant in light of the fact that until 1967, when BP made a large issue of shares to finance the acquisition of certain interests of the Distillers Co. Ltd., the Government with 51·6 per cent. of the equity capital held effective voting control of the company anyway. Its holding is now 48·9 per cent. The veto power is, in essence, only an alternative to the appointment by the Government of the number of directors to which the size of its shareholding would ordinarily entitle it. By virtue of its 69·5 per cent. shareholding in Shorts, by contrast, up to eight of the twelve directorships of the company are in the gift of the Government, and special controls are therefore unnecessary. To these directors, whom it appoints to the board of S.B. (Realisations) Ltd. and who then appoint themselves as directors of Shorts, the Government in 1955 issued a directive[47] requiring them, while carrying on the business in conformity with the best commercial principles, to obtain the consent of the Ministry (now the Ministry of Technology) to certain major commercial decisions such as the exercise of borrowing powers, and also to their selection of a chairman of the board of Shorts. On the chairman personally was placed the additional duty of seeking the approval of the Ministry before entering upon a course of action which, however appropriate to a purely commercial undertaking might, in the case of one substantially owned by the State, raise controversial public issues.

A Government director was also nominated to the board of Fairfields (Glasgow) Ltd. prior to its absorption into Upper Clyde Shipbuilders, but he enjoyed no greater powers than the other three directors directly nominated by the other shareholders. These four directors appointed the rest of the board, and any one of them could refer to a general meeting of the Company any resolution for which, under the articles, a unanimous vote of all the directors was required. Apart from certain provisions designed to protect its interest as the holder of £940,000 of Unsecured Loan Stock, the Government's only special privilege was that future appointments by the board to the post of chairman needed the approval of the President of the Board of Trade.[48]

THE GENERAL PRINCIPLE OF CONTROL

The diversity of arrangements for control is explicable in part by the very occasional and sometimes accidental nature of Government participation in private industry in the past, which has led to the shape of the resulting mixed enterprise being worked out *de novo* on each occasion. In part, however, it reflects, whether by conscious choice or otherwise, the differing circumstances

47. Its terms are set out in the recent evidence of the Minister of Technology before the Select Committee on Nationalised Industries: Special Report from the Select Committee on Nationalised Industries, (1967–68) H.C. 298 (hereinafter cited simply as "Special Report"), Evidence, Q. 136.

48. These arrangements were set out in a Parliamentary reply by the President of the Board of Trade, at 724 H.C. Deb., cols. 46–48 (written answers) (February 8, 1966).

which make Government intervention in the affairs of a company or industry
necessary or desirable. Generalisation is always dangerous, but it does seem
that the Government has been satisfied with the powers of an ordinary but
important shareholder—that is to say, voting power, power to withdraw
existing or withhold additional capital, power to nominate, and if necessary,
to instruct directors—only in those cases where the sole or predominant
purpose of its investment is to promote the profitable operation of the company concerned and hence its continuance in business. Such a purpose, and
such a measure of control, are best seen in conjunction in the arrangements for
the Government participations in Fairfields shipyard and in Short Brothers
and Harland. More commonly, however, the public interest which dictated
the foundation of a mixed enterprise is not consistent in all respects with the
vigorous pursuance by that enterprise of an orthodox commercial policy. The
British Sugar Corporation and MacBraynes provide convenient examples. In
the former case, the Government policy of protecting sugar-beet growers by
providing a guaranteed market, and the ordinary policy of maximisation of
profit likely to be pursued by a sugar-manufacturing company, would pull in
opposite directions. Such a company might wish to amalgamate factories and
to buy only from low-cost producing areas at lowest possible prices. Likewise,
the whole point of the creation of David MacBrayne (1928) Ltd. was to find
an acceptable way of continuing the Government policy of cheap transport for
the Hebrides, which necessitated running the steamer services unprofitably.
In such cases, which form the majority to date, the Government has sought
to protect the public interest not by the use of its powers as a shareholder, nor
through its representation on the board of the enterprise, but by conferring
upon the appropriate Minister additional specific powers taken either under
statute, as under the Sugar Acts 1936 and 1956, or by virtue of contracts such
as undertakings under the Highland and Islands Shipping Services Act
1960[49] and if the Computers Merger Scheme is any precedent, support
agreements under the Industrial Expansion Act 1968.

THE GOVERNMENT DIRECTOR[50]

What results follow from this method of determining how Government control of a mixed enterprise is to be operated? One result is to leave the
Government-appointed director, whether full-time or part-time, free to

49. This is not a purely negative task of restraint: its positive side is shown by the
efforts made, under the incentive agreement of 1964 between the Government and the
British Sugar Corporation (S.I. 1964 No. 561, varied by S.I. 1966 No. 1223) and
the 1961 undertaking between the Secretary of State for Scotland and MacBraynes, to
effect a reconciliation between Government policy and the preservation of commercial
incentives.

50. See Davies, "Government Directors of Public Companies," (1938) 9, P. Q. 421;
and for American experience, Schwartz, "Governmentally Appointed Directors in a
Private Corporation—the Communications Satellite Act of 1962" (1965) 79 Harv.
L.R. 350.

participate fully with his colleagues on the board in promoting the commercial success of his company. Such participation is demanded of him by virtue of his position as a member of the board: as such, like any other director, he may receive fees for his services, is the agent of the company and, most important, is responsible for the conduct of the company's affairs to the whole body of shareholders.[51] The responsibility does not rule out the taking of a slightly different approach to problems coming before the board—this may be expected of the Government director by reason of his special awareness of the needs of the public interest—but it does demand, as a minimum, that he should not do anything to impair the achievement of the ordinary commercial objectives of profit, expansion and stability that the shareholders, among whom the Government may be included,[52] would wish to see pursued. If, however, the powers necessary to ensure that the public interest always prevails (which must amount to the power to veto any decision of the board deemed to be inconsistent with it) are placed in his hands, he may often be called upon to act in just this way. Such powers should therefore be located outside the enterprise. The Government has shown itself aware of the need to avoid imposing conflicting responsibilities upon its directors, implicitly in the past in the way it has shaped the mechanisms of control, explicitly at the present time. In the Lords' debate on the Industrial Expansion Bill, Lord Shackleton, speaking for the Government, said that Government directors must have regard to the prospects of their companies; "It is not possible to appoint a director solely to look after the public interest."[53]

One apparently exceptional case calls for special comment. There is at least the possibility that the public interest which dictated the Government's investment in BP, *viz.* the provision of secure and economical oil supplies for the Navy, might not always coincide with the most obvious path to the maximisation of the company's profits; yet protection of this public interest is confided in the first place to the *ex officio* directors appointed by the Government. That there is no evidence of special difficulties experienced by such directors in combining the tasks of shareholders' representative and Government representative may be ascribed chiefly to the very restricted view of the needs of the public interest that the Government has always had.[54] It may also be noted that their role has been rather to advise, to inform and to provide a channel through which information and views can pass between Government and company, than themselves to determine what action is required in

51. *Cf.* the speech of Sir John Reith, the Government-appointed Chairman of Imperial Airways, at its annual general meeting on November 14, 1938, quoted in Davies, *"National" Capitalism* (1939), p. 257.
52. The main reason for the maintenance by the Government of its shareholding in BP now appears to be its profitability as an investment: Special Report, Evidence, QQ. 102, 125, 130 (Minister of Power).
53. 292 H.L. Deb., col. 424 (May 16, 1968).
54. *Cf.* citation at note 52, *supra,* and for details of this restriction, the discussion of parliamentary control that follows.

the public interest.[55] The power of veto, which they possess for use in emergencies, and which has never been exercised, is in their hands suspensory only, and cannot have permanent effect without confirmation by the Government following an appeal by the rest of the board; and it would seem that informal decisions also, whether to put pressure on the company to change a particular course of action, or to acquiesce in it, are taken by the Government—though they are doubtless taken on the basis of information supplied by the *ex officio* directors, and may be carried out through them. The system of control of BP therefore, while, as will be seen, creating difficulties from the Parliamentary standpoint, is less of a departure from the norm than might at first appear; for where, according to the usual practice, Ministers are charged directly with the protection of the public interest, they must rely hardly less heavily for the performance of this function on information and advice conveyed by the Government director on the spot. Indeed, such Government directors have sometimes been given, by virtue of their position, a special role or special *ad hoc* responsibilities in the running of their company,[56] which has apparently never occurred with BP's *ex officio* directors.

PARLIAMENTARY CONTROL

This pattern of Government control also provides the framework for the exercise of Parliamentary supervision over mixed enterprises. The first result is that for any act of the mixed enterprise which seems inconsistent with the relevant public interest, the relevant Minister can be held accountable. Thus if the British Sugar Corporation were to decide to cease buying beet from Scottish producers, or if MacBraynes were to put up (as they frequently do) their passenger fares and freight rates, the Secretary of State for Scotland

55. Thus Lord Inchcape, one of the *ex officio* directors from 1914 until 1925, sought the approval of the Treasury before consenting to the termination by Anglo-Persian of a contract whereby certain services in Persia were performed for it by an independent agency. This appears from the report of *Anglo-Persian Oil Co.* v. *Dale (Inspector of Taxes)* [1932] 1 K.B. 124, in which the company successfully maintained (with the help of Lord Inchcape's evidence) that the payment necessary to terminate the contract constituted revenue rather than capital expenditure.

56. In his evidence to the Select Committee on the Western Highlands and Islands of Scotland, Sir Josiah Stamp, Chairman of the London, Midland and Scottish Railway, saw the Government director as fulfilling a financial function, an alternative to audit of his company's accounts by the Comptroller and Auditor-General: (1928) H.C. 117, Evidence, Q. 264. The annual return of MacBraynes has in fact usually been signed by its Government director, and a Home Office Memorandum in 1955 stressed the financial aspect of his functions: Special Report from the Select Committee on the House of Commons Disqualification Bill, (1955–56) H.C. 349, Appendix 2, at p. 230. At the same time MacBraynes has been obliged, under the mail contracts and the 1961 undertaking, to open its books to the scrutiny of the Comptroller and Auditor-General if requested to do so. Also, when the relations between Imperial Airways and its pilots were the subject of debate in Parliament, it was promised that the system employed by the company for dealing with its staff, particularly the arrangements for the consideration of staff grievances, would be discussed by the Secretary of State with the company's Government directors, one of whom was at the time of the debate out of the country on an inspection tour of working conditions of pilots of foreign airlines: 329 H.C. Deb., cols. 478–479 (November 17, 1937).

would be clearly responsible, for his approval is, by virtue of statute or of agreements concluded under statute, necessary before such action can be taken.[57] Where the pattern is departed from, as in the case of BP, referred to above, the result is a blurring of lines of responsibility. The exercise of power by way of reports, instructions and advice passing between Ministers and persons who are servants not of the Government but of a distinct and independent legal entity may be administratively convenient, but is perfectly calculated to conceal from Parliament the authorship of any particular decision. In cases where actions of BP have seemed to be at variance with Government policy,[58] it has seldom been clear to Parliament whether the reason was the failure of directors to report to the Government, the failure of the Government to act on the report, or the failure of the directors to implement, or to get the whole board to implement, the Government's instructions or advice. Admittedly, the confusion and disquiet in Parliament on such occasions as the raising of petrol prices in 1929[59] and the raising of BP's interim dividend in 1955 immediately after the Chancellor had called for dividend restraint[60] owed something to failure by the House to appreciate the implication of the Government's undertaking not to interfere by way of its veto in the commercial affairs of the company other than in certain exceptional cases; but even after the publication to the House in 1929 of the Treasury letter of May 20, 1914 in which the undertaking had been given,[61] the matters in relation to which the veto might be exercised remained far from clear, and in any event the Government did not thereby commit itself to refrain from seeking to influence the company's decisions on commercial matters otherwise than by way of veto. Indeed, as holder of nearly half of the very substantial equity capital, it cannot but be concerned about such matters, but it has never acknowledged responsibility for the exercise of any power or influence stemming from this concern. It is this cloak of secrecy in which the Government has shrouded its dealings *quo* shareholder with BP and its *ex officio* directors that has been one of the principal causes of Parliamentary dissatisfaction.[62] In

57. For an acknowledgment of such responsibility, see 725 H.C. Deb., col. 2099 (March 9, 1966).

58. *e.g.* alleged sales of oil to Italy during her invasion of Abyssinia—see 307 H.C. Deb., cols. 739, 1131–1132 (December 10 and 12, 1935)—and to Japan in 1940—see 360 H.C. Deb., co. 6 (April 23, 1940), 364 H.C. Deb., cols. 1280–1281 (August 21, 1940), 373 H.C. Deb., col. 802 (July 22, 1941).

59. See 226 H.C. Deb., cols. 558–570 (March 7, 1929).

60. See 545 H.C. Deb., cols. 1996–1999 (November 10, 1955).

61. 226 H.C. Deb., cols. 2261–2264 (March 26, 1929). The Government indicated that the veto would be used "only in regard to matters of general policy, such as— (i) the supervision of the activities of the company as they may affect questions of foreign, naval or military policy; (ii) any proposed sale of the company's undertaking or proposed change of the company's status; (iii) the control of new exploitations, sites of wells, etc; (iv) sales of crude or fuel oil to foreigners, or such exceptional sales to other persons on long contracts as might endanger the fulfilment of current Admiralty contracts."

62. The Select Committee on Nationalised Industries suggested that there should be an inquiry into BP's relationship with the Government: Special Report, paras. 64–71. This was not implemented: see 777 H.C. Deb., cols. 1181–1274 (Feb. 11, 1969).

theory, similar problems of assigning responsibility could arise by reason of the obligation laid on the chairman of Shorts by the 1955 directive to obtain the consent of the Government to commercial decisions capable of provoking public controversy. That they have not is attributable to the width of the powers of control over the company's major decisions that the Government can exercise under the other provisions of the directive, powers which, by reason of Short's position as an unsuccessful member of an industry all of whose members, publicly owned or not, depend very heavily on Government orders and assistance,[63] have of recent years been used to the full, to the point of imposing a major re-organisation of the company and requiring the resignation of its chairman. For the use of its powers of proprietorship in this drastic way, the Government has accepted responsibility before Parliament.[64] By this route the commercial affairs and prospects of Shorts have come to be frequently discussed on the floor of the House of Commons.

Such discussion is unusual. The second result of applying the general pattern of control, whereby Ministers are made responsible for the protection of the public interest, while the Government-appointed directors participate on behalf of the public in the conduct of the company's commercial affairs, is that such commercial affairs escape to a considerable degree the scrutiny of Parliament, to which those directors are responsible neither directly nor through the relevant Minister. In some ways, this freedom from scrutiny is most beneficial. It gives the enterprise some immunity from political pressures directed to securing the reversal of decisions which may be commercially sensible but are politically inexpedient. The deadening effect of accountability to Parliament on initiative and risk-taking in management, so commonly advanced as a reason to justify the transfer of services from Government departments to public corporations, is also avoided. There is, however, an objection of principle: that it is improper that the commercial success or failure, and the commercial policy generally, of enterprises in which a considerable amount of public money is invested should not be an appropriate subject for discussion in Parliament. To this one might reasonably reply first, that where the public interest in the commercial success of the enterprise is exactly the same as the interest of the private shareholders it may appropriately be protected in the same way, by the exercise of the Government's powers as a shareholder, for which it is responsible to Parliament; second, that to make the enterprise itself, or its directors, or any of them, responsible to Parliament would be to ignore the element of private participation and risk, the "mixed" character with which the enterprise was deliberately endowed; and third, that

63. See Report of a Committee of Inquiry (Plowden) into the Aircraft Industry, Cmnd. 2853 (1965). The Committee found that the airframe sector of the industry was being stifled by the very stringent controls by which the Government sought to protect its massive financial interest, and recommended as a solution the taking up of a Government shareholding in the major airframe companies. The companies concerned opposed this suggestion, and the Government has not so far done anything to implement it.

64. See e.g. 750 H.C. Deb., cols. 419–423 (July 11, 1967).

in any event, as will be seen, lack of commercial success usually creates opportunities for more rigorous and far-reaching Parliamentary scrutiny. Each part of this reply calls for comment and amplification.

(i) If the Government, with its organisation, its reserves of expertise, and its unparalleled financial power, cannot effectively use the methods of control which the law confers upon it as a shareholder or creditor, then none can hope to, and the concept of a limited company is in need of radical re-thinking.[65] For the operation of these controls, the Government certainly does acknowledge a responsibility to Parliament, which may be likened to that of the trustees of a fund to its beneficiaries, for the wise handling of the investments made and maintained on behalf of the public. In relation to BP for example, the Chancellor of the Exchequer has given the names and salaries of the *ex officio* directors[66] and has defended the choice of persons to fill the position[67] (but has refused to give Parliament any information about communications passing between the Government and the *ex officio* directors[68]); has given details from time to time of the value of the Government's shareholding and of the income derived from it;[69] and has explained the Government's decision to take, or not to take, further shares in the company.[70] All this information was, however, given in answer to Parliamentary questions asked from time to time, and enquiries of a wider or more searching character have been rare. In theory the opportunity for debate arises whenever public funds are appropriated to the service or use of mixed enterprises. When Government participation is by way of shareholding, however, the funds needed for the initial purchase are normally the only appropriation made until further shares are taken up, or further issues of capital are made by the company concerned, events which may never happen. Furthermore, while this initial purchase is usually, but not always,[71] authorised by legislation specifically

65. Such a reappraisal is in fact going on: see PEP, "A Companies Act 1970?" (1967).
66. 546 H.C. Deb., cols. 762–763 (November 17, 1955).
67. 422 H.C. Deb., col. 119 (written answers) (May 9, 1946).
68. 508 H.C. Deb., cols. 610–611 (November 27, 1952).
69. 635 H.C. Deb., cols. 1350–1351 (February 28, 1961); 728 H.C. Deb., cols. 115–116 (written answers) (May 12, 1966).
70. 740 H.C. Deb., col. 44 (written answers) (January 31, 1967).
71. Thus the Government's participation in Fairfields was authorised only by parliamentary approval of a Supplementary Estimate, which was not debated. While a brief opportunity for debate had previously been given to Parliament—see 722 H.C. Deb., cols. 2102–2107 (December 22, 1965)—full information about the terms of the Government's participation was not provided until February 8, 1966; see 724 H.C. Deb., cols. 46–48 (written answers). Compare the information and opportunities for debate afforded to Parliament in connection with the Government's purchase of shares in Anglo-Persian Oil, note 23, *supra*. The propriety of providing in the Estimates for new expenditure not authorised by legislation is doubtful: Beer, *Treasury Control* (2nd ed., 1957), pp. 48–50. For a recent case on this question relating to a Government shareholding (the formation by the Ministry of Agriculture, without statutory sanction, of a wholly-owned company, the National Seed Development Organisation Ltd.); see Third Report from the Committee of Public Accounts, (1967–68) H.C. 314, paras. 79–82.

passed for the purpose, when further appropriations are made the sums involved simply appear as a tiny part of the vast mass of votes in the Annual Estimates or (possibly) the Supplementary Estimates. No connection between the subject-matter of debates on Supply Days and on the Consolidated Fund Bill and the Estimates and appropriations themselves is now necessary,[72] and even where a particular Estimate is debated as such, it is rare for Parliament to select an item which is not unusual or controversial. The inquisitorial techniques of the Estimates Committee are also unavailable, since consideration of policy decisions is there precluded and the Government so categorised the 1966 decisions to take up its substantial shareholding in Fairfields and additional holdings in BP.[73]

(ii) BP is, of course, a highly successful company. The usual complaint voiced in Parliament is that it is too successful. It is probably large enough and powerful enough to survive the sale by the Government of its 48·9 per cent. shareholding. Few of the other mixed enterprises that have been here discussed can be in a similarly independent position.[74] The whole or a very large part of the value of private holdings in most of them is, in other words, dependent upon the maintenance by the Government of its financial interest in the enterprise. That interest has in many cases been taken to implement a particular Government policy and its maintenance is guaranteed for as long as that policy seems attractive. In such circumstances there is an element of unreality in talking of the need to have regard to the private interests in an enterprise which give it its "mixed" character. The risk for private participants is not that normally associated with equity capital—bad management, adverse market conditions, etc. It is the quite different risk of a change in Government policy.[75] This makes it less surprising that certain of these mixed enterprises have been submitted to a degree of Parliamentary scrutiny which, in effect if not in form or intention, ignores their mixed character in that it operates so as to call in question the whole running of their business and not simply the actions of the Government in relation to them. The scrutiny is exercised under a variety of forms, principally through the House of Commons' financial procedures, and finds its foothold in the regular

72. See House of Commons S.O. 18 (5) (1967), implementing the recommendations of the Select Committee on Procedure (1965–66) H.C. 122, para. 6.

73. Second Report from the Estimates Committee (Spring Supplementary Estimates) (1965–66) H.C. 108, para. 5.

74. With BP should perhaps be classed International Computers and any other mixed enterprises which may be created in its image under the Industrial Expansion Act, with Government shareholdings designed primarily to secure the maintenance of British ownership and control of profitable activities, as opposed to the continuance of unprofitable ones.

75. Thus, the Select Committee on Nationalised Industries thought that Shorts, having been acquired by the Government to enable it to survive, should be "regarded as by implication to some extent underwritten in the same way as the nationalised industries"; and the Minister of Technology, in his evidence before the Committee, did not press with any vigour the point that different principles should govern an inquiry into Shorts by reason of the minority private shareholding there: Special Report, para. 99 and Evidence QQ. 133, 157.

or reasonably frequent application of public funds as subsidies to or loans to provide working capital for mixed enterprises.

(iii) In every case where subsidies or loans are made directly by the central Government, they must be charged to a departmental vote and the expenditure accounted for to the Comptroller and Auditor-General and through him to Parliament—in fact to its Committee of Public Accounts. Recent proceedings relating to Short Brothers and Harland show that examination of the "wisdom, faithfulness and economy"[76] of this Governmental expenditure can involve the Comptroller and Auditor-General and the Public Accounts Committee in detailed scrutiny of the past performance and future prospects of the enterprise that is being assisted, as well as of the adequacy of the measures being taken by its management to alleviate the difficulties creating the need for assistance.[77] In this case, the Committee confined itself to interrogating the Accounting Officer of the department concerned, but, given the Committee's readiness at the present time to call before it representatives of firms carrying out contracts for the Government[78] there seems no reason of principle why in future cases, or in further inquiries relating to Shorts, the Committee should not take evidence from directors of the firm also. A limit is placed on all these inquiries, however, by the fact that the Comptroller and Auditor-General, on whose expertise and facilities for investigation their effectiveness must depend, has no statutory right to audit the accounts of mixed enterprises.[79] It was lack of this facility that caused the Committee to abandon as unprofitable its attempts to examine the economy of spending by statutory public corporations generally.[80] There is a precedent, however, for a right of access to the books of an enterprise to be conceded to the Comptroller and Auditor-General as part of an agreement between Government and the enterprise. This right is presently enjoyed in relation to MacBraynes under the terms of the 1961 undertaking, and was previously enjoyed by virtue of express stipulation in the various mail contracts through which the subsidy was formerly administered. The writer has not discovered any inquiry into the administration of MacBraynes' subsidy which has made use of such an inspection by the Comptroller and Auditor-General, but this may be explained by the fact that a special form of Parliamentary supervision of the subsidy has existed ever since the formation of David MacBrayne (1928) Ltd. and even before it.

76. The functions of the Committee and of the Comptroller and Auditor-General were thus described by a member of the Committee in 1902 and the description remains accurate: Chubb, *The Control of Public Expenditure* (1952), p. 78. See also Normington, *The Accountability and Audit of Governments* (1966).

77. Fifth Report from the Committee of Public Accounts, (1966–67) H.C. 647, paras. 66–70, and Evidence, QQ. 3951–4044.

78. See *e.g.* Second Special Report (Bristol Siddeley Engines Ltd.), (1966–67) H.C. 571, and Third Special Report (Bristol Siddeley Engines Ltd.) (1967–68) H.C. 192.

79. His general statutory powers of audit are set out in the Exchequer and Audit Departments Act 1921 (11 & 12 Geo. 5, c. 52), s. 1.

80. Gutch, "Nationalised Industries and the Public Accounts Committee" (1953) 31 *Public Administration* 255.

Under Standing Orders 92 and 93 of the House of Commons, contracts entered into by the Government for the carriage of the mails by sea were not binding until approved by a resolution of the House. The renewal, at approximately ten-year intervals, of MacBraynes' mail contract thus provided the House with occasional opportunities, always taken, of reviewing critically and in detail the whole performance of the firm during the currency of the previous contract. (A feeling that such Parliamentary criticism of a private firm was inappropriate was one of the reasons for the abandonment of the coastal trade by the original firm of MacBraynes, a fact which emphasises the public character of the present successor company.)[81] The new arrangements for direct subsidy continue this mechanism of Parliamentary review, as any grant under section 2 of the 1960 Act which is over £10,000 is subject to an affirmative resolution of the House of Commons. The debate preceding the passing of such a resolution relating to MacBraynes in 1961 was no less sweeping in its scope than those formerly held on the mail contracts.[82] Another specialised avenue of accountability to Parliament exists in relation to the British Sugar Corporation. The Sugar Board includes in its annual report to the Minister of Agriculture, Fisheries and Food and the Secretary of State for Scotland a summary of the Corporation's activities during the year under review and a statement of its accounts, in the same form as presented to its shareholders. Opportunities for debate on the affairs of the Corporation are thereby afforded to the House.

The characteristics common to these three modes of scrutiny should be noted. First, the ostensible purpose of the Parliamentary process, in each case, is to examine the actions of the Government or a public corporation in giving financial support to a mixed enterprise, rather than the activities of the mixed enterprise itself; although it is in practice impossible to separate the two things. Secondly, these modes of scrutiny apply, or could be made to apply, regardless of the size of the Government's shareholding (if any) in the enterprise. In particular, it is irrelevant whether the Government is a majority or a minority shareholder. A new form of scrutiny proposed by the Select Committee on Nationalised Industries in its recent special report on its Order of Reference[83] would, in its application to mixed enterprises, differ from the established forms on both these points. In this report, the Committee formulated the principle—

"That Parliament should be able to examine through one of its Committees all bodies which are or could be subject to control by the Government; and that where any such body, by reason of the fact that it disposes of an income arising from its operation, falls outside the Order of Reference of the

81. See the correspondence published as Appendix 1 to the Report of the Select Committee on the Western Highlands and Islands of Scotland (1928) H.C. 117.
82. 651 H.C. Deb., cols. 99–170 (December 11, 1961).
83. (1967–68) H.C. 298.

Estimates Committee or the traditional field of the Committee of Public Accounts, it should be brought within the Order of Reference of the Nationalised Industries Committee."[84]

Applying this principle, the Committee recommended the extension of its Order of Reference so as to include eleven new bodies ranging from the Bank of England to the Horserace Totalisator Board and including the mixed enterprises, BP and Short Brothers and Harland.[85] The practice of the Committee has been to look not only at relationships between sponsoring Ministers and the nationalised industries for which they have responsibility, but also directly at the general organisation and conduct of affairs of the industries themselves, and it seems that inquiries of similar scope would be pursued in relation to any new bodies brought within their order of reference.[86] Here is the first difference. As to the second, in theory all mixed enterprises could fall within the general principle set out above, but in fact the Committee excluded all but BP and Shorts by treating size of shareholding as the sole test of control where limited companies were concerned. Indeed, even BP was admitted only by way of exception (the Government shareholding now being marginally below 50 per cent.) because of the continuing existence of the *ex officio* directors' power of veto, and the Committee wished to confine its inquiry in this case to a single investigation of the extent to which the Government's powers over the company had been or could be used.

Without questioning the general principle on which the Committee acted in making its recommendations, one may ask whether, if it is thought that full and direct Parliamentary examination of the activities of some mixed enterprises is desirable, it is appropriate or sufficient to apply a single test of size of Government shareholding to determine which shall be so examined. Size of shareholding alone can give no clue either to the purpose for which Government control was obtained or to the actual measure of its exercise, and this does not indicate whether a mixed enterprise is essentially a private company in which the Government has a proprietary interest, or a public body organised under private forms and with private participation. The Government's behaviour over the years, and the Minister of Power's recent evidence to the Select Committee,[87] clearly indicates that BP, in which the Government has its second largest percentage shareholding, falls into the former category; equally, the fact that MacBraynes and the agricultural securities corporations, in which the Government has no direct shareholding, and the British Sugar Corporation, in which its direct shareholding is only 11·25 per cent., were brought into being at Government instigation to implement specific Government policies, puts them into the latter. Other mixed enterprises may be

84. Special Report, para. 117.
85. Discussed in paras. 64–71 and 90–103 respectively.
86. Special Report, paras. 12–14, and Evidence, QQ. 5, 156 (remarks of the Chairman of Sub-Committee B, Col. C. G. Lancaster).
87. See note 52, *supra*. And see now 777 H.C. Deb., Cols. 1181–1274 (Feb. 11, 1969).

viewed as falling at various points between these two extremes. Drawing a line on this spectrum between "public" bodies whose affairs a Parliamentary Committee may properly examine and "private" bodies in relation to which such examination would be constitutionally inappropriate, requires a more complex and subtle calculation than the simple arithmetic of percentages.

LEGAL CONTROLS

The treatment that mixed enterprises receive in the courts is, unlike the Parliamentary controls just described, homogeneous in character. They are subject to the same rules of common law and of legislation as private enterprises of the same status, that is, private companies, both in relation to their external contacts and their internal organisation. Failure by the courts to develop any special legal attributes which would correspond to the existence of Government participation in a company or to the differences already remarked which exist as between mixed enterprises no doubt owes something to the absence in Britain of a separate administrative jurisdiction, whose existence would make it necessary to classify such enterprises as "public" or "private" in relation to any action or activity of theirs that was the subject of litigation.[88] The methods by which, within the context of our unitary system, the courts have taken account of the public character and mission of certain bodies are not capable of application in this sphere. Mixed enterprises do not enjoy statutory powers, and are therefore unaffected by the rules developed to reconcile the effective exercise of these powers with ordinary principles of contractual or delictual liability.[89] They could hardly make any claim to be acting in the service of the Crown and thus to enjoy the Crown's privileges and immunities in civil litigation,[90] or its exemption from tax. It is the element of private participation and benefit that makes this status unthinkable, even for those

88. Compare the French case, *Société "Entreprise Peyrot"* c. *Société de l'Autoroute Esterel-Côte d'Azur*, Tribunal de Conflits, July 8, 1963, [1963] *Dalloz (Jurisprudence)* 534, conclusions Lasry, note Josse, also discussed in Fabre and Morin, *supra*, note 20. On the division of competence between ordinary and administrative courts in France see generally, Brown and Garner, *French Administrative Law* (1967) pp. 55–76; Vedel, *Droit Administratif* (4th ed., 1968) pp. 61–153.

89. *Ayr Harbour Trustees* v. *Oswald* (1883) 8 App. Cas. 623; *Virtue* v. *Police Commissioners of Alloa* (1873) 1 R. 285. See generally Mitchell, *The Contracts of Public Authorities* (1954); Street, *Governmental Liability* (1953); Robinson, *Public Authorities and Legal Liability* (1925).

90. Although BP received an undeserved bonus from its Government shareholding when it successfully asserted an immunity from service of process in a United States investigation into an international oil cartel of which it was allegedly a member, in interlocutory proceedings the US District Court, relying on the reasons for the Government purchase of shares in Anglo-Persian Oil set out in the 1914 Memorandum (see note 23, *supra*), held that BP had a "Governmental function" and was "indistinguishable from the Government of Great Britain" and thus partook of its sovereign immunity: *Re Investigation of World Arrangements with Relation to the Production, Transportation, Refining and Distribution of Petroleum*, 13 F.R.D. 280, at pp. 288, 290–291 (1952), quoted in Kronstein, Miller and Schwartz, *Modern American Anti-Trust Law* (1958) pp. 257–258.

enterprises, such as MacBraynes, identified as essentially "public" in character according to the tests already suggested.

The privileges and immunities of the Crown are not in any event appropriate to mixed enterprises or necessary for their proper functioning. What may, however, be necessary are limitations imposed in the interest of the consumer or client, where an enterprise enjoys a monopoly position, or in the interests of competitors, where an enterprise financed in part with public money operates in a competitive context. Neither of these situations, which are economic rather than organisational, is special to mixed enterprises. In neither situation have the methods and concepts of the common law been able to provide the protections needed. In the case of public utilities such as gas, electricity and rail transport, protection against the improper exercise of monopoly power was afforded when they were in private hands by statutory provisions regulating the conditions of access to their facilities, forbidding undue preference or discrimination, or even introducing price-fixing régimes, and such provisions continued in force (and were reinforced by arrangements for consumer representation) when the activities were taken over by public corporations.[91] Likewise, special statutory and administrative provision has been made to ensure that public corporations are seen not to subsidise the activities in which they compete with private enterprise from surpluses made in areas of their business where they enjoy a monopoly.[92] The experience of the last twenty years has shown that such provisions are useful, and possibly necessary, to protect customers and competitors, even given the guarantee of fairness and moderation in business provided by public ownership and control.[93] The analogous guarantees which the appointment of Government directors to the boards of companies enjoying a Government-sponsored monopoly is in part designed to afford are arguably in need of similar reinforcement, which has indeed been provided for MacBraynes and the British Sugar Corporation not by way of the imposition of legal duties not to discriminate, to provide reasonable facilities, and so on, but in the form of the detailed Ministerial controls over prices, charges, purchasing and the provision of facilities already discussed.

91. An excellent critical account of such provisions relating to the railways is provided in Milne and Laing, *The Obligation to Carry* (1956).

92. See *e.g.* Electricity Act 1947, s. 46; Report of Central Electricity Authority for period ending March 31, 1949, (1948–49) H.C. 336, p. 111 (Ministerial directions as to form of accounts); Report of the Minister of Fuel and Power for 1956–57, (1956–57) H.C. 284, p. 6 (recording agreement with the electricity boards on the adoption of a more detailed form of accounts for retail trading activities).

93. Cases like *British Oxygen Co. Ltd.* v. *S.W. Scotland Electricity Board*, 1956 S.C. (H.L.) 112 (subsequent proceedings reported at 1959 S.C. (H.L.) 17) and the recent argument about the legality of preferential long-term coal contracts for aluminium smelters, provide spectacular examples, but at a more mundane level, the reports of an area electricity consultative council will show how pervasive and continuous is the effect of the undue preference provisions of the Electricity Acts on tariff-making in the industry. For an example, see Report of the Eastern Electricity Consultative Council for 1952–53 (published with the Report of the Eastern Electricity Board), (1952–53) H.C. 256, paras. 15–17.

What appears to be more of a problem, if only by reason of the frequency with which, given existing Government policy, it is likely to recur, is the possibility of unfair competition by the mixed enterprise operating with the help of Government subsidies or grants, or on cheap or free Government credit. Are not competing firms which do not enjoy such facilities unfairly disadvantaged? Certainly they are disadvantaged, but so too is any firm which does not secure Government financial assistance of whatever kind, in relation to a competing firm which does. The giving of such assistance can only be regarded as productive in itself of "unfair" competition on the premise that the financial disciplines of the free market are the only framework within which "fair" competition can take place; and since active Government intervention by way of assistance to selected companies is based on the premise that these disciplines may operate counter-productively and contrary to the national interest, to talk of "unfair" competition may simply be another way of stating general opposition to the Government's policy of intervention.

Even if the Government's premise is accepted, however, there is room for unfairness, productive of unfair competition, in the methods by which recipients of assistance are selected and in the use to which the funds granted are put by beneficiary enterprises. One of the main preoccupations of the Advisory Committee established under section 5 of the Industrial Expansion Act will be with the right methods and criteria for selecting recipients of assistance under the Act,[94] and it is to be hoped that they will also consider the second possibility of unfair competition. The need here is for arrangements to be worked out which will ensure that where assistance is given for specific projects, which is one of the types of industrial investment scheme envisaged by the Government,[95] it is clearly seen to be applied only to those projects and not to improve the general competitive position of the firm concerned. In this sense, clause 9(b) of the Minister of Technology's support agreement with International Computers[96] makes his obligation to provide grants towards the group's research and development expenditure conditional upon the maintenance of certain levels of such expenditure (which is itself carefully defined in a Schedule to the agreement) over a period of years, and provides for its certification to the Minister by the group's auditors. Whether analogous arrangements, if adopted as common form, would provide a check on the faithfulness of application of Government assistance sufficient to satisfy competitors and also Parliament is doubtful. It might be strengthened by following the precedent established in the case of MacBraynes and stipulating that the Comptroller and Auditor-General should have access to the books of

94. *Cf.* the similar functions of the Board of Trade Advisory Committee in relation to building grants and general loans and grants for firms establishing themselves in development areas: ss. 3 and 4 of the Local Employment Act 1960 (8 & 9 Eliz. 2, c. 18).

95. Samuels, "Government Participation in Private Industry" (1968) J.B.L. 296, at p. 298.

96. S.I. 1968 No. 990, Sched., Pt. 2.

the enterprise concerned: the alternative safeguard that suggests itself, requiring beneficiary enterprises to publish much fuller accounts which would
show that other activities were not being cross-subsidised by those in respect
of which assistance was given, might prove difficult to reconcile with the
tradition which has been reinforced by restrictive practices legislation,[97] of
non-disclosure of information bearing on a firm's competitive position.

CONCLUSION

The temptation to draw detailed comparisons between the mixed enterprise
and the public corporation as vehicles of Government participation in commerce and industry has here been resisted. One general observation of a comparative character will however be offered. The diversity of form and purpose
which characterise Government participations productive of mixed enterprises means that any general principles of Governmental, Parliamentary and
judicial control of such enterprises must be constructed not only upon the
legal status of limited company which they all share, but also, indeed primarily, upon the policies which produced them and upon their economic
characteristics and situation. The problems of control to which these principles provide solutions are the same as those which the experience of the
industrial and public corporations has rendered so familiar: the proper
apportionment of functions and responsibilities as between Government and
enterprise, the proper extent of accountability to Parliament, the proper way
for the public character of the enterprise, and its access to Exchequer finance,
to be taken into account in law. These public corporations, again, are hardly
more homogeneous, in economic terms, than the mixed enterprises which have
been here discussed. An approach to their study, by lawyers and political
scientists no less than by economists, which would go beyond the legal and
organisational features they all share and seek to identify the imperatives of
control and regulation (or of freedom from regulation) imposed by the
economic characteristics and relationships of each, might therefore produce
a clearer and more rational picture than is available at present of the operations
of existing controls and of the precise improvements to the system that may
be necessary.

97. Particularly by s. 5 of the Restrictive Trade Practices Act 1968 (c. 66) (information agreements).

CHAPTER 4

MINISTERIAL CONTROL
OF THE NATIONALISED INDUSTRIES*

1. INTRODUCTION

IT is widely recognised that the relations between the Government and the legislature on the one hand and publicly owned industries on the other is of central importance. I have closely observed public enterprise in many countries, and everywhere one finds the same problems arising in slightly different forms. One problem is how to give public undertakings of an industrial or commercial character a large measure of independence in their day-to-day activities, while reserving for the Government the final decision in matters of major policy. Another problem is how to encourage or permit the management to follow commercial principles while ensuring that social, political and economic goals are pursued when the national interest so requires.

The tendency in Britain, as in other countries, has been for Ministers to intervene in many different ways, regardless of whether they possessed the legal power to do so. The Government is usually in so powerful a position and has so many opportunities for persuasion or inducement at its disposal that it can almost always influence a public enterprise to do what it wants whatever the legal text may say.

This is the background against which the recent report from the Select Committee on Nationalised Industries, on Ministerial Control[1] should be seen.

Hitherto all the reports from the Select Committee have dealt with a single industry or undertaking. Now for the first time the Select Committee have carried out an inquiry across the board into Ministerial control of all the nationalised industries. This fact, combined with the importance of the subject, makes the report one which demands very serious attention.

The report is a curious document. It is highly abstract, doctrinaire, and non-political in the sense that it seems to leave out of account some essential political aspects of Ministerial responsibility for the nationalised industries.

The report deals mainly with two topics of the subject. One relates to the

---

* By Professor W. A. Robson, formerly Professor of Public Administration in the University of London. Reprinted by kind permission of the Editors and Publishers from *Political Quarterly*, Vol. 40, No. 1, at p. 103 (January–March 1969).

1. Vol. I, Report and Proceedings of the Committee, 371—I. HMSO £1 net. Vol. II, Minutes of Evidence—II. HMSO £4. Vol. III, Appendices—III. HMSO £1. 2s. 6d.

governmental structure through which Ministerial control should be exercised. The other relates to the kinds of control which Ministers should exercise and the methods, purposes and objectives which they should use. The Committee's aim has been to consider whether existing institutions and procedures are well designed "to fulfil the underlying purposes of the creation of public corporations responsible to Ministers."[2] These purposes they deem to be that Ministers should to some extent exercise control, but that the public corporations should have some degree of managerial autonomy which would limit the scope of Government intervention.[3] This is the nearest the Committee get to enunciating a theory of the public corporation or analysing the role of public enterprise—and it is not very far.

2. THE PRESENT SYSTEM CONDEMNED

The nationalised industries have a dual obligation: on the one hand to be mindful of the public interest and on the other to operate as efficient commercial bodies. The Committee declare that Ministers have duties to ensure that both these obligations are achieved as far as possible, though the two goals will sometimes conflict. The public interest is of course a vague expression which can include many different policies.

The Select Committee are highly critical not only of the manner in which Ministers have exercised control but of the whole system. They state that Ministers are not aware of the reasons for the powers they possess; that there is confusion about the purposes and methods of Ministerial controls; that there is an absence of coherent principles among sponsoring departments; that Ministers give little or no guidance on questions of policy but show an increasing tendency to encroach on the details of management; and that it is quite wrong to expect a sponsoring department to combine the twin functions of overseeing efficiency and of ensuring that public corporations observe the public interest. Indeed, the whole system of sponsoring Ministers is attacked and rejected. In reading this report one can see how wide of the mark Mr. David Coombes was in his book[4] on the Select Committee in saying that it is an informative rather than an investigatory body, that it has sought to describe rather than to solve the main problems facing the industries. For in this report the Committee put forward what they regard as the proper lines on which Ministerial control should be conducted.

3. CAN MINISTERS "ENSURE EFFICIENCY"?

It is in my view very doubtful whether Ministers either are or can be responsible for overseeing and ensuring the efficiency of the nationalised industries. There is certainly nothing in the legislation which places this duty

2. Para. 28.
3. Paras. 33 and 60.
4. *The Member of Parliament and the Administration.*

on them. Ministerial powers are explicitly related to particular matters such as the appointment of chairman and board members, the approval of capital investment programmes, research programmes, training and education programmes, laying down the form of the annual report and accounts, appointing the professional auditors, and so forth. Ministers will, of course, normally exercise these powers with the intention of promoting the effectiveness of the undertaking, for this is in everyone's interest, including that of the Government. But how far is it realistic to expect a government department to be able to ensure or promote the efficiency of British Railways or BEA or the BBC? They have neither the staff nor the know-how to be able to do so in any meaningful sense. The Post Office has been entirely controlled by the Postmaster-General, yet this complete and comprehensive Ministerial control did not ensure a satisfactory level of efficiency and so the Government has decided to transform it into a public corporation. Why should the Government now be able to ensure its efficiency when it was unable to do so previously? Why should the Government be able to ensure the efficiency of the British Airports Authority when the Ministry of Civil Aviation and its successors made such a mess of the design, construction and administration of London Airport and have aroused almost universal criticism by its handling of the Stansted proposal?

The Select Committee do not ask, much less attempt to answer, awkward questions of this kind. They merely lay down a series of propositions which indicate what they regard as the criteria of efficiency. These consist almost entirely in the application of specified techniques for investment decisions and price policies. There are some general observations to the effect that Ministers must be concerned with the efficiency with which the industries carry out the public policies and financial, economic, and social obligations imposed on them, but there is no indication how this is to be done except in regard to investment and pricing policy (other than that Ministers should be authorised to carry out "occasional special efficiency studies"). It seems to have escaped the Committee's notice that all the efficiency studies which have been carried out in the past have been made by outside bodies, such as the Herbert Committee on Electricity Supply, the Fleck Committee, the Stedeford Committee, the Pilkington Committee, management consultants, academic economists or political scientists.

4. The Setting of Financial Targets

The present system of financial control stems from the White Paper of 1961 on "the Financial and Economic Obligations of the Nationalised Industries" (Cmnd. 1337). This introduced a series of specific annual financial targets laid down quinquennially for each of the public corporations, after consulting the board and taking into consideration all the relevant circumstances likely to affect its performance. It is quite true that the ability of a public corporation to achieve its target, or even the target figure itself, cannot be regarded as a reliable index of efficiency. A deficit may equally well be due to adverse circumstances rather than bad management. Nevertheless, the introduction of targets was generally welcomed as a great improvement on the vague statutory enactments which required the nationalised industries not to make a loss on current account taking one year with another—and left it at that.

Economists have criticised the setting of financial targets as lacking significance. They contend that if correct methods of appraising investments are used, and correct pricing policies applied, the financial result of the year's trading is irrelevant. The weakness of this analysis is that it ignores the demoralising effect on the personnel and directors of a large industrial undertaking of substantial deficits on the annual trading account. It also ignores the extreme importance attached to an annual surplus or deficit by business men, the Press, politicians and the general public. To the man in the street and to most politicians success or failure in public enterprise is judged to no small extent by whether a public corporation shows a profit or a loss.

5. INVESTMENT AND PRICE POLICY

In 1967 a second Treasury White Paper appeared dealing with the "Economic and Financial Objectives" of nationalised industries (Cmnd. 3437). This introduced the notion of scrutinising investment programmes by means of the discounted cash flow method with a test rate of return of 8 per cent. Any proposed capital investment which survived this test would be approved; any which did not would be rejected, unless it could be justified on non-commercial grounds. The object was a simple one: to prevent the misallocation of national resources by allowing public enterprise to embark on investments which would yield less advantageous returns than other forms of capital expenditure in either the public or private sectors. The DCF method is to be associated with the highly speculative cost-benefit analysis which attempts to assign money values to everything in the world, including the imponderables. Professor William G. Shepherd, an American economist who has made a special study of public enterprise in Britain, remarks that the calculations rest on predictions of cost and revenue which are little more than guesses. "Screening the resulting predicted rate of return is often therefore an empty exercise."[5] Also, why should a uniform test rate of return be applied to projects which differ greatly in risk?

The 1967 White Paper dealt at length with pricing policy. It urged that while prices should cover overall accounting costs wherever possible, they should reflect the costs of particular goods or services. There could be justifi-

5. "Alternatives for Public Expenditure" in *Britain's Economic Prospects* by Richard E. Caves and Associates, pp. 388–389.

able exceptions to this based either on grounds of principle or of practical expediency; but cross-subsidisation is in general undesirable because it means taxing remunerative services in order to cover the losses on other services. The Treasury gave several instances where charges could justifiably differ from costs. Then followed the statement: "*In addition to recovering accounting costs*, prices need to be reasonably related to costs at the margin and to be designed to promote the efficient use of resources within industry. Where and when there is spare capacity, as there may be at some points in the business cycle, or excess demand, short run marginal costs (*i.e.*, the additional costs of increasing output in the short run) are relevant; the object is to persuade customers to make use of spare capacity or to curtail demand."[6] This was followed by a warning that strict adherence to long run marginal costing in, let us say, gas or electricity when new technological developments can greatly reduce long run marginal costs, would lead to substantial revenue deficits requiring heavy subsidies from general taxation which would be hard to justify. Moreover, the huge public industries cannot be modernised quickly and a rapid reduction of prices might stimulate demand and cause a break-down on the supply side.[7]

6. MARGINAL PRICING THE ROAD TO UTOPIA

The Select Committee has transformed this farsighted and balanced statement into a series of dogmatic statements which they assert with all the fervour of converts to a new-found faith.

A Treasury witness had said that without financial targets the nationalised industries would lack guidance and revert to the bad habit of low earnings of earlier years.[8] But, asked the Committee, "what does a financial objective add except a measure of past performance?—as though this was a useless and unnecessary indicator. Sir Alec Cairncross, then head of the Government Economic Service, stressed the limited scope of pricing and investment criteria as instruments of control, and insisted on the importance of financial targets in instilling keenness and cutting costs. He urged that the interactions of all three factors should be considered together. This remark by a distinguished economist with much practical experience the Committee dismissed contemptuously as meaning no more than that "one should lay down criteria of pricing and investment and calculate the financial objective from them, but that if this produces a result one does not like one should go back and fiddle the arithmetic."[9] It is this kind of remark which reveals the lack of common sense or political sensibility in the report.

6. A Review of Economic and Financial Objectives, Cmnd. 3437/1967, para. 21. [My italics.]
7. *Ibid.* para. 22.
8. Report, para. 223.
9. Para. 224.

The responsible Ministries saw quite clearly the political and other difficulties of fully accepting the doctrine of marginal pricing as the only road to salvation. To abandon the covering of average costs would in some instances contravene the statutory duty to avoid making losses. The Ministry of Power said their enthusiasm for marginal cost pricing had to be matched against their enthusiasm for a reasonable degree of financial probity. The Ministry of Transport had been forced to adopt a pragmatic pricing policy charging what the traffic would bear—as the railways had so often done under private ownership. They had to pay attention to competition, and marginal cost pricing might result in pricing a service out of the market.[10]

Any uncertainty or faltering in subscribing to their new-found faith seemed to the Select Committee a heresy based either on confusion of thought (a frequent term of censure in the report) or on a failure to accept the pure and undiluted doctrine of marginal cost pricing. The probable or possible results of its application were nowhere considered. They ignored the political consequences both inside and outside Parliament of heavy deficits in industries which may be capable of making a surplus by other methods; and they did not consider the effect on the popular image of nationalised industries caused by their failing to show up reasonably well on their annual trading account.

Even more striking is the absence in the report of any of the reservations, qualifications or opposition to marginal cost pricing which have been expressed by economists.

A recent article in *Economica* puts one powerful argument against it as follows: "The standard case for marginal cost pricing by a public enterprise requires, among other things, that prices equal marginal costs in the rest of the economy, and it implicitly assumes that any resulting profit or loss is acceptable. In fact, the requirement is not met, and the assumption is invalid. There is often a close relationship between a public enterprise and private industries which do not sell at marginal cost, and public enterprises are normally set financial targets."[11] The Select Committee nowhere inquire into the question whether private industry applies marginal cost pricing, and if so to what extent. And if it does not, whether this affects the position of public enterprise. The report assumes that if the theory is applied in the public sector alone the optimum allocation of resources will result. The report makes no reference to the theory of the second best which has been the subject of much discussion among academic economists. A well-known article[12] by Professor Lipsey and K. J. Lancaster, published more than ten

10. Para. 231.
11. "Second-Best Rules for Public Enterprise Pricing" by R. Rees, *Economica*, August 1968, p. 260.
12. "The General Theory of Second Best" by R. G. Lipsey and K. J. Lancaster, *Review of Economic Studies*, Vol. XXIV—1956–57. See also "The Influence of Marginal Cost Theory on Pricing and Investment in British Nationalised Fuel Industries" by Sheila Bhalla, *Applied Economic Papers*, Osmania University (March 1964), Vol. 4, No. 1.

years ago, demonstrated mathematically that in the real world with its imperfect markets the determination of output on the basis of marginal cost pricing is as likely to lead away from the optimum allocation of resources as towards it. In other words, "to apply to only a small part of the economy welfare rules which would lead to Paretian optimum if they were applied everywhere, may move the economy away from, not toward, a second best optimum position. A nationalised industry conducting its price-output policy according to the Lerner-Lange 'Rule' in an imperfectly competitive economy may well diminish both the general productive efficiency of the economy and the welfare of its members."[13] Nancy Ruggles, in her article on marginal cost pricing which Ralph Turvey has reprinted in his recent collection of readings on public enterprise, concludes that the search for a panacea in the shape of a single simple rule by which to guide all conduct in these matters, is a vain search and even a foolish one. "A set of tools," she remarks, "is available with which to accomplish a complicated job. A better job can be done if each tool is used where it is appropriate, instead of throwing away all but one and expecting it to serve all purposes."[14]

Yet this is just what the Select Committee have done. After reviewing a number of exceptional circumstances which might justify a departure from the norm, they conclude that "in the long run, the economically justified pricing policy for most of the nationalised industries would be marginal cost pricing. They are satisfied that, if this pricing policy was applied wherever possible, the efficiency of the industries would be improved and the optimum allocation of resource secured."[15] The Committee therefore recommend that "the use of marginal cost pricing policies and the use of DCF appraisal . . . for investment control should be the *standard* policies for the economic control of the nationalised industries."[16] [Their italics.]

It is difficult to avoid a suspicion that the members of the Select Committee were taken for an intellectual ride and being on unfamiliar ground they lost their way and were overready to accept simple solutions to complex problems.

But a different interpretation is possible. The Select Committee are anxious to reduce or eliminate much of the intervention now commonly exercised by Ministers. They would like Ministerial control to be limited in the financial and economic sphere to laying down and ensuring the application of simple formulae such as those relating to investment criteria and pricing policy.[17] The whole process would then become largely self-operating and there would be no need for Ministerial scrutiny except as a check on whether the formulae were being strictly applied.

13. Lipsey and Lancaster, p. 17.
14. *Public Enterprise*, ed. by R. Turvey (Penguin Modern Economics), p. 43.
15. Para. 276.
16. Para. 280.
17. Para. 407.
    D

7. A Ministry of Nationalised Industries

With this in view the Committee make sweeping proposals for changes in the machinery of government. Sponsoring departments would disappear, and the Ministry of Power would be abolished. In their place a Ministry of Nationalised Industries is recommended to deal with all the public corporations. It would be responsible for supervising and ensuring the efficiency of the entire range of nationalised industries. Its principal functions would consist of appointing and dismissing the members and chairmen of all the Boards; defining the pricing and investment policies to be adopted by each industry and agreeing their financial targets; reviewing investment programmes and approving capital projects; approving capital structures and borrowing; promoting co-ordination and co-operation between the nationalised industries to improve their commercial efficiency; conducting a general oversight of the structure and organisation of the industries, including the adoption of new management techniques such as critical path analyses, the use of computers, and so forth; making efficiency studies or arranging for them to be carried out by outside bodies such as PIB; approving programmes of research, training and education; approving the form of the accounts and being responsible to Parliament for the nationalised industries.

Any other Minister could try to secure that the public interest as he sees it is pursued by a nationalised industry. Thus, if a railway line were required to be kept open for military reasons, the Ministry of Defence would negotiate with British Railways and pay the cost. If BOAC or BEA are to be persuaded to purchase a foreign aircraft instead of a British plane the Treasury or the Ministry of Technology would compensate the airline for forgoing their preference. The Select Committee do not regard these payments as subsidies but merely as "commercial transactions between the Ministers concerned and the Boards. The Ministers desire a service, namely the provision of certain social or public interest benefits; the Boards are able to provide it. The Minister concerned should therefore negotiate with the Board and agree a contract for the provision of the service . . . at a contracted price . . . ."[18]

8. The Model of Private Enterprise

Throughout their Report the Select Committee project public enterprise in the image of private enterprise. To them, nothing matters compared with commercial efficiency expressed in terms of marginal cost pricing and investment criteria based on a rate of discount designed to treat public enterprise on a par with private enterprise. Even the national interests which Ministers are expected to safeguard would be subjected to the higgling of the market

18. Para. 744.

and negotiated. The feeble system of professional audit is to be maintained, and the salaries of board members are to be increased substantially so as to bring them into line with those paid in private industry—regardless of what is paid to Ministers, civil servants, the higher judiciary, or the law officers.

Efficiency in any sense beyond the narrow economic criteria mentioned in the Report seems to be outside the Select Committee's comprehension. It would be quite possible for all their economic or financial criteria to be satisfied by the Post Office and yet for the telephone service to be as inefficient technically as it is today. The Committee believes that productivity is an inseparable part of general efficiency, but this is a matter which they consider should be left entirely to the management of the public industries. Yet the productivity of London Transport, for example, has been deeply affected by its failure to innovate in regard to the manning of buses or the introduction of new technology during the post-war years. Is a public corporation to be left in undisturbed somnolence in such circumstances as these?

A basic defect of the Report is therefore that while it claims that one of the two main objects of Ministerial control is to oversee and ensure efficiency of the nationalised industries, its concept of what constitutes efficiency is abysmally narrow and rigid.

To concentrate responsibility for, and power over, all the public corporations in a single Minister will mean that his department will know far less about the sphere in which each undertaking operates than the sponsoring departments do at present. On the other hand, a greater consistency of treatment might be achieved by a single department.

9. THE ITALIAN EXPERIENCE

It is odd that the Committee make no mention of the position in Italy, where a Ministry of State Holdings (Ministro della Participazioni) was created in 1956.[18A] The aim was the same as that which the Select Committee have in mind—to promote the operating efficiency of the public corporations and to achieve unified control. The Ministry was intended to be a supervisory body. What has happened in Italy is that a standing Ministerial Committee, presided over by the Prime Minister, decide most of the important questions, such as the goals to be pursued by the State holding companies and indirectly by their subsidiaries. Amalgamations, disposals, the establishment or purchase of undertakings, the approval of new projects, etc., are generally decided by the Committee of Ministers, and not by the Minister of State Holdings. The Committee are not supposed to determine questions motivated only by technical or economic considerations, since the latter are for the management of the enterprise.

18A. See *post*. Chap. 8, at page 147.

Only the Committee of Ministers are entitled to issue directives defining the aims of public enterprise; and it is they who see that funds are allocated for new projects. They also review the financial results of the great Italian public corporations (ENI and IRI). The Minister of State Holdings acts as a channel of communication between the Committee and the public enterprises, but he occupies a subordinate position. The chief centre of authority and policy-making lies in the interministerial Committee. I have described the situation in Italy more fully in an article in *The Times Business News* of August 26, 1968.

The Select Committee's proposal for a Ministry of Nationalised Industry was strongly opposed by the Treasury on several grounds described in the report. It seems probable that the sponsoring departments will oppose the severance of responsibility for securing public interests from responsibility for efficiency, which the Treasury do not consider it possible to separate. The reaction of other departments is not, however, mentioned in the report. The alternative of giving the Treasury wider functions is not considered, though much of the recent economic thinking about nationalised industry has been done in that department.

10. AN AMERICAN ECONOMIST'S COMMENTS

The limited outlook and superficial thinking of the Select Committee's report can be seen by comparison with the much more profound reflections of Professor William Shepherd, whose studies of British public enterprise seem to have escaped the notice of the Committee. In his book, *Economic Performance under Public Ownership: British Fuel and Power*,[19] he cast doubts on the much-vaunted principle of subsidies payable by government to public corporations for unremunerative activities by analysing some of its drawbacks, such as the possibility that such open and rational subsidies might become as entrenched, irrational, and deadening to efficiency as most subsidies to private industries already are (the position regarding housing subsidies is relevant here). He mentions several other drawbacks to the policy of payments from taxes for particular services and deliberately proposed cross-subsidisation within the firm as an alternative. In his concluding chapter, Professor Shepherd declared that "a preoccupation with internal efficiency for public corporations, especially from the viewpoint of commercial criteria, lends itself to superficiality, sterile controversy, and misemphasis among policies."[20]

In his contribution to the Brookings Institute Study entitled *Britain's Economic Prospects*,[21] Professor Shepherd looks at some of the investment and pricing policies of the nationalised industries from a much wider angle

19. Yale University Press, 1965, pp. 48, 144.   20. *Ibid.* p. 145.
21. George Allen & Unwin (1968).

than the Select Committee's report. He considers that the exceptionally and unnecessarily capital-intensive substitution of nuclear power for coal involves a use of limited resources which will yield only modest gains in fuel economy and a relatively small release of miners for other industries. He regards the investment programme for electricity, and especially for nuclear generation, as excessive and urges its reduction.[22] This is irrespective of the Treasury screening method and test discount ratio. A rapid expansion of gas investment during 1968–73, both for conversion and direct use, with a slowing down of colliery closures, could replace a substantial portion of the nuclear investment programme. The unit cost savings in the AGR nuclear cost estimates over conventional stations are only slight, but the capital costs are much higher.[23] "Yet the electricity system's tendency to invest more, and to do so more capital-intensively, than energy policy requires would not be automatically corrected by raising the Treasury's test rate of return."[24]

Professor Shepherd also makes some interesting comments on price policies. He considers British pricing policies in telephones, electricity and gas to be as efficient as any in the world. Further study might show that the deliberate overpricing of business postal services and subsidising of some telecommunications services would promote long-run efficiency.[25]

Surely this is the breadth and quality of thinking we need to inform Ministerial control of the nationalised industries, rather than the narrow concepts and abstract formulae adopted by the Select Committee.

11. IMPLICATIONS OF THE REPORT

In conclusion, we may note one important reaction to the report. *The Times* greeted it in a leading article which described it as "a very good report." Shortly afterwards *The Times* published a long first leader in support of Mr. Enoch Powell's proposal to denationalise the industries by distributing shares to private citizens. The leading article contended that the Select Committee's report abolishes the original case for nationalisation, which rested on the idea that the Government should be able to control or influence certain basic industries or services if they were state owned. The report, wrote *The Times*, "recommends separating these industries from political influences by detaching them from their present controlling Ministries. The effect of this is to create independent corporations which can pursue normal commercial policies. The principle is to commercialise industries which have been damaged by political interference. This in itself makes a strong case for denationalisation. If what we want to do is to make the state undertakings resemble private corporations as closely as possible, then the obvious way to

22. *Op. cit.* p. 393.
23. *Ibid.* pp. 394–396.
24. *Ibid.* pp. 397–398.
25. *Ibid.*, pp. 389, 403.

do it is to turn them into private corporations by disposing of the equity."[26]

It is ironical that a report issued by a Select Committee presided over by Mr. Mikardo, usually regarded as a left-wing Socialist, should provide the opponents of public enterprise with so much ammunition. It is indeed true that the report does at almost every point seek to make the public corporations resemble ordinary joint stock companies. This is seen in its recommendations on investment appraisal, price policy, the salaries of board members, the exaggerated emphasis placed on managerial autonomy, the rejection of an efficiency audit in place of the professional audit, the concentration on economic and financial factors as criteria of efficiency. Above all, the view that Ministers should negotiate, purchase, and enter into contracts with a public corporation in order to induce it to carry out social, political or economic activities in the public interest which it would not otherwise pursue, follows precisely the procedure which the Government observes in dealing with a commercial company. It would be interesting to know on what grounds the case for nationalised industry now rests in the view of Mr. Mikardo and his Labour colleagues on the Select Committee.

It is greatly to be hoped that the Government will think not twice but several times before adopting the recommendations contained in this report.

N.B. For Professor Robson's comments on developments since the above was written, see Appendix, *post*, page 339.

26. *The Times*, September 14, 1968.

CHAPTER 5

THE HIGHLANDS AND ISLANDS DEVELOPMENT BOARD: A BRITISH EXPERIMENT IN SOCIAL ENGINEERING*

1. THE NORTH AND ITS PROBLEMS

THE area for which the Highlands and Islands Development Board has responsibilities covers the counties of Argyll, Caithness, Inverness, Orkney, Ross and Cromarty, Sutherland and Zetland, and such other areas of Scotland as the Secretary of State may designate by statutory instrument.[1] These seven counties are the same as those named in the definition of the term "crofting counties" in the Crofters (Scotland) Act 1955,[2] but the term is not used in the 1965 Act.[3] This may be because of the underlying aim to eradicate any idea that these counties shall in the future live mainly by crofting, although, of course, agriculture as such must remain an important part of the Highland economy.[4] However, for convenience, the present writer will use the term from time to time in referring to the Highlands and Islands.

These seven crofting counties, with a mere 276,000 inhabitants, (a density of twenty per square mile, compared with 910 in Central Scotland) or 5 per cent. of the entire population of Scotland, extend to some nine million acres,[5] nearly one-half of Scotland or one-sixth of Great Britain. From north to south, the greatest length is about 420 miles; from west to east, the greatest breadth is about 150 miles.

The problems of the Highlands have confronted Governments of Scotland and of the United Kingdom for centuries.

In the present century various attempts have been made to pump money into the Highlands. Some of these attempts are part of a general pattern covering the whole country, such as the crop grants, and the subsidies paid to hill farmers as individuals, and the rate support grant paid to local authorities. Other devices have been related more particularly to the crofting

---

* By H. McN. Henderson, M.A., LL.B., Faculty of Law, University of Edinburgh.
1. s. 1 (2) of the Highlands and Islands Development (Scotland) Act 1965, c. 46.
2. 1955, c. 21, s. 37 (1).
3. The term, which was used by several speakers in the debates in both Houses, is the one adopted traditionally by administrators and others to describe this area. The seven crofting counties are covered by six parliamentary constituencies.
4. See the Board's First Report, para. 20, and frequent public statements by the Board to this effect.
5. Of these nine million acres, one-and-a-half million already belong to the State—the Secretary of State is the largest single landlord in the Highlands.

counties themselves, devices such as the Highlands Advisory Panel, started in 1947,[6] the Highland Fund, the new Crofters Commission, and so on. Yet incomes in the crofting counties remain low.[6A] A pamphlet produced a few years ago by the former Highlands Advisory Panel on "Land Use in the Highlands and Islands," quoted in Parliament, envisaged an income of £750 per year from a holding, with capital invested in buildings and fixed equipment alone in the region of £15,000 to £20,000. This return, which is much the same as an agricultural worker's wage, is obviously much too low for anyone to consider such an investment as a practical proposition—a building society investment pays much the same, without the expenditure of any further effort.

It is all too easy to say that the inhabitants of these counties are mere pensioners of the Exchequer. The Rate Support Grant for the county of Zetland, to take an extreme case, is equal to a rate of £14 in the pound. But it must be remembered that central government expenditure on national items (such as Royal Dockyards, central government buildings, research establishments and the like), which pours tens, if not hundreds, of millions into more favoured centres in the south, is virtually unknown in this area—the developments at Dounreay and Fort William are outstanding exceptions. If similar expenditure were lavished on the crofting counties there would be no problem, no emigration, no massive Rate Support Grants.

It is possible to derive some sort of a picture of the size of the economic problem of the Highlands and Islands when we consider that the total rateable value of Scotland was only £105 million before the revaluation which came into effect in 1966–67 (by which the rateable value of Scotland as a whole was increased to approximately £135 millions), and that of the crofting counties a mere £2·2 million, or £4·2 million including the boroughs.[7]

The question may be asked whether there is any point in focusing attention on, and trying to solve, the problem of the Highlands and Islands when a greater return might more certainly be obtained from similar expenditure in decayed industrial regions further south.

An answer may be found in the pages of the Report of the Commission of Enquiry into Crofting Conditions, published in April 1954.[8] The late Principal Taylor of Aberdeen University was chairman of the Commission. This Report was followed by the passing of the Crofters (Scotland) Act 1955, mentioned above, which re-established a Crofters Commission for the seven crofting counties.

6. Replaced now, by the Highlands and Islands Development Consultative Council, under the 1965 Act, s. 2 (2).

6A. The Board's Third Report indicates that *per capita* incomes in this area, though rising fast were still in 1964–65 34 per cent. below the U.K. average.

7. The rateable value of the City of Westminster alone is £106 million. The figure for the crofting counties may be compared with those of Leatherhead UDC or the Borough of Crewe.

8. Cmd. 9091.

The Taylor Commission stated: "We have thought it right, however, to record our unanimous conviction, founded on personal knowledge and on the evidence we have received, that in the national interest the maintenance of these communities is desirable, because they embody a free and independent way of life which in a civilisation predominantly urban and industrial in character is worth preserving for its own intrinsic quality. We put this first because we believe that the crofters feel it to be true and are indeed often capable of expressing it, and because we are convinced that those who fail to recognise it will never begin to understand the Highland situation or make helpful proposals for its improvement."[9]

The population of the crofting counties fell, in the century from 1851 to 1951, from 395,540 to 285,647,[10] with wide variations at different times and in different localities, and indeed some increases in certain towns. The trend continues, with perhaps accelerated emigration from the more inhospitable areas. In the forty years from 1925 to 1965 the population of the Western Isles fell from 38,000 to 26,000—a decline of 30 per cent., while the population of Scotland as a whole rose from 4,880,000 to 5,200,000.

A disturbing feature of the age distribution[11] noted by the Taylor Commission was the abnormally high proportion of elderly people and the abnormally low proportion of children. One witness had indicated to the Commission that there seemed to exist in each community a certain minimum number below which the community ceases to be viable.[12] When this stage is reached, any effort for improvement must come from outside. To get industry in particular into the Highlands, it has been said that we require hothouse development to get it started.

In modern times life in the Highlands has been immeasurably improved by the activities of the North of Scotland Hydro-Electric Board which was established under the Hydro-Electric Development (Scotland) Act 1943.[13] Ironically, it has its head offices in Edinburgh, not in the north.

It originally functioned only within "the North of Scotland District," as defined in the Second Schedule of the Act. Its powers, duties, and the area under its control were extended by the Electricity Act 1947, to cover approximately all Scotland north of a line drawn roughly from the south of Loch Lomond to the Firth of Tay, just east of the city of Perth. This is of course an area considerably greater than that covered by the Highlands and Islands Development Board.

9. Para. 12. Although strictly these remarks apply only to the crofting communities, they are broadly applicable to the population of the Highlands and Islands in general.
10. Para. 46. Over 51,000 emigrated between 1911 and 1931, but fewer than 4,000 in the next 20 years of depression and war. The loss in the decade ending in 1961 exceeded 8,000.
11. Para. 47.
12. Para. 101.
13. C. 32, S. 1.

The Hydro Board (as it is popularly termed) has a statutory obligation so far as its powers and duties permit, to "collaborate in the carrying out of any measures for the economic development and social improvement of the North of Scotland."[14] In this respect it may be contrasted with the Foresty Commission, which has in fact done much good work in the crofting counties, but has no such statutory obligation. The Hydro Board is also required to have regard to the desirability of preserving the beauty of the scenery and any object of architectural or historic interest, and of avoiding as far as possible injury to fisheries and to the stock of fish in any waters.[15]

None of the institutions created earlier, however, was authorised to deal comprehensively with all the varied problems of this area. It was for this reason that the Highlands and Islands Development Board was conceived.[16]

2. THE HIGHLANDS AND ISLANDS DEVELOPMENT (SCOTLAND) ACTS 1965 AND 1968[17]

(1) Introduction

The Highlands and Islands Development (Scotland) Act 1965, which originally appeared as the Highland Development (Scotland) Bill, was given its Second Reading debate on the floor of the House of Commons on March 16, 1965. This fact was in itself significant, for it surely indicated the importance attached to the Bill by the Government, not merely in the context of Scottish legislation, but rather as marking the birth of a new type of British public corporation. As the Secretary of State had written some years ago, "It may well be that the Highland development authority which we set up will become a pattern for other areas."[18] Presumably he had in mind regions such as the southwestern peninsula and the northwest of England, for when the Bill was published he also said that it was a prototype for powers which would be given to similar boards to be set up in other parts of the country.

It was therefore desirable that it should be discussed on the floor of the House, and this move was welcomed by the leading opposition speaker, Mr. Michael Noble, himself a former Secretary of State.[19]

The original Act of 1965 was subsequently found not to have given the Board adequate powers to invest in equities, and, as will be seen, an amending Act was passed in 1968.

14. s. 2 (3).
15. s. 9 (1).
16. The setting up of a Highland Development Authority was proposed in the Labour Party's election programme in 1959 and on earlier occasions. Mr. Malcolm MacMillan. H.C. 16.3.65, col. 1121.
17. c. 51.
18. In an article in *The Glasgow Herald* on February 12, 1964.
19. H.C. 16.3.65, col. 1096.

It appears that at present there are some thirty Government departments and other public agencies employed on particular aspects in the Highlands. The creation of the Board adds yet one more.

(2) The provisions of the Acts of 1965 and 1968

The Act of 1965 establishing the Highlands and Islands Development Board is of moderate length, a mere nineteen sections and two Schedules. Although it was much criticised in detail in both Houses, it contains few provisions which are not without parallel in modern legislation. It is important to remember that many powers are inserted in order to provide what Ministers delight in calling a "long stop."

The first section opens with the following words which embody the spirit which permeates the whole Act: "For the purpose of assisting the people of the Highlands and Islands to improve their economic and social conditions, and of enabling the Highlands and Islands to play a more effective part in the economic and social development of the nation, there shall be established a Highlands and Islands Development Board, which shall have the general function of preparing, concerting, promoting, assisting and undertaking measures for the economic and social development of the Highlands and Islands, and have such other functions in pursuance of that general function as are conferred on them (*i.e.* the Board) by this Act." These functions are, initially at least, to be exercised in what we know as the seven crofting counties. The Board came into existence on November 1, 1965.

The Board consists of a chairman who is also its accounting officer, and not more than six other members, all of whom are appointed by the Secretary of State, the latter after consultation with the chairman. Schedule 1 contains detailed provisions as to the constitution, meetings and proceedings, office, officers and servants, etc., of the Board. This Board is relatively small, but this number was chosen because of the belief that a small number was necessary if an executive body of this kind was to be effective. The Board is one member below full strength, but in a written reply on April 10, 1968, the Secretary of State indicated that he did not intend to make a further appointment at the present time.

As is usual in statutes establishing public corporations, there is a provision that the Board shall give effect to directions of a general character given by the Secretary of State after consultation with the Board itself.[20] As might have been expected, the first three reports of the Board indicate that no such "section 2" directions were given in the periods covered by these reports. This accords with the usual practice of government departments in their dealings with a public corporation.

Another usual feature is the provision for a consultative council to advise

20. s. 2 (1).

the Board on the exercise and performance of its functions.[21] Schedule 2 contains provisions as to the constitution of the council, which is appointed by the Secretary of State himself, without limit of number. The secretary of the council is appointed and employed by the Board.

The duties imposed on the Board by section 3 require it to keep under review all matters relating to the economic and social well-being and development of the Highlands and Islands; to submit proposals to the Secretary of State for the economic and social development of the Highlands and Islands after appropriate consultations, and ensure their implementation; and to advise him on such matters relating to its functions as he may refer to it or it may think fit. An annual report relating to each calendar year is required to be made to the Secretary of State. Finally, the Board is required in exercising its functions to have regard to the desirability of preserving the beauty of the scenery of the Highlands and Islands.

The Board is given wide powers to acquire, manage and dispose of land.[22] Acquisition may be by agreement or compulsorily. Although the Board may not acquire any business by compulsion it could perhaps in theory acquire the land on which a business stands—a hotel for example—and so acquire the buildings on that land. But this seems to be contrary to the spirit of the Act and is probably politically imprudent to attempt.

Buildings may also be erected by the Board, equipment and services provided, and these may all be managed and disposed of in any normal way.[23]

In this connection, the Scottish Industrial Estates Corporation may act as agent for the Board.

The Board is given, under section 6, very wide powers to carry on business, subject of course to the approval of both the Secretary of State and of the Treasury. It may acquire a business by agreement, but not by compulsion— unless it adopts the devious route mentioned above—and carry on that business, or it may set up and carry on any business. The Board may act as agent or through an agent, or directly. At the end of the day, it may dispose of the business, again subject to the approval of both the Secretary of State and of the Treasury. The only test which the Board is required to apply is that in its opinion the business will contribute to the economic or social development of the Highlands and Islands. The enterprise need not therefore be strictly commercial, but might well be something related to tourism, such as the provision of facilities for sea-angling or sand-yachting.

The section 6 powers of the Board appear to be very wide, but they proved to be inadequate to meet a need which was soon required of it, namely, the provision of risk capital. This defect was remedied by the passing of the

21. s. 2 (2).
22. s. 4.
23. s. 5.

Highlands and Islands Development (Scotland) Act 1968.[24] Section 1 of the Act of 1968 indicates that the section 6 powers include the power to form or promote a company (or join any other person in so doing), to subscribe to, acquire, hold and dispose of any stocks and shares. However, by requiring the consent of the company concerned to any such acquisition, it gives the directors of public companies the privilege already to be found in the articles of association of private companies to decline in their absolute discretion to register the transfer of shares. There can thus be no compulsory acquisition of shareholdings.

It is perhaps doubtful whether much will be achieved as a result of this measure, because changes in the fiscal system have reduced the attractiveness of the incorporation of family business into limited liability companies.

The Government had thought that the original Act gave the Board the necessary powers, but when the Board wished to invest in the equity of Cairngorm Sports Development Ltd. (a service industry, it should be noted), it was advised to take £25,000 worth of debenture shares—and the chairman of the Board went on to the board of directors.

The Board is also authorised, under section 7, to provide advisory services to people engaged or intending to engage in business in its area. This is particularly important because of the remoteness of businesses from the mass markets and the sources of raw materials; all these difficulties put a premium on efficiency of management and marketing.

The Board may promote and encourage publicity relating to the Highlands and Islands, and to its own functions.[25]

There are "necessary and proper" clauses,[26] which permit the Board to engage in such other activity as it may deem expedient for the development of enterprises in its areas and to do all such things as are incidental to or conducive to the attainment of the purposes of any of its functions. Although this limits the risk that any activity may be *ultra vires*, learned counsel advised that the purchase of equity shares is not within the scope of the provisions of the Act; hence the need for the Act of 1968.

The powers to make grants and loans under section 8 are again subject to the simple test that in the opinion of the Board the beneficiary will contribute to the economic or social development of the Highlands and Islands. The Board may act in accordance with arrangements approved by the Secretary of State and by the Treasury. It will be possible for the Board to adopt more flexible criteria than those applied by MOTAC under other legislation. In

24. c. 51, passed on, and in operation from, July 26, 1968. The Bill was sponsored by Mr. Robert MacLennan, M.P. for Caithness and Sutherland.

25. An outstanding example of such publicity was the floating exhibition called "Highland Fling" at Tower Pier in January 1969. Some of the £45,000 spent in mounting this were recovered in entrance charges and drawings in the restaurant and bar.

26. s. 7 (c) and s. 9 (1) (d).

fact, the Board will be able to supplement the activities of the Ministry of Technology under the Local Employment Acts.[27]

The provisions of sections 10 and 11, relating to powers of entry and to obtain information, were much criticised in Parliament. There seems to have been a fear that those powers might be improperly used as a cloak to industrial espionage, but the safeguards laid down in section 12, which include the possibility of severe punishment for their infringement, should prove adequate.

The Board and the public it serves may be assumed to act reasonably most of the time, but provisions to deal with the recalcitrant are always necessary in legislation of this type. It should be noted that the privacy of information is protected by the provision for appeal to the sheriff on the ground that the information requested is not reasonably required by the Board, and the sheriff may confirm, quash or vary the notice requesting the information as he thinks fit.

The Act contains, in section 13, customary provisions regarding the keeping of accounts and records, their submission to the Comptroller and Auditor-General, and inspection of books on behalf of the Secretary of State.

In order to avoid conflict between the Board and a local planning authority which could lead to the thwarting of the functions of the Board, there is an important provision in section 14 (2) that proposed development by the Board which requires planning permission shall be the subject of consultation between the Secretary of State and the local planning authority concerned. Of course, consultation is a word which has many shades of meaning in the mouths of Her Majesty's Ministers. It is the Secretary of State who here has the final say, and his approval (subject to any conditions which he may attach) will have effect as if he had granted planning permission under the planning legislation.

Finally, the creation of the Board is an "open-ended" commitment, unlike, for example, the Italian Cassa Per Il Mezzogiorno, which is created for a period of years which has been extended from time to time. No ceiling is laid down in the Act restricting the eventual financial commitment of the Government, or the taxpayer.

(3) Comment

The Highlands and Islands Development Board came into existence on November 1, 1965, and at the time of writing the first three reports of

27. s. 2 of the Act of 1968 provides that the conditions imposed under s. 8 (2) of the Act of 1965, in making a loan, may include conditions providing for the indebtedness to be discharged wholly or in part by issue, to the Board, of stocks or shares in the borrowing company. The risk that the Board might misuse its power by favouring some companies in which it had an interest, at the expense of others, could be avoided by the appointment of independent nominees to the boards of companies in which shares are taken up. There may, nevertheless, be occasions when the public interest may require a measure of partiality.

its activities have been published. It is already beginning to make a considerable impression on the life and politics of the Highlands and Islands. It has already been suggested that some county councils fear it as a potential rival, and much thought will have to be given to the relationship between the Board and the statutory Scottish Tourist Board—will responsibilities overlap, or will the Highlands and Islands Development Board act as regional agent of the Scottish Tourist Board?

The Board naturally has close contacts with the Scottish Office, originally being supervised by the Department of Agriculture and Fisheries for Scotland (DAFS),[28] on whose vote its expenses were carried. This Department had the necessary network of officials already on the ground, and so it was logical to link the Board at first with this Department. However, supervision was transferred on November 11, 1968 from this Department to the Scottish Development Department, because of the increasing relevance of many of the Board's operations to the functions of the latter Department.[29]

It is through the responsible department that the Board has its main links with other departments of the central Government. Thus a query concerning educational policy in the Highlands will be addressed in the first instance to the responsible department—the Scottish Development Department—in Edinburgh, which will pass it on to the appropriate quarter.

The chairman is also a member of the Scottish Economic Planning Council. Collaboration with the Countryside Commission for Scotland, including financial assistance to the Commission, where the interests of the two bodies overlap or coincide, was promised after a meeting of the two chairmen at Perth (the headquarters of the Commission) on May 8, 1968.

The Consultative Council consists of thirty people, including the chairman, the Hon. Lord Cameron, who had been chairman of the former Highlands Advisory Panel. Schedule 2 requires the Council to include members representative of local authority interests, which must include appropriate representation of the northern and western isles.

The Council has been most skilfully constructed to represent a fascinatingly wide range of political and other interests. About 25 per cent. of its members are Gaelic speakers.

The Council meets in plenary session about once a quarter, but it has several sub-committees. The reports indicate the nature of the subjects considered by it.

There is at times a suspicion that the consultative councils of public

28. It should be remembered that these departments within the Scottish Office are purely administrative in character, not statutory. They replace, in effect, the old statutory boards and departments whose functions were vested in the Secretary of State under the provisions of the Reorganisation of Offices (Scotland) Act 1939. See Appropriation Act 1968, vote 2 of Class V.

29. The Secretary of State, in a Written Answer, November 8, 1968; see Appropriation Act 1969, vote 2 of Class VI.

corporations are the chairman's poodle rather than the consumer's watchdog, but one is probably justified in concluding that this Council will behave as a genuine watchdog after perhaps a year or two of "honeymoon" while the Board has an opportunity to get under way.

The Council can of course help the Board enormously in its public relations. Its members are approachable and well-known. Some are known to be outspoken in expressing their views on the problems of the day.

The Board acts as agent for the Board of Trade in the making of building grants up to £50,000 under the Local Employment Acts; above this sum the Board of Trade itself acts.

Loans are provided by the Board for buildings, plant and machinery, to provide working capital and bridging loans pending the receipt of a grant or loan from other sources, or to cover settling in costs or a training period. Here the ceiling, without the intervention of the Scottish Office, is £25,000. The rate of interest is 5½ per cent., which is of course considerably below the present overdraft rate charged by the Scottish banks.

A notable achievement of the Board is that 25 per cent. of the new jobs created as a result of its help are in manufacturing, while only 10 per cent. of the working population in its area is so engaged. So far, about a thousand new jobs have been created each year on projects approved for financial help.

There are rules to prevent a person from receiving both grants and loans for the same building work, or assistance from the Board of Trade and the Highlands and Islands Development Board, or again from shopping around from one to the other within a short time. Generally however the latter Board may operate more flexible rules and supplement the activities of the Board of Trade.

The annual reports show that by the end of March 1967 (*i.e.* in the first seventeen months of its existence) the Board had made grants and loans totalling £663,606 out of a total outlay of £863,496.[30] This may be contrasted with the 70 million dollars expended by the Tennessee Valley Authority in the first year of its existence. By 1968–69 the Government expected expenditure by the Board to have risen to about £1 million. The Scottish Office and the Forestry Commission already spend some £35 millions annually in the crofting counties. But it is not so much how much money is spent as where it is spent, and whether it is spent wisely, that will put new life into this area.

The Board has not yet had to resort to compulsory purchase, but it has had to use its power to enter on land in connection with the well-known projects for the introduction of a major industrial complex at Invergordon, in association with the wider regional development scheme known as Moray Firth

30. The income and expenditure accounts and balance sheets (relating to the financial year) published as House of Commons Papers in the early months of each year, as well as in the later annual reports (relating to the calendar year) indicate that actual expenditure is considerably lower than the amounts of approved grants and loans. By December 31, 1968, the Board had approved a total expenditure in grants and loans exceeding £4·5 million.

Development (MFD). The proposals for industrialisation, as was to be expected perhaps, have met with opposition in certain quarters. It is difficult for the outsider to gauge the strength or genuineness of this opposition. Some of it may be tactical. Farmers may oppose, in the hope that if their land is taken they will receive higher compensation (after years spent in bemoaning the hard lot of agriculture), or because of fear that modern industries will attract away their employees with high wages and shorter hours of work.

The Board's activities were at first to some extent hampered by lack of staff. At the end of 1966 the total amounted to no more than forty-two in all. It rose at the beginning of 1968 to eighty-four permanent staff and five temporary. The Board now employs a permanent staff of 154, and a temporary or seasonal staff of fourteen.[31] This is still small in comparison with many public corporations. To a certain extent it will be essential in the view of some of the Board's officials to have more staff than might at first seem justifiable, because of the burden of consultation with applicants for assistance and other authorities. There is the physical task of merely covering the ground to see people and their land and buildings when a telephone call is not a suitable means of communication.

The personal element is very important. It may be that an application as phrased is unacceptable, but if suitably altered it might come within the scope of the Board's plans and receive more sympathetic treatment.

A virtually inescapable difficulty is that the Board cannot answer criticism publicly. As is indicated in paragraph 70 of the first report, the Board does not give reasons to applicants for decisions on their applications. Even all the responsible staff may not know the reasons for a particular decision which may occasion comment in the press. Disclosure of reasons—which may be subjective, but none the less real for that—could lead to fruitless controversy, or disclose valuable information to competitors of the applicant. It is understood that on occasions adverse press criticism has had an unfortunate effect on the morale of the staff, but this could perhaps be remedied by improvements of internal communications.

If the Board is to succeed, it is essential that much of its work be conducted under a cloak of confidentiality. A former Secretary of State, Mr. Woodburn, has said that it is desirable to deal with the problems of the Highlands more democratically and publicly.[32] This may be true, but it would require a very considerable alteration in British traditions of administration if it were to come about.

(4) Controls

Contributors to this series of essays are asked to consider what hidden or informal controls are exercised over the activities of the Board? If this question is posed in a pejorative sense, the answer is probably "none."

31. H.L. 27.2.69, col. 1201.   32. H.C. 16.3.65, cols. 1112–1113.

It is perhaps significant that so far no proposals made by the Board to the Secretary of State have been turned down. There is now some risk that meritorious proposals may be rejected, but such rejection would be because of the current financial crisis.

Of course, it may be argued that no proposals will be submitted unless they have been cleared informally beforehand. In the Board's early days, a DAFS representative used to attend Board meetings. He would be (at least in theory) in a position to warn the Board off, should it be considering any unwelcome proposals. However, no Scottish Office representative now attends these meetings, and so this potential threat to the Board's independence appears to have been removed.

According to the reports, as indicated above, the Secretary of State has so far given no official "section 2" directions. On the other hand, suggestions can be made to the Board from all sorts of pressure groups, directly or through the Consultative Council. But in the atmosphere of the crofting counties this can be achieved in a civilised manner, in a low key, so that many of the concepts of high-pressure lobbying which may be relevant in heavily industrialised and commercialised regions have no place here.

(5) The Future

It is too early to say whether the Board has been a success, but there are grounds for optimism. Its policy appears to be flexible. It may be said to make its policy as it goes along. Life in the Highlands is still leisurely enough for this to be possible. Each case can still be genuinely decided on its merits, rather than according to blanket regulations.

It is to be hoped that it will become, as Franklin D. Roosevelt hoped the TVA would become, "a corporation clothed with the power of government, but possessed of the flexibility and initiative of private enterprise." The problems to be solved will certainly make full demands on the powers, flexibility and initiative of the Board. It cannot hope to industrialise the Highlands as a whole. Not everyone in the Highlands wants to be summoned to work by a factory hooter, any more than do those who live elsewhere.

The Board (like the Norwegian Government, faced with similar problems) may eventually, and sooner rather than later, have to consider the need to evacuate people from townships even on the mainland where it is not really a practical proposition to try to maintain the standard of living which is now generally accepted as desirable.

It is necessary to strike a balance. The social cost of economic depression in the crofting counties and of the ever-expanding boom in the English south-eastern "coffin" is not to be overlooked, and the words of the Taylor Commission, quoted above, are surely relevant here too. To a considerable extent indeed the problem of the Highlands is a problem of under-use of existing resources, and a thorough and systematic survey of natural resources is urgently needed.[33]

Even within the area for which the Board is responsible, it will be necessary to guard against the danger that growth points, instead of radiating activity to smaller areas outside, may attract labour from the more remote and isolated areas, accelerating decay and unplanned depopulation of the poorer crofting areas.

Scotland is famous for its investment trusts. This is an organisation which may eventually develop some of the features of a trading company, a finance house, and an investment trust—and presumably, through the dispensation of grants, to some it already seems to be a fairy godmother.[34]

33. H.C. 16.3.65, col. 1125.
34. The writer wishes to express his appreciation of the kindness of Mr. R. D. King and Mr. Stuart Edmund to him during his visit to the offices of the Board, and to thank them for their patience in supplying information and giving answers to his queries, both then and in subsequent correspondence.

Part II

The Continent
of Europe

CHAPTER 6

PUBLIC ENTERPRISES IN FRANCE*

A STUDY which appeared in 1954[1] dealt with the term *établissement public* in France, an expression which was translated as "public corporation." But to-day it seems that this expression *établissement public* is both too wide and too narrow to be regarded as being exactly identical with the English "public corporation." It is too wide because *établissements publics* are divisible into two categories, *établissements publics administratifs* and *établissements publics industriels et commerciaux*, and it is really only the second category, those subjected partially to private law, that can properly be compared with "public corporations." *Etablissements publics administratifs*, subject exclusively to public law, and having objectives exclusively of a public service character, can only with difficulty be likened to public corporations.[2] The term is also too narrow because some enterprises have the status of commercial companies while their capital is partially or completely publicly owned, and these should also be here considered, although they do not, nor could they have, the status of *établissements publics*.

It is for these reasons that it is preferable to use the expression *"entreprise publique"*. It is true that in French law *entreprise publique* does not normally possess any very precise meaning. It is an economic and not a juridical expression because above all the term *entreprise* is itself not a juridical expression. But we are here in a field where juridical rules are in the course of being formulated in an empirical manner, as the result of a long process. If there is no status as such of *entreprise publique* and if the expression seems to include differing juridical concepts, nonetheless a single uniform concept is gradually being formulated. This uniformity has its roots in economic and political origins, and it also comes from what one might call "the greatest common propensity" of juridical institutions; finally this unification is due also to the status of *entreprises publiques* at the European level, within the European Economic Community.

It is desirable first to ascribe a definition to the term *"entreprise publique."* For the moment this definition will be synthetic, but it will become precise in the course of this essay. An *entreprise publique* is an enterprise the whole or the majority of whose capital belongs to the State or other public agencies. By

* By Professor R. Drago, Faculty of Law and Economics, University of Paris, translated from the French by Professor J. F. Garner.
   1. R. Drago, "The Public Corporation in France" in *The Public Corporation*, ed. W. Friedmann, Toronto, 1954.
   2. A. Martin-Pannetier, *Eléments d'analyse comparative des établissements publics en droit français et en droit anglais*, 1966, pref. R. Drago.

reason of its industrial or commercial activities it is basically subject to private law (and particularly to commercial law), as are private enterprises, but, because of its public nature, it finds itself subjected to a certain degree of dependence on and control by public authorities.[3]

And so we may define *entreprise publique* by reference to three elements:

(a) public ownership of its capital,

(b) its subjection to private law, and

(c) its relative dependence on public authorities and the control exercisable by them over the enterprise. This last question is so important that it is dealt with specially by Professor Lévy in Chapter 7.

Defined in this way *entreprises publiques*, operating together with the more important private sector of industry, are concerned with more than 11 per cent. of the internal production of raw materials in France and employ more than a million persons. They have a dominant role in certain sectors: power (90 per cent. of the electricity produced, 95 per cent. of the gas, 34 per cent. of the petroleum extracted), and transport (a monopoly in railways, 90 per cent. of national air travel, 25 per cent. of sea travel). They also occupy a not insubstantial place in other sectors: engineering (36 per cent. of motor vehicles, 50 per cent. of aircraft production), chemicals (61 per cent. of nitrogen fertilisers, an important part of organic chemicals, all the sulphur and all the potassium fertilisers) and finance (52 per cent. of savings banks, 40 per cent. of insurance policies). They also play an important part in other sectors: building construction, motorway construction, the armament industry, publicity, cinemas, hotels, electric cleaning equipment, printing, etc.

The importance of this "public sector" of industry has posed at both the national and the local level a certain number of problems of an economic and social kind, which have been the cause, since about 1965, of a number of reforms or proposals for reform. These problems have also prompted the Government to establish a "working party," presided over by M. Nora, charged with an examination of the position of the *entreprises publiques*, in particular in relation to structure, economy and finance. The report of this working party (referred to herein as the "Nora Report"[4]) was published in November 1968, and is one of the most important factors indicating a determination of the future structure of *entreprises publiques* in France at the national level.

In order to study the problem of the *entreprises publiques* it will be convenient first to analyse the new elements in their status since 1954. While taking into consideration the most important reforms or proposals for reform

3. V. Delion, *Le statut des entreprises publiques*, 1963; J. M. Auby and R. Ducos-Ader, *Grands services publics et entreprises nationales*, Vol. I, 1969, pp. 74 *et seq.*; see also Dufau, "Remarques sur la notion d'entreprise publique", *Actualité Juridique droit administratif*, 1956–I–89.

4. Working party of the Inter-Ministerial Committee on Public Enterprises, *Rapport sur les entreprises publiques* (April 1967), 131 p., Ed. Doc. française, 4ème trimestre 1968.

it will also be possible to investigate what may be the future of *entreprises publiques*.

1. EVOLUTION OF THE STATUS OF ENTREPRISES PUBLIQUES FROM 1954 TO 1969

Taking account of the developments that were considered in my former article,[1] four questions arise:

(1) The creation of *entreprises publiques*;
(2) Juridical form of *entreprises publiques*;
(3) Their organisation and constituent law;
(4) The legal regime and fiscal status.

(1) The creation of entreprises publiques

The creation of *entreprises publiques* by national or local public authorities depends essentially on the concept of the State; that is to say that an *entreprise* will be created for political motives. From the juridical point of view, one can however distinguish three sources, which, while they react on one another, it is convenient to distinguish; that is to say, unilateral creation *ex nihilo*, nationalisation, and participation by the State directly or indirectly in the affairs of a private enterprise.

(i) *Unilateral creation* ex nihilo

The industrial and commercial activity of the entreprise in this instance is the result of the unilateral wish of some public authority. They create an economic enterprise, either in a field where no similar private enterprise exists (*e.g.* atomic energy), or in a field where there are already private enterprises of the same kind. The problem is, however, different according to whether the enterprise is created by the State or by some other public agency.

(*a*) *Creation by the State.* In principle before 1958, it was the legislature which gave birth to enterprises of this kind, in such a manner that its decision was not capable of being contested by any means, and was dependent merely on political majority decisions in Parliament. It was pointless, in particular, to ask if such a creation attacked the principle of liberty of commerce and industry proclaimed by the law of March 2–17, 1791, which has been interpreted as prohibiting public agencies from engaging in private activities.

Since the coming into force of the Constitution of 1958 and the distinction it draws between the legislative sector and the "regulations" sector (*le domaine réglementaire*) in Articles 34 and 37, the position has been different. In effect, except for certain matters reserved by Article 34, the creation of new public services can be the result of the exercise of an autonomous power to legislate by regulation. In this situation it is theoretically possible to attack the creation of economic enterprises by central government administrative authorities in the administrative courts. One is led to this as a hypothesis, but it should be observed that to date the case law has not given any examples of any such attacks.

(b) *Creation by public authorities other than the State.* In this case, on the contrary, the law of March 2–17, 1791, as it has been interpreted by the Conseil d'Etat, prohibits local authorities from creating economic enterprises, except in a case of failure on the part of private enterprise. Until about 1930 the Conseil d'Etat had made itself the defender of economic liberalism in construing this law very narrowly. Certainly the decree laws of November 5 and December 28, 1926 allowed communes to create economic services in a variety of fields, but these provisions did not stop the administrative courts from continuing to apply their former case law. But the evolution of ideas and the necessities born in the crisis of 1930 led the courts progressively to admit the creation by local authorities of services directly competing with private enterprises, subject only to the condition that they should be provided in the public interest. The more recent case law has gone a very long way in this direction, and has allowed the creation of a cinema,[5] a petrol station,[6] and a camping site.[7]

(ii) *Nationalisation*

This implies the transfer to national ownership (with or without compensation) of a private enterprise, or even of all the private enterprises operating in a particular economic sector. Such a process, the result of a *dirigiste* concept of the State, is comparatively new in France. Except for the cases of 1936 (nationalisation of munitions factories and aircraft establishments) the political concept of nationalisation began in France in 1944. Its justification is to be found in the preamble to the Constitution of 1946: "Any enterprise which has or has acquired the characters of a national service or of a monopoly, should become the property of the community." If there is a question of transfer of ownership only the legislature is competent to act, and this situation has not been modified as a consequence of the coming into force of the Constitution of 1958, Article 34 of which expressly deals with the case of nationalisation. Therefore nationalisation depends on exclusively political considerations, and it is this which explains the fact that the only nationalisations realised between 1944 and 1947 were those concerned with the more important sectors of the national economy, namely, electricity, gas, coal, the Banque de France and four deposit banks, thirty-two insurance societies and the Renault car undertakings.

5. C.E., June 12, 1959, "Syndicat des exploitants de cinématographes de l'Oranie, A.J.D.A., 1960—II—85, concl. Mayras.
6. December 18, 1959, "Delansorme", *ibid.* p. 213, concl. Mayras; Dalloz, 1960, 371, note Lesage.
7. April 17, 1964, "Commune de Merville-Franceville", AJDA, 1964—II—304.

(iii) *Participation by the State directly or indirectly in the affairs of a private enterprise*

This process is the one most frequently used today in important sectors. The State (or other public authorities) has created enterprises of a mixed economy in which it retains a majority participation. As an alternative a public authority may directly or through the intermediary of an *entreprise publique* take an interest in a private enterprise. This may perhaps be achieved by a unilateral act (*e.g.* the creation by a law of a company of a mixed economy, such as Air France), but more often this will be the result of some private law action (such as the creation of companies according to ordinary commercial law; see below).

(2) Juridical form of entreprises publiques

These forms have at the present time attained a considerable diversity and any classification must necessarily be somewhat artificial. One can distinguish four principal varieties: the industrial undertaking (*régie*), the industrial and commercial public corporation, the national company and the company with a mixed economy. However, it is also necessary to take account of the financial interests held by public enterprises in private enterprises; this phenomenon of subsidiaries is certainly one of the most important of the new activities of the State in the economic sector (see below).

(i) *Industrial and commercial undertakings*

These are public undertakings of an industrial and commercial character, carried on directly by the State or other public authorities, which do not have any corporate personality. There is no comprehensive code of law for all the State undertakings; on the other hand, undertakings created by the communes are subject to the provisions of Articles 355–374 of the Code of Communal Administration. Today they possess a lesser importance than those of other forms of State activity.

By reason of their commercial activity, some of these undertakings have been entrusted with financial autonomy, so that independent accountability can demonstrate their results. Such is the case with the alcohol service and the administration of the posts and telephones (PTT), each entrusted with a separate budget.[8]

(ii) *Industrial and commercial public corporations (établissements publics)*

In this case the undertaking has corporate personality and financial autonomy of such a kind that it may more easily conduct its affairs according to commercial principles. Such an undertaking may resemble some administrative public corporations, but it is distinguished from them by its constitution being regulated almost exclusively by commercial law (see below). This kind of

8. See A. G. Delion, "Les services industriels en régie de l'Etat," *Droit Social*, 1965.

établissement public appeared at the end of the last century, but has not been developed since. Some were created *ex nihilo* (the national inter-professional office of cereals; ORTF (radio and television office)), while the largest number and the most important were the result of nationalisation laws (Electricité de France, Gaz de France, Charbonnages de France (coal mines), Houillères de bassins (the coal beds), etc.)[9] The names of these undertakings must be registered every year at the same time as the Finance Bill (law of July 18, 1949). In addition the elements of a common code are to be found in Articles 151, 152, 153 and 190–225 of the decree of December 29, 1962, which makes general regulations about public accountability.

(iii) *National companies*

These comprise companies which are subject to ordinary company law but of which the State is the sole shareholder. The most important are the result of nationalisation statutes (Bank of France, nationalised banks, nationalised insurance companies, the National Renault Company).

(iv) *Companies with a mixed economy*

After a relatively modest appearance between the two World Wars these companies take, as we have already said, the most original and most dynamic share of the industrial activity of the State and other public agencies. In most of these cases, the State or agency hold from 51 to 99·9 per cent. of the share capital. Their development at the present time is considerable in all sectors of national and local activity (research and exploitation in petroleum, transport, motorways, national planning and housing construction).[10]

Their creation corresponds to what the *Cour des Comptes* (Court of Accounts) has called "the fragmentation of the administration," although because of these companies it seems desirable to introduce into administration a principle of "mission" as well as the existing idea of an undertaking. The danger of this is that it implies a certain commitment of public money in private commercial enterprise. Guarantees are taken together with control which will have a tendency to increase, as is shown by the Circular of August 17, 1964, cited in the notes. On the other hand court decisions are also compelling these companies to submit to the rules of public law imposed to protect the general interest.[11]

9. See R. Drago, *Les crises de la notion d'établissement public*, pp. 66 *et seq.*; pp. 200 *et seq.*; R. Connois, *La notion d'établissement public*, 1958.

10. J. Branger, "Participations financières de l'Etat (sociétés d'économie mixte)," Rapp. au Conseil économique, p. 48, 1958; Fabre, Morin and Serieyx, *Les sociétés locales d'économie mixte et leur contrôle*, 1963; Circular of August 17, 1964, relating to the creation, operation and control of companies of a mixed economy (*Journal Officiel*, September 6, 1964).

11. See Trib. Confl., July 8, 1963, *Sté Entreprise-Peyrot c/ Sté de l'autoroute Esterel-Côte d'Azur*, AJDA, 1963, p. 484 and the commentary by J. Fabre and R. Morin, RDP, 1964, pp. 767 *et seq.*

(3) Organisation and constituent law of entreprises publiques

The rules relating to organisation and constitution vary from one enterprise to another. It is, however, clear that one can find a certain number of constant features, at least in the case of the three forms of *entreprises publiques*, because the functions carried on most frequently follow a classic hierarchic administrative structure.

The feature most commonly found at present is that of decentralisation and autonomy of the enterprise itself. There is at the top an administrative council (*conseil d'administration*) which is the deliberative organ. Under the authority of the council a director or director-general is the executive organ and the executive staff are subordinate to him.

The administrative council is constituted on a representative basis according to the rules of "tripartite management" (State, employees, consumers) used by the enterprises created by the nationalisation statutes. This principle has a number of variations, although the councils always include representatives of the State and of the employees of the enterprise (about one third each); they also include persons qualified in the field of activity of the particular enterprise, and in the case of companies of a mixed economy, representatives of the private shareholders. All the nominations of members of the councils are made by decree of the Prime Minister.

The composition of these councils is not without certain difficulties:

(i) The representatives of the State are nominated by the Ministers concerned with the undertakings carried on by the enterprise to the extent that each Minister insists on having his say in the selection of the council, and this means that the representation of the State is not homogeneous, and that the role of arbitrator that these representatives ought to play is not always assured.

(ii) The representatives of the employees are appointed from persons nominated by the strongest trade unions, and their selection results from the application of criteria defined in Article 31 (*f*) of the Labour Code (law of February 11, 1950), namely, competence, independence and attitude during the German occupation. These relatively vague criteria give a wide discretion to the Government in the choice of those nominated.

(iii) The representation of users and consumers has always been difficult to legislate for precisely, as consumers are not organised at either national or local level. Therefore the Government choose these representatives from persons nominated by local authorities, consumer industries and family associations.

(iv) The presence of qualified persons on these councils dates primarily from the reforms of 1953. It has had the effect of decreasing the influence of the representatives of consumers and often implying as it does a wide liberty of choice, of increasing the influence of the Government in these councils.

The powers of the council of administration of an *entreprise publique* are very wide, as it has power to determine the activities of the enterprise, to take decisions about the employment of its capital, to declare the amount of dividends and to pass the profit and loss account. In practice, however, those councils which meet less often and whose members are often opposed to one another by divergent interests, will leave the reality of power to the director-general.

The director-general is appointed by a decree of the President of the Republic or of the Prime Minister, in some cases on the nomination or advice of the council of administration. His status is by reason of this fact one of public law. He conducts the general direction of the enterprise and in practice very frequently has a very wide power to make decisions, and he exercises his authority over all the personnel of the enterprise.

This system is however liable to evolutionary changes in structure which can be instituted by application of Articles 118 *et seq.* of the law of July 24, 1966, in the case of commercial companies. By this means the Mining and Chemical Enterprise (EMC), created by decree of September 20, 1967, is governed by a directory and a supervisory council. The council consists of twelve members; two representatives of the Minister of Industry, two representing the Minister of Economics and Finance, one representing the Minister of Agriculture, four persons chosen by reason of their experience, and three representing the employees of the enterprise or of its subsidiaries.

The employees of the *entreprises publiques* are as a body governed by rules of private law. Certainly in the case of some enterprises, there are legal provisions that are the result of regulations (for example, electricity, gas and mines), but the relationship between the employees and the enterprise remains basically one of private law, even for the senior officials,[12] except for some contrary provisions in special statutes. The only restriction is concerned with the right to strike in relation to those public enterprises that are concerned with the undertaking of a "public service." For these enterprises (see Section D, below) the right to strike is limited by the requirement of a five-day warning and a prohibition on "staggered" strikes, introduced by the law of July 31, 1963. In addition, when the enterprise is concerned with services involving the "fundamental needs" of the public and the strike threatens a sufficiently severe attack on those needs, the Government has power to requisition personnel.[13]

Property law is comparatively complex but it can perhaps be described in the following manner.[14] The property of enterprises undertaking services (*en régie*) falls basically within the public sector, that is to say, it is inalienable and cannot be taken in execution. It is in principle the same for the property of

12. C.E., March 8, 1957, *Jalenques de Labeau*, Dalloz, 1957, 378, concl. Mosset, note of Laubadère.
13. C.E., October 26, 1962, *Le Moult et Syndicat "Union des navigants de ligne,"* p. 580, for the Company Nationale Air France.
14. See L. Jacquignon, *Le régime des biens des entreprises nationales*, 1956.

enterprises having the form of industrial and commercial *établissements publics*.[15] However, enterprises having the form of companies, either national companies or companies with a mixed economy, hold their property "in commerce" and are subject to the ordinary law. It seems moreover that the industrial and commercial *établissements publics* have a tendency at the present time to become assimilated with companies and in the interest of their commercial relations they accept the principle that their property should be liable to be taken in execution.[16] Finally, it can be accepted that, with the exception of the undertakings, the property of the *entreprises publiques* is subject to ordinary private law. There is, however, one limitation: the enterprise must be capable of carrying out the tasks with which it has been entrusted by its constituent statute (or by the administrative act that has created it), and in these conditions it could not be presumed that the directors should be able freely to dispose of the property of the undertaking to the extent of compromising these tasks. Put another way, it may be said that the property *ut singuli* is subject to the ordinary law, but the total of the undertaking's property must be reserved so that the mission of the enterprise may be carried out.[17]

(4) The legal régime and fiscal status

In principle the *entreprises publiques*, whatever may be their juridical form, are subject to the ordinary common law; that is to say, commercial law for all that concerns their external affairs, such as contracts concluded with their customers and their suppliers; responsibility towards their customers, their suppliers and third parties. Indeed, it is because of these external relations that the courts originally decided to apply the common law.[18] At the present time, however, although the question had previously been contested, the *entreprises publiques* have the quality of merchants and are registered in the Commercial Register.[19]

It can also happen that some public administrative agency has in part an industrial and commercial activity. The courts then must decide which part of such an activity is subject to public law and which part is subject to private law, according to a "collection of tests."[20]

15. Cass. com., July 9, 1951, Sirey, 1952—I—125, note Drago.
16. Trib. civ. Douai, June 11, 1952.
17. See opinion of the Conseil d'Etat, March 16, 1948, in sub-note Sirey, 1949—I—77 and note Drago, above. In another opinion of November 19, 1963 (n. 288325), it decided concerning ORTF, that it " has become the owner of the goods and installations dependant on radio and television services and formerly belonging to the State; in the case where certain installations would have formed part of the public ownership before the transfer they could only become the property of ORTF in the sense that they retain the status of public ownership".
18. Trib. confl., January 22, 1921, *Sté commerciale de l'Ouest Africain*, Sirey, 1924—III—34, concl. Matter, case called the "bac d'Eloka."
19. Art. 48 of the new commercial code, Dinet, March 23, 1967.
20. Trib. confl., November 23, 1959, *Sté mobilière et immobilière de meunerie*, RDP, 1960, p. 676, note Waline; CE, July 1, 1960, *Assemblée permanente des présidents des chambres d'agriculture*, AJDA, 1960—II—330, concl. Fournier.

One can imagine the possibility of liquidation of those enterprises that have the character of commercial companies. For them liquidation is theoretically possible, but in practice it is barely possible, because the State would certainly come to the assistance of such a company in difficulties, if only by reason of its economic importance, and the State would then proceed with its reorganisation on a different basis.

If then the commercial régime is applied to all these enterprises, it should not be forgotten that they are, according to the apt expression used by Dean Vedel, "public merchants"; that is to say, the State which has created them cannot dis-interest itself from the "mission" which it has entrusted to them, above all, when they are destined to be "pilot" enterprises in those economic sectors within which they have been created.

There should be a distinction between the enterprises that carry on a public service and those which do not carry on such a service. This distinction may seem to be otiose since all these enterprises can be qualified to carry on public services of an industrial and commercial character, but it becomes clear when one appreciates the basic nature of these institutions.[21] First, it is clear that the enterprises *en régie* carry on a public service and benefit from this fact by possessing all the prerogatives of a public corporation, with which they may be confused. So far as the others are concerned, the best test consists of asking whether they are or are not *concessionaires* of a public service. Thus by using this organic test which is in consequence an easy one to apply, we arrive at two major categories of enterprises which are quite independent of their juridical form. On the one hand there are *concessionaires* which are either *établissements publics* (Electricité de France; Gaz de France) companies with a mixed economy (SNCF—the French Railways—and Air France) or subsidiaries of those companies; on the other hand other enterprises are not *concessionaires* but are *établissements publics* (Charbonnages and Houillères), national companies (banks and insurance companies) or companies of a mixed economy (petrol companies).[22] Those in the second category enjoy a legal régime of private law concerning their internal affairs, while those in the first category because they are concessionaires of a public service, have an internal régime that is partly public law. Their projects are public and their construction work is subject to the régime of public contracts. They can exercise powers of compulsory acquisition in the public interst, etc. Public law rules as to strikes by their personnel apply by virtue of the law of July 31, 1963.

21. And therefore the Tribunal des Conflits (January 15, 1968, *Compagnie Air France c/ époux Barbier*, AJDA, 1968, pp. 225 and 233) decided in relation to a rule made by the Council of Administration of the company, according to which the marriage of an air hostess meant that she had to lose her job, that the administrative courts were competent to determine questions concerning the legality of this rule, "which as it concerned the organisation of a public service, possessed an administrative character."

22. See on this point, R. Drago, *Définition de la notion de service d'intérêt économique général*. Report to a colloquium on the relations between the public and the private sector in the European Economic Community, Brussels, 1963.

This division of the *entreprises publiques* into two categories has always been essential. It acquires today a capital importance which is underlined by the Nora Report,[23] where it refers to the desirable attitudes that should be adopted by these enterprises in future. This document distinguishes "those enterprises that are subject to strict controls in the interests of the public service," for which it is necessary to lessen the excessive weight of preventive controls and to increase their freedom to make decisions, and on the other hand "enterprises in the concurrent sector" in relation to which it is necessary above all to institute structural reforms so as to give them a wider outlook over the whole national economy (see second part of the Report).

The fiscal régime of all the enterprises is that of the common law (patents, company tax, and taxes on a number of transactions) as is expressly provided for in most of the constituent laws and repeated in Articles 206-1 and 1654 of the general Tax Code. On the other hand, the undertakings created by local authorities which do not have legal personality, would seem to be exempt from taxes by virtue of Article 207-1, 6, but the courts have expressed the opinion that this exemption applies only to those services that the local authorities "have a duty to provide," that is to say, those that have for their object the exploitation or execution of a service which is indispensable to the satisfaction of the collective needs of their inhabitants.[24]

So far as their financial régime is concerned this is intimately bound up with control and is more closely examined in that context. However, we would underline the importance of a few principles. With the exception of those undertakings (*régies*) that do not possess corporate personality, *entreprises publiques* are generally distinguished by their corporate personality which makes them distinct from and independent of the legal person that created them. So far as concerns *établissements publics*, their financial régime is identical with that of similar private enterprises. All these enterprises dispose of resources resulting from the income of their products and services. Of course they may be entitled to benefit from State subventions either at the time of their creation or as part of an investment policy.[25] On this point again important reforms are contemplated particularly in relation to groups of *entreprises publiques*.

2. THE FUTURE OF ENTREPRISES PUBLIQUES

The years 1967–69 will certainly mark a turning point in the life of *entreprises publiques* in France. The concentration which has been achieved by these enterprises has caused the appearance of the phenomenon of "groups" of *entreprises publiques* and also that of "public holdings." The publication of the Nora Report and the various proposals presented to the Government

23. Nora Report, *op. cit.* pp. 89 *et seq.*
24. CE, January 16, 1956, ADJA, 1956—II—80.
25. See P. Bauchet, *Propriété publique et planification,* 1962.
E

presage a complete reform of the status of enterprises. Finally they will have to find their place in the Common Market and adapt themselves to several relevant provisions in the Treaty of Rome. Such then are the three questions with which it is convenient to deal.

(1) The groups of entreprises publiques and the "public holdings"

Entreprises publiques of different categories (except for those *régies* or under-takings which do not possess corporate personality) have always established subsidiaries; that is to say, they have taken majority or minority interests in private enterprises, whether these are existing enterprises or, more often, by the creation of new enterprises resulting from an agreement between an *entreprise publique* and one or more private enterprises. For example, Houillères du Nord (Northern Coal) and Houillères du Pas de Calais have twenty-three subsidiaries,[26] and so the parent public enterprise, besides its own direct concerns, becomes the head of an important industrial group. This is also the case for Renault with its two principal subsidiaries, Saviem (lorries) and SNR (ball bearings).

Whatever may be the form of the parent enterprise, the subsidiaries neces-sarily have the form of a commercial company. According to the rules laid down in the decrees of August 9, 1953 and August 26, 1957, the expense of acquiring the interest must be approved by decree, if the amount of the interest is equal to, or more than, 50 per cent. of the total capital of the new enterprise. When this interest is fixed at a lower level, Ministerial approval only is required.

But this phenomenon has today taken on an altogether greater importance. It is linked up above all with a movement for the concentration of *entreprises publiques*, a concentration designed to give to certain enterprises a European stature. Thus, a decree of May 25, 1966, has decided that two national banks, the National Bank for Commerce and Industry and the National Savings Bank, should be merged to form a new bank—the National Bank of Paris.

Further, a decree of February 16, 1968 has decided that the Minister of Finance and Economics should be empowered to determine the constitution of groups of insurance enterprises to be formed by the merger of the nationalised insurance companies. Under this decree, the Union of Paris Insurance (UAP) and the Group of National Assurances (GAN) have been formed out of thirty-two existing national companies. A merger of the same magnitude will be undertaken under the control of Charbonnages de France, so as to regroup seven coal fields in three groups. Already, since October 13, 1966, all the commercial activities of enterprises concerned with combustible minerals in the chemical sector have been re-grouped under the control of a single company, the company Charbonnages de France—Chimie. Concen-

26. See F. Asseman, *Les participations financières des entreprises publiques*, thesis, Lille, 1962, and the references cited in note 10.

tration should also take place in the aeronautical and air space fields. Indeed, on February 19, 1969,[27] the Government decided to concentrate into a single company as from 1970, the three national companies concerned with space travel construction: Sud-Aviation, Nord-Aviation, and SEREB (Company for the study and manufacture of ballistic missiles).

Within the same range of ideas the State has been persuaded to create enterprises whose role is exclusively financial and which consists of taking interests over the whole of a particular sector of the economy. These are the true "public holdings,"[28] which exist principally in three fields: the construction and planning of sites through the intermediary of a Construction and Planning Company (SCET), itself a subsidiary of the *Caisse des depôts et Consignations*; petroleum policy, by the intermediary of the enterprise for research into and conduct of the petroleum industry (ERAP) created by a decree dated December 17, 1965, and the policy adopted for the chemical industry by means of the mediation of Mining and Chemical Enterprise (EMC) created by decree of September 20, 1967.

And so a new phenomenon has appeared, that of grouping of *entreprises publiques*, constituted not only around an enterprise with a specialist function (charbonnages, régie Renault, SNCF) but also around holding enterprises which influence a whole sector of the economy. We may take as an example EMC (mining and chemicals). This enterprise was the result of a merger of two enterprises having the form of *établissements publics* of an industrial and commercial character, the Potassium Mines of Alsace and the National Office for Industrial Nitrogen. It has itself the form of an industrial and commercial *établissement public*, and carries on its activities by means of three subsidiaries constituted in the form of limited liability companies: a sales organisation for the mining products, and two companies to administer the industries (potassium and nitrogen).

We may see the same arrangements in the petroleum industry, with ERAP and its 150 subsidiaries regrouped under the control of intermediate enterprises, the principal two of which are the General Union of Petroleum Oils (12 per cent. of all refining and distribution) and the National Company of Petrols of Aquitaine (natural gas, sulphur, artificial textiles, pharmaceutical products, etc.).

The birth of these "groups" poses juridical problems of the first importance; especially in determination of the status of subsidiaries in the second or third rank, which adds to the difficulties of control and means there is a risk that the interests of the public will be lost sight of. The desire to avoid these abuses on the financial plane has in some cases resulted in the creation of financial statements and balance sheets consolidated for the whole group of enterprises, which then present by reason of the "transparency" that

27. See *Le Monde*, February 21, 1969.
28. See M. Vasseur, *l'Etat, banquier d'affaires*, 1962.

these imply, a complete picture of the financial position for the administration of the group and the controlling bodies (decree dated December 17, 1955, Art. 12; decree dated September 20, 1967, Art. 11).

(2) The possibilities of reform of the entreprises publiques

The régime of the *entreprises publiques* thus involves several ambiguities. If it would have been possible twenty years ago to formulate a status which would include all these enterprises,[29] it must be admitted today that such a status is no longer necessary, as it would crystallise an evolutionary process where empiricism plays an important part. Apart from juridical formulas it is admitted in practice and by the courts, that a common status and régime does exist. Moreover, the details of the juridical régime are nowadays assumed to fit into the public sector in the national economy. In an earlier study[30] we concluded in the following terms: "The essentials of this problem are to know whether, by these processes, the State really dominates this huge public sector, or whether on the contrary the State is in the hands of a public technocracy more powerful than its civil servants, or indeed whether the private economy does not play in this sector the role of a Trojan Horse."

On the economic plane, the *entreprises publiques* find themselves today faced with major questions which they are not always capable of resolving; these include price fixing, choice of investments, salary and employment policy and financial solvency. Operating within a free economy but subject to a sensitive system of national planning, they frequently find themselves in an equivocal situation. Their status ought to become better adapted to this situation and to the questions they must solve.

One of the principal problems is that of the simplification and co-ordination of controls which is tackled separately. But this question is not the only one and structural reforms have been announced by the Government, particularly some based on the Nora Report.

It seems evident today that the pattern to be followed will be that provided for in Articles 118 *et seq.* of the law of July 24, 1966, concerning commercial companies; a supervisory council whose members will partly be appointed by the State, but which will be subject to the conduct of affairs to the organs of *tutelle* (*i.e.* Ministerial supervision), and there will be a directorate which implies that the executive will be carried on by a number of persons in a collegiate manner.

So far as those enterprises that are engaged in the concurrent sector are concerned, these structural reforms will be accompanied by rules ensuring that public shareholding in policy may be secured.[31] The existing sectors will

29. See M. Virally, "Remarques sur le projet de loi portant statut général des entreprises publiques," Rév. Adm. 1950, p. 355.
30. R. Drago, *Le régime des activités commerciales et industrielles des pouvoirs publics*, 7th international congress of comparative law (1966), French contributions, p. 460.
31. See Nora Report, *op. cit.* pp. 104 *et seq.*

have to be better arranged at the same time so that a more active policy of shareholding may be followed. Put another way, the State must be capable of having at its disposal instruments which are able to realise a policy of business being conducted by means of a financial portfolio. It would be a question first of rationalising each branch of the existing shareholdings and this rationalisation would then have to avoid duplication and co-ordinate the action of concurrent *entreprises publiques*. It would further be a question of extending the principle of financial holdings, which would then have a predominant position over the whole of a sector of the economy. We might even ask whether the entirety of national policy in this field ought not to be placed under the supervision of a single Minister, as is done in the case of the Minister of Public Holdings in Italy.[32] The Nora Report does not discuss the problem from this angle but it envisages the possibility of establishing a "Central Holding Company" which would administer the entire public share ownership and control all the enterprises dealing with public share-holding.

It is clear that such a solution would introduce a powerful element of coherence into the conduct of *entreprises publiques* and their subsidiaries, but it would also bring serious dangers of rigidity. Moreover, the choice so open to the public is a political one. "If public opinion," says the Nora Report, "interprets or is persuaded so to interpret, an active policy of shareholding as a declaration of an ideological war on 'private enterprise,' or as a committed step towards disguised de-nationalisation, this action would provoke reactions which would be more harmful than useful."

In fact at present the Government seems to be moving towards the constitution of groups and the creation of "holdings" in particular sectors. But this certainly does not exclude structural reforms of an individual *entreprise publique*, such as the reform of SNCF announced by the responsible Minister, at the same time as the revision of the agreement that puts it under State control.[33]

(3) The French entreprises publiques and the Common Market

The Treaty of Rome of March 25, 1957, setting up the European Community, contains a certain number of provisions concerning the *entreprises publiques*. These include Article 37–1 relating to an obligation to make progressive arrangements for national monopolies of a commercial character; Articles 54–3 (g) and 58 relating to the co-ordination of legislation concerning "corporations subject to public law"; Article 90–1 compelling the States to enforce no rule contrary to the provisions of the Treaty relating to "*entreprises publiques* or other enterprises to which (the States) accord special or exclusive laws"; Article 90–2 concerning the application of rules relating to "enterprises entrusted with the conduct of services that are of general economic concern";

32. Compare Chap. 4, p. 87 and Chap. 8, p. 147.
33. See *Le Monde*, October 12, 1968, January 22 and February 22, 1969.

Articles 72 *et seq.*, relating to the prohibition of subsidies by the States, etc. . . .

These provisions have and will have a number of effects on the régime of French *entreprises publiques*. But the principal result will be to alleviate the differences between the enterprises in other countries of the Community and to establish a model of a European *entreprise publique* valid for all six States. Proposals are at present being studied in the offices of the Community concerning either individual branches of undertakings entrusted to *entreprises publiques* or else a co-ordination of legislation in the States.

For all the reasons that have here been indicated, the French *entreprises publiques* are in the course of acquiring a new look. For the most part created a quarter of a century ago for a variety of reasons and possessing differing constituent statutes (often improvised), they are in the course of acquiring at the present time a greater cohesion in their juridical structures and at the same time in the economic policy which the State aims to carry out through them. However, it is not one of the least significant paradoxes that they should acquire more freedom to carry on their own affairs while continuing to comply with this policy. But the evolution is not complete. One can anticipate the future without being able to describe it exactly.

CHAPTER 7

CONTROL OF PUBLIC ENTERPRISES IN FRANCE*

THE main principle behind the setting up of public enterprises in France is that of autonomy in the conduct of their business. Certain undertakings of an economic character must be subjected to the public sector either exclusively (nationalisation and the grant of monopoly) or concurrently with the private sector, but such undertakings cannot be entrusted to administrative bureaus directly attached to Ministries. Unity, which is an essential feature of enterprises, and the need for economic efficiency, lead to a recognition of the right to manage their affairs themselves and to make decisions freely within the scope of activity which has been entrusted to them (compare Drago, *ante*, p. 107).

However, autonomy remains subject to some control on the part of the State. This control in theory has a double object. The first is to ensure that in its conduct of affairs the public enterprise applies the terms of the legislation and regulations currently in force in a proper manner. The second is to ensure that those objectives of a public character laid down by the establishment of these enterprises should not be abandoned as a consequence of their independent management, and also so as to make certain that the enterprises should pursue a course of policy which is integrated harmoniously with the general lines of political economy decided upon by the responsible organs of the State.

So it is difficult to achieve equilibrium between autonomy and control. If the first object of control preponderated, supervision would become essentially a control over legality in a wide sense, but in practice the second aspect of control has been developed to its maximum so as to approach by many interventions, and by the character of those interventions, a system of *tutelle* where the considerations of policy most frequently play a determining role. It has been said[1] that "in fact the authorities exercising *tutelle* fix limits on competence and initiative" concerning the management of a public enterprise, and that their "interventions are so numerous and so direct on all matters concerning the determination of investments, of methods of finance, of prices, salaries, production objectives and sales policy, that the powers of management can more easily be defined by differentiation than by enumeration."

* By Professor D. M. G. Lévy, Professeur à la Faculté de Droit et des Sciences Economiques de Paris, translated by Professor J. F. Garner.

1. *Rapport sur les entreprises publiques*, published by *Le groupe de travail du Comité interministériel des entreprises publiques* (April 1967) p. 80. Published with a supplement in *Notes et Etudes Documentaires*, 1968 (the "Nora" Report).

This evolution has resulted in two consequences. The first is the importance of control which tends to substitute itself for any power of action on the part of those responsible for the enterprise, and the second is the multiplicity of formulas used in order to exercise this control.

This has led to the result that the classical distinctions established by the jurists and especially those concerned with administrative law in this field, have become without any real meaning for they do not correspond to present-day reality.

The classical distinction between controls *a priori* and controls *a posteriori* has, in particular, lost any character of a precise line, not only because the importance of the controls *a priori* have tended always to become much greater, but also because certain restrictive procedures belong to both types. The permanent controls are no longer neatly opposed to occasional controls, as the multiplicity and frequency of the latter are such that they can be classified among the permanent controls. Further, financial controls go outside their strict domain so as to operate on technical matters. Finally, we have already underlined that the distinction between *tutelle* and control in the strict sense of the term does not permit of any very precise analysis, and in fact there is a tendency to integrate control into a more and more fully developed form of *tutelle*. Certainly there still exist differences and one can still admit that *tutelle* is exercised by an intermediary of the executive power and by his representative within the enterprise, whereas on the other hand, control is vested in Parliament, the *Commission de Vérification des Comptes des Entreprises Publiques*, and only in some cases in the Executive Government. But all these provisions are inextricably inter-twined, so that any necessarily limited explanation such as the present, which tried to separate them all out, would be extremely confused; that is why it has seemed preferable to take as a central feature the nature of those organs which exercise control. A presentation based on an organic distinction would appear to be simple, but it is the only one which can explain in a somewhat condensed manner, the reality of the provisions whereby controls are exercised. We will therefore be obliged to consider successively Parliamentary control, the control exercised by the *Commission de Vérification des Comptes des Entreprises Publiques*, and finally Governmental controls.[2]

PARLIAMENTARY CONTROL

Parliament has, since the beginning of the development of public enterprises, wished to exercise control over their administration. Since public enterprises are enterprises of the State, the representatives of the State should, according

2. Some readers would perhaps have expected some information about juridical controls exercised over public enterprises. We will not speak of them because this control is of an occasional character and it is left to the initiative of a particular plaintiff; also it does not present any special characteristics.

to them, be in a position to verify the manner in which those affairs are conducted. Sometimes the members of the Assemblies have shown a strong distrust of the manner in which the nationalised industries, in particular, have been functioning. These crises have been due for most of the time to the difficulty that Parliamentarians who are not generally specialists have not understood the problems presented to them by technicians. This has often resulted in bad feelings between the controlled and the controlling Members of Parliament. Further, strong political views and the taking up of preconceived ideas by some parties, have affected the way in which control has been exercised.

During the first phase of the Fourth Republic, soon after 1947, Parliamentary control was strengthened by the creation in each of the two Chambers of a Parliamentary Sub-Committee comprising deputies (or senators), members of the *Commission des Finances* and deputies or senators who were members of the specialised Commissions concerned with public enterprises. These Sub-Committees were given the duty of following and understanding "the conduct of affairs"[3] of the nationalised industries and of the *sociétés d'économie mixte*. They had very extensive powers of enquiry and could require information on all necessary matters, and in particular could take evidence from officials without going through the intermediary of the responsible Minister.[4] Each year one of the two Sub-Committees submitted a report to Parliament.

After 1955 Parliamentary control became even stronger. The Law of April 3, 1955 provided that the powers of these Sub-Committees should be increased and that the officials should not be able to refuse to reply by hiding behind any exigencies of secrecy. Further, after 1957 the nationalised industries were submitted to a financial control by Parliament in connection with budgetry discussions. Since 1958, however, conforming with the tendency to diminish the powers given to the legislature which is a characteristic of the Fifth Republic, Parliament has exercised a less developed control. However it is far from being deprived of any power of action. The permanent Sub-Committees have disappeared, but it is possible for Parliament to decide to create a control committee in cases where it considers this to be necessary. These committees are set up in order to examine the conduct of administrative, financial or technical affairs of a particular public enterprise. They have a duty to inform the Assemblies which created them as to the results of their examination.[5] Further, Parliament receives a whole series of documents concerning the enterprises, notably a complete list of nationalised undertakings of an industrial and commercial character and of the *sociétés*

3. Laws of March 21, 1947 and July 3, 1947.
4. Arts. 68 and 70 of the Law of March 21, 1947, modified by Arts. 1 and 2 of the Law of July 3, 1947.
5. Ordinance of November 17, 1958, relating to the functioning of the Parliamentary Assemblies, Art. 6, para. 3.

d'économie mixte with all their various subsidiaries.[6] Finally, Parliament has for its information each year the report of the *Commission de Vérification des Comptes des Entreprises Publiques*[7] which is discussed below. Of course the members of Parliament also retain the possibility of putting written or oral questions to Ministers, but in modern practice this is used relatively rarely.

Parliamentary control under the Fifth Republic no longer plays a very substantial role. This is a consequence of the fact that Parliament has seen its importance decline. It is also a consequence of the general evolution of the control exercised by the executive over the enterprises, which associates the Government with the formulation of decisions and even transfers to the Government the most important decisions. In a matter where Parliament is anxious to act it will more willingly intervene on occasions where the discussion concerns general principles governing public enterprises, than on matters of detail of their conduct, it being in the former case where it could exercise a real control.

2. THE CONTROL OF THE COMMISSION DE VERIFICATION DES COMPTES DES ENTREPRISES PUBLIQUES

The *Commission de Vérification des Comptes des Entreprises Publiques* corresponds for public enterprises to the functions of the *Cour des Comptes* concerning administrative public bodies. This Commission was created by Articles 56–62 of the Law of January 6, 1948, and its modern name has been given to it in the Regulations of July 19, 1948. The Law of June 22, 1967, concerning the *Cour des Comptes* sets down in Article 12 the composition of the Commission. "It will be convened in the *Cour des Comptes* under the Presidency of one of the Presidents of a Chamber of the *Cour des Comptes*; its Councillors will preside over the sections and the majority of members having a decisive vote will be judges of the *Cour des Comptes*." Therefore one sees that this Commission, although distinct from the *Cour des Comptes* has very close links with it. It is divided into specialised sections according to the major categories of the enterprises, power—transport and communications—credit, insurance and information—mechanical industry—chemicals and miscellaneous enterprises. Within each section there is a further specialisation according to particular enterprises. In addition to the judges of the *Cour des Comptes*, one finds officials who have a right to vote. Further, certain representatives of the State take part in the deliberations with a right to be consulted—a representative of the Minister exercising *tutelle*, the State controller[8] of the enterprise subjected to control, and a representative of the *Commissariat au Plan*. Finally experts are used as *rapporteurs* for particular matters.

The Commission possesses extensive powers of investigation. It receives

6. Ordinance of December 30, 1958, Art. 164, para. I.
7. Ordinance of December 30, 1958, Art. 164, para. IV.
8. *Cf. infra*, p. 129.

the accounts and balance sheets of the enterprises and also of the principal accounting parties. Further, all the reports from the other organs of control are communicated to the Commission. It can proceed by enquiries. The role of the Commission is particularly important as it ensures in the first place the regularity of the accounts and it then should estimate the commercial value of the manner in which the enterprise is being carried on and its commercial future. It can, if it considers it desirable, make suggestions in order to improve the affairs of the enterprise. Its investigations result in two series of reports: first a report addressed each year to the Prime Minister, to Parliament and to the *Cour des Comptes*, and secondly it addresses an individual report to each enterprise which is not published but which is sent to the Minister concerned.

The control of the Commission is thus a control *a posteriori*, which has indirect effects over the functioning of public enterprises as it provides an opinion for Parliament, and above all, for the government, on the information it has discovered.

3. GOVERNMENTAL CONTROLS

These are certainly the most important. It has already been indicated that the executive exercises a considerable interest, thanks to these controls, over the public enterprises. A study of such controls includes the examination of the various organs through which they are exercised, then a study of the legal provisions according to which they are applied, and finally a critical appreciation.

(1) The organs of control

The characteristic of governmental control over public enterprises is that it is exercised at two levels. Control is practised, as we have already said, from the exterior. But supervision can also be closer in the sense that beyond the organs of external control one meets organisations charged with control within the enterprises themselves.

(i) *External controls*

We mention first the existence of certain administrative committees which exercise control in certain particular fields. These committees watch over the activity of an enterprise in the particular field in question and grant any necessary authorisation in particular cases. These are particularly those concerning contracts and dealings in land. Further, in matters of investment, those enterprises which are enabled to apply for grants from the "Funds for Social and Economic Development," are subjected to the control exercised by that organisation. But these controls present a character complementary to the principal control exercised by the central administration. Every enterprise is attached, so far as concerns the technical control of the Minister, to a Ministerial Department termed that of *tutelle*, but the Minister exercising *tutelle* is not the one whose control is the strongest. Besides him and, one could almost say, above him, is to be found the Finance Minister. In the final analysis it is the Minister exercising *tutelle* and the Minister of Finance who are responsible, but control is normally exercised by Ministerial directions which raise the problem of co-ordination of action between the Ministers.

The Directions which are concerned with Finance are those of the Budget, of the Treasury and those concerning prices. Each in its own sector supervises the enterprise and represents the decisions of the Minister. Until November 1966 it was the Minister's private office which was responsible for co-ordinating all the various controls. Since this last date a reorganisation of officials has been introduced and established a permanent Secretariat which allows for better co-ordination.

The Ministers exercising control use their powers in many different ways; one can count almost a dozen, such as industry, national defence and agriculture to quote only the essential. A certain co-ordination can exist when several Directions come under the same Minister but it is more difficult to ensure this if they come under different Ministers. All the same, co-ordination may be very close between the control exercised by the directives of the Minister of Finance and those of the technical Ministers as it can be exercised at the level of the Funds for Economic and Social Development.

(ii) *Internal controls*

In principle there exist two organs of control within the enterprise. The Minister exercising *tutelle* is represented by a *Commissaire du Gouvernement*.[9]

Besides this official there is also another organ of control in the centre of the enterprise, namely the *Contrôleur d'Etat*.

(a) *The Commissaire du Gouvernement.* He is not found in all cases and certain public enterprises would know nothing of his existence. In each case his presence and his powers are fixed by the statute relating to the enterprise. It is his duty to represent the technical Minister and in principle to exercise a control in the fields which are concerned with a particular activity, but his activities can also be seen at the level of supervision over economic activities of the undertaking. When there is a *Commissaire du Gouvernement* he is entrusted above all with the duty of effecting liaison between the supervising Minister and the enterprise itself; most frequently the *Directeur* of the Minister exercising *tutelle* sets out the duties of the *Commissaire du Gouvernement*. As a rule the *Commissaire* has a seat on the Council of Administration of the enterprise, so that he can make known the views of the Government

9. It is necessary not to confuse these functions with those exercised before the contentious section of the *Conseil d'Etat* by the member of the court entrusted with the duty of presenting conclusions in the case. Here the *Commissaire* does represent the Government, as is the case before administrative bodies or before Parliament. Of course, these different *Commissaires* may be, and most frequently are, distinct persons.

on any questions which are raised. In fact he appears most often as a kind of director representing the State.

(b) *The Contrôleur d'Etat*. The control of the State has been organised by a general statute, namely the Decree of May 26, 1955. By virtue of these provisions the Minister of Economy and Finance can nominate for each enterprise a *Contrôleur d'Etat* or a control commission consisting of several members. This *Contrôleur* or Commission exercises three forms of directions giving control over public enterprises. The office is normally entrusted to senior officials but their functions are not really defined. No one is charged with co-ordinating the instructions they receive, their activities are not supervised and are scarcely controlled at all. "Each administration in the absence of considering the *Contrôleur* as its instrument entitled to receive and to give information, is tempted to address itself directly to the enterprise. This increases the isolation of the *Contrôleurs d'Etat* and side-tracks them into a role which in its turn justifies the attitude of the central administration."[10]

The *Contrôleurs d'Etat* are essentially concerned with supervising the economic and financial activity of the enterprise but each *Contrôleur* has a particular understanding of his own task. Some of them are concerned above all, and almost exclusively, with an examination of an entirely formal character, others, on the contrary, occupy themselves with problems of administration and of economic decisions. Yet others appear, after considerable time passed within a particular enterprise, as if they were in fact representatives of the enterprise and have a tendency to take on the defence rather than to act as true controllers.

The *Contrôleurs* should annually report to a committee of experts and give an account of their activities to the Minister of Finance.

(2) The legal provisions for control[11]

The extent to which a control can be effective varies according to the legal provisions where it is established, and this is affected by the practical necessities of the situation. When economic circumstances cause the State to carry the larger part of a financial burden resulting from the activities of an undertaking, control is very strong. On the contrary, in the case of enterprises in the form of *société d'économie mixte* the control is very considerably lighter and it is exercised only over the powers of the principal officials of the corporation. This is essentially the case with the great public enterprises such as *Electricité de France* or *Charbonnages de France*.

These enterprises are then subjected to a double technical, economic and financial control. This control takes the form in principle of a group of

10. See the report cited in note 1, *supra*, at p. 83.
11. On this point, the *Rapport du groupe de travail du Comité interministériel* contains some very interesting suggestions, and the developments which follow were inspired by their recommendations.

decisions which have to be approved, and other matters over which the administration has the possibility of exercising a right of veto. The powers of approval vary with each enterprise and are theoretically determined by the statutes relating to them. They ought not to take the effect of restricting the autonomy of the corporation by a control. In fact, let us repeat, this *tutelle* goes very far. It is not limited to a simple control over legality but extends also over policy. It is necessary to be able to appreciate the main purpose behind a particular decision of administration if *tutelle* is not to have an illusory character, but there is more than this. The control tends to substitute itself for the direction of the enterprise and to take its place in fundamental decisions. Moreover, economic considerations tend more and more to be superimposed on technical points of view in the course of the exercise of control and so the control of the Minister of Finance comes to over-ride that of the so-called Minister exercising *tutelle*.

(i) *The undertaking of control over the conduct of affairs*

The public enterprises have only very rarely had the possibility of deciding themselves on their rates of charges. The controlling authorities have decided these matters, as it might be necessary for a subsidy to overcome a deficit caused by too low a level of charges. Thus the enterprises have had to renounce almost completely any autonomy in the matter of prices and salaries. So far as investment is concerned, the control is a little less strong as the enterprises can make propositions and defend them in argument with the Ministries exercising control and the departments of the *Plan*, but the final decision is taken away from them. The remainder of the activity of the enterprises, for example, contracts and land dealings, need preliminary approvals which considerably slow up proposed activities when they do not completely prevent them.

This taking away of the effective powers of decision of an enterprise in favour of the organs of control has been made more noticeable by the existence of the organs of control within the enterprise itself. When the *Commissaire du Gouvernement* represents the State on the Council of Administration of an enterprise, there may then be considerable confusion between controller and controlled. One sees then a loss of autonomy and a substitution by the authorities of control for the directors of the organisation. But, as we shall see in a moment, not all of the controlling authorities benefit equally from this transference of power.

(ii) *The preponderance of financial control over technical control*

Technical control and financial control have theoretically distinct domains and objectives. Technical control has the function of elaborating a general policy within the particular sector with which it is concerned and of ensuring that the activity of the enterprises which it controls falls within these objectives. It should also examine the repercussions of financial matters so as to avoid conflict with the Minister of Finance.

The control of the latter is more limited but deeper since it is concerned with financial regularity and solvency as much for each enterprise as in the entire national economy. In fact, when an enterprise shows a certain level of deficit, or when its needs appear to be too great in the investment field, the Ministry of Finance is encouraged to examine the decisions of the enterprise very closely. And so, any act of the administration or any initiative susceptible of having financial repercussions, concerns this second *tutelle*, which tends to become overgrown and to substitute itself for the technical *tutelle* which is considered at this stage as being inferior. So then we may describe the Directions of the Minister of Finance as coming to assume the taking of the greater part of decisions, which each operate so as to protect particular objectives of their own, often without relating them to the necessities of the technical controls and the enterprise itself. So at a first estimation one could consider technical control as being relatively homogenous, but financial control is disparate. It has been said that since 1966 co-ordination has been exceptional; since then it can be effected only in the best conditions and more generally at a global level and not enterprise by enterprise. The only field where co-ordination between technical and financial control has a possibility of becoming effective under relatively satisfactory conditions is by means of the *Fonds de Développement Economique et Social*, but the experts are of the opinion that the present day functioning of this Board "presents the double inconvenience of being used clumsily for the co-ordination of financial *tutelle* on the one side and on the other of making to some extent unsatisfactory the technical *tutelle*."[12]

(3) Appreciation of government control

The results of the several controls have not been completely bad in spite of the criticisms that one can make of them. They do not give complete satisfaction either to the enterprises, the technical controllers, or to the financial controllers, but they have not resulted in a complete catastrophe or a total paralysis. Everyone complains, but they are not unbearable, and everyone could and has been able to adjust affairs to meet them. In particular the administrators of the enterprises and the technicians who work under their orders do not find them too bad, as these controls assure for them a protection against the eventual responsibilities which they might incur under an autonomous situation where they would be completely responsible. Further, the systems and their tendencies do not have any absolute character, and often the personal authority of a particular official of the enterprise and the

12. *Rapport sur les entreprises publiques*, p. 87.

importance of the enterprise at whose head he is working, will give him the possibility of making his opinions prevail over a Minister who is less assured as to the extent of his own activities.

However these considerations ought not to make one lose sight of the inconvenience of the present system. If the *régime* is bearable at the level of a particular enterprise it has nonetheless regrettable consequences; in particular in its effect on the position and role of public enterprises in the national economy.

On the one side the transference of powers which happens in fact to the advantage of the organs of control, "bring about the dilution of responsibilities and attenuate any need for good administration. When losses get below a certain level and tend to become permanent, the directors of the enterprise experience difficulties in trying to stimulate efforts to reduce the cost of administration."[13]

On the other hand "the conviction that the last word remains with the Minister of Economy and Finance does not encourage the Directions of the technical *tutelle* to exercise at their level the preliminary role of economic arbitration which ought to be exercised by them."[14]

The technical directions thus do not always result in a good administration from a technical point of view because of their subordination to the considerations of finance and capital, and their relative powerlessness in discussions in which they may be opposed by the representatives of financial control. These representatives, who are led to trespass into the technical field for which they have little competence in fact by reason of the training of their personnel, may often commit serious errors.

The *Groupe de travail du Comité interministériel des entreprises publiques* has formulated propositions in order to improve the control system, which may be summarised as follows:

(i) to restore to public enterprises an objective conforming with their nature as enterprises, and giving them such autonomy as is indispensable to them to enable them to carry out their activity;

(ii) to confer on the technical controllers the responsibility of policy decisions within their sector and also the means of exercising this;

(iii) to permit the financial controllers to exercise fully the role of arbitrator which belongs to them, while freeing them from tasks for which they are not adequately equipped.[15]

From a general point of view these changes ought not to overlook any longer the necessity to harmonise and unify control in such a manner as to facilitate the objectives of the enterprise and to diminish costs both direct and indirect.

13. *Ibid.* p. 85.
14. *Ibid.* p. 87.
15. *Rapport*, p. 89.

CHAPTER 8

THE PUBLIC CORPORATION IN ITALY*

WHAT IS A PUBLIC CORPORATION

THE organisation of public administration in Italy follows an intricate pattern in which new devices are intertwined with traditional authorities. In principle, on one side stand the Government departments, deprived of any legal personality of their own, as distinct from that which is recognised to that all-embracing entity which is the State, in domestic as well as in international law. Some agencies within a Government department, such as the Post Office or the railways, do, however, enjoy some sort of autonomy. On the other side may be counted tens of thousands of legally incorporated bodies, which are considered to be of a public nature and to form part of the administrative organisation, in consideration of the link existing between the purposes they pursue and the general purposes of the State. They range from the incorporated regions, provinces and municipalities, to welfare institutions. The last decades have also witnessed the growing up of a large number of joint-stock companies, the shares of which are wholly or for the greater part held by the Government, either directly or indirectly, through other public bodies. These companies are not, properly speaking, part of the administrative organisation, but they are so closely connected to it, as to make the distinction sometimes fictitious and irrelevant. These are henceforth called "private companies." To complete the picture one might mention the companies or individuals who remain such but are given by law or act of the administration the exercise of some public function or service, from the collection of taxes to the running of bus lines.

The presence of these various bodies each having some similar features helps to blur the nature of public corporations. But their definition is often of fundamental legal importance. They stand mid-way between the State and private companies, having some elements in common with both and others different. The State itself is a public corporation, the public corporation *par excellence*, and public corporations may even share some of the attributes of sovereignty; but they are legally independent from the State. In a highly developed system of administrative law, like the Italian, a public corporation may thus carry out administrative acts, *viz.* acts unilaterally modifying the legal sphere of third parties, be subject to the jurisdiction of administrative courts, be directly liable for the tortious actions of its agents, and they may

* By Professor G. Treves, Institute of Public Law, University of Turin.

be considered to be public agents and have a special status, and may own goods which are the object of a particular régime, concerning their use and alienation, in view of their destination to a public aim, etc. All these aspects may be found in some public corporations, only some in others, and possibly none in the remaining. This shows the great richness of the scene, ranging from the possession of powers of sovereignty to the position of private persons.

When is then a corporation to be called public, not merely for the sake of some scientific tidying up, but to make it possible to recognise in it the subject of some of the rights and duties which have just been enumerated as being characteristic? Its public nature derives from the law, as a public corporation is part of the administrative set-up of the country. When Parliament defines a corporation as public, then there is no problem. Such is the case of regions, provinces and municipalities, public assistance and social security boards and a host of other social and even economic bodies. But in the past, legislative qualification was not the rule, and even to-day may occasionally be lacking. Parliament has not always followed the same criteria to include a corporation within the administrative organisation. When a corporation is directly and individually incorporated by the law, when it is considered to be equivalent to a State agency, for instance from the point of view of taxes, or when it is endowed with a supremacy power, such as the issue of by-laws, administrative decisions or certificates, the levy of taxes, etc., then the corporation shows features which seem to correspond to those of a public nature. In other cases, and especially when its activity is wholly governed by private law, recourse is made to the aims fixed for a corporation, an element which has always been deemed to be of paramount importance. But this is often a question of values and degree, where it is not possible to draw a clear-cut line. Education, assistance and economic initiative are entrusted to both public and private bodies, according to the Italian Constitution itself. A public corporation or a private company may be set up by the State to run an industry, and many public charitable institutions are founded by private individuals. This being the situation, the courts have shown an inclination to make a kind of algebraic sum of those symptoms in favour and those against the public character of a corporation, a method, of course, which is not refined and is of practical value only in doubtful cases. Litigation used to be particularly frequent and difficult soon after the Second World War in connection with employment relationships that had to be classed as either public or private not only from the point of view of substantive law, but also so as to determine which judge had jurisdiction.

There are no intermediate bodies between public and private corporations, like the French *établissements d'utilité publique*. Public administration to-day is not always placed on a platform higher than the citizens and issuing orders to them. It includes many agencies tendering services to them or carrying out all sorts of financial, industrial and commercial activities, which fall beyond the area of public law.

At the beginning of the century public bodies were still very few—local government authorities, chambers of commerce, charitable institutions, professional corporations and some banking concerns. But, little by little, the State increased its holding on society, qualifying as public all kinds of social institutions, national and local, whose objects range from culture to sport and from health to tourism. Some are individually established by statute, both legally and in fact. In other cases, a statute may generally recognize legal personality subject to the ascertainment of some requisites to be met in each instance. Sometimes their establishment is compulsory and at other times facultative. Some are associations, including a number of individuals who take part in their operations. Others are simple foundations, in the sense that legal personality is conferred upon a fund. But the personal and material elements may be variously combined. There are bodies sharing Government functions and others pursuing circumscribed or ephemeral or even doubtful public objectives. Some are really dismembered parts of the Government, whereas local government bodies have to be self-governing in a democratic society.

Public corporations may be grouped together through the appointment of a common chairman or some joint directors, by a merger of their administration, or by a federation or common membership of a non-incorporated association. Municipalities and provinces may combine in syndicates for joint administration of some common services or works. Parliament may go a long way towards regulating the life of a public corporation, but often each body issues a statute of its own, to be approved by the Government. The relevant legislation is often patchy, but it would be rash to make recourse to the rules applicable to other bodies when the interpreter of other rules finds himself at a loss. The proliferation of these bodies may be accidental or due to many different reasons, but it also reflects different State interests which may call for different means to be realised.

Local government authorities, *i.e.* the regions, the provinces and over 8,000 municipalities, usually called territorial bodies, may be left outside the scope of this discussion, even if they are in one sense typical public corporations. The independence they enjoy, guaranteed by the Constitution itself, the width of their powers and the political issues they involve, raise problems of a peculiar nature, the solution of which is not always helped by an outdated and entangled legislation. They do not easily lend themselves to a description together with other bodies.

A further selection may also exclude charitable institutions and many other public bodies, in order to compare English public corporations with their Italian counterparts. The analysis may therefore be more usefully confined to those modern bodies operating a public service or an economic activity.

SEMI-INDEPENDENT STATE OR LOCAL AGENCIES

Historically the first services to be undertaken by the administration were carried out by the central Government. Postal, telegraphic and telephonic services, the tobacco and salt monopolies, the railways, the national highways and some minor services were given an autonomy unknown to normal departments and now constitute special agencies or administrations. The formula has been dropped since the last war, but it is still followed by municipal authorities. This autonomy was thought necessary if the services had to be run smoothly and be efficient, as private enterprise is supposed to be. The rules for the accounting and financial control of Government agencies are so old and clumsy, that they are completely unsuitable to this purpose. These special agencies are administered by a chairman, who is usually the Minister in charge of the department to which the agency is attached, and a board, mainly composed of officials with advisory functions. Their personnel, although being Government personnel, may have a special status. Financial autonomy finds its expression in a separate budget, which, however, is annexed to the national budget and submitted for parliamentary approval. Prior Treasury auditing is dispensed with. Each agency has its own revenue, consisting of Government grants, taxes, payment for services, etc. It may even issue bonds and turn to private banking for credits. The railways, the highways, the forests, etc., remain State property, and the agency merely manages them. There is a call for more freedom, similar to that which is conferred on public corporations.

Midway between the usual Government departments and these special agencies stand some funds which are separately administered or have separate budgets or simply separate accounts, showing revenue and expenditure. Arsenals and other defence factories and laboratories have what is called a "functional" autonomy within the framework of programmes established by the Ministry on which they depend. Sometimes these funds are not recorded in the national budget and their returns may be employed in further operations.

Similar arrangements are provided for semi-autonomous agencies mainly depending on municipal authorities. They are entrusted with the management of some industrial or commercial services, often on a monopoly basis, such as transport, gas, water, milk, etc. Their administration, budget and accounts are distinct from those of the municipality, and they may enter into contracts and sue and be sued in the ordinary and the administrative courts in connection with their tasks. Their main functions are vested in a board of administrators and a managing director. This organisation scheme has some points in common with the distribution of powers among local government authorities. The municipal council as well as the prefectures control the agency. Profits go to the municipality, which also makes good the losses. Employment is ruled by private law, in the absence of special regulations. Some regions, and especially Sicily, also have established organisations of this kind. But local government authorities show now a preference for private companies endowed by them and empowered to exercise a public service.

Some public banking institutions administer special purpose funds on parallel lines.

In cases like these the distinction between a legal person and its agencies or organs loses some of its original sharpness. The process goes further when one of these semi-independent State agencies is also granted a legal personality of its own, for property reasons, or a Government department also manages a public corporation, as is the case of some pension schemes. The universities are public corporations enjoying a considerable degree of administrative, didactic and disciplinary autonomy, but their staff is composed mainly of State personnel. This is also the status of university professors, with the exclusion of those teaching in a limited number of privately endowed faculties.

THE ECONOMIC PUBLIC CORPORATION

This is the device which was adopted at the time of the First World War to finance private rearmament industries out of public funds. A great public life assurance institution was shortly afterwards set up to influence that market without nationalising it. However, economics was still fundamentally a matter for private initiative, and the Government intervened only when prompted by public interest to control, limit or encourage individual activity without substituting itself for private enterprise. The depression of the thirties marked the turning point. The main instrument of the new policy was the Institute for Industrial Reconstruction (IRI), a public corporation created by statute in 1933 to look after the technical, economic and financial reorganisation of the country's industries, and empowered to advance medium and long term loans previously granted by the banks. IRI's task was the "healing" of the financial market, an operation which led it to become a major shareholder in a number of private companies. Other tasks were subsequently assigned to IRI, and always undertaken with the same mechanism. A similar corporation was established in 1953, the National Hydrocarbons Board (ENI), for the research and utilisation of this natural gas, with monopoly rights over operations in the northern part of Italy. Its development is second only to IRI and also is carried out through a complex system of shareholding.

The third large public corporation is the National Electricity Board (ENEL) directly operating the electric power industry, nationalised in 1962—the second example of nationalisation after the railways, which occurred in 1905.

Another important corporation of a commercial type was created in 1966 to carry out "Government interventions in the agricultural market" (AIMA), in connection with the realisation of the European Common Market. It mainly operates through co-operatives, combines and other suitable organisations.

As well as some minor holdings and industrial or trading corporations, there is a considerable network of savings banks, regional banks and other financial institutions granting medium or long term credits in specialised sectors. They all are of a public nature. A body of a particular kind is the Fund for the South (Cassa per il Mezzogiorno), planning and financing the development of that region. Legal personality confers on them a remarkable freedom of action, subject only to State control.

The organised activity these bodies exercise is considered to fall within the definition of "enterprise" given by Article 2082 of the Civil Code, in so far as it constitutes their main object. They are characterised by the fact that they have practically no governmental powers in their relationships with third parties, which are governed by civil law. Following a common process of personification, these bodies exercising an enterprise are themselves called enterprises, and more precisely public enterprises, or public economic corporations.

The capital of these bodies comes from different sources, the principal being, of course, the national budget. The "endowment fund" of IRI and ENI and other corporations is entirely supplied by the Treasury, for which a certain share of the profits should be reserved. This fund has been often substantially augmented. In this way the State meets those risks that private shareholders face with regard to private enterprise. This money is to a large extent used for the implementation of programmes not promising immediate returns. A considerable amount of resources is also obtained through the issue of bonds, guaranteed by the Treasury or enjoying other favoured conditions. On the other hand, some banks derive their capital from ancient foundations. The capital of ENEL corresponds to the properties transferred to it as a result of nationalisation. In other cases, further public or private bodies may participate in their capital, with or without the Treasury. Although a certain social structure may here be detected, no question arises of a company being established. Those who subscribe capital may receive a yearly dividend if there is any profit, and appoint some directors, but their powers are as a rule restricted in comparison to those retained by the Treasury and other Government departments, with regard to the administration and the winding up of the corporation.

The public holding corporations, such as IRI, ENI, are entirely concerned with the management of a number of enterprises, each having the status of a limited company. The ENEL, exercising a large-scale national industry, unlike, in this respect, the Central Electricity Board in Britain, has a single central organisation. This is, however, "functionally articulated and territorially decentralised," especially with reference to distribution, in order to assure the greatest efficiency, "with due respect to its unity." The centre is divided into several services, and the field organisation is composed of eight large departments, including some thirty districts and 180 operating units, in direct contact with the public.

The banking institutions have of course a number of local branches. Some of the special credit sections may even be endowed with separate legal personality.

The appointment of the administrators of the economic corporations is mainly in Government hands. For example, the chairmen of the two largest holdings, IRI and ENI, are chosen by the Council of Ministers, and the members of the boards of directors by the various Ministers concerned, with the addition of some experts, chosen by the Minister for State Holdings. Although wide powers are vested in the board, both the chairman and the managing council composed of himself and some of the experts retain a considerable freedom of initiative.

The conditions of employment of the personnel of these public corporations are as a rule based on the civil code or collective labour agreements, but the employers as part of the public administration of the country keep some control over their own organisation. But the Supreme Court of Cassation and the *Consiglio di Stato* have not yet agreed on whether these labour relationships should be considered as private or public, *viz.* falling within the jurisdiction of the ordinary or the administrative courts, respectively, in cases of disputes. To avoid doubts, some recent laws define the employment as private for all purposes, both substantive and procedural.

Public corporations of this kind pay taxes as if they were private companies, with some exceptions. But profit is not the aim expressly set them by the law. This is rather a general or public interest and the profit motive may be excluded by the very nature of the corporation's function. If it is provided that profit, if any, should be reserved for some further public utility aim, as is the case with the saving banks, this does not mean that profit, and not the increment of small savings, is their ultimate goal. Holding corporations and the whole system of public enterprises are supposed to be run according to criteria of *economicita*, a vague word, which is deemed to cover economic viability, efficiency, productivity, a relationship between the results attained and the means employed, a long term economic equilibrium. The five-year national economic plan stresses that they are called upon to develop an "active entrepreneur's function", provided a social purpose has not to be pursued.

The magnitude of public enterprise in Italian economic life may best be measured by recalling that some of these corporations are public holdings, controlling a large number of private companies. The reason for this extension of the "public hand" may even appear contradictory, and in some cases it is difficult to find out the public interest which should lie at the root of any public operation of this kind. The reduction of unemployment is certainly one. Different trends have marked the various stages. In times of crisis, it is private initiative itself that has repeatedly asked for Government intervention. But Government action, which in the past was casual, has now become part of a deliberate policy. The recent example of nationalisation of the electric power plants reveals the work of political ideas very close to those that have accompanied similar operations in Great Britain. There is a tendency towards the control of some key-sectors in the industries, the development of the depressed South, and investments in the public interest that private initiative would not consider to be sufficiently remunerative. Some recent events have given the impression that public enterprise is extending its sway to new fields, such as the chemical industry, through the purchase of shares on the market. This expansion is accompanied by rationalisation and concentration. The phenomenon, of course, is not exempt from sharp criticism, ranging from the financial privileges granted to these enterprises, the lack of a dividing line between social and economic undertakings, their competition with private initiative and the narrowing sphere left to it, to relationships too close to the political ruling class.

On the whole, State semi-independent agencies, public corporations and the dependant companies have obtained almost complete control over the sources of power, such as electricity, methane, liquid hydrocarbons and coal, over communications, railways and air transport, and over pig iron, and medium and long term credit. The majority of the steel production and of maritime traffic, half of the life assurance business, and a large share in the shipbuilding industry and short term credit are also in public hands. All this has been done only occasionally by nationalisation, but more often as a result of devolution of old or new economic activities, by statute, or just as the outcome of a set of circumstances, as already mentioned.

PUBLIC SHAREHOLDING IN PRIVATE COMPANIES

The participation of the Government in the capital of private companies limited by shares was at the beginning merely the result of executive procedures taken against insolvent debtors or of the transfer of *bona vacantia*. As pointed out before, the shares of companies requesting financial aid were later on held as guarantee, and subsequently retained. We witness to-day a direct constitution of new private companies on the part of large public holding corporations. Even minor public corporations have been transformed into private companies, and these, as well as private companies owned by the State, with one main exception, the "Cogne" coal and steel concern, have been transferred to one or other of the big holding corporations. The law actually prescribes that these shares should be transferred to these holdings. The credit sector is excluded. This is some kind of a "flight" into private law whereby public ends are to be obtained through private means. The Government exploits the private joint-stock company, which is an instrument of private capitalism, as an instrument of its intervention in the economic field. The associated form, the possible participation of private capital in these companies, and the employment of another capitalistic device, the financial holding company, should not hide the wide socialistic flavour which the Italian economic system has gradually and often unwittingly acquired. Like the public corporations holding their shares, these companies do not pursue profit as their aim and do not enjoy monopoly rights, even if in fact they may come very near to this in several fields; but they may run public monopolistic services as a result of a concession by a public authority. On the whole, government participation in these companies is indirect, through the public holding corporations.

Public shareholding may be said to be the third in time and at present the most favoured legal form followed for State intervention, after the Government semi-independent agency and the public economic corporation.

The three types have prevailed almost in successive waves, without following methodical lines and with many reciprocal interferences, but fundamentally responding to the need of a more accentuated decentralisation. The machinery of State administration is too antiquated, cumbersome, rigid and slow to lend itself to the fulfilment of the new demands of a modern society. Novel arrangements are taking place all the time and the field is apt for experimentation. But on the whole one might go very near to reality in maintaining that special Government administrative units are still carrying out some traditionally essential public services. Public economic corporations are now mostly limited to the financial and nationalised sectors but in some cases dress themselves as holdings. Private companies practically dispense with legislation and secure the flexibility, possibility of manoeuvre and speed of the private firms with which they are very often competing. But they may join together autonomy and the pursuit of public interest only as long as they remain under close control from a public holding, thus being dominated by the State in an indirect way.

Some years ago these companies were not referred to as public enterprises, but now the definition is usually extended so as to include them, provided their capital is wholly or at least as to its majority in public hands. The definition also covers companies with private minority shareholding. A public minority participation remains out of the picture, unless it may command a control of the company. This makes it possible to consider together a large and complex variety of organisms, all having in common a public purpose, if the "public hand" has thought it fit to intervene, even if the grounds for this are open to discussion, as in the typical case of a newspaper. Their capital is largely public. It is natural then for the companies to be submitted, directly or indirectly, to public control, to attain their tasks. As they are part of the "economic group of the State," legislation may consider them jointly with public corporations in several respects. More often any differences are questions of form, rather than of substance. It would be an empty convention to exclude them from administrative organisation.

This comprehensive notion of public enterprise does not entail any strict legal consequence, but corresponds to the one which seems to be favoured in other countries, and especially in the other member States of the European Common Market, where public intervention widely takes the form of a private company. This notion should also merit the acceptance in the interpretation of Article 90, section 1, of the Rome Treaty, which equiparates public and private enterprises, with some exceptions, for the application of the regulations against restrictive practices. It is impossible, however, to go so far as to include under this common denomination those enterprises which operate a public service under a concession from a public authority, when their capital is in private hands, or those groups of private enterprises that are submitted to special controls, only in view of their relevance to the public interest. The latter is the case of banks or industries receiving State subsidies, such as ship-building or film production.

Coming now to the structure of the public corporations holding shares in private companies, attention should be mainly concentrated on the two concerns, the IRE and the ENI, that have raised considerable attention outside Italy. The former was the first and still remains the major body of this kind. It now holds the totality or the majority of some 150 main companies and a number of minor companies, employing about 300,000 people. It is the fourth largest undertaking in western Europe, and the largest public enterprise in the Common Market in consideration of its turnover. Among the companies it controls are the three "national interest" banks, which already collect almost one-fifth of the total national savings, the radio and television and the air transport companies, exercising State monopolies, the companies building and running auto routes, and five private holding companies, or group leaders. These are charged with the direction, technical co-ordination and control of a series of companies operating in homogeneous sectors, such as telephones, shipbuilding, steel and mechanical industries, and sea transport. These private financial companies own, often jointly with IRI, all or part of the shares of the operating companies, which, in their turn, may hold the shares of other dependent companies.

The ENI, whose institutional task is the promotion and implementation of initiative in the national interest in the field of hydrocarbons and natural gas, holds the shares of only three large group leaders, which are at the same time operating companies and private financial holdings, owning the shares of some one hundred major companies and of some minor ones, often mixing their capital. ENI's participation may thus follow a crossed pattern, whereas that of IRI is more lineal.

This may give rise to two or even three or four tier structures. Private capital is often called upon to participate in large measure. Obviously, the capital conferred by other undertakings of a group is not wholly and genuinely public, but it allows the group to impose its control over a company through the machinery of participation, even if a company's capital may in fact result in the whole being composed of a large amount of money coming from private sources. The public corporation may hold all the shares of the private holding company and, directly or indirectly, of many dependant companies. Usually the group owns the majority of the shares, more seldom half, as in the case of foreign investments. A minority shareholding is to be found in a number of smaller undertakings not included in the consolidated balance-sheet. A careful balance is kept by the holding between the issue of bonds and shares, in order to retain the control of the companies in its hands. Shares are especially offered in companies promising good returns. The public has shown a keen interest in these companies, combining the public interest with a business-like spirit free from any bureaucratic complex. Self-financing is also widely followed, and borrowing from the banks is considerable. The Treasury contributions to the "endowment fund" of the holding complete the picture.

Public holding corporations of a lesser scale group some mineral springs, cinema and mechanical undertakings. But several other public corporations, including banks, have taken a noticeable participation in private companies. When statutory authority is lacking, care has to be taken to secure that this is not a contrivance employed by the corporation to go beyond its institutional aims or avoid the controls imposed over it.

The companies under ultimate public control are not subjected to any special regulation. Their relationships with the public holdings are almost entirely determined by the Civil Code. Both the public and the dependant private holdings exercise their influence through their shareholders' rights. This makes it possible for them to appoint the members of the boards of directors of the various companies, to establish their financing, to organise them and fix their production policy. One of the holdings' tasks is that of raising a diaphragm between the companies and political pressure. Private shareholders may of course exercise their rights in due measure. When the whole capital belongs to a group, the general meeting becomes a private affair. No special privileges are granted to these companies, apart from some tax exemptions in favour of private holdings. The IRI and ENI companies withdrew from the industrialists' confederation to join two newly formed federations, one for each group, thus splitting the employers' front and allowing the trade unions to press for better conditions. According to Article 43 of the Constitution, the State may reserve to itself or to public bodies some enterprises related to essential public services, sources of power or monopolistic situations, and having a character of a pre-eminently general interest. Their exercise has in some cases been conceded by statute to companies under public control, and this may be thought to alter their equality status.

On the whole, the holdings control several profit-making companies. But the dividends these pay to the former may be used to make up the losses of other companies of the group or develop further enterprises not economically promising. This means that the share of net profits which the public holdings have to pay over to the Treasury for the public money invested is exceedingly small.

OTHER PUBLIC CORPORATIONS

Among the public associations, a mention may be made of the professional men's councils that are entirely self-governing. Their membership is compulsory for the exercise of a profession. Similar structures are to be found in land reform syndicates and some confessional congregations. Public corporations, including local government authorities, may also combine in other public corporations, and the controls over the former extend to the latter.

Much thicker is the forest of bodies which may be considered as foundations of a public character. They are under the supervision of different Government departments, according to the particular activity. Some groups have received a uniform regulation whereas other bodies are governed by individual and often piecemeal legislation. A reform of this sector is required, but it should not lead to a general levelling, in so far as these bodies may differ in regard to aims and means. Social insurance boards are particularly important. They administer the relevant legislation and are very large. Together with other social assistance bodies they are criticised because of their excessive personnel expenditure and the superimposal of their activities. Proposals are advanced for some streamlining.

An example of this new trend is offered by the very recent establishment of the hospital boards, whose realisation is on the way but still depends on the practical settlement of controversial issues of various kinds. They are entrusted with public hospital assistance in favour of all, citizens and aliens alike. Public assistance and charitable bodies solely caring for the sick are recognised as hospital boards by law and declared such by State or regional authorities. Private foundations and associations may apply to be recognised by the same authorities. University and religious institutions remain disciplined by previous legislation, but the former are also, and the latter may ask to be, submitted to some of the new principles. New hospital boards may be set up and those existing merged by the above mentioned authorities.

Each hospital board comprises one or more hospitals "functionally autonomous." They are classified as general, i.e. area, provincial and regional hospitals, or specialised hospitals, and hospitals for chronic or convalescent patients, all with different equipment.

The modernisation of other sectors should follow.

PARLIAMENTARY CONTROL

Parliament cannot stand aside before the development of public corporations and enterprises. In the first place, a corporation is established and regulated by statute and the requisites for its recognition also have to be so prescribed. It is also by statute that their aims and means, the main directives and often the rules for their organisation and activities are fixed.

Secondly, under a parliamentary form of government, such as the Italian, a Minister is responsible to the two Houses for his actions with regard to the bodies depending on his department.

A further intervention derives from the fact that Parliament receives the accounts of the largest public corporations of all kinds, often attached to the accounts relating to the department supervising it. The public holdings also present reports on the work done as well as their programme of future action, revealing the situation of the dependent private companies as well. The Court of Accounts, a body carrying out an extensive financial control and audit on all organisations receiving Treasury funds, also sends to Parliament a report on its findings.

If Parliament has for a long time not shown a great inclination to debate the problems of public corporations, and no serious problem has really arisen, its interest in them has lately been getting keener, especially as a consequence of the greater speed with which the Court of Accounts now publishes its closely documented reports. This fact has opened up new fields of political controversy.

The British distinction between policy, for which a Minister may be held accountable, and day-to-day administration, was accepted in principle, although it would have been difficult in practice to draw a neat line, especially in view of the general supervisory powers of the Minister. But it may soon become rather obsolete. Parliament is now receiving the papers and the programmes from the corporations, annual surveys from the Ministries concerned, and annual reports from the Court of Accounts. Parliamentary committees have also the power of requesting fresh information from the Government or the corporations themselves. Parliament can thus form its political opinions about the administration of a corporation and the way in which it has performed its statutory tasks, as well as about the Minister's controls over it. No legal or technical fetters may hamper its work.

In examining the Court of Accounts' reports the Senate (the Upper House) has recently followed a new line. The Senate standing committees dealing with the relevant branch of the administration will consider the reports and pass their remarks to the finance committee, which will offer to the House a more comprehensive view of public finance. The utility of this may be gauged from the fact that the budgets of local authorities and public corporations exceed in their size the national budget, and that some sort of financial unity ought to be reconstructed, even if a work of synthesis is difficult to accomplish. New steps are being taken in the other House as well for a better political check. The possibility of hearings is viewed with favour.

The observations of Parliament find their main addressee in the Government. It is the Government that has the power of introducing the necessary legislation, of issuing instructions to the corporations, and of taking direct steps for the redress of their administration and the grievances advanced, but Parliament may take action on its own initiative, although so far it has not proved to be too bold.

Governmental Direction and Control

Local government authorities are self-governing, and the Government is constitutionally bound to respect the foundations of their autonomy. Controls are necessary, but they should be restricted, as far as possible, to checking on the observance of the law, without entering into policy or discretionary matters and certainly without becoming directors of the local authorities. Public associations and charitable foundations have only some points in common with them, and the Government has to see to it that the general interest and the intent of the founders are respected. The intensity of this interference depends in the main on the degree of interest that the State professes to have in the body. This interest should be greater for the bodies established by Parliament itself. In some cases, it might even be hard to separate control from direction and management.

With regard to public economic corporations, their statutes are not always explicit. They provide for a Government "supervision," which cannot imply an overall control of all their acts, even if limited to the grounds of strict legality. The expression is more likely to indicate which is the Minister exercising the main control over the corporation and responsible for it to Parliament. As a rule, the principal acts of a corporation, e.g. budgets, annual accounts, statutes, financial operations, etc., are required to be authorised or approved by the Minister, before they can become effective. Their convenience as well as their legality may be examined. Ordinary operations are free from control. But the problem of control of public enterprises, in the strictest sense of review, has to a large extent been superseded by that of direction. Should the Minister check the decisions of a commercial undertaking, which is supposed to act with a certain amount of speed and secrecy, before they may be carried into effect, as is the case of local government, the attainment of the enterprise's goals would be considerably affected. On the other hand, these bodies have been to a high degree established out of public funds and pursue aims which have a public relevance. The co-ordination of their activities may best be secured through direction. A defence of their independence is often deprived of any meaning, outside the strict operative field which ought to remain autonomous. These bodies are substantially Government agencies, personified as a measure of expediency. No general principles on the degree of their dependence can be stated, as the incidence of State interest, the trends prevailing when a body was set up, the policies of the day, the nature of the activity carried out, and other particular circumstances, may contribute to differentiate between the various bodies. But the tendency is towards greater uniformity.

In 1956 a new Government department was set up, the Ministry for State Holdings, to which the main powers of direction and control in relation to public holding corporations were transferred. The Minister may issue general instructions to them.

It was formerly only through the corporations that the Minister's instructions could reach the dependent companies. But he has now received a power of summoning the chairmen and the managing directors of the corporations as well as those responsible for the administration of the depending companies. He may obtain from them information on their situation, control the implementation of programmes and instructions, and authorise the assumption of share participations in new companies or the handing over or transfer of existing shares. In this way he is now in direct contract with the operating companies.

The Minister's influence is very great at law, since it is only with his consent that the major events in the enterprises' life may occur. But his position may better be measured after a fuller examination of governmental powers. At any rate, public economic corporations and public-owned companies that are not grouped in public holdings are not subject to his control. The banks, in particular, remain tightly in the hands of the Treasury.

The Minister of Economic Planning may also require extensive information from public enterprises of all kinds, and the planning agencies are entitled to examine their specific programmes and results. Several other Ministers may exercise more powers over them. The consent of the Treasury is necessary for major financial operations of public corporations, and their accounts as well as some regulations on the economic status of the personnel have to receive its approval. Moreover, public industries may be submitted to some sort of regulations common to the private sector. Thus the Ministers' committee for prices may fix the price of some goods and services, the Ministers' committee for credit and savings must authorise the issue of bonds, and the Ministry of Industry may issue instructions to some industries, public and private alike. Again, the Foreign Ministry will give instructions to the broadcasting and television company, the Minister of Transport to the air lines, and technical details may be settled by others. But the overall supervision remains vested in the Minister for State Holdings. His place is taken for other corporations by the competent Minister, such as the Minister of Industry for the ENEL.

The Minister in charge very often has authority to revoke the appointments of administrators of a corporation in case of repeated infringements of relevant laws and regulations.

Now the system has been strengthened in view of the realisation of the national economic plan, 1966–70, which has statutory force. Public enterprises must conform their decisions to it, as they are "instruments of the policy directed to approach and attain aims and objects established by the plan." As a result, not only does the Ministers' committee for economic planning check whether the programmes of the public holding corporations comply with the national economic plan, and examine the way in which they are carried out, but it also formulates the general directives of particular importance for their execution, with special consideration for the priorities assigned by the plan, and appraises the social aims of public enterprises. It is then a matter for the Minister to issue the directives necessary for the implementation of these decisions and to control their execution. The public holding corporation may pass these directions on to the private holding companies and thence to the operating companies. The Ministers' committees for prices and for credit and savings also take notice of the general directives of the planning committee.

In this set-up, the Minister for State Holdings, who always was bound by the overall economic decisions of the Cabinet, has become a sort of link between the Ministers' committee for economic planning, of which he is a member, and the public enterprises. He has now the task of detailing to them the guiding lines drawn by this committee, and of submitting to the latter their investment programmes for approval. His functions may be reinforced from the point of view of their effectiveness, but his figure is fading before that of a higher authority. The problem of this Minister's powers is, in reality, centred on the personality of the people involved and the vigour of the managers' groups. The head of one of the big holdings may in practice feel himself strong enough to by-pass the Minister and enter into direct contact with the Ministers' committee and the Minister for the Treasury, who holds the strings of the public purse. Hence the impression that the public economic power has not only succeeded in freeing itself to some extent from political power, but is getting the upper hand over the latter.

Economic planning is now making its influence felt in non-economic fields as well, such as the hospitals. Their five-year programme is linked to the national plan and fixes the requirements and distribution of beds, according to regions and specialisations, and the financial contributions made available for buildings and modernisation works. The Minister of Health is entrusted with wide supervisory powers.

Thus it may be seen that a new closely-knit system is emerging, and it is expected that it will prove effective and eliminate interference among the various controlling authorities.

Directives and instructions are not the only way in which the Government controls the corporations. The Ministers on which they depend have the power of choosing their directors. They are, in a way, the trustees of the Minister who has appointed them, being persons enjoying his confidence. If they are officials of the department concerned, their position may become ambiguous, as they are at the same time responsible to the head of their department and to the corporation. This dual allegiance is enough to condemn the figure of the "controller controlled." It may be added that these people are already very busy officials, often on the boards of several corporations and lacking commercial experience. The administrators chosen from outside the Civil Service should enjoy more freedom, as they are likely to survive the Minister who has appointed them, but it is a widely levelled complaint that they may owe their position to political pressure in what is a sphere of "under-government," rather than to personal merits or experience.

Representation of the personnel and the consumers is unknown to Government semi-independent agencies, public corporations and private companies in public hands, with some limited exception, such as ENI. The statute nationalising electric power plants provides for ENEL to hold periodical meetings for the consultation of local and economic representatives, and of local government authorities, trade unions and scientific bodies in particular. The administration of the hospital boards is composed of members elected by the local authorities, plus some members representing the original foundations, if they exist. These boards are advised by medical councils, including the heads of departments and representatives of their assistants. On the whole, however, the inclusion of experts in public corporations is rare.

FINANCIAL AUDIT

Audit of public corporations is carried out by three main bodies—the corporation's board of auditors, the Treasury, and the Court of Accounts.

The Treasury and some Ministers as a rule appoint their officials to sit on the board of auditors, generally carrying out their functions along the lines set by the Civil Code for private companies. Here again we may have a problem of dual responsibility. The auditors are supposed to conduct a control from the inside, without forgetting their status as civil servants. It is their duty to pay attention to the attainment of the statutory aims of the body, following its management and timely criticising its initiative, and also to keep the Ministers informed, in an endeavour to prevent illegality, rather than to repress it.

A financial control is also carried out from the outside by the Treasury over all public bodies which could affect the State budget, directly or indirectly.

F

An inventory of all of them is not available. The auditing is carried out by general finance inspectors, who are Treasury officials, conducting inspections and dealing with personnel problems and financial contributions. The inspectors' remarks are notified to the Ministers concerned and to the Court of Accounts, when its intervention is required.

A third and more important type of control is exercised by the Court of Accounts. The three controls should be better co-ordinated and simplified. The Court of Accounts has wider powers than the British Comptroller and Auditor-General, in so far as it accomplishes not only a prior control over Government expenditure, but also it has judicial functions. According to Article 100 of the Constitution, it participates as well in the financial control of any bodies "to which the State ordinarily contributes." Being "the eye of Parliament," the Court reports the results of its audit directly to the two Houses. An Act of 1958 has regulated this matter, with particular reference to the public bodies concerned. They are reckoned to amount to about 2,000, but less than 200 have so far been subjected to the Court's control.

Two main categories of corporations are classified in the Act. The first includes all bodies, public and private alike, receiving a contribution inscribed for more than two years in a Government department's budget, and also bodies empowered to impose taxes or other contributions. The second refers to those public bodies that have received a capital contribution or a financial guarantee from the Government. Both categories must send their annual accounts and balance-sheets, accompanied by the directors' and auditors' reports to the Court. In addition to this, the representatives of public administrations sitting on the boards of the bodies of the first category are bound to forward to the Court all the information they may obtain, at its request, and the Court itself may ask the bodies themselves or the competent Ministers for all information and documents concerning their finance. With regard to the bodies of the second category, the Court may appoint one of its judges to be present at meetings of the directors' and auditors' boards.

According to a literal interpretation of the statute, and to the intent of Parliament, it seems that the public economic corporations, mostly belonging to the latter category, are not to be subjected to the stricter controls dictated for the former. But the Court has decided that it is is empowered to exercise far-reaching and more effective controls over them. These controls are supposed to be direct and uninterrupted, and the judge should be allowed to examine any sort of documents concerning the corporation subjected to his oversight. Anyway, the distinction should not affect the biggest holding corporations, as they are also receiving large contributions engaging the State budget for over two years. It could perhaps be abolished without any harm, and the matter seems to be ripe for revision. The extension of the Court's audit to financial institutions has not been met with favour, as the banking system remains a reserve of the Treasury and the Bank of Italy.

The *Consiglio di Stato* has jurisdiction over litigation concerning the Government's decree assigning a body to the control of the Court. Apart from some appeals of this kind, there are practically no instances of cases concerning relationships between public corporations and the Government. Only the Constitutional Court has sometimes had to decide on the constitutionality of legislation granting special powers to the corporations, such as the television monopoly and nationalisation of the electric power.

The control of the Court of Accounts is of a paramount significance, in view of the authority and independence of the agency. The Court itself has construed its tasks as implying a valuation of the activities of a body in connection with its institutional goals, without thereby stepping out of a strict legality control. Legality, in fact, also covers the correspondence of decisions to the aims set forth in the statutes. But the distinction between legality and convenience or policy is getting somewhat flimsy, when the Court takes into consideration a series of operations as well, *e.g.* the management of a corporation. Nevertheless, a control over the economic efficiency of enterprises, which is as useful as a financial control, escapes the powers of the Court. In any case, the Court being traditionally trained to the latter type of control over Government departments, perhaps is not the most appropriate agency for the former, without a reform and a strengthening of its present structure, for instance, with the addition of experts. The Court cannot punish infringements discovered, but may merely denounce them to the Ministers and to Parliament, and also cannot issue instructions to the corporations.

A reform of book-keeping, imposing standard forms of budgets and accounting, would certainly facilitate the work of the Court and Parliament.

The Court sends its remarks to the Minister for the Treasury and the Minister in charge of controls over a particular corporation, should it find any irregularity or deem it necessary, and it also reports annually to Parliament. These reports, as well as the programmes and balance-sheets of public enterprises, are made available to the public. The Court's work has been delayed in the past by the corporations or the Ministers themselves, but progress is now being made. These reports show that the Ministers' control is not always as effective as it was supposed to be, and that the administration of public corporations is not always above reproach, having been too costly and overstepped its statutory limits.

The private joint-stock companies controlled by a public holding are only indirectly submitted to the Court's supervision, at least through the examination of the consolidated balance-sheet of the latter, and of the relationships between the corporation and the depending companies.

There are signs that the Court's reports are received by Parliament and the Government with closer attention than formerly.

SELECT BIBLIOGRAPHY

Literature in English is mainly concerned with the economic aspects of public enterprise. Reference may however be made to:

V. Lutz, *Italy. A Study in Economic Development*, London, 1962.
W. A. Robson, *Nationalised Industry and Public Ownership*, 2nd ed., London, 1962, Appendix.
G. H. Hildebrand, *Growth and Structure in the Economy of Modern Italy*, Cambridge, Mass., 1965.
A. Shonfield, *Modern Capitalism*, London, 1965, pp. 176–192.
M. Deaglio, *Private Enterprise and Public Emulation*, London, 1966.
M. V. Posner and S. J. Woolf, *Italian Public Enterprise*, London, 1967.

Some papers may be found in *Review of the Economic Conditions in Italy*, published every two months by the Banco di Roma.

Italian literature is of course very extensive. Information on public corporations in general may be found in textbooks on administrative law, such as:

M. S. Giannini, *Corso di diritto amministrativo*, Milan, 1965.
G. Treves, *L'organizzazione amministrativa*, 2nd ed., Turin, 1967.

The following is a selection of the most recent law books dealing with public enterprise:

S. d'Albergo, *Le partecipazioni statali*, Milan, 1960.
S. Cassese, *Partecipazioni pubbliche ed enti di gestione*, Milan, 1962.
G. Pescatore, *L'intervento straordinario nel Mezzogiorno d'Italia*, Milan, 1962.
G. Zangari, *Natura delle partecipazioni statali*, Milan, 1964.
F. Merusi, *Le direttive governative nei confronti degli enti di gestione*, Milan, 1965.
F. Roversi Monaco, *Gli enti di gestione*, Milan, 1967.
G. Guarino, *Scritti di diritto pubblico dell'economia*, Milan, 1968.

There also are some collective works:

F. Vito (ed.), *Il controllo dell'impresa pubblica*, Milan, 1960.
Il controllo sugli enti pubblici economici e sulle aziende municipalizzate, Milan, 1967.
Le baronie di Stato, Turin, 1968 (economic).

A useful addition to the foregoing list is the predominantly economic and political book by G. Petrilli, *Lo Stato imprenditore*, Rocca S. Casciano, 1967.

The Ministry for State Holdings publishes an annual report on the trends of the enterprises under its control (Ministero delle partecipazioni statali, *Relazione programmatica*, Rome).

Among the Acts of Parliament and delegated legislation concerning public enterprise the following are worth mentioning:

Decree No. 5 of January 23, 1933, establishing IRI (whose last statute is approved by Decree No. 51 of February 12, 1948).
Law No. 136 of February 10, 1953, establishing ENI (whose statute is approved by Decree No. 1523 of December 22, 1954).

Law No. 1643 of December 6, 1962, establishing ENEL, and Decree No. 1670 of December 15, 1962, on its organisation.

Law No. 1589 of December 22, 1956, on the creation of the Ministry for State Holdings.

Law No. 259 of March 21, 1958, on the control of the Court of Accounts.

Law No. 218 of February 27, 1967, on the organisation of the Ministry of Economic Planning, completed by Decree No. 554 of June 14, 1967.

Law No. 685 of July 27, 1967, approving the national economic plan, 1966–70.

A collection of legislation is contained in R. Coltelli and A. De Stefano, *Codice delle partecipazioni statali*, Milan, 1959, brought up to date to 1968 by three Appendices.

CHAPTER 9

PUBLIC ENTERPRISE IN GERMANY*

THERE are at least two reasons for approaching the subject of the German public enterprise cautiously. The first reason is, of course, that there is no equivalence between the public corporation in the English sense and the German *öffentliche Unternehmen*.[1] These are really different categories, particularly in view of the federal structure of the country on one hand,[2] and the distinction drawn in Germany between public law and private law on the other. The second reason is that there are many forms of public enterprises in Germany but no general theory which could be applied to all of them.

We shall therefore examine the scope and forms of public enterprise in Germany before considering the rules of organisation and control.

1. SCOPE AND FORMS

(1) Economic Classification

From an economic viewpoint, one can distinguish the following kinds of public enterprise:

(1) Credit institutions and savings banks.

(2) Enterprises of the "public service" kind (*Versorgungsbetriebe*) and fiscal monopolies.

(3) The Federal Railways (*Bundesbahn*) and the Federal Post (*Bundespost*).

(4) Radio and television.

(5) The industrial enterprises of the State subject to private law.

(i) *Credit institutions and savings banks*

The Federal State, the *Länder* and the municipalities have established a number of credit institutions, as follows:

(a) The Federal State has created or inherited various credit institutions of a public law form so as to encourage particular economic, social or political action, with the help of the capital market.

The Reconstruction Loan Corporation (*Kreditanstalt für Wiederaufbau*) provides medium and long-term credits for the reconstruction of private enterprises.[3] It has been further transformed into an institution which is

---

* By Professor J. H. Kaiser, Director of the Institute of International Law, University of Freiburg.

1. The translation of *öffentliches Unternehmen* should perhaps be "public enterprise," in order to stress the activity rather than the legal form.

2. Therefore "State" or "public authorities" refers to the Federal State (*Bund*), the member States (*Länder*) or the municipalities (*Gemeinden*).

3. *Gesetz über die Kreditanstalt für Wiederaufbau* (18.10.1961/BGBl I, p. 1877). The State owns 80 per cent. of the capital.

empowered to make loans for "development."[4] It is not subject to the supervision of credit and to the other provisions of the federal law concerning credit.[5]

Credit facilities for agriculture are provided by the *Landwirtschaftliche Rentenbank*, the *Deutsche Landesrentenbank*, and the *Deutsche Siedlungsbank*. Credits for co-operative societies are supplied by the *Deutsche Genossenschaftskasse*. The construction of houses is financed by the *Deutsche Pfandbriefanstalt*.

The "Equalisation of Burdens Bank" (*Lastenausgleichsbank*) makes loans to refugee enterprises and persons.

These are all public law institutions of the *Anstalt* type, 'even the *Kreditanstalt für Wiederaufbau*, although it is designed as a corporation (*Körperschaft*) in its statute, for it lacks an organ capable to express the corporative will. In the same manner, the *Deutsche Pfandbriefanstalt* is considered as an *Anstalt* and not a corporation in spite of its statute, in view of the predominance of the State which is a majority share-holder and retains considerable powers of control.

The German Federal Bank (*Deutsche Bundesbank*) has a rather different construction. According to paragraph 2 of the *Bundesbankgesetz*,[7] it is a federal public law legal person (*bundesunmittelbare juristische Person des öffentlichen Rechts*), difficult to classify between *Antalten* and *Körperschaften*. It has the right and duty to give advice to the Federal Government on important monetary matters. It is in fact the autonomous "guardian" of the purchasing power of the *Deutsche Mark* and is supported in this function by public opinion which has lately become increasingly sensitive to internal and external monetary affairs.[8] It has subsidiaries in the different *Länder* (*Landeszentralbanken*).

(b) At the level of the *Länder*, there are many public law credit institutes, like the *Pfandbriefanstalten der Länder* or several *Bausparkassen* (building savings banks).

(c) At municipality level, the savings banks, since the reform of 1931–32 are autonomous establishments of public law and have considerable economic importance.[9]

(ii) *Enterprises of the "public service" kind and monopolies*

The *Länder* and municipalities have set up a number of public enterprises to supply gas, water and electricity on a limited territorial scale.

4. Law of 16.8.1961 (BGBl I, p. 1339).
5. Law of 10.7.1961 (BGBl I, p. 881).
6. "The *Anstalt* or establishment, is a durable organisation of technical and human means used by a public authority for a specified public purpose" (O. Mayer). "The main difference between an *Anstalt* and a *Körperschaft* is that the personal tie prevails in the latter. A *Körperschaft* or corporation has members, not an establishment" (Hettlage in *Staatslexikon*, Verlag Herder).
7. *Gesetz über die Deutsche Bundesbank* of 26.7.1957 (BGBl I, p. 745).
8. See Spindler-Becker-Starke, *Die Deutsche Bundesbank*.
9. Heinrich Frick, *Die Staatsaufsicht über die kommunalen Sparkassen*.

These are mostly enterprises belonging to the Federal State, the *Länder* or the municipalities, or mixed enterprises (*Gemischtwirtschaftliche Unternehmen*).[10] Those producing electricity, for instance, are organised according to private law, but their autonomy is limited. They have to submit to the supervision of the "Energy supervision authority" (*Energieaufsichtsbehörde*) composed of the Economy Ministers of the *Länder*, especially with regard to their public service tasks and their price policy. It is therefore possible to apply public law in some cases to the relationship of public enterprises with users, *e.g.* the principle of the least possible encroachment, which makes it an obligation for public authorities to restrict any encroachment upon private rights to what is absolutely indispensible, even in the case of comprehensive powers.

Production of energy is thus carried out by private law enterprises with public law obligations, while distribution of energy at municipal level is achieved through enterprises organised under public law, particularly through enterprises belonging to the municipalities and called *Eigenbetriebe*. The *Eigenbetriebe* are not autonomous legal persons, but are special funds of the municipalities endowed with some measure of autonomy by reason of their integration in the general market economy. Municipalities and rural districts can also join in creating an administrative local union called *Zweckverband*, which is empowered to operate such public service undertakings. The *Zweckverband* is a public law corporation which extends beyond the limits of the municipality the legal construction and function of the *Eigenbetrieb*.

At federal and Land level, the form of the *Eigenbetrieb* is replaced by the so-called "article 15 enterprises," *i.e.* enterprises following the provisions of article 15 of the *Reichshaushaltsordnung* (RHO). These are special funds which have some autonomy but no legal personality. Examples include the federal printing-works and various transport, supply and other undertakings. The most unusual is the spirit monopoly (*Bundesmonopolverwaltung für Branntwein*), which is a public[11] monopoly with autonomous administration under the Minister of Finance.

The other State monopoly, the match monopoly (*Zündwarenmonopol*), is on the contrary organised according to private law, but endowed with certain public powers. The difference between these two monopolies is mainly historical.

(iii) *The Federal Railways and the Federal Post*

These two bodies are special funds of the Federal State endowed with some autonomy (*verselbständigte Sondervermögen*). They are empowered to trade

10. It is generally considered that public authorities should retain at least 25 per cent. of the capital and thus be able to influence the management of the enterprise.
11. On the federal monopolies see Joseph H. Kaiser, "Staatliche Handelsmonopole in der Dynamik des Gemeinsamen Marktes," in *Europarecht* 1967, Heft 1, p. 1.

and to sue in the private law courts. In theory they are not public law persons, but this is little more than a fiction.

(iv) *Radio and television*

A distinction can be made between the radio and television corporations which are operated as public law corporations on the one hand, and their subsidiaries entrusted with the advertising and commercial activities on the other, which are mostly corporations under private law, specially in the form of limited companies (*Gesellschaften mit beschränkter Haftung*). The radio and television corporations were generally organised by the *Länder*, with the exception of the *Deutschland Funk* and the *Deutsche Welle* which were created by federal law. All are autonomous corporations with a right to self-administration through a board (*Rundfunkrat*) which is composed of representatives of the interested Governments (Federal State or *Länder*), of the churches, of trade-unions, industrial associations, arts and other branches of economic, social and intellectual activity (press).

(v) *Industrial enterprises subject to private law*

The Federal Government is the owner of a number of industrial corporations which have a private law status. These corporations represented in 1963 2·7 per cent. of the total German industrial turnover. The most important are the *Salzgitter AG*, the *Saarbergwerke AG*, the *Vereinigte Industrieunternehmungen AG* (VIAG), the *Deutsche Lufthansa AG*. The interference of the State is particularly important in the fields of aluminium production, ironroe, coal, naval works, nitrogen, and electricity.

(2) Legal classification

Besides an economic classification, there is, naturally, a legal classification of public enterprises.

From the start we should distinguish between what we would call the indirect public service economic activity of the State, *i.e.* the activity conducted by means of independent private enterprises charged with specific functions in the national interest (*beliehene Unternehmen*),[12] and the immediate or direct activity of the State, conducted through its own enterprises.

Public enterprises may also be classified according to their degree of independence from the controlling public authority. This usually leads to the following distinction:

(a) administrative enterprises of the municipalities (*Regiebetriebe*), *e.g.* archives, small electricity supply undertakings;

(b) public utilities or public service undertakings of the municipalities (*Eigenbetriebe*), *e.g.* the larger electricity and water supply enterprises;

12. "The *beliehene Unternehmen* is a private law person entrusted with definite tasks and powers of public administration in relation to its own economic activity and in virtue of a delegation" (E. R. Huber, *Wirtschaftsverfassungsrecht*, J. C. B. Mohr, 1953, p. 533).

    (c) autonomous administrative enterprises of the Federal State and of the *Länder* (*verselbständigte Regiebetriebe*), *Bundesdruckerei, Bundesanstalt für Milchwirschaft*;

    (d) public law establishments (*Anstalten*) without legal personality: *Bundespost, Bundesbahn*;

    (e) public law establishments or corporations (*Körperschaften*) with their own separate personality: banks, insurance companies;

    (f) enterprises in private law form: *e.g.* Salzgitter A.G., Saarberwerke A.G.

All legal classifications refer to the form of organisation of public enterprises as given by statute. Another usual distinction separates autonomous legal persons from non-autonomous enterprises:

The autonomous legal persons use the existing forms of private law or public law. Private law forms are the joint-stock company (*Aktiengesellschaft*), the company with limited liability (*Gesellschaft mit beschränkter Haftung*) and the limited partnership (*Kommanditgesellschaft*). Public law forms are the *Anstalt* and the *Körperschaft*. None of these forms is especially appropriate to public enterprise, and it is often necessary to write special provisions into the constituent law of the enterprise.

Non-autonomous forms often prove more appropriate: they include the *Eigenbetrieb* or the organisational form of the *Bundespost* or the *Bundesbahn*. These forms take into account both the necessity of obligations of a public nature, and the advantages of economic independence and administration according to the standards of private economy (efficiency).

The recent trend is to use the more elastic form of private law corporation and to introduce into the statute all necessary public law regulations. The advantages of private law companies are evident in economic transactions; in particular their legal capacity, and general flexibility. It is not surprising therefore that one should witness what has been called "the migration of the State into private Law."[13]

Whatever form is chosen, public enterprise generally carries out functions of general interest. Which naturally brings us to the criterion of the object or purpose of public enterprise.[14]

"Public purpose" (*öffentlicher Zweck*) appears as the condition of municipal participation in an enterprise or municipal economic activity in the *Deutsche Gemeindeordnung* of 30.1.1935. It is today recognised that municipal enter-

---

13. Arnold Köttgen, *Das Verwaltungsrecht der öffentlichen Anstalt*, Veröffentlichungen der Vereinigung der Deutschen Staatsrechtslehrer, Heft 6, 1929, p. 135. On the economic significance of the legal form of public enterprises, see Karl Oettle, "Die ökonomische Bedeutung der Rechtsform öffentlicher Betriebe," in *Archiv für öffentliche und freigemeinnützige Unternehmen*, Band 8, Heft 3, 1967.
14. Interesting considerations on this and other themes concerning public enterprise are to be found in "Verwaltung mit Unternehmen," Heft 10, *Politik und Verwaltung* (Nomos Verlag), and particularly in the following contributions: Hartwig Bülck, "Öffentliche Unternehmen im deutschen und europaischen Recht"; Hans Hämmerlein, "Unternehmen aund Verwaltungsführung."

prises can be created or expanded only when a "public purpose" justifies the enterprise, when this enterprise is proportionate to the possibilities of the municipality and to public demand, and when the "public purpose" is not or cannot be satisfied by a private enterprise.

Conditions are somewhat similar for participations of the Federal State and of the *Länder*. They are: an "important interest" of public authorities, the assurance that such a participation will not turn to the disadvantage of the Federal State (or *Land*) and that the proposed goal will be attained through this very participation, and finally the "necessary influence" that the Federal State (or *Land*) must retain in the administration of the enterprise (and particularly in its supervisory board).

If we take the view that public enterprise can be considered as a technical entity of the administration launched by a political decision into the general process of production and consumption, we have to admit that such an operation is regarded with suspicion in the régime of the *soziale Marktwirtschaft*,[15] in which economic liberalism somewhat blurs social objectives, and the trend of political decisions rather pushes public enterprise back into private property.

However, the principle of "the subsidiary character of state enterprises" in front of private enterprises is controversial.

2. ORGANISATION AND CONTROL

The Federal Treasury Ministry (*Bundesschatzministerium*) was established in 1957 to administer economic participations of the Federal State. Until then various Ministries were competent. The new Ministry is not however an instrument of central management. Its main task is to lay the practical foundations of "denationalisation" (*Privatisierung*), and it has been called a "liquidation office." Management is decentralised to the enterprise itself, particularly when this enterprise trades in the competitive sphere.

There is also no unity in controls. Controls vary according to the legal forms of public enterprises, as well as to their organisational autonomy. They are carried out at federal, at regional, and at municipal level, but also, in some cases, at international level. They are institutional or personal, economic or political.

We shall hereafter point out the elements of control relating to the constitution and transformation of public enterprises, to their organisation and management, to their relations with their personnel and with third parties, and more generally with the economic, political and international world.

1. The creation of public enterprises, provided that the necessary conditions and financial means are supplied, is formally achieved through an act of organisation of the supporting public authorities for the *Regiebetriebe*, through

15. On the *Soziale Markwirtschaft*, see for example: Müller-Armack, *Wirtschaft-sordung* (Verlag Rombach); Carlo Mötteli, *Soziale Marktwirtschaft*.

a law for the public law moral persons, or through the usual formalities of commercial and civil law for the private law corporations. The constituent law of the Federal Railways is the *Bundesbahngesetz* of 13.12.1951, and the Federal Post was organised by the *Postverwaltungsgesetz* of 24.7.1953.[16]

2. The transformation of private enterprises into public enterprises does not entail any particular problem if the enterprise retains the form of a private corporation. In that case the State buys a majority of the shares and so acquires a leading influence in the company.

If however such a move determines an encroachment upon the rights of the former owners, then certain limitations are to be observed. Nationalisation can be achieved only through expropriation (art. 14 GG)[17] or, in very rare circumstances, through socialisation (art. 15 GG),[18] and involves compensation. This compensation is determined with consideration to the interests of the community and of the parties, and the question of amount can be brought before the ordinary courts, whereas the administrative courts are competent as to the validity of the act of acquisition itself. The constitutional guarantee works as a protection for private enterprises, and there has consequently been no notable nationalisation of private enterprises in the Federal Republic.

Much to the contrary, we can witness a general move towards de-nationalisation (*Privatisierung*).

This trend derives from the thought that the State should not play the part of a business firm, since this is contradictory to a free market economy. From a constitutional viewpoint the existence of public enterprises is perfectly valid. However, public opinion demanded and—to a certain extent—obtained that industrial enterprises of the State should in principle be handed over to private ownership. The decisive step was the creation of the *Bundesschatzministerium* in 1957. Even socialist-governed *Länder*, like Hessen, have de-nationalised some of their enterprises (*e.g.* Buderus, Wetzlar).

Two methods have been used up to now: the sale to private persons or private groups (thirty-two public enterprises were sold in this way between 1949 and 1958), and the so-called "social de-nationalisation" (*soziale Privatisierung*), the aim of which was to build up capital in low income social classes. This was achieved through the creation of a new type of share, the "popular share" (*Volksaktie*), which was to be subscribed in priority and on very favourable terms by the members of the said classes.

16. *Bundesbahngesetz*: BGBl I, p. 955 and "Änderungsgesetz zum Bundesbahngesetz" of 1.8.1961: BGBl I, p. 1161. *Gesetz über die Verwaltung der Deutschen Bundespost*: BGBl I, p. 676.
17. German Federal Constitution, art. 14: "(1) Property and the right of inheritance shall be guaranteed. ..." See J. H. Kaiser, "Verfassungsrechtliche Eigentumsgewähr, Enteignung und Eigentumsbindung in der Bundesrepublik Deutschland," in *Staats- und Privateigentum*, Cologne–Berlin, 1960.
18. German Constitution, art. 15: "Land and landed property, natural resources and means of production may, for the purpose of socialisation, be transferred to public ownership or other forms of publicly controlled economy by way of a law which shall regulate the nature and extent of compensation. ..."

The main examples of de-nationalisation are the Preussag, the Volkswagen and the Veba companies.[19]

3. There is no unique type of *management organisation* of German public enterprises. In fact there are nearly as many forms of management as there are different enterprises. They are generally given in the constitutive law or statute.

(1) Administrative enterprises, Bundesbahn and Bundespost

The municipal public utilities (*Versorgungsbetriebe*) belong to the general administration. Their managers are civil servants or administrative employees, who receive directions from their superiors. Control is achieved through inserting receipts and expenses in the budget.

By the so-called "article 15 enterprises" (enterprises organised according to article 15 *Reichshaushaltsordnung*), which are also considered as "inferior services of the general administration," management is also diversely organised according to the nature and the size of the enterprise. Only predictable profit or loss need be entered in the budget. Control is achieved through the statement of accounts, which is examined by the Federal or Regional Court of Accounts.[20]

The larger enterprises at municipal level are severed from the rest of the general administration, at least in budgetary matters.

The organs of the *Eigenbetriebe* are the enterprise management (*Werkleitung*) which settles ordinary business, the municipal council (*Gemeinderat*), which controls the enterprise management and sees to important matters, the enterprise committee (*Werkausschuss*), which names the accountant entrusted with the examination of yearly accounts, and the municipal director (*Gemeindedirektor*), who has a right to issue directions in matters affecting municipal administration.

Control is exercised principally by the municipal council, which has an unlimited right to request information, and wide possibilities to inspect accounts.

The Federal Railways (*Bundesbahn*) have a board of management (*Vorstand*) and a board of directors (*Verwaltungsrat*). The board of management settles current affairs according to the decisions of the board of directors, which is also competent for major economic issues. Both organs are supervised by the Minister of Transport, who is responsible in all matters of political relevance, and is empowered to control as well as to object to any measure of the railway administration.

Accounts and activity are submitted to independent inspection. The yearly

19. See Vialon, *Haushaltsrecht* (Verlag Franz Vahlen) 2, Auflage, p. 717; J. H. Kaiser, *Die Verwaltung der öffentlichen Unternehmen*, XIII. Kongress des Internationalen Instituts für Verwaltungswissenschaften (Hektografiert).

20. See Vialon, *op. cit.*, on the Federal Court of Accounts: *Gesetz über Errichtung und Aufgaben des Bundesrechnungshofes*, of 27.11.1950 (BGBl I, p. 765).

statement is published after it has been brought to the knowledge of Parliament. Although examination by the Federal Court of Accounts (*Bundesrechnungshof*) is foreseen, it is replaced by an inspection carried out by the "inspection service" of the *Bundesbahn*. The main "inspection service" of the *Bundesbahn* is basically independent. The Federal Court of Accounts retains the right to take part in the examination, to request the checking of particular accounts, or to lay down rules for this examination (for instance so as to ensure that all inspections of public enterprises follow the same procedure). Finally, the Court of Accounts makes a report to the Minister of Transport and to the Minister of Finance, who present the accounts and report to the Government. The Government then decides upon the discharge of the Railway boards. The yearly statement, the economic plan and the employment programme of the *Bundesbahn* are brought to the knowledge of Parliament.

The Federal Post (*Bundespost*) is headed by the Minister for Post and Telecommunication, who is assisted by a board of directors (*Verwaltungsrat*) composed of twenty-four members (five representatives of the *Bundestag*, five representatives of the *Bundesrat*, five representatives of economic organisations, seven representatives of the personnel, and a number of experts). The Minister is obliged to submit some of the more important problems to the board of directors, and can exercise a right of veto to ensure that due regard is paid to federal interests. The fixing of telephone taxes in 1964 caused the Minister to intervene; however public opinion forced him to reduce tariffs after he had increased them.

(2) Moral persons of public law

Corporations (*Körperschaften*) are administered by organs composed of their members. The "supporting" (*Träger*) public authority is responsible for the observance of law and statute.

Establishments (*Anstalten*) are managed by organs nominated by the supporting public authority and directed by them. Independence is the exception in the case of *Anstalt*: it has however been conceded to central banks and radio-television establishments.

These public law institutions are always subject to control by the Courts of Accounts (Federal or *Länder*).

(3) Moral persons of private law

These are mainly joint-stock and limited companies.

The joint-stock company is managed by a board of management (*Vorstand*), which is responsible to a supervisory board (*Aussichtsrat*), generally composed of share-holder representatives, *i.e.* representatives of public authorities. The management board is limited only by the provisions of company law. The fact that public authorities are represented on the supervisory board does not generally restrict the freedom of the management board. When civil servants represent the State on the supervisory board, they are theoretically supposed to follow the instructions of their superiors, while at the same time respecting the interests of the company. Conflicts of duties may arise from this situation, and there is no consensus in theory as to how they should be resolved.

The influence of public authorities is also reduced by the coexistence of representatives of the *Bund* and of the *Länder* on the supervisory board inasmuch as they own shares, as well as by the application of the laws on the participation of workers (*Mitbestimmungsgesetz* and *Betriebsverfassungsgesetz*). When these laws apply to a joint-stock company, the State cannot appoint a majority of members of the Board even if it owns 100 per cent. of the shares. In fact these companies are not very different from private companies.

Detailed instructions for the control of State companies are laid down in article 48 and article 110 of the still valid *Reichshaushaltsordnung* (budgetary regulation) of 1922, as well as in the prescriptions concerning the checking of accounts in the economic enterprises of the State of 30.3.1933.[21]

The only admissible private law forms of State company are the joint-stock company, the company with limited liability, and the limited partnership (*Kommanditgesellschaft*), *i.e.* those forms in which partners have limited liability and, what is more significant, for which relatively clear legal provisions exist concerning management, control and accounting.

When founding or joining such a company, the State should manage—possibly through particular written arrangements or through a modification of the articles of association—to retain "the necessary influence" on the management. That does not mean however that responsibility should shift from the company management to controlling State organs. The State should—as much as possible—dispose of the majority of supervisory board seats. This, we have seen, is practically impossible in all companies, subject to the application of the laws on "participation" in the coal and steel industry. The problem is therefore to adjust and to harmonise budgetary obligations and company law. As to the question of accounts, for example, definite provisions concerning the extent and the nature of financial control generally introduce the budgetary regulations into the company statute, or are separately agreed upon in writing. Company accounts must be examined by a chartered accountant who is chosen in agreement with the competent Minister (and the President of the Federal Court of Accounts). Federal authorities can also, of their own initiative, commission a chartered accountant to investigate the accounts of the company.

It is also assumed that the supervisory board will meet four times a year, and it must meet at least once a year. Further provisions make it obligatory

21. *Vorschriften über Prüfungspflicht der Wirtschaftsbetriebe der öffentlichen Hand.* See Vialon, op. cit., p. 1031.

for the State to enforce its controls, not only over the companies of which it is a direct shareholder but also over subsidiary corporations of these companies (indirect participations). These controls are comprehensive and range from a simple order to conduct additional enquiries, to inspection "of the enterprise, its accounts and papers" (article 113 RHO).

4. With regard to questions of personnel there is no general statute, even in public law enterprises, which are, however, generally headed by a civil servant while for the rest the staff consists of employees and workers. There are some examples (the federal stationery office: *Bundesdruckerei*) where the head of the enterprise is either a civil servant or an employed person. The former distinction between civil servants and employees is today somewhat blurred. There remains a difference in the legal nature of their activity (civil service or contract) and in the identity of the competent courts in cases of dispute (administrative courts or industrial courts).

The various laws concerning the participation of workers (*Mitbestimmungsgesetz, Mitbestimmungsergänzungsgesetz* and *Betriebsverfassungsgesetz*) are enforced in public enterprises in the form of joint-stock companies.[22]

Participation in this sense concerns all economic measures of a social character and all questions relating to employment. Its application varies according to which of the participation laws is valid for a given enterprise.

The *Mitbestimmungsgesetz* provides that the personnel must have as many representatives as the shareholders on the supervisory board, and that they have a right of veto over the appointment of a "labour manager" (*Arbeitsdirektor*), who is a member of the management board (*Vorstand*). This legislation applies to the coal and steel industry.

The *Betriebsverfassungsgesetz* applies to all other public joint-stock companies. The personnel has a third of the seats on the supervisory board.

These rights of participation and collaboration of workers constitute a limit to the action of public authorities as well as to the action of private shareholders.

Participation of the workers and employees in the public service (that is in administrative enterprises or public law establishments) is regulated by the *Personalvertretungsgesetz*, which provides for the election of a "personnel committee." This committee is meant to ensure that all texts and measures in favour of personnel shall be applied in the enterprise.

5. In its economic relations with clients, suppliers, and third parties, the German public enterprise usually follows the rules of private law (civil or commercial law). The public law relationship between the Post and its users is a historical exception. All lawsuits (except those concerning postal services) are therefore brought before the civil courts and any public enterprise has a

22. *Gesetz vom. 21. Mai* 1951 (BGBl I, p. 347); *Gesetz vom 7. August* 1956 (BGBl I, p. 707); *Gesetz vom 11. Oktober* 1952 (BGBl I, p. 681); *Gesetz vom 5. August* 1955 (BGBl I, p. 477).

right to settle disputes by agreement. When an enterprise is conducted in private law form, it is subject to the normal rules of compulsory liquidation and winding up.

There are no special privileges for public enterprises in German law. It is, however, usual for the State to give subsidies, particularly to the Post and the Railways, which are sometimes compelled to operate below cost. The Federal Railways and the Federal Post also enjoy a right of expropriation for the carrying out of their duties, and they are not subject to the provisions of the law on restrictive trade practices (neither are the *Bundesbank*, the *Kreditanstalt für Wiederaufbau*, or the monopolies).

The "principle of speciality," in the French meaning, is a limit on the activity of public enterprises. Although it is not as developed in Germany as in France, it is a direct consequence of the fact that each enterprise has a definite "field of economic activity" according to its statute. If an enterprise conducts business outside this field, it transgresses its statute and its organs of management will be called to account by the supervising authorities. Affairs conducted out of the proper "sphere" or not covered by the proper "object" of public enterprises in private law form are, however valid, since their outside activity is unlimited and since business partners must be able to trust the managing organs with which they deal. The solution is different for public enterprises in public law form and business transacted outside the proper field of the enterprise is not considered as having any effect at law since the capacity of such enterprises is precisely limited to their powers and duties, as determined by statute.[23]

6. As a general rule only those public enterprises which are legal entities are entitled to own property. However, although non-autonomous, the *Bundesbahn* and the *Bundespost* have their own budget and accounts, and their property is a separate fund (*Sondervermögen*) of the Federal State. Practically all types of public enterprises can dispose of part of their property, but there are narrow limitations for the "*Eigenbetriebe*."

The fiscal treatment of public enterprises is somewhat privileged, particularly when they carry out functions of a public nature, although the system of free competition implies equality of treatment for all enterprises, whether public or private. Administrative enterprises of the municipalities are not liable for taxes when they have no legal personality, but *Eigenbetriebe* are exempted from capital tax only when they are not of the public utility kind. Joint-stock companies are not liable for capital tax when the State is sole owner: in other cases, they are treated like private companies.

Public enterprises, however, are not always content with playing a merely passive role in the economy. There are some examples which show that the State is conscious of the possibilities offered by a dynamic steerage of the

23. The basic decision is the decision of the *Bundesgerichtshof* of 28.2.1956 (BGHZ 20, 119).

corporation. Such an attitude is not without merit in a market economy: in 1961, the management of the Volkswagen company (in fact General Manager Nordhoff), then in the majority ownership of the State, raised automobile prices against the will of the Government, and the Federal Government Minister Erhard, while he respected the management's decision, did not hesitate to lower custom duties on foreign cars so as to expose its own enterprise to harder competition on the German market.

The example of the Federal Railways shows that the State can intervene, economically, in at least two respects: it can use public enterprise to carry out a policy of structural development, and it can make public enterprise an instrument of crisis management.

If using the Federal Railways for promoting under-developed regions raises no special problem, it is however understood that public enterprises should be managed with a view to economy and rentability, and that services rendered under cost should be compensated. The recent "Stability Act" of 8.6.1967 has gone a step further and compels *Bundespost* and *Bundesbahn* to follow an anti-crisis investment policy, namely in receiving and investing additional credits in times of economic stringency. It is too early to know if this is really the beginning of a new conception.[24]

7. Public enterprises are naturally subject to political control. This control takes place with the vote of the yearly Budget by the Parliament. Members of the *Bundestag* also have the right to put questions to the Government. Parliamentary control is only a part of political control, which also covers control by the executive, *i.e.* by the Government, by virtue of its general rights of supervision, control by the political parties (and we must not forget that the political majority varies in the different *Länder*, not to speak of the municipalities), and control by public opinion, *i.e.* mainly, by the press. An example of political control was the affair of the *Bundesbahn* unprofitable lines in 1964. The socialist party, then in opposition, had heard unofficially that the *Bundesbahn* was going to close several financially non-operational secondary lines. This gave occasion to a wide controversy which spread in the papers and in the political circles, and eventually caused the project to fail.

We have already mentioned various forms of control: legal and formal controls, that is control by the courts, the administration, the Parliament and the Government; but there are also economic and social controls, such as those limits which result from measures of "denationalisation," "participation," or "planification." We should like now to put the emphasis on two complementary notions which have recently undergone considerable development, namely "functional control" and "sectorial control."

Sectorial or professional control is no novelty. The concept of the economic

24. See "Public Enterprise as an Instrument of Administrative Planning," in *Planung III*, edited by J. H. Kaiser (Nomos Verlag) with German contributions from Stukenberg, R. Schmidt.

sector, however, is certainly gaining in importance with the opening of wide markets and the possible blotting out of national frontiers. All enterprises concerned with coal and steel, for example, have to follow common rules, that is the rules of the European Coal and Steel Community, and in this case it cannot be distinguished as between public and private enterprises. The criterion is no longer the ownership of the company, but its function.

Thus, in article 66 (7), the ECSC Treaty provides that: "As far as may be necessary, the High Authority is empowered to address to public or private enterprises which, in law or in fact, have or acquire on the market for one of the products subject to its jurisdiction a dominant position which protects them from effective competition in a substantial part of the Common Market, any recommendations. . . . " In the same way, article 80 stipulates: "The term enterprise, as used in this Treaty, refers to any enterprise engaged in production in the field of coal and steel within the territories mentioned in the first paragraph of article 79 and . . . to any enterprise or organisation engaged in distribution." And article 83: "The establishment of the Community does not in any way prejudice the system of ownership of the enterprises subject to the provisions of this Treaty."

The wording of the Treaty of the European Economic Community is not very different in its article 222: "The Treaty shall in no way prejudice the system existing in member States in respect of property." The attitude of the European Economic Community towards public enterprises is however complex. It is certainly to be wished that all enterprises should be on the same footing as to community regulations, especially as to the common rules concerning free competition (arts. 85 and 86 EEC), with few exceptions (art. 90 EEC). An interesting case is the case of commercial and fiscal monopolies, and an interesting solution is the process of progressive adjustment to the market provided for in article 37 concerning the former. We cannot go into details, however, and must refer to what we have written elsewhere on these problems.[25]

It is clear that "sectorial and functional controls" take on a new meaning when one considers economic units of the size of the European Communities. New regulations and new limitations evolve, but new fields are opened and new forces are born; control over Government enterprise to-day should take into account these developments in a world of large areas, technostructure and planning.[26]

25. See note 11 and *Les entreprises publiques et l'économie du marché*, Semaine de Bruges 1968.
26. On planning and public enterprise, see also *Planung I* and *II*, edited by J. H. Kaiser (Nomos Verlag). On technostructure, Galbraith: *The new industrial State* (Houghton Mifflin 1967). Other publications on German public enterprise include: Albert Schnettler, *Öffentliche Betriebe* (Verlag W. Girardet 1956) and *Betriebe, öffentliche Haushalte und Staat* (Duncker & Humblot 1964); Centre Européen de l'Entreprise Publique, *Les entreprises publiques dans la Communauté Economique Européenne* (Dunod, Paris 1967); Horak, *Die wirtschaftliche Betätigunug der öffentlichen Hand in der BRD und ihre Probleme* (Cologne 1964).

CHAPTER 10

THE PUBLIC CORPORATION IN SWEDEN*[1]

1. DIFFERENT FORMS OF PUBLIC ENTERPRISE

SWEDISH legal notions are strongly influenced by continental doctrine, and therefore differ in many respects from Anglo-Saxon conceptions of law. In consequence, it is not easy to find the Swedish term corresponding to "public corporation." In Sweden we are accustomed to speak about three main types of corporate bodies of public law (except State, church and municipalities): public associations, institutions, and foundations (*offentliga korporationer, anstalter och stiftelser*). But the present author doubts whether any of these doctrinary types exactly corresponds to the conception of "public corporation." The last-mentioned term is more appropriate to some modern types of public enterprise, which are characterised by legal independence. These are, in Sweden, sometimes given the form of a public institution but most commonly that of a State-controlled company. The "public companies" have been the object of increasing attention in recent Swedish jurisprudence, but they are not yet acknowledged as a specific type of corporation of public law. Nevertheless, in an account of the Swedish equivalent to the "public corporations" these companies must take a dominating place, while certain other Swedish "legal persons of public law" can be passed over (*e.g.* the many societies and associations with more or less pronounced public functions).

The public corporation and the "public company" may be regarded as alternative legal forms of enterprise. There are two ways of establishing a corporate body with a public purpose: either its organisation may be determined by special legislation, or the forms of organisation offered by the private law may be used. In the first case, the result will be a public corporation in a strict sense; in the second, the corporation created is formally one of private law, but its organisation may show features which indicate more or

* By Professor Håkan Strömberg, Faculty of Law, Lund University.
1. As for Swedish literature concerning this subject see Herlitz, *Föreläsningar i förvaltningsrätt* II (1948) pp. 281–330, and the works there quoted, especially Sundberg, *Den korporationsrättsliga regleringen i Sverige* (Strödda uppsatser, 1943, pp. 23–71)— Nyström, *Statliga och kommunala bolag* (*Förvaltningsrättslig tidskrift*, 1939, pp. 147–161) and Tersman, *Statsmakterna och de statliga aktiebolagen* (1959). The subject has been treated in English by Douglas H. Verney, *Public enterprise in Sweden*, Liverpool University Press (1959) (reviewed by Holmgren in *Förvaltningsrättslig tidskrift*, (1960), pp. 161–167). An important source of knowledge is a series of official reports in the publication *Statens offentliga utredningar* (abbreviated SOU), especially the following numbers: *Statsägda aktiebolag i Sverige* (SOU 1956: 6), *Statsägda företag i utlandet* (SOU 1956: 24), *Statens reproduktionsanstalt* (SOU 1956: 59), *Statens vattenfallsverk* (SOU 1957: 26), *Betänkande med förslag till reformering av de nuvarande statliga företagsformerna* m.m. (SOU 1960: 32), *Postverkets organisation* (SOU 1962: 52), *Kommunala bolag och andra särskilda rättssubjekt för kommunal verksamhet* (SOU 1965: 40), *Affärsverken* (SOU 1968: 45, 46).

less clearly its public functions. The latter form has most commonly been chosen in Sweden, and the most frequent form of organisation is that of a joint-stock company (*aktiebolag*, abbreviated *AB*), often with the State as a shareholder and always under dominating State influence. As a matter of fact only two forms of public enterprise are generally discussed: governmental bodies or joint-stock companies. Only in a few cases have public corporations of a specific type been created by a legislative Act. This circumstance makes it rather difficult to define precisely the characteristics of the "public corporation," especially to draw an exact line between "public" and "private" companies. But although the difference between these two kinds of companies seems to be only a difference of degree, certain typical features characterise the organisation of the public companies.

In Sweden, as everywhere else, there is a tendency towards increasing State activity. But the scope for public enterprises in the form of corporate bodies is subject to certain limitations. To begin with, some important branches of activity, which in several other countries are managed by special corporations, are in Sweden pursued in the form of direct State administration. These branches of public administration, called "the commercial enterprises of the State" (*statens affärs drivande verk*), are the following: *postverket* (postal administration), *televerket* (administration of telecommunications), *statens järnvägar* (state railways), *vattenfallsverket* (administration of waterfalls, *i.e.* of electricity production through water power), *domänverket* (public domain administration), *försvarets fabriksverk* (administration of military factories), and *luftfartsverket* (air-traffic administration). As with most Swedish State authorities, they are not parts of the Ministries but separate entities within the State organisation. They enjoy a certain economic liberty of action, and the State budget states only their profits or losses.[2]

From these governmental bodies we have to distinguish the institutions of the Diet (*riksdagens verk*), especially the National Bank (*Riksbanken*) and the State Debt's Office (*Riksgäldskontoret*). They also are State institutions, but they stand under the direction and guarantee of the Diet.[3]

Another important feature is that, although socialistic ideas have great influence in this country, direct nationalisation has been almost completely avoided. The natural resources and the heavy industries are still

2. It has been proposed to give these branches of administration a financial status more akin to that of private enterprises; *i.e.* they should have to pay to the State treasury an amount corresponding to income tax on private enterprises (*Affärsverken*, SOU 1968:45,46). Since January 1970, their common policy is managed by a delegation (*affärsverksdelegationen*), practically identical with the board of the State trust company as mentioned below (see page 173.)

3. The traditional dualistic notion of the State in Swedish constitutional law has made it difficult to characterise the legal status of these institutions. In a judgment of 1959 the Supreme Court has declared the National Bank to be a corporate body separate from the Crown (*Nytt juridiskt arkiv I*, 1959, p. 385). Prescription of a claim against the Bank could, consequently, not be avoided by notifying the claim to a governmental State authority.

predominantly in private hands. Socialism works in other ways: through taxes, regulations and subsidies. Certainly the State is the owner of forests, mines and factories, but in competition with private undertakings, whether these assets be administered directly by the State (as the forests) or by State-owned companies (as the mines). In consequence, there is in Sweden almost no analogy to the British public corporations managing nationalised industries.

Another circumstance of importance is to be observed in this connection. When it is not found advisable that the State itself should manage a particular public service this function is generally entrusted to the municipalities. Thus most social services are operated by the municipalities, which often are provided with special administrative organs for these purposes.

Consequently, the activity of the Swedish public corporations and public companies generally lies in the fields normally covered by private enterprise. The separate position of these enterprises is due to the fact that private enterprise is legally or actually excluded. In some cases a certain kind of activity may not be carried on legally without the permission of the Government or some other public authority, and permission is given only to one company, the organisation of which is determined either by legislation or by conditions imposed by the Government. In some other cases, the activity in question cannot be carried on without the financial initiative or support of the State; and as the State provides the capital stock or an important part of it, it determines the organisation of the enterprise by legislation or by special conditions. These are the two main ways in which the State puts its stamp on the organisation of independent enterprises. It is therefore necessary to distinguish two types: monopolised enterprises and State-supported enterprises. As for those State-owned companies which manage enterprises in free competition with private undertakings, there is generally no reason to describe them as "public corporations."

2. PUBLIC CORPORATIONS PROPER

As typical representatives of the Swedish public corporations proper there are to be mentioned some financial institutions which enjoy a unique position. Sweden has a complicated hierarchical organisation of mortgage-banks, the function of which is to provide capital for agriculture, house-building, etc. The lower echelons have the form of associations with the borrowers as members or partners, and at the top of this we find three central mortgage-banks, each with its own sphere of activity, which provide the capital to the associations (*Sveriges allmänna hypoteksbank, Konungariketscoll Sveriges stadshypotekskassa, Svenska jordbrukskreditkassan*). As security for the bonds issued by these central banks (in addition to the mortgage-security) the State has offered them their original funds in the form of State bonds, which, however, are still in the possession of the State. In this regard the banks are State-supported.

For the rest, their economy is quite independent. The organisation of the central mortgage-banks is determined by special legislation. They are then public corporations in a proper sense. Of the same type is the Swedish ships' mortgage-bank (*Svenska skeppshypotekskassan*), although it is not subdivided. A similar institution is also the savings banks' security fund (*Sparbankernas säkerhetskassa*), made up by compulsory contributions from the savings banks.

The degree of State influence upon the administration of these corporations varies. Generally, the State has to appoint some of the board members and auditors or, in some cases, all of them. But the connected organisations (in the last resort the borrowers) also have a certain influence. They have to elect or at least nominate some of the board members and auditors, and they generally have to grant discharge to the board (in the case of the savings-banks' security fund, however, the discharge is granted by the Government). As a manifestation of this influence, some of these corporations are formally organised as public associations, with the lower associations as members or partners (*Sveriges allmänna hypoteksbank, Svenska jordbrukskreditkassan*). But most of them formally have no members or partners, and consequently they may be called "independent public institutions" according to Swedish terminology.

Under the Social Insurance Act of 1962, the local administration of social insurance is entrusted to public insurance funds (*allmänna försäkringskassor*), which are organised as a kind of public corporation. The former sick-relief funds, which were originally private societies, have been transformed into corporate bodies of public law without any individual members. The board of each fund is composed of three members appointed by State authorities and four members appointed by the provincial assembly. Of the three auditors one is appointed by the State Insurance Board (which is the supervising authority) and two by the provincial assembly.

Proposals have been made to organise the postal administration as a public corporation and to give the municipalities the possibility to organise their enterprises as public corporations, but these proposals have not yet given any results.[4]

3. STATE CONTROLLED COMPANIES

As already mentioned, the ordinary legal form of an independent public enterprise in Sweden is that of a State-controlled joint-stock company. Typical examples of public enterprises managed by such companies are the Swedish tobacco and spirits monopolies.

In conformity with an Act of 1961 the manufacture of tobacco is a State

4. *Postverkets organisation* (SOU 1962: 52); *Kommunala bolag och andra särskilda rättssubjekt för kommunal verksamhet* (SOU 1965: 40). *Cf.* the Post Office in the United Kingdom.

monopoly, the use of which can be granted by the Government to an independent enterprise. In fact, the monopoly right is exercised by a joint-stock company (*Svenska Tobaks AB*), with the State as the main shareholder. In a contract between the State and the company detailed precepts are given about the exercise of the monopoly right.

According to a royal ordinance of 1954, the sale of intoxicating liquors may be managed only by special companies, approved by the Government. The wholesale and retail sale respectively is reserved for two companies, licensed by the Government for a period of at most six years (*partihandelsbolag* respectively *detaljhandelsbolag*). The articles of these companies must assure a dominant influence to the State. The wholesale right is granted to a company named *AB Vin- & Spritcentralen* and the retail sale rights to a company named *Systembolaget AB*. Special contracts between the State and the companies contain the conditions necessary beyond the precepts of the ordinance. In fact the State holds nearly all the shares of these companies.

Licences for serving intoxicating liquors in restaurants are given by the provincial governments. As for the so-called popular restaurants, such licences may be granted only to a central restaurant company (*restaurangbolag*), having a number of affiliated companies in the provinces. The central restaurant company must be approved by the Government for a period of at most four years, and its articles must give the State a dominating influence. Shareholders may be only the State or Swedish citizens who have been granted this privilege by special permission of the Government. The approbation of the Government has been given to a company named *Sveriges Centrala Restaurangaktiebolag*. As for the forms of State influence, reference may be made to what has been said about the wholesale company.

A feature common to all these monopoly companies is that the dividends are limited and that the surplus must be handed over to the public treasury.

The monopolies so far treated are legal monopolies. But there are other types of factual monopolies, where the Government has given permission to carry on a certain activity to only one enterprise, although the law does not require a monopoly.

According to a royal ordinance of 1939 lotteries may not be organised without the permission of the Government, except in the cases specified in the ordinance. In fact, the permission to arrange lotteries with pecuniary prizes of considerable amounts is given exclusively to a special company, *AB Svenska penninglotteriet*, of which the State is the main shareholder. According to the company articles, which may not be altered without the consent of the Government, and the concession given by the Government, the dividends are limited, and the surplus goes to a public lottery fund, from which the Government distributes grants for cultural purposes.

The concession to arrange a special form of lottery, the football pool, has been given to another company, *AB Tipstjänst*. The articles of this company are confirmed by the Government and may not be altered without its consent. Any annual profits must be used for the encouragement of sport.

A related kind of monopoly is exercised by the Swedish Broadcasting Company, *Sveriges Radio AB*. According to an Act of 1966, a permission by the Government or the Royal Telegraph Board is required for possessing or using radio establishments. The technical equipment of the broadcasting service (except the studio equipment) is in the possession of the Telegraph Board (*i.e.* the State) but is placed at the disposal of the Broadcasting Company. The company manages the programme activity in virtue of a concession given by the Government, containing certain general directions. The expenses for this activity are defrayed through a part of the licence charges collected from the listeners by the Telegraph Board. The shares of this company are in private hands and are held by representatives of Press and radio industry. But the company articles give to the Government the right to appoint the majority of the Board and two of three auditors. The Government also appoints a supervising council (*radionämnden*), which has to consider representations from the listeners and supervise the general programme activities.

Finally, the State is interested in a number of industrial or commercial enterprises managed in free competition with private undertakings, *e.g. Luossavaara-Kirunavaara AB* (iron mines), *Norrbottens järnverks AB* (iron works), *AB Statens skogsindustrier* (wood industries) and *AB Sveriges kreditbank* (commercial bank). Although the articles of such companies in some cases may assure a more or less dominating influence to the State, the purposes and legal status of the companies do not separate them clearly from private companies. Thus they are hardly to be regarded as a kind of "public corporation."

Altogether, the State is the main share-holder of about forty companies. The co-ordination of these activities is quite imperfect. The State-owned companies fall under seven Ministries. A better co-ordination has been proposed in an official report in January 1969.[5] It recommends that under the Ministry of Industries a trust company (*förvaltningsbolag*), should be formed to hold the shares of most of the State-owned companies and co-ordinate their activities, irrespective of the monopoly or commercial character of the companies. The board of the trust company will be appointed by the Government, and all shares of the company are to be held by the State. For co-ordination between the State-owned companies and "the commercial enterprises of the State" (see above) a consultative board is to be organised under the Ministry of Industries, called "*affärs verksdelegationen*" (delegation of commercial enterprises), consisting of the board of the trust company and a representative of the communication enterprises of the State.[5A]

5. *Förslag till samordning avgivet av Företagsdelegationen* (stencilled reports of the Ministry of Industries, 1969: 1); Kunglig proposition 1969: 121.
5A. In January 1970 a trust company named *Statsföretug AB* was formed in accordance with these proposals.

4. LEGAL CHARACTERISTICS OF PUBLIC ENTERPRISE

As will appear from the account given, the Swedish enterprises corresponding to the "public corporations" form a very heterogeneous group. Their "public" features can be more or less pronounced and it is not easy to distinguish them clearly from private companies. The best example of public corporations proper are the central mortgage-banks, the organisation of which is fixed by special legislation. As for the "public companies", they are all organised according to the Swedish Joint-Stock Company Act of 1944, which permits by-laws deviating from the usual pattern. But the scope for the existence of such companies is often limited by law. There can legally exist only one tobacco monopoly company and only one alcohol wholesale company. And the Government legally possesses and has made use of the power to give the concession of certain kinds of lottery to only one company. So these companies have a status as unique as that of the central mortgage-banks. In addition, the law often prescribes the content of the company by-laws or at least gives to the Government the power to demand a special type of by-law.

In those cases when the public features of the organisation have no such legal basis, the "public nature" of the companies is more dubious. Where the State has only used the technique of private law in order to assure a dominating influence to itself, the companies may be regarded as public in fact, but not in law. Perhaps one may regard a company as public in the not infrequent cases when the permanence of the public influence is assured by making the articles and by-laws as well as their amendment subject to confirmation by the Government. However, the companies dominated by the State and serving a public purpose are of interest as a form of public enterprise outside the ordinary State administration.

As already mentioned, there are mainly two forms of public enterprise discussed in Sweden: direct State administration and joint-stock company. When the latter form is chosen, that is generally for two reasons. Firstly, a company can be more flexibly managed than a government department. Secondly, the company provides a simple way to engage private capital in a public enterprise. In both regards, however, the public interest asserts itself: the freedom of the board and the influence of the private shareholders are limited by statutory rules, articles, concessions or contracts.

In spite of the State influence, the public corporations and public companies enjoy an entirely independent legal personality in the sense of private law. In consequence, the liability of the State for their engagements is limited to the amount of the funds offered by the State, or the amount of the shares held by the State. And a legal action between the State and a corporation or between two corporations is possible, although the competence of the ordinary courts is often excluded by an arbitration clause.

The public corporations and companies enjoy a higher degree of managerial independence than government institutions proper. Certainly they have to some extent to obey the orders of the Government or other public authorities. But they are not formally part of public administration. And the State prefers to use its influence in an indirect way, by instructions to the board members appointed by the Government.

None of these organisations are regarded as public authorities in a strict sense. The central mortgage-banks are classified as independent public instiutions. As for the companies, the legal doctrine offers no other label than that of a private joint-stock company, but it is admitted that the companies in question are actually managing public enterprises of great importance. To the general public, however, there is no great difference between the State and the public companies. The man in the street, buying his bottle of spirits in the "*systembolag*," certainly discerns the severe countenance of the State behind the counter.

5. EXTENT OF STATE CONTROL

The relations between the State authorities and the public corporations or companies cannot be described in a general formula. In some cases, *e.g.* the tobacco and spirits' monopolies, the activity in question is regulated by legislative Acts or royal ordinances; in other cases by concessions or contracts. Sometimes the board of the enterprise has to obey the orders of a public authority; the alcohol sale companies, for example, are subordinated to the Royal Control Board. But there is no general duty of obedience; thus it would be considered as improper for the Government to interfere in the programme activities of the Broadcasting Company in any concrete case.

To a great extent the State influences the activity of the public enterprise in more indirect ways: by exercising its rights as a shareholder or by instructions to the board members appointed by the Government. As mentioned before, this kind of influence is often assured by the content of the company articles.

As a guarantee for the performance of the duties imposed on the public enterprises it is generally prescribed that the enterprise may lose its monopoly right, concession or subsidies in case of negligent conduct of its affairs.

The financial relations between the State and the public enterprises vary considerably. Most of the monopoly enterprises give a good revenue to the State, not only through dividends (which are limited to a certain percentage) and through indirect taxes, but also through the surplus, which has to be delivered to the public treasury. Other enterprises receive yearly subsidies from the State. A special form of subvention is enjoyed by the Broadcasting Company, to which a certain part of the radio licence charges is granted.

Auditing is generally done by private auditors. The auditors are mostly elected by the shareholders (or, in the case of the mortgage-banks, by the associations connected with them, representing the borrowers), but in some cases the Government has reserved to itself the right of appointing the majority of the auditors. In five state-owned companies (*Svenska Tobaks AB, AB Vin- & Spritcentralen Systembolaget AB Sveriges Centrala Restaurang AB and Statsföretag AB*) the State debts' delegates of the Diet (*riksgälds-fullmäktige*) appoint some of the auditors. These are, however, formally functionaries of the enterprise not of the State. Generally, the right of granting discharge to the board for its administration of the enterprise rests with the shareholders' meeting.

The State auditors elected by the Diet (*riksdagens revisorer*) have repeatedly demanded the right to look into the affairs of the State-controlled companies, but as yet without success (except in the case of the railway restaurants company, *AB Trafikrestauranger*). Only if the companies receive subsidies from the State, are they, according to a royal ordinance, bound to submit their accounts to the State auditors on special demand. But this applies equally to anybody in receipt of State subsidies.

Similarly, the functions of the three legal attorneys of the Diet (*riksdagens justitieombudsmän*), whose duty it is to supervise the execution of their legal duties by judges and civil servants, are limited to officials of the State, municipalities and public corporations, proper, and they have nothing to do with the functionaries of State-controlled companies.

6. CONCLUSIONS ON LEGAL STATUS

In conclusion, what is the legal status of the public corporations and companies in comparison with that of private companies? It has already been mentioned that the former as well as the latter have an entirely independent legal personality in the sense of private law. The extent of State influence and control has also been dealt with. For the rest, their legal situation in some respects differs from that of private companies. But this is to be regarded as an exception, not as a rule.

There is no general principle of immunity from taxation for these kinds of enterprises. Any exemption from taxes must be founded on explicit rules in the relevant legislation. This is sometimes done. For example, the ships' mortgage-bank and the above-mentioned lottery companies are free from State income taxes and also from municipal rates, except for land tax.

The public corporations and companies generally do not exercise any kind of public power, except that some of them have to collect indirect taxes (*e.g.* the tobacco, alcohol and lottery taxes), and to hand them over to the public treasury. But generally these enterprises have no such functions, and that is the reason why they do not rank as public authorities.

In consequence, they are in principle subjected to the same liability in contract and in tort as private companies. From the point of view of Swedish law this is not remarkable. The situation would be the same if the State itself had managed these enterprises, because the State is immune from liability only when exercising public power.

This does not mean, however, that their relations with the general public (the customers) are determined only by the rules of private law. On the contrary, freedom of contract is often limited. Thus the monopoly companies are not free in fixing their prices, and they no doubt have a legal duty to offer their services to the customers without discrimination.

As for the legal status of the personnel, they are not in general public servants. Only the board members and the higher officials of the public corporations proper are subjected to the criminal responsibility of civil servants (Swedish Criminal Code of 1962, ch. 20, s. 12). The employees of the public companies have no such responsibility. Therefore, the trade unions, in which they are generally organised, have an unrestricted right of collective bargaining on behalf of the personnel.

7. GENERAL CONCLUSIONS

The conception of the public corporation as a specific form of enterprise, governed by special principles, has no place in Swedish law. The public corporations appear as anomalies, and a departure from the normal pattern of State-controlled companies. And even these companies are not subjected to any common rules of public law. Their "public" features are considered only as modifications within the general type of joint-stock company. Their form of organisation savours of a compromise. But in Swedish eyes this is no fault. Practical considerations, not juristic doctrine, have determined the choice of the legal forms for public enterprise. And it is not very probable that there will be any great demand for a unification of the legal forms of public enterprise.

Generally, the forms of organisation here described have been proved satisfactory and efficient. Of course, there have been complaints about bureaucracy, in spite of the relatively flexible management of the independent public enterprises. But if there is a certain risk of bureaucracy, this is not necessarily due to the State influence. Every enterprise, public or private, which has a dominating position in its field and carries an extensive organisation is in the same danger.

Part III
Other Countries

CHAPTER 11

THE PUBLIC CORPORATION
IN THE UNITED STATES*

1. HISTORICAL BACKGROUND

USE of the public corporation in the United States is not new. Neither is it so rare as some have believed. Nevertheless it is true that it has not been and is not now a routine governmental mechanism. The explanation of this, though perhaps complex, is not complicated in the context of American constitutional and historical development. Its consequence, on the other hand, is to render description of the American experience vastly complicated since the largely *ad hoc* use made of the corporate device means that there has been no general principle, almost no general pattern, around which description can be integrated.

As with so much else in connection with American political institutions, one needs to keep in mind the respective roles of the Federal Government and of the State Governments. Both have made use of the government corporation sporadically and, it would seem, hesitantly. The instances for use and the grounds for neglect each exhibit variations which seem to correlate significantly with contemporaneous notions as to the appropriate functions of the States and the Federal Government respectively. The first is perhaps more familiar and for that reason only it will be first examined.

Marshall's opinion in *McCulloch* v. *Maryland*[1] is generally accepted as having settled the constitutional power of the United States to grant charters of incorporation. Whether in doing so it did not, like other of his judicial products, unsettle what had theretofore been the law is another question. The rejection of Madison's proposal, in the Philadelphia Convention in 1787, expressly to grant such a power to the Federal Government and disregard of North Carolina's suggested amendment withholding such power leave one in the dark whether specification either way, and if so which way, was regarded as redundant. They and the attendant discussions disclose clearly enough, however, the prevalence of a deep-seated and widespread sentiment as to the impropriety of the Federal Government's becoming active in that connection. So strong was the opinion that, except for chartering municipal corporations for local self-government (a matter outside the scope of the present discussion) in the District of Columbia, there was no attempt to grant

---

* By Albert S. Abel, Professor of Law, Toronto University.
  Gabriel Wilner has carried out the revisions to this article originally published in *The Public Corporation*, 1954.
  1. 4 Wheat, 316, 4 L. Ed. 579 (1819), U.S.

federal charters, except for these very banks of the United States the existence of which was challenged and sustained by the *McCulloch* case. The bank was not strictly speaking a public corporation. It was instead a federally chartered corporation in which the United States was a substantial though minority stockholder. Management was in private hands. Furthermore, it harkened back to precedent of the era of the Continental Congress. Still the decision was so entangled with politics that however firmly it may have settled the existence of constitutional power, it gave equal assurance that the power would not be exercised while the political views of the exasperated Jackson and his political heirs were in the ascendant. A climate of opinion antagonistic to the very grant of federal charters of incorporation *a fortiori* precluded engaging in Government enterprises through that instrumentality.

In 1846, however, Congress did set up the Smithsonian Institution as a corporate instrumentality for administering the welcome but embarrassing bequest of James Smithson, seemingly with misgivings, as the only compromise solution for curing the finger itch of a host of public servants with private projects. This was the precursor of other establishments—the National Academy of Sciences, the National Home for Disabled Volunteer Soldiers, the National Training Schools for Boys and for Girls—of a charitable or eleemosynary character conducted in corporate form as adjuncts of the Federal Government. Part of the support of these institutions comes from public funds, either those of the United States or those of the District of Columbia, and there is characteristically some provision for reporting to and for supervision by federal officials. Further generalisation is impossible. Governing boards are variously constituted by executive appointment, *ex officio* designation, or succession to named incorporators. The granted heads of federal power to which such agencies are incidental vary. There is no regularity in the particulars of federal financing and supervision. There has not even been a consistent policy of using the corporate form for such purposes. Related activities, for example, Saint Elizabeth's Hospital and Howard University, have been incorporated within the area of action of the Department of Health, Education and Welfare. Use of the corporation here resembles the election made by some States to exercise similar functions, for instance, the operation of institutions of higher education or of sanatoria, through the medium of corporations. The conduct of such activities is out of the main stream of concern in a discussion of public corporations. Accordingly neither the State nor the federal manifestations will be further explored. The real significance for the present discussion is that such institutions initially occasioned resort to public corporations by the Federal Government.

2. FEDERAL CORPORATIONS—SCOPE OF ACTIVITIES

Time and events had erased the sentiments provoked by the Bank controversy enough that, during the Civil War, federal charters were freely issued for national banks and for transcontinental railways. The charter of the Union Pacific even provided for representation of the Government on the board of directors. Still there were no public corporations on the federal plane. Neither was the mechanism used by the Confederate States even though the latter did engage in substantial business and manufacturing undertakings to which the public corporation would seem to lend itself readily.

It was by acquiring stock ownership of the Panama Railroad Company and the Alaska Northern Railway Company, both existing non-federal corporations, in 1904 and 1915, respectively, and continuing operations thereunder that the United States embarked on the operation of corporate enterprises outside the area of charities. Such activities, ancillary to exercise of control over the territories and outlying possessions, were historical accidents rather than first fruits of a new policy. In each instance, facilities to serve Government personnel were needed. The need existed outside the boundaries of any State. Private enterprises chartered to furnish such facilities already existed. But they existed under circustances never or no longer attractive enough to induce the requisite flow of investment for their continued maintenance. Their continued operation in their original status but under new management was rather a matter of convenience than of reasoned choice.

All this marginal activity nevertheless eroded the basis for opposition in principle to federal public corporations and by the time of World War I the United States was prepared to and did employ the public corporation as a normally available alternative for the carrying out of federal functions. There emerged the United States Emergency Fleet Corporation, the United States Grain Corporation, the United States Housing Corporation, the War Finance Corporation, the Sugar Equalisation Board, the Spruce Production Corporation, and the Russian Bureau, Incorporated. Their missions were those either of war procurement or war financing in contexts where it was apprehended that private enterprise would prove either uninterested or inadequate and where legal limitations on the ordinary Government agencies deprived them of needed flexibility. Their characteristics were various—some originated in statutory authorisation, some in presidential or other administrative directives; some were federally chartered, others were chartered under State (New York, Delaware, Connecticut, Washington) or District of Columbia corporation laws. All were regarded as emergency in character and were designed to be temporary in duration, and all disappeared as soon after the war as they could conveniently be liquidated, except for the Emergency Fleet Corporation which was in 1927 transmuted into the Merchant Fleet Corporation. Thus, little survived in the way of new institutional arrangements; but the episode provided a firm tradition of recourse to the public corporation as a technique for dealing with emergency situations involving federal interposition in financial or marketing arrangements.

Coeval with these war corporations arose the Federal Land Banks, also aimed at an emergency—the emergency of farm financing. They were, however, created as a permanent part of the financial structure. Federal participation in them was envisaged originally on a temporary basis. This expectation was abandoned when they failed to attract private capital. Instead they became regular public corporations, with the Federal Government holding fluctuating proportions of their stock, but confirmed in control of the directorate. The Federal Intermediate Credit Banks established in the early twenties were patterned after them as an adjunct farm financing instrumentality. They and the Inland Waterways Corporation were the only instances, between World War I and the onset of the great depression, of federal institution of public corporations. Inland Waterways did not represent an expansion of Governmental activity but a continuation in corporate form of barge line operations formerly carried on by the Director General of Railroads and the War Department successively. Like the territorial railway enterprises, it was an attempt to preserve, by methods regarded as extraordinary, a system of transportation where the public interest was strong, but the prospects of profitable operation so weak that private investment interest was lacking. What was unprecedented about it was that its concern was with operations within and between States of the Union. In dealing with the territories and external affairs, in the exercise of the war power, and in its supervision of banking and credit institutions, the Federal Government has been traditionally recognised as possessed of fairly sweeping powers. None of these circumstances was present, except peripherally, in connection with the Inland Waterways Corporation. Its large though then unrecognised importance was that for the first time the United States was using the Government corporation to engage in business operations of a continuing character and outside the standard categories where specialised doctrines of federal power prevailed. A shift in attitude was manifest.

The extent and potentialities of the shift revealed themselves more fully after the crash in 1929 when rapidly worsening economic conditions called forth federal intervention of progressively expanding scope. Most although not all the situations where the public corporation was used had identifiable prototypes in the earlier history which has just been traced. What was novel was less the specific applications than the tremendous proliferation of such corporations and their acceptance as simply a member of the class of administrative devices. Undoubtedly the commonest use of the public corporation was in the familiar area of banking and credit. Even before the New Deal, the Hoover administration launched the Reconstruction Finance Corporation on its long and initially honourable course, and RFC proceeded to spawn its subsidiary Regional Agricultural Credit Corporations. Under President Roosevelt, the agencies designed to shore up collapsing values by extension of credit became so various and extensive as to preclude their listing in a summary survey. Prominent among them were the Home Owners Loan

Corporation, the Production Credit Corporation, the Commodity Credit Corporation and the Export–Import Banks of Washington. Insurance came within the range of federal activity; at first collaterally to banking by establishment of the Federal Deposit Insurance Corporation, and then in unrelated areas, as with the Federal Crop Insurance Corporation. The Federal Subsistence Homesteads Corporation and Tennessee Valley Co-operatives, Inc., were essentially industrial development corporations aimed at the active promotion of entrepreneurial production by groups or in forms accorded a preferred position on policy grounds. Distribution and marketing were the primary concern of the Electric Home and Farm Authority, Inc., and the Federal Surplus Commodities Corporation—the former designed to stimulate purchases, the latter to serve sellers. In production, the Government's activity was much more limited—but there was activity. There was, for example, the Federal Prison Industries, Inc., formed in 1934 to co-ordinate production in federal penal institutions with that of private industry so as to shield the latter from adverse market impacts.

Above all—and perhaps most extensive, certainly most dramatic, of all federal public corporations—there was the Tennessee Valley Authority. This unique venture involved nothing less than the resource development of an entire region, a comprehensive programme of industrial and social activation of the widest scope. Its constitutional validation in *Ashwander* v. *Tennessee Valley Authority*[2] is strongly reminiscent of *McCulloch* v. *Maryland* in what ensued. There was the same momentous and abiding enlargement beyond traditionally received notions of the potential range of permissible federal activity, as a matter of constitutional doctrine. There was the same grudging acceptance of the holding by opponents of the programme and the same relentless opposition to further exercises of the power was thus recognised. At present the TVA's operations can roughly be divided into two categories, namely, (1) power operations; (2) non-power activities, which include flood control, navigation improvements, fertilisers and munitions development. Its three sources of funds are: appropriations by Congress, revenues from its operations, and the issuance of electric power bonds. As of 1961, it had fixed assets of two and a half billion dollars. From the beginning the TVA, under its board of directors, appointed by the President, has had the authority to use the revenues from the sale of power, fertiliser or any other product, and the disposition of all property. In this and in a number of other areas, the TVA is exempt from the direct Government controls to which all the other federal public corporations are subject.

Technical disputes as to how much credit is due the TVA must be resolved by those with greater technical qualifications than those of the author, although it is clear that for some reason or another the region where it operates has advanced industrially and economically relatively faster than the country

2. 297 U.S. 288, 56 S. Ct. 466, 80 L. Ed. 688 (1936).

as a whole. Outside the United States, there seems to be a general consensus that it is almost uniquely valuable among recent American contributions to the governmental process. Nevertheless, there have been no later replicas. Other "valley authorities" have been projected only to be rejected; and even where comparable federal enterprises have been put in operation, as in the Bonneville Power Administration, they have been set up with narrower powers and within the hierarchy of the federal departmental structure rather than on the TVA pattern.

A miscellaneous clutch of ephemeral corporations—the Defense Homes Corporation, the Rubber Development Corporation, the Petroleum Reserves Corporation, the U.S. Commercial Company—were set up incidental to the conduct of World War II and discontinued early. All were merely adaptations in detail of World War I precedents. After the great burst of activity outlined in the preceding paragraph, the use by the United States of the Government corporation has been waning. That trend will probably continue in the near future. Scandals in the operation of the Reconstruction Finance Corporation, which caused or at least occasioned its termination, have put Federal Government corporations as a class on the defensive before public opinion. Theories of administrative organisation, broached in the 1937 Report of the President's Committee on Administrative Management and culminating in the recommendations of the Hoover Commission (many of them now translated into law), were antagonistic to the existence of autonomous administrative units and markedly biased in favour of a closely co-ordinated executive branch. In fulfilment of this philosophy, Government corporations have been folded into the regular departmental structure. For example, the Saint Lawrence Seaway Development Corporation was established in 1954. Its main purpose after construction of the Seaway was to co-operate with its Canadian counterpart in the control and operation of the Seaway. However, in 1966 it was placed in the newly created Department of Transportation and, subjected to the direction and supervision of the Secretary of Transportation.

The decline in the use of the public corporation by the Federal Government—but not its disappearance, since some, i.e. the Federal Deposit Insurance Corporation and the Tennessee Valley Authority will continue to exist—has been matched by an attempt to achieve similar ends by using the private corporation. Similar techniques had been tried several times previously in connection with the Second Bank of the United States in 1816 and the Union Pacific Railroad in 1862. The Space Communications Satellite Corporation was incorporated under the District of Columbia Business Corporation Act. Its creation was anticipated in the Communication Satellite Act of 1962. Controversy over the use of the private corporation form for such an activity was fierce, as demonstrated in the extended hearings before a number of Congressional committees. Regulatory provisions set out in the Act, are repeated in the articles of incorporation. They include control by the

United States Treasury over the sale of stock, submission of reports to the President, and appointment by the latter of three of the fifteen corporate directors. Fifty per cent. of the ownership of shares is in the hands of the communications common carriers and the other 50 per cent. in the hands of the public. While critics have already commented upon the serious defects of this technique, Comsat has been referred to as "semi-public" or "semi-private" and has been lauded as a model for the future.

Nevertheless, in July 1968, with all the alternatives before it, a ten member Presidential Commission on Postal Organisation urged the creation of a Government-owned corporation to operate the postal service on a self-supporting business basis, free from politics, and under modern management practices which would include, "not only greatly improved mail service but the early elimination of the postal deficit and far better career opportunities and working conditions for the individual postal employee." Traditional opposition to the creation of a public corporation is exemplified by the re-action of the chairman of the Appropriations Subcommittee of the House of Representatives: "Congress will think for a long time before it turns the Post Office over to a corporation."

3 CONSTITUTIONAL PROBLEMS

The plenitude of constitutional power for the United States to undertake to do, by means of the public corporation, whatever seems of sufficiently important public concern to induce a Congressional majority and the President to undertake it is substantially established. It is no more likely that there will be a retreat from this judicial position than there was from *McCulloch* v. *Maryland* during the long years of its practical desuetude. The federal power has become no more restrictive than the State power has been all along. This fortifies the significance of the States' experience with the public corporation.

The remote antecedents of some of the States themselves may be found in the charters to merchant adventurers of the Tudor and Stuart eras, a species now extinct save for the Hudson's Bay Company, but of which the Virginia Company and the Plymouth Company were also members. By 1776 these were largely of antiquarian interest. Anyway, the association of charters with monopolies and the royal prerogative did not tell in their favour at the time of achievement of American independence. Charitable corporations and municipal corporations for local government were of course widespread, but the corporate form was used hardly at all in business enterprise, even by private persons. Some of the frontier States associated themselves with State banks in the way the Federal Government had with the Bank of the United States. The débâcle of those banks produced instances of State control of such corporations ordinarily for purposes rather of liquidation than of opera-tion though a few, for example, Kentucky and Alabama attempted the latter.

Seven States, mostly in the South and West, were active in the early construction and operation of railroads. This natural extension of the States' historic concern with highway developments and navigation improvements, including canals, was not long-lived, and has left as its sole significant survival Georgia's interest as non-operating lessor in the Western and Atlantic Railroad "the same relation . . . as owner, that any company or corporation . . . (occupies) . . . to its railroad." The power of the States to engage in business enterprise through government corporations was distinctly affirmed in *Briscoe* v. *Bank of Kentucky*[3] but, aside from sporadic exceptional situations, such as have been mentioned, they remained conspicuously inert throughout the nineteenth century.

This lack of activity was partly due to certain provisions of State constitutions or the operation of provisions in the United States Constitution. Rigid notions of the separation of powers, recognised to some extent in most of the State constitutions, precluded participation in the designation of directors and thus created irrelevant constraints on organisations calculated to discourage the use of Government corporations. More important was the influence of the contract clause of the United States Constitution. This provision that "no State shall pass any law impairing the obligation of contracts" (a restriction not placed on federal legislation) was read, in the *Dartmouth College* case,[4] to include corporate charters within the term "contracts." On circuit, Justice Story, deciding *Allen* v. *McKean*,[5] applied the doctrine in a situation where no rights of private benefactors were involved. These decisions, though made in connection with charitable corporations, attributed to corporate charters a character of irrevocable commitment whose natural tendency would be to make the States hesitate to use the corporate device. Municipalities and minor political units such as counties meanwhile were busily competing with each other for railroads and business enterprises by subventions which often involved the acquisition or under-writing of corporate securities, sometimes stock although more often bonds. The great majority of these ventures proved ill-advised and collapsed. The disillusioned local governments then attempted to back out of their commitments, only to be met in case after case by the ban of the contract clause, sternly applied by the United States Supreme Court. This experience so disgruntled their citizenry that nearly half of the States inserted in their constitutions, and currently have, provisions forbidding the State or any of its municipalities or subdivisions from becoming a subscriber, shareholder or joint owner with others in any corporation. The contract clause decisions thus gave rise to these State constitutional restrictions. Actually, they are ordinarily read not to prohibit the States from the conduct of corporate enterprise but only to forbid their associating themselves with

3. 11 Pet. 257, 9 L. Ed. 709 (U.S. 1837).
4. *Trustees of Dartmouth College* v. *Woodward* [1818], 4 Wheat. 518, 4 L. Ed. 629 (U.S. 1819).
5. 1 Fed. Cas. 489 (C.C.D. Me. 1833).

others in such conduct. Even so they do limit the range of State discretion as to available modes of action. A few go further, adding to the common provision an outright exclusion from specified types of enterprise—in Tennessee, for instance, banking, in Virginia, works of internal improvement—or all corporate enterprise, as in Louisiana.

At the other extreme are constitutional provisions expressly authorising corporate business activity either in sweeping terms or by specification. They would seem to add little if anything to the substance of State power in this connection. States whose constitutions are more typically silent on the matter have in practice been about equally ready to establish Government corporations and their capacity to do so has never been seriously challenged for want of explicit constitutional authorisation. Indeed, even in Louisiana, where the most sweeping constitutional restrictions are found, the Board of Commissioners of the Port of New Orleans has substantially corporate attributes. On the other hand, differences in constitutional language very well may indicate prevalent attitudes toward the policy of State conduct of corporate enterprise. Thus, the amplest recognition of such power is that expressed in the constitutions of Arizona, Oklahoma, and North Dakota, all of them relatively new western States reputedly entertaining heterodox views of appropriate relations of government and business.

4. STATE GOVERNMENT CORPORATIONS

Instances of State government corporations, or public authorities, as they are frequently called, have been increasingly frequent since about the end of World War I, and more particularly since the great depression of the 1930's. In New York, for example, the Port of New York Authority, created in 1921, is the oldest of approximately thirty-five public authorities characterised as "public benefit corporations" presently active. These include six bridge and tunnel authorities; The Power Authority of the State of New York; seven water authorities; the New York Thruway Authority; the Buffalo Sewer Authority; the Dormitory Authority; the New York Transit Authority; four State port authorities; eight parking authorities; and most recently, The New York Job Development Authority; The Saratoga Springs Authority; the New York State Atomic and Space Development Authority (1964); The Metropolitan Transportation Authority (1967); The New York Higher Education Assistance Corporation (1967); and Vehicle Pollution Control Corporation (1967).

The basic reasons for the use of public authorities are set out in the Staff Report submitted to a New York Commission studying the subject.[6] The financial reasons relate to financing public improvements without resort to

6. Staff Report on Public Authorities, Temporary State Commission on Co-ordination of State Activities (New York State, 1956).

additional taxes so that only users pay for such improvements; financing improvements without conflicting with State constitutional debt limitations; and taking advantage of federal loans and grants. The administrative reasons concern the desirability of removing the administration of enterprises from direct control by politically responsible officers (the degree of success has varied in this) and "to provide a more flexible administrative instrument to manage commercial type public enterprises." The jurisdictional reasons relate to the use of the public authority to fill bi-State or multi-State needs.

In fact, a good many of the State government corporations, which presently number in the hundreds, are rather special in character and of correspondingly limited significance. Some have been used as convenient means of executing traditional functions of State government more commonly handled by administrative boards or officials wearing no corporate cloak, as, for instance, the construction of highways and bridges, the maintenance of college dormitories and the operation of State liquor dispensary systems.

Others have been devised to mesh into federal programmes and facilitate receipt of federal aid funds (here highway authorities and housing authorities deserve special mention, although federal assistance has been greatly expanded in many areas) or patterned after outstanding federal models like the TVA, The Grand River Dam Authority in Oklahoma, and the Platte River Public Power and Irrigation District have been of that character, on the State level.

Instances which cannot be so classified merit particular attention. Some are a response to specific new needs, such as control of pollution, co-ordination of urban transportation services and atomic development. The New York Job Development Authority was set up in 1962 to create and improve job opportunities, and provide additional employment, where unemployment is critical, by assisting in the construction, acquisition and improvement of manufacturing and industrial plants, by means of loans financed through the issuance of bonds and notes to local development authorities.

Broad programmes of economic or industrial management have been projected in a few States and appropriate government corporations set up to implement them. The first and still the most sweeping is the programme enacted in North Dakota in 1919 under Non-Partisan League sponsorship. Banking, residential construction and phases of agricultural processing and marketing were entrusted to the Industrial Commission, with *ex officio* membership, to which was given substantially the powers characteristically possessed by a board of corporate directors, as to each of the enterprises established. With some changes of function, both deletions and additions, the original plan has continued. It may not be without significance that despite the marked correspondence between the Commission's grant of authority and ordinary corporate attributes, the legislative purpose is declared to be that the

Commission's acts "shall be the acts of the State of North Dakota functioning in its sovereign capacity" and still more emphatically in connection with one phase of its operations, the North Dakota Mill and Elevator Association "is not a separate agent of the sovereign power, but is the State itself functioning." The situation seems peculiarly adapted to use of the corporate device, the plan of conduct prescribed is that of a government corporation in virtually everything but name, but the State distinctly withholds the name. In *Green* v. *Frazier*,[7] the programme was upheld successively in both the State and the United States courts of last resort, against a variety of constitutional objections. The nearest approach elsewhere has been in the specific field of power development and distribution with corollary commercial activities incident to that field of endeavour. Here (in addition to more limited and local "watershed" projects mentioned in the preceding paragraph) the South Carolina Public Service Authority and the Wisconsin Development Authority are interesting variants. South Carolina's programme encompasses an active operating entity while Wisconsin's has primarily technical planning functions. Special note should be taken of the Virgin Islands Company and the very comprehensive array of "authorities" of corporate character established by Puerto Rico, notably in legislation of 1941 and 1942, extending to all the principal aspects of the island's economy.

Another interesting development has been the use of the public authority as a technique for the management of enterprises of common interest by two or more States. Agreements or compacts between States are permitted by the United States Constitution[8] and such compacts have been made for cooperative ventures ranging from the Palisades Interstate Park Commission (New York–New Jersey) to the Bi-State Development Agency (Illinois–Missouri) and more recently the Mid-Atlantic States Air Pollution Control Compact. These "quasi-authorities," established by interstate compact are not self-supporting, and are created in the form of a public corporation for jurisdictional reasons.

There are only a handful of what has been called "true interstate authorities." These include the Delaware River Port Authority, a number of bridge authorities, but the foremost is the Port of New York Authority. As a statutory corporation of both New Jersey and New York, the Port Authority, is empowered to purchase, construct, lease and operate terminal transportation and other commercial facilities within the port district. It operates four bridges, two tunnels, three airports, six marine terminals, three truck terminals, two heliports and the New York Bus Terminal. All are financed by the issuance of the Port Authority's own bonds. While new projects must have the approval of the legislatures of both States, such approval has been granted with little exception. The Port Authority's most recent project has been the

7. 253 U.S. 233, 40 S. Ct. 499, 64 L. Ed. 878 (1920).
8. Art. I, s. 10.

development of a world trade centre, which involves the construction of buildings and other facilities.

Though this survey reveals that use by the States of the public corporation has not been insignificant either in its frequency or in the nature of the situations where it has been employed, it remains true that it has been occasional and unsystematic. For example, in New York, the State constitution provides that a public authority can only be created by a separate Act of the legislature. The Public Authorities Law is therefore merely a compilation of the Acts creating the State's public authorities. The Staff Report to the New York Commission[9] in commenting on the existing confusion recommended that "to the extent that it may be practicable, general provisions applicable to all public authorities should be included in the Public Authorities Law." The absence of a general organisational structure has its ramification in every aspect of the operations of the authorities, as will be seen in the remaining parts of this chapter.

The States have generally found in the public corporation an *ad hoc* response to particular circumstances without ever developing it as a regular instrument of government. The constitutional constraints already alluded to, whether they be real or apprehended, may partly explain this. Yet, they are at most impediments, curtailing discretion as to organisation and functions. A more fundamental consideration, operative at the national as well as State level, whose impact is undiminished by the establishment of the constitutional availability of the public corporation at both levels, is the issue of the appropriate sphere of Government action.

5. PUBLIC ENTERPRISE AND PUBLIC OPINION

American opinion has always been predominantly hostile to positive government. That position is consistent with, and is indeed an aspect of the pluralistic conceptions which have been a pervasive influence in American social and political philosophy. Moreover, history and predilection have reciprocally re-enforced each other. The publication of the *Wealth of Nations* in 1775 punctuates dramatically the conjunction of the nation's development with the development of the free market economy. Replacement of mercantilist doctrine by *laissez-faire* ideas was just being achieved when autonomous American governments emerged. The way the appropriate relations between government and economic activities were defined in those formative years has remained a powerful influence in the nation's intellectual tradition. Such a tradition was peculiarly congenial to a community like the United States, which was a frontier for much of its history. As a continuously expanding economy its task was one of exploitation of vast spaces and resources by a comparatively sparse population. The explosive though perhaps wasteful

9. See *supra*, note 6.

drives of an utterly open society, with few areas of activity pre-empted by governmental entities, gave the requisite impetus. Institutional evolution responded to the intellectual and physical environment.

Among other effects a prestige system emerged which assigned a relatively inferior role to Government employees. Unadorned by the aristocratic and academic associations which strengthened its British counterpart, the American Civil Service did not attract, or at least was not popularly viewed as attracting, personnel of an order of competence comparable to those drawn to private industry. All these features militated against free recourse to Government corporations. They are durable though not indeed permanent in nature. Some people think some or all of them are waning. The New York Commission Staff Report asserts that "user charges appear to be more palatable when collected by an authority than by a regular department of Government."[10] Until they do dwindle a great deal further in significance, however, it may safely be predicted that neither the United States nor the several States will systematically employ the Government corporation as an administrative technique though their plenary power to do so is judicially settled. Enterprises of the same nature and scope as are conventionally handled by Government corporations elsewhere may quite possibly be undertaken by the United States and the States (as indeed they have been) but, if so, it is likely that they will be placed within the regular Governmental organisation.

6. PERSONNEL PROBLEMS

Major impediments to the operation of public corporations in a business-like manner are encountered in the handling of personnel matters. On the one hand personnel difficulties have arisen from the highly formalised and minutely codified laws and regulations governing the federal Civil Service. The Ramspeck Act[11] enacted in 1940 authorises the application of the civil service laws to employees of federally-owned corporations (with the significant exception of the TVA) at the discretion of the President, which has been extensively employed for that purpose.

On the other hand, at the State level, political and personal influence are often important in administrative staffing policies. Generally, the States follow no consistent policy on the personnel matters of their public corporations. In New York, some are placed under the State Civil Service Commission, others under local civil service commissions, and still others, twelve in number, are exempt from civil service requirements. Among those exempt is the Port of New York Authority which, together with Tennessee Valley Authority on the federal level, has made some of the most significant contributions to modern public personnel administration.

10. See *supra*, note 6.
11. 54 Stat. 1211, 5 USCA s. 631a.

The public corporation gives promise of avoiding both difficulties. Its autonomous character outside the regular Government hierarchy should enable it to operate outside the constraints of the civil service system. At the same time it should be somewhat immunised from the pressures incident to the spoils system, both because its specialised and somewhat isolated functions place it outside the main stream of political attention and because its corporate status is a symbol identifying it with the business corporation, hence with the connotations of efficiency and political neutrality which are accepted as being among the leading attributes of the latter. This view has been expressed in the proposals for converting the general Post Office Department into a public corporation which consider that one of the important innovations of the public corporation would be to abolish political appointment of postmasters and remove other personnel from the general civil service system to a special merit system.

7. FINANCIAL APPROPRIATIONS AND CONTROL

Government operations, both federal and State, in general are dependent on current appropriations, annual or biennial as the law may prescribe. This highly important political safeguard does not, however, fit well into the conduct of a business enterprise. There is the major impossibility of wisely deciding the scope or direction of plant alterations or additions unless long range assumptions can be made and planned for, of projecting the course in detail of business fluctuations and hence of operating revenues and of making essential business commitments in the face of periodic contingent "insolvency" through lack of a fixed capital or a revolving fund. There is also the necessity of covering all funds and unexpended balances periodically back into the general treasury—in short, of operating as a business in the absence of the assumptions of continuity on which normal businesses must and do proceed. Moreover, there is the bother and, to some extent, peril of being called on to make budgetary justifications to the authorities who, in fact, control the details of appropriations bills; the Federal Bureau of the Budget; and the States' various statutory or constitutional equivalents with differing statutory designations or composition; as well as the appropriate legislative committees on both levels. At the very least, time and effort of "top management" is diverted from operational activities. More seriously, the ultimate shaping of the programme down to the very details of operation is left with persons outside the enterprise whose determinations will inescapably be made in considerable part on considerations extraneous to the agency. These may range from merest partisan vindictiveness to a broad-gauged appraisal of the comparative urgency of competing demands on Government resources. In any case, they deprive the enterprise managers of the capacity for effective programming. This is all in sharp contrast to the basic principle of the Government corporation, or autonomous entity operating on behalf of, but not necessarily in, the Government, which would afford a way of divorcing enterprises whose areas of action are analogous to those of private enterprise from the requirements of appropriations and budgeting.

Difficulties have arisen because of the peculiar development of Government auditing in the United States. No valid objection could, of course, be made to requiring that Government enterprises be subjected to examination and verification of their accounts according to standard auditing procedures comparable to those employed by responsible private enterprise nor, for that matter, to the designation by the Government of the authority which should make such audit, even of a common authority for all operating activities of the Government. The plain fact is, the Comptroller-General and the General Accounting Office have never confined themselves to standard auditing operations and, indeed, have stubbornly resisted any attempts by Congress or the courts so to confine them. The tradition as developed by them has been not that of verifying but of approving accounts, of reviewing expenditures or commitments to determine whether they are authorised in the light of the interpretation of the statutes deemed proper by the Comptroller-General. By and large the State auditors have subscribed fully to this notion of their mission as being that of statutory or constitutional glossators. Such subjection to retrospective invalidation of transactions is seriously prejudicial to business operations. On the other hand, the Government corporation, unhampered by the need to submit its transactions to veto for nonconformity with the always intricate constructions of legal authorisations applied in this type of audit, could enjoy the flexibility in contracting and disbursing appropriate to business enterprises. Perhaps justifiable as safeguards in connection with ordinary Government activities, the procedural and other limitations which have resulted from supervisory auditing are incompatible with business operations. In matters where the latter are a dominant factor, the public corporation permits escape from Government "audit" to auditor's auditing.

Existing federal legislation very largely destroys the advantages of Government corporations which have been the principal inducement for their use. The Government Corporation Control Act of 1945,[12] as a leading student of the subject has commented, "goes far toward completing the task of eliminating the features which have made Government corporations useful instruments for enterprise purposes". Broadly speaking, as to wholly-owned Government corporations, the statute sweeps away the feature of exemption from ordinary budgetary and auditing requirements characteristic of the Government corporation. True, it expresses an awareness of the technical and hampering ways in which those requirements have operated by calling for the submission of a "business-type budget," by specifying that operations "shall

12. 59 Stat. 597, 31 USCA, ss. 841–871.

be audited by the General Accounting Office in accordance with the principles and procedures applicable to corporate commercial transactions" and by preserving the authority of the corporation to finance themselves in the manner currently authorised by law, and to make contracts and commitments without reference to fiscal year limitations. To this extent the Act admits of and almost invites an application which would be only mildly destructive of the advantage of Government corporations. Administration in such a spirit for any long period would be counter to American administrative experience, however. No such contradiction has marked the record of this statute. It should be observed that the TVA has been singled out for special exemption in some aspects of the auditing requirement, just as it was with respect to personnel under the Ramspeck Act.

Finally, the Government Corporation Control Act, besides these fundamental matters, imposes secondary though still important limitations on the use of such corporations. Their creation other than by express statutory authorization is forbidden, thus precluding the use of executive orders for the purpose or the establishment of subsidiaries by an existing Government corporation at its discretion or for its convenience. It specifically authorises the Director of the Budget to recommend treatment of Government corporations as standard Government agencies which direction, if approved by Congress, would effectively convert the corporation into a standard Government agency for all budgetary and auditing purposes. Between them, the Government Corporation Control Act and the Ramspeck Act have comprehensively and systematically pared down several of the distinctive features which gave such corporations their utility.

No generalisation can be made as to the States. Typically, their public corporations are created by specific statute, required under the Constitution of some States such as New York. In other States, this procedure is permissible despite the quite common State constitutional prohibitions against the passage of special or local legislation where general laws could be devised and against the legislative grant of special charters, because of the uniqueness characteristic of the corporate object. In many States, it would appear, the statutes are utterly diverse in provisions as to budgeting and auditing, and most of them solve those problems largely by silence. One is remitted to the whole complex background of judicial, statutory and constitutional arrangements and informal administrative practices, special to each State.

In New York several of the handful of general provisions in the Public Authorities Law[13] prescribe that an annual report on operations, an annual budget report, and audit reports every five years must be submitted to appropriate State authorities, namely, the governor, the chairmen of the legislative committees dealing with finance, and the State comptroller. The purpose of these reports is to provide information and it does not appear that State

13. Art. 2500–2503.

control is asserted here. The New York Commission Staff Report[14] recommended that such "... authority information would not and should not require any State approval, and authorities should continue to be free to alter their budgets at any time without the need for State approval." Control by the State is asserted in a number of other ways. For example, it should be noted that the incorporation statute of each New York State authority contains certain restrictions on the sale of revenue bonds. The Saratoga Springs Authority Act, for example, provides that the Authority can issue or refund bonds only after gaining the approval of the State controller-general.

The Port of New York Authority is not subject to the Public Authorities Act and, therefore, financial controls upon it have been developed separately. Article III of the Compact provides for a compulsory annual report to the two legislatures. Its books are subject to examination by the Comptroller of New York State and the New Jersey director of the Division of Budgets and Accounts. Control over its activities stop here. The Port Authority's Board of Commissioners exercise full power, subject only to the veto of the State governors, to make all decisions regarding capital improvements, operating methods, finance and other matters.

One or two special considerations regarding State public corporations deserve comment. It seems to be generally, although not quite universally, assumed that their obligations are not the obligations of the State. Hence, public works projects can be carried on in corporate form without running afoul of State constitutional limitations on indebtedness. Moreover, the public corporation provides a method for potential extra-territorial operation by the State, a possibility which receives perhaps its clearest statement in Article XXIX of South Dakota's Constitution specifically authorising warehouse and elevator ownership "within or without the State."

8. TAXATION AND PUBLIC CORPORATIONS

The taxation of Government corporations has been treated as an aspect of the law regarding taxation of direct Government instrumentalities. There seems little doubt of the power, which is very rarely exercised, of the Federal Government to tax the property, operations, or income of federal public corporations and correspondingly of the States to tax their public corporations. Questions of federal taxation of State public corporations and State taxation of federal public corporations appear to be decided in the light of the varying fortune of the American doctrine of inter-governmental tax immunities. The immunity, where it exists, is now settled to be one which belongs to the corporation and not to those dealing with or for it, such as employees or contractors.[15]

14. See *supra*, note 6.
15. See *Helvering* v. *Gerhardt*, 304 U.S. 405 (1938); *Graves* v. *New York, ex. Rel. O'Keefe*, 306 U.S. 466 (1939).

The test of whether State instrumentalities were subject to federal taxation was, at one time, made to depend on the logically questionable and practically confusing distinction between whether the State was exercising governmental or proprietary functions, immunity attaching, it was said, to the former but not to the latter. The United States Supreme Court found that the sale of mineral waters taken from the spring and bottled by the Saratoga Springs Authority, a New York public corporation, was not immune from federal taxation. It should be noted, however, that the bonds of a State public corporation are immune from federal taxation. For this purpose the courts have included State public corporations as political subdivisions exempt under the United States Internal Revenue Code. In practice this means that State enterprise of a kind which would lend itself to operation as a public corporation can be taxed by the United States. *New York* v. *United States*[16] recast the formula so that now immunity attaches only if the State's activities are of a kind uniquely and peculiarly performed by Government, but not if it is of a kind in which private enterprise frequently or alternatively engages.

Under the traditional test all federal activity was by definition "governmental in character" and so immune from State taxation, because the Federal Government was one of limited and delegated powers. In practice, the rule seems settled that the States do not tax federal corporate activities. Decisions indicate that the immunity of federal instrumentalities from State taxation is a matter for Congress to decide.[17] No doubt the supremacy clause would be found to prevent State taxation which Congress expressly prohibits or where it provides for some type of payment in lieu of State taxes. Sometimes, as in the establishment of TVA, Congress has provided compensation to the States for lost tax revenue. Pursuant to section 13 of the TVA Act, it pays 5 per cent. of its gross revenue from the sale of power to States and counties in which it operates. Waiver of the immunity by agreement of the corporation itself with local authorities or by Congressional authorisation of a limited application of local taxes, as was rather commonly done in connection with corporations whose activities envisaged substantial real estate holdings, is, of course, effective to subject Government corporations to make contributions to local revenues to the extent of the waiver.

9. LEGAL STATUS

The capacity to sue and be sued, that earmark of corporate personality, is intimately linked with the problem of sovereign immunity. The general rule of sovereign immunity shields Government departments and agencies from suit unless there is an express waiver. In fact, most acts of incorporation of public corporations contain provisions permitting them to sue and be sued.

16. 326 U.S. 572 [1946].
17. See *Maricopa County* v. *Valley Bank*, 318 U.S. 357 (1943).

These powers have in turn been considered sufficient to establish waiver of immunity.

The TVA Act provides that it "may sue and be sued in its corporate name." But the courts have not always permitted suit against it, and even when they have, certain remedies, such as those not permitted against regular Government departments have not been afforded.[18]

The status of the United States as real party in interest for purposes of suit and the specific conduct of corporation employees on account of which the corporation could be called to respond in damages or as to which specific relief could be sought are collateral ramifications which deserve mention. Broadly, the approach seems to be analogous to that where activities of standard administrative agencies are in issue. To this extent the litigation status of the corporations is assimilated to that of the United States, despite which it seems fairly clear, that it is not so far identical as to entitle them to whatever remnants of sovereign immunity still persist in the federal jurisprudence.

In most States the doctrine of sovereign immunity still persists, and there is therefore a tendency to attribute to their public corporations the status of agencies of the State rather than of orthodox corporations, as to suability, and thus to shield them from suits in tort, and perhaps to a lesser extent in contract. In recent cases, where the courts have applied sovereign immunity they have stressed the close relationship and interest of the State to the particular activity as well as the absence of a specific waiver of immunity.

Nevertheless, in a number of other States the trend has been away from the doctrine of sovereign immunity. At present almost all public authorities in New York can sue and be sued, and, more specifically, a number of them can be sued in tort before the Court of Claims. The Port of New York Authority was, until 1951, exempt from suit. In that year, however, the legislatures of New York and New Jersey explicitly consented to permit suits against the Port Authority. More recently, this tendency has become more marked as exemplified by *Petty* v. *Tennessee–Missouri Bridge Commission*,[19] a decision which has been followed by other courts. This public corporation was established by means of an interstate compact. The Court disregarded the sovereign immunity doctrine which was still applicable in the two States, but rather looked to the "sue and be sued" clause in the compact which had received congressional approval.

18. See *TVA* v. *Lacy*, 116 F. Supp. 15 (1953).
19. 359 U.S. 275 (1959).

BIBLIOGRAPHY

New York State Constitutional Convention Committee, Constitutions of the States and United States (1938) (Compilation of State constitutional provisions).

(Hoover) Commission on Organisation of the Executive Branch of the Government, Federal Business Enterprises, 1949.

McDiarmid, *Government Corporations and Federal Funds*, Chicago, 1938.

Weintraub, *Government Corporations and State Law*, New York, 1939.

Key, Government Corporations in Marx (ed.) *Elements of Public Administration*, New York, 1946.

Dimock, "Government Corporations: A Focus of Policy and Administration," 43 *Am. Pol. Sci. Rev.* 899, 1145 (1949).

Lilenthal and Marquis, "The Conduct of Business Enterprises by the Federal Government," 54 *Harv. L. Rev.* 545 (1941).

Nehemkis, "The Public Authority: Some Legal and Practical Aspects," 47 *Yale L.J.* 14 (1937).

Pinney, "Government Commercial Corporations," 11 *U. Cin. L. Rev.* 481 (1937).

Pritchett, "The Government Corporation Control Act of 1945," 40 *Am. Pol. Sci. Rev.* 509 (1946).

Seidman, "The Theory of the Autonomous Government Corporation: An Appraisal," 12 *Pub. Ad. Rev.* 89 (1952).

Thurston, "Government Proprietary Corporations," 21 *Va. L. Rev.* 351, 465 (1935).

Staff Report on Public Authorities under New York State, Temporary State Commission on Co-ordination of State Activities, New York State, 1956.

Hanson, "Regional Survey: North America" in *Public Enterprise*, 36, ed. Hanson, 1955.

Gerwig, "Public Authorities in the United States," 26 *Law & Contemp. Prob.* 591 (1961).

Seidman, "The Government Corporation: Organisation and Control," 14 *Pub. Admin. Rev.* 183 (1954).

Lukens, "Controls, Accountability and Administration in the Port of New York Authority," in *Public Enterprise*, 49, ed. Hanson, 1955.

"Applicability of Sovereign Immunity to Independent Public Authorities," 74 *Harv. L. Rev.* 714 (1961).

Leach, "Interstate Authorities in the United States," 26 *Law & Contemp. Prob.* 666 (1961).

Fair, "Port Authorities in the United States," 26 *Law & Contemp. Prob.* 703 (1961).

Goldstein, "An Authority in Action: An Account of the Port of New York Authority and its Recent Activities," 26 *Law & Contemp. Prob.* 715 (1961).

Jones, "The Financing of TVA," 26 *Law & Contemp. Prob.* 725 (1961).

CHAPTER 12

THE PUBLIC CORPORATION IN CANADA*

1. BACKGROUND AND DEVELOPMENT

HISTORICALLY, the business activities of Canadian Governments have been directed to the costly task of binding together a sparsely-populated continental domain. The Government first appeared as the perpetually harassed owner and operator of the canal system upon which "the commercial empire of the St. Lawrence" depended. With the advent of railways the Government at first assumed a relatively passive role, but after 1867 found itself unable to resist pressures which carried it into the railroad business. Between 1870 and 1910 railways and Government were closely intertwined. In 1919 this notorious and lengthy intimacy was formally acknowledged by the creation of a publicly-owned national railway system. The Government in the same year also decided that the corporation rather than the ordinary department was the more appropriate administrative agency to employ for such projects.

Even before this period the municipalities had taken the lead by setting up independent corporations to operate gas, water and electrical utilities, as well as local transportation systems. Today, as an indication of the scope of these activities, one may note that over 90 per cent. of Canadian municipalities have their water supplied by local public authorities. The provinces have also participated in this movement, the pioneer undertaking, that of the Hydro-Electric Power Commission of Ontario, being created as early as 1907. Apart from the nationally-owned railway system "the Hydro" is the largest Governmental enterprise in Canada.[1] Some of the other provinces have copied this model. In addition, the Prairie Provinces have, for many years, operated their own telephone systems; Quebec and Ontario have engaged in the lucrative retail sale of spirituous beverages through corporate agencies, an example now followed by most of the other provinces; and, under a Socialist Government, Saskatchewan in recent years took the lead in exploring the administrative possibilities of the Crown corporation for a great variety of commercial undertakings.

* By Professor J. E. Hodgetts, Professor of Political Science in the University of Toronto and Principal, Victoria College, Toronto.
1. The Hydro-Electric Power Commission has fixed assets valued at nearly 3·2 billion dollars, a staff one-third as large as the whole Civil Service of the Province and, as producer and wholesaler of electrical power has direct contacts with over three hundred local authorities, many rural communities and large industrial consumers. Certainly no other Government agency has exercised such a pervasive and continuous influence over the development of the Province. The only comprehensive survey of federal corporate agencies is by C. A. Ashley and R. G. H. Smails, *Canadian Crown Corporations* (Toronto: Macmillan of Canada, 1965).

Despite the early development of publicly-owned business ventures at all levels of government, it was not until the 1930's that the national Government displayed any marked inclination to experiment extensively with the device of the public corporation. The change in attitude may be attributed to the depression, the criticisms of private enterprise voiced by the newly formed socialist party (The Co-operative Commonwealth Federation), the exciting experiments in the United States under the New Deal and the growing knowledge of the public utility trust employed in the United Kingdom. Between 1932 and 1938, as a result, radio broadcasting, central banking, the marketing of wheat, national harbours and air transport were all brought under partial or complete public ownership and control. During the war the Government became more deeply involved in industrial enterprises but these were operated by Crown companies, a rather special sub-species of the main type of public corporation to which only passing references will be made in this study.[2] That the Canadian Government had become fully convinced of the value of the public corporation during these years is readily revealed in the large crop of such agencies which appeared between 1944 and 1948. In that period no less than eighteen agencies were given corporate status and most of these are still operative.

Throughout the whole course of this development it has been apparent that neither nationalisation nor the use of the public corporation has developed as a controversial issue between the two major parties. The National Democratic Party (successor to the CCF) it is true, from its inception took a firmer line as a matter of principle, although it has been extremely vague in dealing with the type of agency to be set up for administering nationalised undertakings. It cannot be said that any unifying philosophy underlies the use of the public corporation in Canada: the whole development has been piece-meal and pragmatic.[3] Only in the years following World War II, as will appear later, has any effort been made to standardise the form and operations of the corporations or the law relating to them.

Four general features of this development at the national level merit notice.

2. The Government also devised other co-operative arrangements with private business ventures such as "management-fee" contracts and special depreciation allowances for new plant built for supplying Governmental needs. Similar arrangements were authorised for the build-up required by the "cold war."

3. A startling illustration of the pragmatism of the Government was provided in 1947 in an exchange between Mr. Smith on the opposition benches and Mr. C. D. Howe, then Minister of Trade and Commerce who was the most important "corporation launcher" in the Government.
   Mr. Smith: " . . . the Minister has given us no reason why this [The Dominion Coal Board] should be a corporation."
   Mr. Howe: " . . . my hon. friend asked why this commission should take the form of a corporation. I shall have to get a more satisfactory answer to that question than I can give offhand. All I can say is that for a commission to operate and do business it seems to be necessary that [sic] they be formed into a corporation. All the commissions I know of that operate around Ottawa are formed into corporations, I do not know why, other than that a corporation is a convenient form."—
   Debates, House of Commons, Canada, 1947, p. 4249.

First, with a few notable exceptions such as the Canadian National Railways and the National Harbours Board, the public corporations have all started as fresh ventures; they have not been set up, as in the United Kingdom, to administer mature private enterprises which have been taken over by the Government. There are obvious advantages in thus starting with a clean slate: loyalties (or antagonisms) to former employers do not have to be reckoned with nor do the ghosts of past errors rise to plague the new management.

Secondly, the Liberal Government (under which most of the expansion took place) has repeatedly declared that it has no intention of entering into competition with already existing private undertakings. Even the milder version of competition, exemplified in the United States by the Tennessee Valley Authority's "yardstick" standards, has not been stressed. State enterprises are viewed as a means of bridging gaps left by private enterprise, a view which is especially prominent in the many Governmental credit and insurance agencies.[4] While there are a few State monopolies linked with the defence production requirements of the nation, even in this realm the Government has taken full advantage of industrial plants and skills already existing by entering into special financial or managerial arrangements with private *entrepreneurs*. In the novel field of atomic energy, for example, the Federal Government has developed complex relations with private consortia and provincial utilities.[5] It would not be true to say that Governmental enterprise has completely avoided clashes with potentially competitive private ventures, but on the whole such clashes have occurred at the margins of the main operations of governmental agencies.[6]

The third factor conditioning the growth of Government corporations in Canada is the mixed or dual economy which leaves a privately-owned railway system to operate alongside the public system; which envisages a nationally-owned broadcasting system working in conjunction with over 350 private stations; which preserves the privately-owned chartered banks but tops them with a Bank of Canada; which divides air transport between a State system and private operators; and which declares certain harbours to be parts of a national system, while leaving others under local jurisdiction. This preference for preserving a dual system possibly explains the fourth general feature of the public corporation: many of the Canadian corporations emerged with an ambivalent mix of regulatory and operative functions. The Canadian Broadcasting Corporation (until 1958), the National Harbours Board and the Atomic Energy Control Board are illustrations of agencies which appear to

4. See, for example, discussion on the incorporation of the Industrial Development Bank, before the Standing Committee on Banking and Commerce, *Minutes of Proceedings and Evidence*, 1944, pp. 11 *et seq.* A similar view is to be found in *Debates*, House of Commons, Canada, 1951, pp. 2003 *et seq.*

5. See J. E. Hodgetts, *Administering the Atom for Peace* (New York; Atherton Press, 1964), pp. 104–110.

6. In the fields of radio broadcasting and air transport the conflict between private and public enterprise has recently become more pronounced.

have been designed with mixed motives. Just as Canadian Governments have been unable to accept outright nationalisation so too they have been reluctant to break from the older tradition of regulation. The result in the first instance is the dualism already noted and, in the second instance, a curious and often embarrassing combination of commercial and regulatory duties in the one agency (or, at least, with added social policy elements as "chosen instruments").[7] A balance sheet designed to depict the financial health of an agency may be badly distorted when corporations are loaded with supplementary, non-commercial responsibilities or broader social goals which are not amenable to strictly commercial measures of efficiency. The Canadian National Railways and the Canadian Broadcasting Corporation probably endured more criticism on this score than have other public corporations.

2. CLASSIFICATION OF GOVERNMENT CORPORATIONS

The scope and variety of the Federal Government's corporate enterprises make any simple classification difficult. The "General Office Guide," compiled by the Auditor-General in 1946, makes a two-fold division based on the type of control exercised over the corporate "instrumentalities." Some corporations submit to ministerial or Cabinet control and these are described as "executive instrumentalities"; others, described as "parliamentary instrumentalities" are dependent on Parliament in so far as they are statutory creations.[8] The difficulty with this classification is that there are varying degrees of control exercised by both Ministers and Parliament so that in practice the law courts, as will be shown, have rendered a most confusing array of decisions relating to the public corporation.

A more satisfactory classification has been presented in connection with the Financial Administration Act 1951.[9] In Schedules A, B, C and D of the Act will be found a list of Government departments proper (Schedule A); "departmental corporations" (Schedule B); "agency corporations" (Schedule C) and "proprietary corporations" (Schedule D). This classification is based on two factors: the extent of financial independence and the general nature of the activity. The departmental corporations have administrative, supervisory or regulatory functions, closely akin to an ordinary department and are financed by appropriations. Agency corporations undertake trading, service and procurement operations and are usually given controlled "revolving funds." Finally, proprietary corporations manage lending, financial, commer-

7. For the concept of "chosen instrument" see Lloyd D. Musolf, *Public Ownership and Accountability* (Cambridge: Harvard University Press, 1959).

8. *General Office Guide*. Office of the Auditor-General, Canada (Ottawa: King's Printer, 1946) pp. 117 *et seq*. This section "The Audit of Crown Corporations" contains many interesting detailed instructions to audit officers which bear rather widely on the legal and financial position of the corporation.

9. Statutes of Canada, 15–16 Geo. 6, c. 12 (2nd Session, 1951), as amended, 14–15–16 Eliz. 2, c. 74 (1967).

cial or industrial operations and are normally expected to finance themselves from the sale of goods and services.

For the purpose of revealing the general nature of Governmental enterprise the following four-fold classification, based on the type of activity rather than the degree of independence, is presented.

(1) Credit and financial agencies

(1) Farm Credit Corporation (1959), formerly Canadian Farm Loan Board (1935). Originally set up in 1927 as Federal Farm Loan Board.

(2) Bank of Canada (1938). First created as a "privately-owned public trust" in 1934.

(3) Industrial Development Bank (1944). A wholly owned subsidiary of the Bank of Canada.

(4) Exports Credits Insurance Corporation (1944).

(5) Central Mortgage and Housing Corporation (1945).

(6) Atlantic Development Board (1962). (Scheduled for absorption in a department in 1969).

(7) Municipal Development and Loan Board (1963).

(8) Cape Breton Development Corporation (1967).

(9) Canada Deposit Insurance Corporation (1967).

(2) Commodity trading and procurement agencies

(1) Canadian Wheat Board (1935).

(2) Crown Assets Disposal Corporation (1950). Originally War Assets Corporation (1944).

(3) Fisheries Prices Support Board (1944).

(4) Canadian Commercial Corporation (1946).

(5) Defence Construction (1951) Ltd. This agency took over the charter of a previous Crown company, Wartime Housing Ltd. (1941).

(6) Agricultural Stabilisation Board (1958). Originally Agricultural Prices Support Board (1944).

(7) Canadian Livestock Feed Board (1966).

(8) Canadian Dairy Commission (1967).

(3) Producing and business agencies

(1) Canadian National Railways (1919).

(2) Canadian National (West Indies) Steamships Ltd. (1927). A subsidiary of CNR, now virtually moribund.

(3) National Harbours Board (1936).

(4) Canadian Broadcasting Corporation (1936). First set up in 1932 as the Canadian Radio Broadcasting Commission.

(5) Air Canada (formerly Trans Canada Airlines) 1937.

(6) Polymer Corporation Ltd. (1942).

(7) Eldorado Mining & Refining (1944) Ltd.

(8) Northern Transportation Co. Ltd. (1947). A wholly owned subsidiary of Eldorado Mining & Refining Ltd.

(9) Canadian Arsenals Ltd. (1945).

(10) Northern Canada Power Commission (1956). Originally Northwest Territories Power Commission (1948).

(11) Canadian Overseas Telecommunication Corporation (1949).

(12) Atomic Energy of Canada Ltd. (1952).

(13) St. Lawrence Seaway Authority (Statute passed in 1951, proclaimed in 1954).

(14) Eldorado Aviation Ltd. (1953). A wholly owned subsidiary of Eldorado Mining & Refining Ltd.

(4) Management, co-ordination and research agencies

(1) National Battlefields Commission (1908).

(2) Halifax Relief Commission (1918) now virtually inoperative.

(3) National Research Council (1924). A Medical Research Council since 1960, operates virtually autonomously under the same Act.

(4) National Capital Commission (1958). Formerly Federal District Commission (1927).

(5) Director of Soldier Settlement (1931). A corporation "sole."

(6) Unemployment Insurance Commission (1940).

(7) Director, the Veterans' Land Act (1942). A corporation "sole."

(8) Atomic Energy Control Board (1946).

(9) Dominion Coal Board (1947).

(10) Eastern Rockies Forest Conservation Board (1947).

(11) Canadian Patents and Development Ltd. (1947). A wholly owned subsidiary of National Research Council.

(12) Roosevelt-Campobello International Park Commission (1964). A joint venture of the United States and Canada.

(13) Economic Council (1964–65).

(14) National Museums of Canada (1968). Embracing museums and the National Gallery, one of the earliest corporate agencies established in 1913.

It may be noted that in category (3) nearly all the corporations are concerned with providing transportation or communication services, an emphasis that has already been explained in the opening paragraphs of this essay. Most of the corporate agencies in category (4) have been made responsible for managing either a special fund or else certain public properties having special features, e.g. national battlefields or national museums. It is in respect of this group that one may question the use of the corporate form, since many of these agencies are merely adjuncts of a regular government department. This is acknowledged in the classification appended to the Financial Administration Act where most of these instrumentalities are referred to as "departmental corporations" and accorded almost the same treatment as ordinary departments.

3. CROWN COMPANIES

A number of agencies in the foregoing list bear titles which reveal a characteristic which legally sets them apart from all other Crown corporations. Agencies with "Limited" attached to their titles are all Crown companies which have been incorporated under Part I of the Companies Act (1934) like any ordinary private company.[10] This Act places no restrictions on the type of activity upon which a corporation may embark but does limit the number of shareholders, regulates the right to transfer shares, insists that all directors be shareholders and requires that the corporation open its books to the public. During the war the Act proved flexible enough to permit the Government to set up in a great variety of businesses, all connected with war production and supplies. The Minister of Munitions and Supply was given blanket authority by parliament to propose to Council the creation of Crown companies. At the same time the other requirements of the Companies Act enabled the Minister in charge to maintain adequate control over the companies. A token share capital was authorised for each company and shares duly issued to each director who had been appointed by the Minister. Since these shares were endorsed over to the Minister by the directors the control by the Government was potentially very direct and intimate.[11] In addition to the provisions of the Companies Act itself there are three other legal instruments that determine the operations of these companies. An Order in Council is the creative instrument; Letters Patent issued by the Secretary of State provide the legal authorisation for the company to do business under the Companies Act; and the formal agreement between the company and the Minister sets out in detail the structure, financing and powers of the agency. Through this somewhat complicated but convenient administrative form, the national Government at the height of the war, had set in motion nearly three dozen Crown companies. Most of these ventures have since been liquidated although as the previous list reveals, several important agencies such as the multi-million dollar Polymer plant have been retained. Moreover, Parliament has revealed its interest in continuing the use of the device. In 1946 it approved the Government Companies Operation Act,[12] a comprehensive statute intended to unify the

10. *Ibid.* 24–25 Geo. 5, c. 33. The Canadian National (West Indies) Steamships which was created by statute in 1927 was an early forerunner of this, by now, familiar Crown agency.

11. See *Debates,* House of Commons, Canada, 1946, p. 2367. Note also Mr. Howe's statement, *ibid.* p. 1918, concerning Polymer Corporation, Ltd.; he claimed that Polymer's bank account was "cleaned out" every Saturday night and the money sent to the Treasury.

12. Statutes of Canada, 10 Geo. 6, c. 24 (1946). Most sections of this Act were subsequently re-enacted in the all-embracing Financial Administration Act 1951, which covered all Government corporations as well.

legal and fiscal position of these companies. Further, Parliament has conferred on three Governmental agencies the discretion to create additional
Crown companies. The Minister of Defence Production in accord with an
Act passed in 1951, the Atomic Energy Control Board under statute of 1946,
and the National Research Council in its amended statute of 1946, exercise
this privilege of recommending to Council the incorporation of Crown
companies.[13]

The Crown Companies which have all originated through Orders in Council
are exceptions to the rule of incorporation by statute and, in the main, must
be regarded as a group apart from the regular statutory corporations. Since
each corporate agency has its own statute and since these statutes have been
spread over many years, the arguments in favour of this special administrative
device as well as the peculiar form and legal status to be conferred on it have
varied greatly. In fact the observer who attempts to describe the main
characteristics of the public corporation in Canada would have no reason to
quarrel with John Marshall's definition: "A corporation," he declared, "is an
artificial being, invisible, intangible, and existing only in contemplation of
law." That both the law and many official sponsors, over the years, have
"contemplated" the public corporation in different ways and with different
assumptions about its essential value and position requires elaboration.

4. PURPOSES OF INCORPORATION

The reasons for adopting the corporate rather than departmental form are to
be found in certain characteristics of the corporation which, it has always been
alleged, make it a more appropriate agency for embarking on business or
commercial activities. It is clear that the reasons which induced private
entrepreneurs to employ the corporate form are not relevant for the State as
entrepreneur. Access to large amounts of share capital, perpetuity and limited
liability—three important assets from the private businessman's point of
view—are not significant so far as the State is concerned.[14] Nor is the convenient separation of the corporation as a legal entity from the individuals who
own and control it relevant in the context of responsible government. In the
last analysis, no matter how "independent" the agency is supposed to be,
Ministers of the Crown must assume responsibility for the decisions and acts
of their agents.[15] It is this situation which creates the real paradox of the
public corporation. How can it maintain managerial independence (or be

13. Statutes of Canada, 15 Geo. 6, c. 4 (1951), s. 7; 10 Geo. 6, c. 37 (1946), s. 10 and
10 Geo. 6, c. 31 (1946), s. 9.
14. On the point see Report of Royal Commission on Government Organisation,
Vol. V, Ottawa: Queen's Printer, 1963, pp. 69–70.
15. In no instance was this point more dramatically demonstrated than in the highly
publicised disagreement on policy between the Governor of the Bank of Canada and
the Minister of Finance in 1961. See Ashley and Smails, *Canadian Crown Corporations*,
op. cit. pp. 165–170.

"taken out of politics" as the saying goes) and at the same time be held responsible for its policy decisions?

Most of the earlier Canadian public corporations were created with the demands of managerial autonomy in mind. Give the corporation its own funds, allow it to hire its own staff, free it from the nagging controls that confront an ordinary department, and management could be expected to conduct the enterprise on efficient business lines. This was the theory. But practice in Canada, as in Britain and the United States, did not always conform. Nor, as time went on, did it seem altogether safe to rely on managerial autonomy. By 1945 in the United States the Government Corporation Control Act drastically narrowed the managerial independence of the corporations, while in Great Britain with the nationalisation of key industries, management could not be left in political peace to make the vital decisions which would affect the new planned economy. In Canada, the tendency to apply the check-rein to management through the imposition of departmental controls and ministerial directive has not been quite so pronounced. Nevertheless, the public corporation in Canada is far from possessing the full freedoms which are enjoyed by its counterparts in private business. The restriction on corporate freedom mainly takes the form of reducing financial independence rather than in providing for outright Ministerial intervention in policy matters. Within the variable confines of these financial strictures, the boards of public corporations claim, and Ministerial heads generally acknowledge a freedom from direct parliamentary surveillance.

While this has been the general trend, each corporation has had its own history and its own reasons (in some instances "excuses" might be a more accurate term) for leaving the departmental fold. With several of the earlier corporations such as the Canadian National Railways (1919), the Canadian Farm Loan Board (1927), the Canadian Broadcasting Corporation (1932–36) and the National Harbours Board (1936) the determining factor was the concern to create a politically-neutralised administrative agency. Sir Thomas White, in defending the Government's decision to incorporate the Canadian National Railways summarised this attitude when he said: "If it were not for this question of the intrusion of patronage it seems to me that the logical position would be for the Government to administer the system directly, just as the Intercolonial [Railway] was administered. We have been seeking to get away from that position . . . in order to avoid the influencing of administration in a particular political interest."[16] Several drastic reorganisations of the CNR in the years that followed were an indication that the mere act of incorporation did not lessen the political pressures on the administration. Nevertheless, when the Canadian Broadcasting Corporation was set up in 1936, a similar reasoning was used, and great care was taken to insulate management from partisan pressure by setting up a part-time board of directors

16. See *Debates*, House of Commons, Canada, 1919, p. 1634.

between it and Parliament. A rather different set of pressures confronted
the National Harbours Board at the time of its formation in 1936. The local
harbour boards from whom it took over had been exposed to strong and often
undesirable local pressures and the new national board was expected to be in
a better position to ward off local importunates. The periodic complaint from
the localities about the "unresponsiveness" of the national board suggests,
perhaps, that it has managed to fulfil its mission.[17]

In the discussions over the incorporation of more recent Governmental
ventures, much less has been said about the need to place management beyond
the reach of partisan politics. The emphasis seems to have shifted, rather, to
defending the corporate form as the best device for luring competent businessmen into the public service and for escaping some of the central personnel and
fiscal controls to which ordinary departments must submit.[18] The strengthening of this "businessman's approach" to the corporation can probably be
traced to the extensive war-time experience with the Crown Company, which
has already been mentioned.

Clearly, the incorporation of an agency offers many tempting conveniences
to the Government. It permits a flexibility in headquarters arrangements
which the departmental system prohibits. A real administrative need may be
met by locating the headquarters in a commercial environment more congenial
than that of Ottawa or in placing the board in closer proximity to the major
area of activity. But the overwhelming consideration in the minds of most
executive directors of Crown corporations is the independence which they
obtain in the handling of personnel. In their view, it is most important for
management to be in a position to pick up competent personnel when they
suddenly become available and to be able to discharge the inefficient without
fuss. Staff morale and loyalty to the enterprise can be all the more quickly
built up if management has perfect freedom to make such vital decisions.
Most departmental heads might be inclined to adopt the same attitude, for it
is equally hard for them to be forced to bow before decisions made by an
external hiring agency, such as the Civil Service Commission. Indeed, in
1962–63, the Royal Commission on Government Organisation drew this conclusion and, after acknowledging the advantages for public corporations of the
freedom in administering their own staff, proposed that departmental managers
be relieved of the more nagging rigours of central personnel controls. In this
respect, the Royal Commission was intent on moving toward a more unified
public service, in which departmental managers would now share in some
of the managerial freedoms enjoyed by their brethren in the corporations.[19]

17. See, for example, *Debates*, House of Commons, Canada, 1946, p. 3357.
18. For good illustrations of this emphasis see *Debates*, House of Commons, Canada,
1946, pp. 1511 *et seq*. (Mr. Howe's detailed statement in support of the Government
Companies Operation Act); and *ibid*. pp. 1884 *et seq*. (further views of Mr. Howe in
the debate on amending the National Research Council Act).
19. See Report on the Royal Commission on Government Organisation, Vol. I,
pp. 255–256.

5. FINANCIAL CONTROL

Financial autonomy has also been regarded as a major virtue of incorporation. Release from the normal departmental process of estimating financial needs for one year in advance is, of course, the main freedom sought by incorporation. Departments must annually haggle with the Treasury Board over their estimates and then must confront Parliamentary scrutiny of these requests. They must adhere rigorously to the "allotments" into which their appropriations are sub-divided; their expenditures are watched closely by officials drawn from the Comptroller of the Treasury's Office; unexpended balances lapse at the end of the fiscal year and must be re-voted; and their books are carefully examined by the Auditor-General who is empowered to report as an officer of Parliament to the legislature. These are the main controls imposed on the ordinary department. The public corporations escape most of them, especially if their activities bring in substantial revenues. Most corporations, however, submit to the ministrations of the Auditor-General; many of the purely administrative and regulatory corporate agencies are financed through appropriations and consequently have no greater financial freedom than ordinary departments; and the Treasury Board and/or the Department of Finance normally has some power to intervene in the larger financial transactions of all the corporations.

The extreme variety of the provisions in each statute covering the financial operations of the public corporations has been subjected to some rationalisation in Part VIII of the Financial Administration Act of 1951. This legislation which manfully grapples with the vast complexities of financing government as a whole, has reserved this one Part for the Crown Corporations. The Appended Schedules "B," "C" and "D" which provide for three types of corporations henceforth to be known as "departmental corporations," "agency corporations" and "proprietary corporations," have already been noted. For the corporations listed (or to be listed in future by Order of the Governor in Council) in the Schedules to the Act an attempt has been made to lay down uniform provisions governing their finances. There are sections dealing with the financial year, budgeting procedure, bank accounts, surpluses, loans, contracts, accounts, reports and audit. Inconsistencies between these general provisions and the specific provisions appearing in each separate statute of incorporation are rectified by giving priority to the specific Acts.[20] On the other hand general supervision of corporate financial transactions is clearly established in the Act. The Minister of Finance, Treasury Board and Auditor-General have their responsibilities for the corporations set out in general terms. These simply consolidate and systematise arrangements which had appeared in some but not in all of the Acts incorporating the separate agencies.

20. Two important corporations omitted from the list and therefore not subject to the Financial Administration Act are the Bank of Canada and the Canadian Wheat Board.

It is probable that this general statute goes about as far as is desirable in providing a unifying frame of reference which still leaves room for individual variations. In this respect, also, the Royal Commission on Government Organisation found merit in conferring on departmental managers some of the same fiscal flexibility accorded public corporations. Thus, with respect both to personnel and financial management departments and corporations tend to come closer together, as on the one hand the former autonomy of the corporations is curtailed and on the other, the former stringent controls on departments are somewhat relaxed. The financial check-rein on the public corporation would appear to be tighter than that exercised over the finances of most British Crown corporations but somewhat less than that foisted on the corporations in the United States by the Government Corporations Control Act 1945.

6. Legal Status

An argument frequently advanced in favour of the corporation is that the public have less difficulty in bringing actions against it than against an ordinary Government department. This has always been a doubtful argument because the courts in Canada have followed two quite opposed lines of interpretation in dealing with corporate entities. Moreover, in recent years the Government has progressively liberalised the traditional conceptions of the immunity of the Crown so that today it would appear that Government departments and Crown corporations are almost equally amenable to the normal judicial processes. Some brief explanation of each of these developments is required.

One line of court interpretation has supported the view that the public corporation is an independent entity, to be treated in precisely the same manner as any private corporate entity. Canadian courts have repeatedly cited as the leading case on this point *Graham* v. *Public Works Commissioners* (a British case decided in 1901).[21] Here it was said that the Crown, as a convenient business arrangement, often gives corporate trading agencies the power to contract as principals rather than agents; for that reason, as Mr. Justice Richards declared in his dissenting opinion in *Oatway* v. *Canadian Wheat Board* (1944),[22] the corporation is given "the advantages as well as the liabilities of such (private) corporation in its dealings with third parties." This view of the corporation acting in its own, rather than an agency, capacity has been upheld in a number of decisions involving the Canadian National Railways and the Canadian Broadcasting Corporation.[23]

21. Cited in *Re C.B.C. Assessment* [1938] 4 D.L.R. 764, at pp. 789–90.
22. *Oatway* v. *Canadian Wheat Board* [1944] 3 W.W.R. 337.
23. In *Michaud* v. *C.N.R.* [1924] 3 D.L.R. 1 the court stated in part: "Parliament having deliberately divorced the management of the railway from the control of the Government, having taken away the jurisdiction of the Exchequer Court and having

Unfortunately, the courts have also pursued an opposite course which seeks to identify the corporation with the Crown and thus place it in a position comparable to a Government department as a so-called "emanation of the Crown." The courts have in these instances sought to establish the degree of control exercised by the Government over the agency; if there is extensive control then the courts take the position that the corporation is really an agency of the Crown and can be proceeded against only in the same manner as one would proceed against an ordinary department. A leading case which established this line of judicial analysis was *Halifax* v. *Harbour Commission* (1935)[24] in which it was decided that "the mere fact that an agent of the Crown is a corporate body whose statute of incorporation provides that it may sue and be sued does not give the right to bring action against it in the ordinary way." In 1941 a decision involving the Canadian Broadcasting Corporation devoted many pages to establishing the fact that the CBC *was* the Crown because the Act instructed it to carry out a service of national broadcasting *for* the Minister of Transport. The court also emphasised the various controls exercised over the Corporation by the Governor-in-Council and came to the conclusion that as an emanation of the Crown the CBC could not be assessed for local taxes.[25]

Some clarification of the paradox created by these legal decisions may be expected as a result of recent legislation. Prior to 1950 the position was that if a corporation was declared to be an emanation of the Crown and thus entitled to the legal immunities of an ordinary department, an aggrieved citizen had to petition the Governor-General in order to carry his case before a special federal court—the Exchequer Court. In the Statute Law Amendment Act of 1950 Parliament provided that corporate Crown agencies could sue and be sued in provincial courts of competent jurisdiction without a fiat of the Governor-General.[26] It is important to note that this statute for the

---

repealed the necessity of a fiat being obtained, I cannot help coming to the conclusion that it fully intended that the Corporation should in all respects stand in a similar position before the courts of the country as any private corporation would." The courts pursued the same reasoning in *Gooderham and Worts* v. *C.B.C.* [1939] 4 D.L.R. 241: "in view of the wide power of contract conferred on the Canadian Broadcasting Corporation by its creating statute, the Corporation is not immune to actions in the ordinary courts for breach of contract notwithstanding it is an emanation of the Crown." This position was even adopted towards a Crown company in *North and Wartime Housing Ltd.* v. *Madden et al.* [1944] 4 D.L.R. 161. In this instance even though the company was wholly owned by the Dominion, even though an Order-in-Council declared it an "emanation of the Crown" and a delegated agent acting for the Minister, it was nevertheless amenable to suit like a private company.

24. [1935] S.C.R. 215.
25. *Recorders Court* v. *C.B.C.* [1941] 2 D.L.R. 551.
26. Statutes of Canada, 14 Geo. 6, c. 51 (1950). This legislation was designed especially to clarify the position of corporations acting in the name of Her Majesty and in their own name. Proceedings can now be taken against Crown corporations without a fiat regardless of whether the corporation acted in its own right or in the name of Her Majesty. It should, perhaps, be pointed out that when Canada set up the Federal Exchequer Court in 1887 it established a unique precedent followed 60 years later in Britain. The Court could hear every claim against the Crown arising out of any debt, injury to the person or property, or any public work resulting from negligence of any officer or servant of the Crown while acting within the scope of his duties or employ-

H

first time permits citizens to bring actions against Crown corporations before provincial courts, as distinct from the federal Exchequer Court which previously alone held jurisdiction. In the following year a further step was taken in the Petition of Right Act which brought the ordinary department closer to the legal position recently conferred on the public corporation.[27] Suits against Government departments could now be taken before the Exchequer Court without having to rely on the fiat of the Governor-General. A final stage was reached in 1953 when Parliament approved the Crown Liability Act to make the Government liable for torts of its servants, thus bringing its legal liabilities into line with specific provisions already written into many of the statutes regulating the separate public corporations.[28] The end result of these changes appears to be that the difference between the independent Crown corporation and the regular department with respect to legal immunities has been considerably narrowed. Federal departments and public corporations now equally share one other legal peculiarity: they are both immune from taxes levied by local or provincial Governments.[29] Since many of the federal corporations must do business within the boundaries of the provinces or municipalities this claim to immunity has raised considerable controversy. It is true that Crown corporations "have been instructed to negotiate arrangements with municipalities for allowances in lieu of taxes that are fair and equitable having regard to all relevant circumstances."[30] But these are *ex gratia* payments to which the taxing authority has no legal right. Refusal of the Crown to abandon this important mark of its legal omnipotence has possibly caused more grumbling against the corporations than has any other feature of their operations.[31] It should be pointed out, however, that this immunity would

---

ment. While the claims were limited to the tort of negligence in fact nearly all cases arising against the Crown appear to fall into this category. Crown corporations also came under the Exchequer Court Act unless their own statutes specifically provided for suits in tort to be carried before the ordinary courts. (For such cases see debate on National Harbours Board, *Debates*, House of Commons, 1936, pp. 3106 *et seq.*). In practice a rigorous construction of the term "public works" restricted the citizens' legal access to the Government, a situation which was altered by deleting the term from the Exchequer Court Act in 1938.

27. Statutes of Canada, 15–16 Geo. 6, c. 33 (1st Session, 1951).

28. An extremely valuable brief history of this whole development is provided by Mr. Garson, the Minister of Justice, on the second reading of this measure. See his speech on January 29, 1953, *Debates*, House of Commons, Canada, pp. 1470 *et seq.* See also Statutes of Canada, 1–2 Eliz. 2, c. 30 (1952–53).

29. This immunity can be traced to section 125 of the British North America Act, which reads: "No lands or property belonging to Canada or any Province shall be liable to taxation."

30. See Mr. Abbott's comments in the debate on the Municipal Grants Act, *Debates*, House of Commons, Canada, 1951, pp. 4216 *et seq.*

31. The corporations that draw the most anguished criticism from Members speaking for their tax-hungry constituencies are the CNR, Central Mortgage and Housing Corporation and Polymer Corporation Ltd. When Mr. Graydon, a leading member of the Opposition inquired what would happen if the Crown corporations decided not to make an agreement for payment in lieu of taxes the Minister replied "They [the municipal authorities] would not have any taxes." See *Debates*, House of Commons, Canada, 1951, p. 4380.

not prevent a provincial Government from taxing its own corporate agencies, nor has it prevented the Federal Government from making its "proprietary corporations" (listed in Schedule D to the Financial Administration Act) liable for federal income tax.[32] Indeed, the Federal Government having put its best foot forward, now expects that the provinces will make similar provisions with regard to their own proprietary corporations.

The autonomy of the public corporation in Canada has been circumscribed in a number of ways. As the foregoing paragraphs have indicated the decisions of the law courts have often tended to discount the independence of corporate agencies. In addition, where corporations sell goods or provide services on a national scale they generally must submit to some external regulatory body having the characteristics of a court. For example, the Board of Transport Commissioners, subject to the over-riding jurisdiction of the Cabinet, fixes the rates to be charged by the Canadian National Railways (as well as the privately-operated Canadian Pacific Railway). The same is true of transportation by air where Air Canada is regulated along with all private operators by the Air Transport Board.[33] An outstanding highly controversial exception to this pattern, until 1958, was the Canadian Broadcasting Corporation which regulated both its own stations and those operated by private *entrepreneurs*. In 1958, a Board of Broadcast Governors assumed the regulatory functions, which were clarified and extended in 1968 by the creation of the Canadian Radio Television Commission.[34]

7. GOVERNMENT SUPERVISION

No public corporation is able to evade some form of executive influence or supervision. The usual powers conferred by statutes on the Governor-General-in-Council (*i.e.* cabinet) include the following:

(1) appointment and removal of the members of the board;

(2) approval of all by-laws passed by the board;

(3) authorising all expenditures in excess of a fixed maximum;

(4) approving contracts and expenditures on capital account which involve large outlays;

(5) approving short-term loans or advances to the corporations.

The Minister of Finance also occupies a rather special position in relation to the affairs of most corporations. He may prescribe the form in which the

32. Statutes of Canada, 1 Eliz. 2, c. 29 (1952). One of the proprietary corporations, Air Canada sponsored a measure to circumvent this Act: it advanced a Bill that would amalgamate its profitable domestic service with its financially less successful trans-atlantic service, thereby reducing its taxable profits.

33. In 1967 a new "umbrella" regulatory agency, the Canadian Transport Commission, was established (14–15–16 Eliz. 2, c. 69) to succeed three separate regulatory boards—the Board of Transport Commissioners, the Air Transport Board and the Canadian Maritime Commission; these, along with two new regulatory operations for Water Transport and Motor Vehicle Transport, were ensconced as "Committees" within the new all-embracing Transport Commission.

34. See Statutes of Canada, 1967–68, c. 25.

operating and capital budgets (required by s. 79 of the Financial Administration Act 1951) are prepared; he may approve the special bank accounts which a corporation wishes to establish; and he may direct the corporations to prepare their accounts according to any standard form which he wishes to develop. The Minister who is required by law to act as the spokesman for the corporations in the House is also given certain powers. In conjunction with the Minister of Finance and the Cabinet he is empowered to direct a corporation to pay any surplus to the Receiver-General. He is normally entitled to request from the corporation such detailed accounts, books and papers as he may require and, of course, it is through the Minister that each corporation reports annually to Parliament. The clear-cut powers of direction which have been conferred on Ministers by legislation in the United Kingdom have not normally appeared in Canadian statutes but there is, nonetheless, a wide, though varying range of opportunity for executive control, particularly over the financial affairs of the corporations. Even the power to issue directions has been accorded in some statutes.[35]

Another external agent with whom most public corporations have to contend is the Auditor-General. Several of the larger corporations are entitled to employ a private firm of auditors,[36] although by the terms of the Financial Administration Act the Auditor-General may now be eligible as an auditor or joint auditor for such corporations.[37] The normal arrangement is, however, that the financial affairs of the Crown corporations now take their place alongside the departmental accounts as a section in the annual volume of the Public Accounts and may be scrutinised by the Public Accounts Committee.

8. PARLIAMENTARY CONTROL

Parliamentary control over the corporations has been deliberately restricted

35. The Canadian Overseas Telecommunication Corporation Act (3 Geo. 6, c. 10 (1949, 2nd Session)) reads: "The Corporation shall comply with any directions from time to time given to it by the Governor-in-Council or the Minister with respect to the exercise of its power." A similar power expressed in a different form appears in the Surplus Crown Assets Corporation Act (13 Geo. 6, c. 38 (1949)). Here it is stated that the Minister's powers are delegated to the corporation and are subject to his "specific or general instructions." The original Central Mortgage and Housing Corporation Act was amended by 15 Geo. 6, c. 13 (1951), sub s. 5 (5) of which reads: "The Corporation shall comply with any directions from time to time given to it by the Governor-in-Council or the Minister respecting the exercise or performance of its powers, duties and functions." The Government made its intentions quite clear in relation to this section when the Minister said: "On matters of policy, and in fact to the extent defined by this section, the Minister or the Governor-in-Council shall have direct control over the operations of Central Mortgage and Housing Corporation." *Debates*, House of Commons, Canada, 1951, p. 4284. The most significant addition of Ministerial direction powers came as an aftermath to the fracas between the Governor of the Bank of Canada and the Minister of Finance. An amendment to the Bank of Canada Act (14–14–16 Eliz. 2, c. 88 (1966–67, s. 14), spells out with more than usual rigour a section headed "Government Directive."

36. The major exceptions are the Bank of Canada, Canadian National Railways, Central Mortgage and Housing Corporation, the Canadian Wheat Board, and Air Canada.

37. See s. 77 (2) of 15–16 Geo. 6, c. 12 (2nd Session, 1951).

in pursuit of the earlier ideal of managerial autonomy and freedom from partisan pressure. Parliament can, of course, discuss the annual report of each corporation when it is tabled but in practice a full debate, comparable to the debates in the British House on a motion for concurrence, never takes place. The question period, one instrument of parliamentary control, has been restricted, as in England, by applying the Ministerial formula: "this is a matter involving an independent agency and I can answer only in so far as the agency sees fit to provide me with the information." Occasionally, responsible Ministers have been able to sweeten this negative reply by suggesting to inquisitive Members that they can best obtain the detailed information they are seeking by raising the matter before special or standing committees. There are already in existence enough appropriate standing committees of the House to look after the reports from all corporations. The affairs of the Bank of Canada, the Wheat Board, Air Canada, the Canadian National Railways, and Atomic Energy of Canada Ltd.—to mention a few outstanding cases—could and have been explored in a relevant standing committee. Special or select committees have also been used, notably in the case of the Canadian Broadcasting Corporation, to permit both organised private interests and the staff of the Corporation to present their views to the legislature. One standing committee which has not been employed as effectively as it could be, is the Committee on Public Accounts. In the past this Committee has not been characterised by the vigour and success of its counterpart in the United Kingdom. However, beginning in 1950, there were indications that the Public Accounts Committee would henceforth bring under its consideration the financial reports of various Crown corporations. Since these reports now make up part of the public accounts, there would seem to be no reason why this Committee could not usefully occupy itself with inquiries into the financial performance of the corporations. Some members of the Committee have, in fact, asked to have the standing orders of the House altered so as to make reference of these reports to the Committee completely automatic. The Government has taken the position that the Public Accounts Committee may use its own discretion in considering the reports of all those corporations that appear in the Public Accounts and that the Opposition ought to be satisfied with that arrangement.[38] At the same time, it should be added, that no effort has been made to initiate, on the UK model, a select committee on nationalised undertakings.

It is appropriate when dealing with Parliament's relations with the corporations to comment briefly on the attempts to establish relations with the public.

38. On this point see the discussion in Parliament, *Debates*, House of Commons, Canada, 1951, pp. 2004 *et seq*. Note Mr. Macdonnell's complaint: "After all, let us be realistic about this, Committees always have a government majority and do not meet unless the Government wishes them to meet," *ibid*. p. 2005. Note also the interesting discussion in the Public Accounts Committee over its power to examine the accounts of Crown corporations. Standing Committee on Public Accounts, *Minutes of Proceedings and Evidence*, 1950, pp. 64 *et seq*.

Canada has not attempted to follow the experiments made in the United Kingdom with consultative committees and consumers' councils. Some corporations have used advisory committees rather sparingly. In the case of the
Wheat Board, to select one outstanding example, representatives of organised
agriculture have stated a preference for representation on an advisory council
rather than on the Board itself.[39] Clearly this preference will persist only so
long as the organised interests believe that the Board is really prepared to
accept the advice of the committee. The Canadian Broadcasting Corporation
has also used advisory committees to help in the planning of programmes
directed to special listeners such as the farmers or adult education groups.
The Corporation receives fairly direct dividends from this policy of consultation, for it wins enthusiastic friends at court when its affairs are being critically
scrutinised by parliamentary committees.

9. INTERNAL ORGANISATION

Turning now to the internal features of the corporation one may appropriately
start at the top with the board of directors. The appointment of board members raises no real problems. In nearly every instance the appointing power
is confided to the Governor-in-Council. Tenure is generally stated to be "at
pleasure"—either of the Minister or more usually of the Governor-in-
Council. In a few cases a technically more permanent form of tenure "on
good behaviour" has been granted. This type of tenure is usually associated
with long-term appointments, e.g. the seven-year terms of the chairman of the
board of governors of the CBC and the ten-year terms of the members of the
Harbours Board. Where large boards exist part-time directors are generally
appointed on staggered three-year terms which can be renewed. Most of the
statutes are vague or entirely silent in dealing with the conditions which would
qualify or disqualify members of the board.

Boards vary greatly in size, ranging from a "corporation sole" to the
twenty members on the National Capital Commission. In a few instances
where a small full-time board (usually three members) exists, responsibility
for the special aspects of the corporation's work is allocated to each member.[40]
On the larger boards part-time members outnumber the permanent members
and the board, meeting only a few times a year, is strictly policy-forming or
even advisory. The inevitable gap between management and board produced
under these circumstances is reduced in a few instances by the appointment

39. For a strong expression of this view see comments of the Minister of Agriculture
(Mr. Gardiner) in the debate on the Agriculture Prices Support Board, *Debates*, House
of Commons, Canada, 1944, pp. 5577 *et seq.*
40. The National Harbours Board, for example, informally allocates to each
specialist member responsibility for general administration, financing and engineering
respectively. Roughly 80 per cent. of the Board's work is handled by circulation of
memoranda between the three members.

of an executive committee which, meeting more frequently than the full board, is able to maintain closer contact with day-to-day issues. It is difficult to determine from Canadian practices whether there is an optimum size for a board: so much depends upon the size of the enterprise, the number of policy issues raised and the amount of supervision required. Judging from recent experience, the Government seems to favour a board ranging between five and nine members.

Little effort has been made to set up representative boards. The statutory requirement approximating this emphasis is to be found in the Acts governing the CBC and the Bank of Canada where the governors are to be selected "to give representation to the principal geographic divisions of Canada." Occasionally organised labour and agriculture have requested representation but the Government has refused to make any formal commitments to the principle of representation, including now even geographic representation.

The outstanding feature of the boards of many Canadian corporations is the presence on them of senior permanent departmental officials. The group of financial corporations without exception follow this pattern, and several others also support the practice. Were these primarily "departmental corporations" with little or no autonomy this arrangement would appear to be logical and legitimate. (Although one might then raise the question: why have a corporation at all?) But agencies like the Bank of Canada, Central Mortgage and Housing Corporation or the Industrial Development Bank scarcely fall into this category of departmental satellites. Clearly, no senior civil servant should be placed in a position where, as a member of a corporation, he is compelled to join in an opinion that may be opposed to that of his own political chief. Such administrative ambivalence is neither healthy, necessary nor feasible.[41] Mr. Howe, whose experience with Crown corporations makes his opinion worth noting, as early as 1936 argued that he would never appoint his own deputy Minister to the board of a corporation which had to report to him as the responsible Minister.[42] Mr. Howe and the various Ministers of Finance have long since ceased to practise his earlier precept. Two recent examples, Export Credits Insurance Corporation and the Canadian Commercial Corporation, carry to an extreme the principle of seconding senior civil servants to the boards of Crown corporations: in both cases the board, apart from its

41. A leading financial critic on the Opposition, Mr. J. M. Macdonnell, singled out this feature of the membership of boards for adverse comment. See *Debates*, House of Commons, Canada, 1951, p. 2007. For amplification of this situation see J. E. Hodgetts, "Responsibility of the Government Corporation to the Governing Body," *Proceedings of the Fifth Annual Conference*, 1953, Institute of Public Administration of Canada.

42. See *ibid*. 1936, p. 2183 where Mr. Howe stated that he would not put the Deputy Minister of Railways on the Board because: "The government intends to see to it that the directors are in a position to discuss freely and among themselves any and all matters coming before them"; note also in *ibid* 1946, at p. 2481, Mr. Howe's case for keeping his own Deputy Minister off the board of any Crown company owned by his department.

executive director is nothing more than a glorified interdepartmental committee of high permanent officials.

It might be suggested that this preference for the permanent expert on the board is an illustration of the advancing "managerial revolution." And, indeed, the relations established between boards of Crown corporations and the senior executive officers of the corporations are further evidence of this transformation. In the 1930's corporate organisation—both private and public—was based on the assumption that administration and policy-formation could be separated. The arrangements made in 1936 for the CNR and the CBC best exemplify this theory of separating management from the board. In both cases the chief executive officer was not included on the board and in both cases the scheme subsequently proved unworkable.[43] Both in private and public corporations recent alterations reveal a marked preference for including on the board one or more senior executive officers. In a number of instances present arrangements call for a part-time board with a full-time chairman who is also chief executive officer. In fact, many of the recent corporations include more than one representative of management on the board.[44] Where, as in the unusual case of the Bank of Canada, the governor (and chairman) of the bank is empowered to veto decisions of the full board one seems to reach the climax of managerial domination. It would appear that the board's function of acting as a buffer between those responsible for day-to-day administration and external political pressures is adversely affected by this trend to elevate managerial officials to top-ranking positions on the board. The combination of chief policy-former and chief administrator in one person may, however, lend greater weight to the corporation's representations to the Cabinet or the responsible Minister.

Indeed, there are some critics who would strengthen the point of contact between board and Parliament by placing the responsible Minister on the board—preferably as chairman. When this proposal was strongly pressed by Opposition Members during a debate in 1946 on the Atomic Energy Control Board, Mr. Howe made these strong objections to the plan:

"For example, sitting on a board of five the Minister might be overruled and outvoted four to one, which would hardly be consistent with the line of authority. Then if a recommendation came from a board of which the Minis-

43. The CNR informally acknowledged the unworkability of the plan by amalgamating in practice (but without statutory change) the positions of chairman of the board and president of the corporation. The CBC went through a more formal reorganisation after the general manager had dominated the board without actually being a member of it. After numerous experiments, the president of the board is chief executive officer. It is interesting to observe that the Hoover Commission Report on the Reorganisation of Government in the United States continued to express confidence in part-time policy boards with no representation for management on the boards.

44. For example, the two executive officers of the Bank of Canada and the Central Mortgage and Housing Corporation, the three executive heads of the National Research Council and of Surplus Crown Assets sit on the respective boards of these corporations. Several others follow the same pattern.

ter was a member and it became the duty of the deputy Minister to overrule
the decision of the board or to recommend to the Minister that he overrule
that decision, there will be some difficulty. I am strongly of the opinion that
the board will function very much better if no Minister of the Crown is a
member of it."[45] While this view seems to have been accepted without qualification at the national level, one might observe that many provincial corporations deliberately make room for the Minister at the board table.

It has already been pointed out that one of the privileges most cherished
by the managers of a public corporation is their freedom from civil service
regulations in dealing with personnel. The most recent available statistics
show that, as compared with a total roster of 202,427 salaried Governmental
employees (March 31, 1966), there were 143,179 persons employed by the
Crown corporations. While this shows a significant number of officials in the
employ of the corporations, it should be noted that about 80–90 per cent. of
this total are in one corporation, the Canadian National Railways.[46]

The freedom accorded corporations in personnel matters does not appear
to have led to any extensive experimentation or innovation in this field.
Escape from the rigorous confines of the civil service classification and pay
scales has enabled corporations to adapt their salaries to market requirements.
But for ordinary clerical and routine work, salaries approximate those in the
civil service. Release from the jurisdiction of the Civil Service Commission
probably has cut down the delay which inevitably attends centralised recruitment methods. The fact that management maintains a close guard over
individual salaries—consistently refusing to reveal these to Parliament—
suggests that corporations attach much importance to payment in accordance
with individual merit rather than in accordance with a set "class" of positions.[47]

Pension plans for the corporations have been authorised on a piece-meal
basis. The Crown companies, such as Polymer, obviously must follow the
practices pursued by similar private concerns (*e.g.* the pension scheme of the
oil companies close at hand). For that reason they are empowered to formulate
their own plans and submit them for approval to Council. Some corporations
have been designated as part of the Civil Service for purposes of pension under
the regular Civil Service Superannuation Act. Others have been permitted by
their statutes or by special Order in Council to create their own pension

45. *Debates*, House of Commons, Canada, 1946, pp. 2482–2483. One might logically
ask why these same criticisms could not be directed to the practice, already mentioned,
of placing deputy Ministers on boards.

46. See *Canada Year Book*, 1968. By far the largest corporate employers are in the
category of "proprietary corporations" which includes such agencies as the CNR, Air
Canada, the CBC, etc.

47. The corporation have answered questions in parliament concerning the salaries
of the higher officers. On March 6, 1953, the Prime Minister tabled Orders-in-Council
which authorised increases in salary to several important corporation officials. The
president of the CNR and the Governor of the Bank of Canada each with annual
salaries of $50,000 then occupied the enviable position of being the highest paid public
servants in Canada.

schemes. It would be impossible here to make any general assessment of the relevance of these separate plans to the peculiar needs of each staff group or of the difference between such plans and the rather satisfactory pension plan provided for the Civil Service.

Until 1967, corporations have had to pay a price for autonomy in the management of personnel. Unions and demands for collective bargaining could not be side-tracked as readily as was possible in the regular Civil Service for nearly a century.[48] The larger Crown corporations which have had to deal with employees whose work was similar to that undertaken in private enterprise, have long since come to accept unions and collective bargaining. The CNR, for example, has had to deal with the well-entrenched railway brotherhoods and, indeed, has had to face strikes or near strikes.[49] The National Harbours Board facing a polyglot labour force engaged in various port activities has had to negotiate with over thirty different unions. Some of the other corporations, notably the Canadian Broadcasting Corporation, have faced up to this issue much more reluctantly. However, in 1948 an amended Industrial Relations and Disputes Investigation Act included a new section which left the reluctant corporations little choice but to accept collective bargaining agents for their staffs.[50] While this legislation excluded employees in departments, ten years later even this difference was eliminated in the rather sudden acceptance of collective bargaining for the entire Public Service.

10. SUMMARY AND CONCLUSIONS

Looking now to the future, what possibilities are opened up for the public corporation? It appears most likely that the uneasy equilibrium between public and private enterprise will continue, regardless of the party in power. For this reason, extensive nationalisation projects will probably be set aside in favour of the present programme of filling gaps left by private enterprise. The experiments with atomic energy were originally thought to involve a close control and even outright State monopoly extending from the raw materials

48. There is a confusing multitude of staff associations in the civil service and since 1944 a joint council (a modified version of the British Whitley Council Scheme) has been the formal negotiating instrument for the staff. However, following three years of agitation, a committee report, and strikes amongst postal workers, a new era was ushered in by the Public Service Staff Relations Act of 1967. This Act recognises collective bargaining and provides for conciliation and arbitration procedures and even authorises strike action. (Statutes of Canada, 14–15–16 Eliz. 2, c. 72.)

49. See *Toronto Globe and Mail*, March 17, 1953, for a story about the CNR's concern for improving unsatisfactory wage-bargaining relations because of their impact on the railway rate structure.

50. Statutes of Canada, 11–12 Geo. 6, c. 54 (1948), s. 54. The provisions of the Act concerning the right of every employee to join a union and the provisions governing certification of a bargaining agent were to "apply in respect of employees of such corporation, except any such corporation, and the employees thereof, that the Governor-in-Council excludes from the provisions. . . . " s. 55 of the same Act excludes "employees of Her Majesty in right of Canada." This last section has been overtaken by the legislation of 1967 (see note 48).

to a wide range of products for domestic use. It was for this reason, presumably, that power to create Crown companies was vested in the National Research Council and the Atomic Energy Control Board. However, as peaceful uses of atomic energy evolved, Government assumed a more *laissez-faire* approach and through its existing agencies has developed an elaborate partnership with private concerns and a provincial utility (Ontario Hydro) in the generation of electrical power. Similarly, should the nation confront a severe depression a more serious clash of forces might be expected in the realm now peacefully, but only partially occupied, by the credit and financing agencies of the Government. An extended programme of public works and subsidies might involve the Central Mortgage and Housing Corporation or the Industrial Development Bank. At the same time the commodity-trading agencies might occupy a much more important position in a deflated economy. In another direction—the development and exploitation of natural resources either in the far North or through co-operation with the provinces—one might expect to see an extension of such corporate utilities as the Northern Canada Power Commission or the Eastern Rockies Forest Conservation Board, which is a joint corporate entity shared between the national Government and the Province of Alberta. Clearly, the contemporary stress on "development" which requires collaborative arrangements between various federal agencies and regions or provinces, suggests the use of corporations in the fourth category which are managerial, co-ordinative and research oriented. There is also a strong possibility (1969) that the venerable Post Office Department will become a public corporation involved with the new and expensive communications satellites.

With the prospect in Canada of continuing and even extending the use of the public corporation it is encouraging to discover that the efforts to systematise the form and clarify the legal position of these administrative entities have been attended with some success. This trend began in 1946 with the Government Companies Operation Act and was broadened in the Financial Administration Act of 1951. The control and financing of various corporate bodies was covered in detail by the legislation. The legal ambiguities created by court interpretations of the amenability of Crown corporations to the normal processes of law have also been largely swept aside by the legislation passed between 1950 and 1953. In the specific area of labour relations, the federal statute of 1948 seems to have settled that problem by placing the corporations (with the exception of those excluded by order of the Governor-in-Council) in precisely the same position as other private enterprises carrying on nation-wide activities. With the exception of the last-mentioned change, for which organised labour had long contended, the other alterations have been worked out behind the scenes by permanent officials of the Departments of Finance and Justice and the Auditor-General in consultation with the interested corporations. Now that collective bargaining has been recognised for civil servants in conventional Government departments, the argument for the separate legal status of the public corporation has been considerably modified. Further efforts to produce uniformity are likely to foster rigidities which it has always been argued the incorporation of administrative entities was deliberately designed to avoid. While the official launchers of corporations invariably look about for suitable models already in existence, it would probably be no advantage to have a "standard model" which would have to be slavishly imitated. Standardisation, then, has probably been carried as far as is consistent with the real need for flexibility and continued experimentation. And, in view of the current efforts to accord some of these managerial freedoms to Government departments such standardisation would run against the tide.

However, this conclusion does not preclude a serious re-examination of some of the uses to which the Crown corporation has been put in substitution for administration by a regular subdivision of a department. In the list of agencies presented above, many of those appearing in group (4) are suspect. The reasons for incorporation, if given at all, are seldom convincing. Indeed some of those who manage such agencies find difficulty in describing the actual benefits which they derive from incorporation. Perhaps no serious harm is done by making such agencies corporations, so long as they are treated exactly like departments. But then, unnecessary complication of the administrative apparatus is not desirable, nor is the use of the corporate form for such non-commercial, non-productive activities likely to enhance the reputation of those agencies which are legitimately granted corporate status. The Government has now begun to face up to these questions and appears, with its legislation in 1967, to have admitted that proliferation of the corporate form as a mechanism for escaping rigid central controls is not the answer. The better solution is to be found in developing central managerial agencies that will place the stress on service and unifying guide lines that do not constrict managerial initiative, whether in a corporation or a department. The end result will be to remove many of the reasons, originally quite valid, for creating corporations as escape mechanisms.

From this general observation one may pass on to somewhat more detailed conclusions respecting the internal structure of and the external controls asserted over the corporation. The major question raised by current practices in relation to the boards of the corporations has to do with the propriety of appointing senior departmental officials to the board. The practice surely cannot be dictated by either a scarcity of competent personnel to man the boards or by a desire to economise; it must now be viewed as a matter of policy. The philosophy underlying this policy has never been expressed: are these departmental watchdogs set up by a Government that is suspicious of its own action in creating an "independent" corporation? If so, why use a corporation in the first place?

Another matter requiring reconsideration, based now on a maturer experience with the form, is the practice of bringing up to the board so many senior executive officials concerned with management. Policy and administration it is true are closely interlinked, but at the same time one must consider whether this practice does not lead to managerial domination of the (usually) part-time board, and also whether the board, in such cases, is a sufficiently strong buffer against political pressures. These at least are questions that ought now to be pondered.

The relation of the executive to the corporation is also a matter which will increasingly demand attention. Clearly, the last few statutes or amendments to earlier statutes of incorporation show a tendency to introduce the Ministerial power of issuing "directives." In this respect Canada is merely following the precedents created by the nationalised undertakings in Britain. But if this is to become the pattern then certainly one safeguard has thus far been overlooked: the requirement that formal Ministerial or Cabinet directives must be fully publicised so that Parliament can know who has made the final decisions. Even this requirement, as British experience has shown, is not entirely satisfactory, but it is at least the minimum which Parliament has the right to demand. Since it is precisely at the point where Minister and board meet that the paradoxical position (*i.e.* combining independence and responsibility) of the corporation strikes with full force, we are not likely ever to arrive at a completely satisfactory arrangement. Nevertheless, Parliament, acting for the total electorate as the supervisor of the executive—the shareholders' trustee, in this case—must not be deprived of its ultimate power to place responsibility where it belongs.

Parliament's role in relation to the public corporation in Canada has not been clearly assessed in the past because of the fear of those enthusiastic supporters of managerial autonomy that parliamentary "interference" would spell disaster to the enterprise.[51] Since the war there have been signs that Parliament has become somewhat restive when asked to assume this neutralist position toward the Crown corporation. When a Bill incorporating a new agency comes before the legislature now, the Government is placed more on its mettle in defending the device. As noted previously, members of the Public Accounts Committee have now enthusiastically seized the opportunity to consider the financial reports of various corporations. Moreover, many members are pressing insistently for the automatic referral of the annual reports of Crown corporations either to the Public Accounts Committee of the House or even to a special committee appointed for that purpose. Parliament's

51. Observe the late Lord Bennett's comments when Prime Minister in 1934: "We have not yet been able to devise, either in this Parliament or elsewhere, any institution that takes the place of the annual meeting of shareholders that subjects the operations of the directors to the scrutiny and their conduct to the criticism that [*sic*] is possible at an annual meeting of shareholders with the directors elected for the purpose of giving effect to their wishes in connection with their enterprise." *Debates*, House of Commons, Canada, 1934, p. 839.

consideration of the annual reports of the Crown corporations would be facilitated by a better timing for the presentation of the reports. Several of the larger corporations, including the Canadian National Railways, Harbours Board, Air Canada, Central Mortgage and Housing Corporation and the Bank of Canada, now report at the end of the calender year. Thus their reports always receive adequate review by appropriate standing committees. Other corporations report normally, along with the ordinary departments, on March 31. This creates a peak load problem for the Auditor-General, delays the presentation of reports and may so postpone the consideration of them that Parliament will find itself dealing with transactions dating back over two years.[52] In practice this often means that the corporations' reports receive no examination by Parliament at all. Finally, it should be noted that some of the Crown companies (notably Polymer Corporation Ltd.), because they have been founded by Order-in-Council offer very little information to the public or Parliament either as to their form, their precise operating terms of reference or their financial affairs. It is even possible for such an agency to launch foreign subsidiaries without Parliament's knowledge or prior approval. If multi-million dollar activities are to be conducted by these Crown companies as a permanent rather than a temporary matter it would be preferable to publicise the legal form and powers of the corporation and also see to it that more substantial reports were properly circulated. This is surely not a private matter between the Minister and the Crown company concerned.

Lord Macaulay long ago admonished the British electors that in selecting their representatives they should choose wisely and confide liberally. His admonition would appear today to apply with particular relevance to the Crown corporation. Parliament and even the responsible Minister must show confidence in the corporation by refraining from breathing down the neck of management. On the other hand, the Canadian system of parliamentary government can impose responsibility only on the Ministers of the Crown. Hence the public corporation cannot be used as a means of evading ultimate responsibility. Where to draw the line between the claims of managerial autonomy and the claims of parliamentary responsibility remains for Canada a problem that has been seriously posed rather than solved by contemporary use of the public corporation.

52. See comments of the Auditor-General before Public Accounts Committee, *Minutes of Proceedings and Evidence*, 1947, pp. 439 *et seq.*

CHAPTER 13

FEDERAL PUBLIC CORPORATIONS
IN AUSTRALIA*

AUSTRALIA was a pioneer in the development of the public corporation. Since 1883, when the Victorian Railway Commissioners were established as a corporation, until the present day, both Commonwealth[1] and State Governments have created hundreds of statutory corporations for a multitude of purposes.

In *The Public Corporation* (edited by Professor W. Friedmann) Professor Sawer traces the early history of the public corporation in Australia and states (at pp. 12–13) that the advantages of a corporation claimed by those who were its advocates were as follows:

"Firstly, the technical legal advantages of a personality with perpetual succession, capable of suing and being sued by ordinary processes of law and of obtaining, owning and giving title to property (including land, shares, etc., where special formalities are required), free from the cumbrous and inappropriate restrictions and immunities of Crown law. . . . Secondly, the political advantage of administration free from the irrelevant issues of partisan politics at any time, with consequent ability to concentrate on short and long-term policies appropriate to the activity, and on technical and managerial efficiency. Thirdly, the administrative advantages of building up a personnel structure free from the rigidities of ordinary civil service rules, giving more emphasis to efficiency than to seniority, encouraging an *esprit de corps* within the organisation instead of resort to parliamentary pressure to gain advantages, and adopting classifications suitable to the technique of the activity. Fourthly, the possibility of representing in the control of the organisation various functional interests or outlooks appropriate to the activity—the technical expert, the statesman, the producer, the consumer and so forth. Fifthly, the advantage of removing from Parliament the temptation to indulge in log-rolling on behalf of consumers, beneficiaries, employees, and others. Sixthly, the possibility of careful accounting practice designed to run the activity as economically as possible, and where it is a revenue-earning activity, to run it on 'business' lines, that is making its income pay for interest on capital, depreciation, reserves for development and running costs."

* By Professor Leslie Zines, Faculty of Law, Australian National University.
1. In this paper "Commonwealth" refers to the Government of the Commonwealth of Australia, *i.e.* the Federal, as distinct from the State, Government.

Since Victoria introduced legislation to allow for actions for tort against the Crown, the first reason given by Professor Sawer is no longer a wholly valid one in Australia. In any case, the question whether a body is entitled to the privileges and immunities of the Crown depends less on whether it is a corporate entity than on the extent to which it is subject to Government control. The third advantage mentioned has been affected in recent years by requirements that the corporation obtain the approval of the Public Service Board before creating various positions within its organisation and by direct and indirect Treasury control. The fourth reason has only limited application in the federal sphere in Australia: the consumer is rarely represented on statutory commissions or boards and functional representation seems to be a policy pursued only in connection with organised marketing schemes for agricultural products. Of the remaining three alleged advantages we find that, in the case of Australian public corporations, Governmental control is such that the principles involved are (at least potentially) capable of being undermined by executive action.

Although the corporation has been resorted to by all Governments in Australia it is proposed in this paper to concentrate only on corporations established by the Commonwealth.

Since the nineteenth century the various Acts setting up corporations, and amendments to those Acts from time to time, have reflected the conflict between the democratic object of Governmental accountability to Parliament and the opposing object of such legislation, namely, independence from political control. As appears to be the case elsewhere, the trend in Australia, at any rate since World War II, has been towards greater Government control and less freedom of action for the corporation. This has not however always been the result of any defined or consistent policy. The policy decisions have been more or less *ad hoc* and it was not until 1955 that a Parliamentary body— the Public Accounts Committee of the Commonwealth Parliament—gave any systematic thought to the general question of the administration and constitution of public corporations.

The various provisions have been enacted haphazardly and the parliamentary debates throw little light on the reasons for the various types and methods of parliamentary or Ministerial control.

Statutory controls on the freedom of action of corporations increased considerably between 1941 and 1949 while there was a Federal Labour Government. This was consistent with the general philosophy of the Australian Labour Party. However, there has been no sudden reversal of this general trend by the Liberal-Country Party Governments which have been in office in the Commonwealth since the end of 1949.

Some of the major corporations established by Commonwealth law are as follows:

(a) Marketing boards for primary products: boards have been established to control the export of apples and pears, canned fruits, dairy produce, dried fruits, eggs, honey, meat, wheat and wine.

(b) Industrial or commercial undertakings: corporations under this heading include the Australian National Airlines Commission, the Commissioner for Railways, the Overseas Telecommunications Commission, the Snowy Mountains Hydro-electric Authority, the Australian Coastal Shipping Commission and the Commonwealth Serum Laboratories.

(c) Credit and financial agencies: these include the Commonwealth Banking Corporation, the Reserve Bank of Australia and the Commonwealth Export Payments Insurance Corporation.

(d) Regulatory and planning agencies: these include the Australian Stevedoring Industry Authority, the Commonwealth Bureau of Roads, the Repatriation Commission, the National Capital Development Commission, the National Standards Commission, the River Murray Commission and the Australian Broadcasting Control Board.

(e) Research and academic bodies: these include the Australian National University, the Australian Institute of Aboriginal Studies, the Commonwealth Scientific and Industrial Research Organisation and the Canberra College of Advanced Education. (To some extent the Australian Atomic Energy Commission might be put both in this category and in category (b).)

(f) Miscellaneous corporations such as the Australian Broadcasting Commission and the Australian Tourist Commission.

CONSTITUTIVE CONTROLS

Commonwealth Acts provide for many forms of control by the Government, or a Minister, over the activities of the corporations. Some of these controls are exercised through the actual setting up of the corporation and the appointment of the members of the corporation. Members of the agencies are usually appointed by the Governor-General for fixed periods, often from three to five years. The office is deemed to be vacated if the member becomes bankrupt, fails to attend three consecutive meetings without leave, or fails to comply with provisions relating to the disclosure of any personal commercial interest in the activities of the agency. The Governor-General[2] is usually given power to terminate the appointment of a member on the grounds of "inability, inefficiency or misbehaviour."

(The Commissioner of Railways is in an exceptional position here. He can be removed only by an address praying for his removal being presented to the Governor-General by both Houses of Parliament. The Minister is given a right to suspend when Parliament is not sitting for "inability, inefficiency,

2. Reference to the "Governor-General" means the Governor-General acting on the advice of the Government of the day.

mismanagement or misbehaviour or refusal or neglect or failure to carry out any of the provisions"[3] of the Act.)

The marketing boards differ from most other corporations in that the members include representatives of the relevant industries. There is also a Commonwealth representative appointed by the Minister. In some cases, the board also includes a member representing employees.

DIRECTION CONTROLS

Sometimes corporations are given powers which are generally subject to the direction of the Minister. This is so in the case of most of the marketing boards and the Australian Atomic Energy Commission. In a few instances the general control of the Minister is limited to matters of policy. With regard to most other corporations, however, there is no provision for general Ministerial control but the exercise of particular powers may require the approval of the Minister or may be subject to his direction. The matters in respect of which ministerial approval or consent is required under the various Acts are as follows:

(a) Entering into contracts for the supply of materials for a consideration exceeding a certain amount. The amount will often vary with the age of the constitutive Act or the type of undertaking. In some cases the consent of the Minister is required to dispose of land. Ministerial approval is often required before the corporation can enter into long-term leases.

(b) Staffing: the relevant Acts, as a rule, contain a general clause giving the corporation power to appoint such officers as it thinks fit. Provision in most of the Acts is made to exclude the operation of the Public Service Arbitration Act 1920–69.[4] A common provision is that which requires that the creation of positions with a salary over a fixed amount (varying from $5,000 to $7,500) shall require Ministerial approval. In some cases provision is made for entry into the service of the corporation by open competitive examination. A provision requiring such examination was inserted in the Australian Broadcasting Act 1942 as a result of an enquiry by a Joint Parliamentary Committee into the Australian Broadcasting Commission. The conclusion of the Committee was: " . . . [I]n order to ensure that all classes of the community may be afforded prejudice-proof opportunities of entering the service of the Commission in these positions [that is positions involving routine and administrative functions], we are of [the] opinion . . . that open competitive examination should be stipulated. . . . "[5] Similar provisions were made applicable to the

3. Commonwealth Railways Act 1917–68, s. 12 (2).
4. This Act provides for the appointment of an arbitrator who has power to determine all matters submitted to him by public service organisations, relating to salaries, wages, rates of pay or terms and conditions of service or employment of officers and employees of the public service.
5. *Report by the Joint Parliamentary Committee on Broadcasting*, (1942) p. 24.

services of the Overseas Telecommunications Commission, the Commonwealth Banks and, in respect of clerical positions, the Australian National Airlines Commission. Acts of more recent years do not include such provisions.

In the case of a number of corporations, including the Snowy Mountains
Hydro-electric Authority, the Australian Atomic Energy Commission, the
Export Payments Insurance Commission and the National Capital Development Commission, the corporations are empowered to determine terms and
conditions of employment, but such determinations are subject to the approval
of the Public Service Board, which of course ensures similarity of salary and
conditions with ordinary members of the Public Service. In the case of commercial and financial corporations conducting undertakings in competition
with private enterprise, such as the Australian Coastal Shipping Commission,
the Australian National Airlines Commission and the Commonwealth Banks,
approval of the Public Service Board in respect of terms and conditions of
employment is not required; however, Ministerial approval is necessary for
the payment of salaries in excess of a specified sum. What is sought in these
cases is not comparability with public servants but with employees in the same
industry. In Australia this is achieved by making the corporations subject to
the general industrial arbitration machinery.

In respect of a number of corporations (other than the "competitive" corporations), tribunals are provided to deal with appeals in matters of promotion
or dismissal.

(c) Directions to supply goods and services: power is sometimes given to
the Governor-General or to the Minister to require various goods or services
to be supplied. Here we strike a conflict between two aims. The power given
to the Government to direct in this regard is of course based on the view that,
whatever the commercial aspects of the matter, it is desirable, for political or
social reasons that the corporation supply the goods or services required. At
the same time one of the reasons for setting up the corporation separate from
the Public Service is to ensure that the corporation will run the undertaking
in a manner similar to other commercial concerns. In a number of the Acts,
the resolution of this problem is attempted by what has been called a "recoup
provision"[6] which was first inserted in the Victorian Railways Commissioners
Act of the last century. One such provision is in the Australian National Airlines Act 1945–66, section 25, which provides as follows:

"25 (1) The Minister may, if he is satisfied that it is in the interests of
the development of Australia so to do, direct the Commission to establish,
alter or continue to maintain any interstate airline service or territorial
airline service specified by the Minister.

(2) If, at the direction of the Minister, the Commission establishes,
alters or continues to maintain an airline service and satisfies the Minister

6. These provisions are discussed by R. L. Wettenhall in *Public Administration* 391
(London).

that the airline service so established, altered or continued to be maintained has been operated at a loss in any financial year and if, after due provision is made for reserves, a loss results in that financial year from the whole of the operations of the Commission, the Commission shall be entitled to be reimbursed by the Commonwealth to the extent of the first-mentioned loss or to the extent of the second-mentioned loss, whichever is the less."[7]

(*d*) Reports and auditing: all the corporations have a duty to open and maintain accounts with a prescribed bank. They are all subject to audit by the Auditor-General; and they are all required to submit annual reports to the Minister.

FINANCIAL CONTROLS

The capital of the corporation is usually defined as being the value of the assets transferred to the corporation by the Commonwealth and any other amounts which are appropriated by Parliament. One type of provision for payments by the corporation to the Commonwealth is that contained in section 29 of the Australian Coastal Shipping Commission Act 1956–69 which is as follows:

"29 (1) Interest is not payable to the Commonwealth on the capital of the Commission but the Commission shall pay to the Commonwealth, out of the profits of the Commission for a financial year, such amount as the Minister, with the concurrence of the Treasurer, determines.

(2) The capital of the Commission is repayable to the Commonwealth at such times and in such amounts as the Minister, with the concurrence of the Treasurer, determines.

(3) In the making of a determination under either of the last two preceding subsections, regard shall be had to any advice which the Commission has furnished to the Minister in relation to the financial affairs of the Commission."[8]

In other Acts provision is made for the Commonwealth to pay money to the corporation on such terms and conditions as the Treasurer determines and those terms and conditions may provide for repayment to the Commonwealth of the whole or part of moneys paid to the corporation.[9]

Different financial methods have been adopted in relation to different corporations depending upon the nature of those corporations. The differences often arise not from specific provisions of the Act but from the discretion

7. Similar provisions are contained in ss. 43, 44 of the Commonwealth Railways Act 1917–68; s. 17 of the Australian Coastal Shipping Commission Act 1956–69 and ss. 19 and 38 of the Commonwealth Serum Laboratories Act 1961–66.
8. Similar provisions are contained in s. 30 of the Australian National Airlines Act 1945–66 and s. 33 of the Commonwealth Serum Laboratories Act 1961–66.
9. See s. 23 of the Export Payments Insurance Corporation Act 1956–66.

given to the Treasurer for repayment of capital and for interest payments. Where, as in the case of the Airlines Commission and the Coastal Shipping Commission, the corporations compete with private enterprise, the provisions for payment of interest and the repayment of capital are presumably designed to ensure fair competition.[10]

The borrowing powers of corporations are considerably restricted by Commonwealth Acts. They may borrow money from the Commonwealth or, for temporary purposes, on overdraft from a prescribed bank. Recently, however, it has become usual to insert a provision permitting borrowing from other sources with the consent of the Treasurer and, in some cases, the Minister.[11]

The liability of the various corporations for taxation varies. The Australian Coastal Shipping Commission is subject to all Commonwealth taxes but not to State taxes; the Australian National Airlines Commission is liable to pay all Commonwealth taxes and such other rates, taxes or charges as the Minister specifies (s. 37). The Snowy Mountains Hydro-electric Authority is subject to Commonwealth taxation other than income tax but is not subject to any State taxation (s. 29). The Overseas Telecommunications Commission is in a similar position (s. 50). The Australian Broadcasting Commission is not subject to any taxes under either Commonwealth or State law (s. 72).[12]

In recent years, there has been greater Governmental control over the expenditure of public corporations than was hitherto the case. For example, before 1948 the Australian Broadcasting Act provided for an Australian Broadcasting Commission Fund into which was paid a proportion of the money collected by the Government as listeners' licence fees (s. 27). The Commission had unrestricted access to this Fund which was expected to finance the bulk of its activities. Under amending legislation in 1948 the Australian Broadcasting Commission Fund was abolished and the Commission is now financed by annual Parliamentary appropriations. The Commission must now submit annual estimates to the Minister in such form as the Minister directs (s. 68). Section 69 (3) provides: "No moneys shall be

10. T. H. Kewley, "Some General Features of the Statutory Corporation in Australia" (1957) 16 *Public Administration* 3 (Sydney). In the case of the Airlines Commission, amendments to the legislation in 1961 require the Minister to determine a profit target. The Minister is to determine a percentage rate on capital which will "represent a reasonable return to the Commonwealth from the operations of the Commission" (s. 32). This is a result of the present system of rationalised competition between public and private airlines in Australia.

11. For example, Australian Coastal Shipping Commission Act 1956–69, ss. 30 and 31; Overseas Telecommunications Act 1946–68, s. 43; Australian National Airlines Act 1945–66, s. 31; Commonwealth Serum Laboratories Act 1961–66, s. 34.

12. In *Australian Coastal Shipping Commission* v. *O'Reilly* (1961–1962) 107 C.L.R. 46, it was held that the Commonwealth had power to exempt corporations which it had validly created from State taxation. The extent to which corporations are subject to taxation presumably depends on whether they are required to be run as a "commercial enterprise" and further whether they are competing with private enterprise. Even taking these considerations into account however it is hard to determine a consistent policy from the above varied provisions.

expended by the Commission otherwise than in accordance with the estimates of expenditure approved by the Treasurer."[13]

A similar provision is in the Atomic Energy Act 1953–66 (s. 26 (2)).

Usually there is a provision to the effect that the net profits of the corporation are to be applied in such manner as the Minister, after considering any recommendation of the corporation and with the concurrence of the Treasurer, directs.[14]

CONTROL OF POLICY

As mentioned above, most of the marketing boards of the Commonwealth are given functions which are expressly subject to any direction of the Minister. This is also true of the Australian Atomic Energy Commission. In law there would seem to be no limit on the matters in respect of which the Minister may give directions in these circumstances. In the case of many other corporations, the power of the Minister or the Government to control the corporation has been limited by statute to the express matters which have been dealt with above. Of course, by virtue of control over these matters it may be possible for the Minister indirectly to control the policy of the corporation, especially where the corporation is dependent for the major part of its funds on annual appropriations by the Parliament.

There has lately been an attempt in Commonwealth Acts to make a distinction between matters of policy and matters of day-to-day management, the former being under the control of the Minister. For example, section 17 (1) of the Australian Tourist Commission Act 1967 empowers the Minister to give directions to the Commission "with respect to matters of policy, including directions with respect to the general nature and extent of the operations of the Commission."

The distinction between matters of policy and detailed administration can of course give rise to considerable disagreement between the Minister and the corporation. It might be useful for the statute to give some guidelines by indicating what matters are not to be regarded as concerning general policy. This is done to some extent in the case of the Export Payments Insurance Corporation, which is required to receive the approval of the Minister before adopting a policy with respect to a number of matters such as the classes of contracts of insurance into which the Corporation will enter and the nature of the risks that may be covered under contracts of insurance with the Corporation. The section, however, goes on to provide that nothing shall be construed as requiring the approval of the Minister to the Corporation entering into any particular contract of insurance or giving a particular guarantee.[15]

13. Broadcasting and Television Act 1942–69.
14. For example, s. 33 (3) of the Australian Coastal Shipping Commission Act 1956–69; s. 48 of the Overseas Telecommunications Act 1946–68; s. 38 (3) of the Australian National Airlines Act 1945–66.
15. Export Payments Insurance Corporation Act 1956–66, s. 11.

An enquiry made some years ago by the Committee of Public Accounts emphasises among other things the desirability of defining, as precisely as circumstances will admit, the controlling power of the Minister or the Government. This Committee is a Joint Committee of both Houses of Parliament. Its duties are to examine the accounts of the receipts and expenditure of the Commonwealth and to report to both Houses with such comment as it thinks fit any items or matters in those accounts, etc. or any circumstances connected with them to which the Committee is of the opinion that the attention of Parliament should be directed. In 1954, the Committee commenced investigation into the accounts of the Australian Aluminium Production Commission which was a statutory corporation consisting of representatives of the Commonwealth and Tasmania. The Committee decided that its investigations into the accounts of the Commission had called for a closer examination of the nature and characters of the statutory corporation. The report[16] of the Committee deals with two major problems:

(a) the general question of the degree of control that a Government should have over a corporation, and

(b) the problem of clearly placing responsibility on defined persons or bodies so as to prevent confusion as to the lines and limits of this responsibility.

The Commission was a corporation peculiar to federal countries in that it was established under both Commonwealth and State Acts.[17] The members of the Commission were appointed by the Governor-General. By virtue of amendments made in 1952 four of the members were to "represent" the Commonwealth and one was nominated by the State to "represent" the State. The Act required the Commission to keep its accounts in a form approved by the Treasurer. A Treasury official was appointed a member of the Commission. The Commission's accounting fell into arrears and the Auditor-General refused to certify the Commission's accounts. The Chairman of the Commission maintained in evidence that on the question of accounts, the Commission was entitled to rely and did in fact rely on the Treasury representative for guidance in matters of finance and accounting. The Solicitor-General advised the Committee that the Treasury official as a member of the Commission had no special responsibilities for the financial or accounting arrangements of the Commission. His status, functions and responsibilities were no different from those of any other member. The Committee pointed to the fact that the Treasury official as a member of the corporation faced a most difficult problem involving a conflict of loyalties. They advised that if the status, functions and responsibility of a Treasury official were no different

16. Commonwealth Parliamentary Public Accounts Committee, 21st and 22nd Reports, Canberra 1955.
17. Aluminium Industry Act 1944 (Commonwealth); Aluminium Industry Agreement Act 1944 (Tasmania).

from those of any other member, there was little purpose in such an appointment. Indeed in this case some confusion resulted because of the presence of the Treasury official.

The more important question, however, was the relationship of the members of the Commission to the Government. This question was also the subject of a written opinion by the Solicitor-General. The Solicitor-General noted that four out of the five members of the Commission were appointed not as individuals chosen to conduct a business enterprise but as "representatives of the Commonwealth" and that they were therefore undoubtedly subject to instruction from the Minister on behalf of the Government. He concluded therefore that if one looked at the legal position alone, the Minister was in a position to make himself just as fully responsible for the operation of the Commission, if he wished, as he was for the affairs of his Department. He then went on however to refer to what he called "constitutional practice". He summarised this constitutional practice as follows:

"(i) that the establishment by Parliament of a public corporation rather than a Department of State as the chosen instrument for the conduct of a business undertaking implies an intention that the corporation should enjoy a substantial measure of freedom from political direction and control;

(ii) that Ministerial control over the public corporation should be restricted to matters of general policy and principle and should not extend to the details of management;

(iii) that in order to promote business efficiency and flexibility it is necessary to accept some derogation from the complete measure of Ministerial accountability to Parliament which is insisted on, in the constitutional systems of the British Commonwealth, in relation to the Departments of State."[18]

The Solicitor-General's view therefore seems to have been that while, legally speaking, the Minister could direct the day-to-day operations of the Commission, constitutional practice prevented him from so doing.

Professor Webb[19] has written that, for a layman, the obvious difficulty was to ascertain the status of the body of principles to which the Solicitor-General referred and also to determine the content of the principles. For the lawyer the task is no easier. The British lawyer is familiar with the notion of "constitutional conventions" which refer to a consistent usage over a period of time that has acquired normative force. In my opinion, however, it is extremely doubtful whether in this area there could be said to be any firm "conventions" in regard to Ministerial control. Experience seems to show that much depends

18. Commonwealth Parliamentary Public Accounts Committee, 21st and 22nd Reports, p. 84
19. (1955) 14 *Public Administration* 158, 161 (Sydney).

on the personality of the Minister. This is of course true even in respect of ordinary Government departments. At one extreme some Ministers are of the "rubber stamp" variety; at the other they may seek to control directly every aspect of the department's functions. If a Minister has general statutory control over a public corporation, the most that can be said is that the very existence of the separate corporation may inhibit his interfering as much as he would with his own department. In any case, it is arguable whether a Minister with *legal* control over a corporation would not be acting in dereliction of duty if he stood by when he was aware of gross mismanagement of the day-to-day affairs of the corporation.[20]

The general confusion that arose in respect of the Aluminium Commission makes it clear that it is unwise, at any rate in the case of commercial undertakings, simply to make a corporation in general terms subject to Ministerial control. Apart from the fact that the degree of control will depend much on how the Minister views his functions, the general vagueness of the power given may result in confusion as to the lines of authority and responsibility. It is not a field in which it is safe to rely on any supposed constitutional conventions.

DISAGREEMENT BETWEEN THE CORPORATION AND THE MINISTER

Generally speaking when an Act requires the approval of the Minister for the corporation to take any particular action or if the corporation in respect of that action is subject to the direction of the Minister, the Minister of course has the last word. In a few cases, however, disagreement between the Minister and the corporation is required to be referred to, and decided by, the Governor-General-in-Council—which as a practical matter means the Cabinet. For example, the National Capital Development Commission is charged under the Act with undertaking and carrying out the planning, development and construction of the City of Canberra as the National Capital of the Commonwealth. Section 12 of the National Capital Development Commission Act 1957–60 requires that the Commissioner keep the Minister informed of the decisions of the Commission with respect to matters of policy; if the Minister and the Commission disagree they are required to endeavour to reach agreement and if they are unable to reach agreement, the Governor-General may by order determine the policy to be adopted by the Commission. A similar provision first appeared in Commonwealth legislation in section 43 of the Commonwealth Railways Act 1917–68. Similarly, in the case of the Government banks, *i.e.* the Reserve Bank (which is the central bank) and the various Commonwealth banks, provision is made for differences of opinion between the bank board and the Treasurer on matters of policy to be submitted to the Governor-General which may by order determine the policy to

20. *Ibid.*

be adopted by the bank. The Treasurer is then required to inform the board that the Government accepts responsibility for the adoption by the bank of that policy and will take such action (if any) within its powers as the Government considers to be necessary by reason of the adoption of that policy. Papers relating to the difference of opinion are required to be tabled by the Treasurer before each House of Parliament.

These provisions are however exceptional. A different form of provision is that in section 11 of the Export Payments Insurance Corporation Act 1956–66 which provides that before adopting a policy with respect to a number of matters the Corporation is required to submit the policy for the approval of the Minister and not to adopt the policy without his approval. Where there is disagreement between the Corporation and the Minister, they are required to endeavour to reach agreement but if agreement is not reached the Minister may by writing determine the policy to be adopted by the Corporation.

PARLIAMENTARY CONTROL

Although Parliament has wide powers to legislate on the attributes of a public corporation, its control, after the enactment, of the activities of the corporation is as a practical matter very limited indeed. The Commonwealth does not have any special parliamentary committee to supervise the operations of these corporations and the role of the Public Accounts Committee is limited. The various Acts require the corporations to render annual reports and financial statements to the Minister who is usually required to table these in Parliament. Similarly the Auditor-General's report is required to be tabled in Parliament. These can provide the occasion for parliamentary debate but this rarely happens.

However, neither the House of Representatives nor the Senate has adopted the British practice of permitting parliamentary questions relating to public corporations only on matters within the responsibility of the Minister or the Government. Questions are constantly being asked on the day-to-day activities of these corporations. Almost invariably, the Minister refers the question to the corporation and the answer is given. It has been suggested that this might appear to result in part from the fact that there are so many points at which the Minister has been granted powers in relation to the corporation's activities.[21]

21. Kewley, *op. cit.* p. 25. On one occasion in 1956, the Treasurer concluded a question with the statement that "It is . . . a question of some difficulty as to how far the [Commonwealth] bank should be called upon to provide detailed information on matters affecting its day-to-day management. Obviously a limit must be observed if the degree of independent responsibility conferred by statute upon the bank is to be maintained" (Commonwealth Parliamentary Debates (House of Representatives) March 6, 1956, p. 543). This statement of the Treasurer does not seem to have stopped questions on the day-to-day administration of corporations.

JUDICIAL CONTROL

As in the United Kingdom, the courts can control statutory corporations through the doctrine of *ultra vires*. The courts can ensure that the corporation only exercises powers which it is authorised to exercise under the Act creating it. Professor Garner has stated that when the powers conferred upon a public corporation are drawn very widely in the legislation it becomes almost impossible for a court to declare an action of the corporation as being *ultra vires*. He points to the fact that in the United Kingdom a number of Acts empower a corporation "to do such things as may seem to them necessary and expedient for the exercise of" the powers granted.[22] On other occasions, while there is not a subjective element in the definition of the powers, they are defined in such a vague and general way that it would be difficult to exercise judicial control.

To some extent, different considerations are involved in the drafting of Acts of the Commonwealth Parliament. This is because the Commonwealth is a government of limited powers. It can only enact legislation with respect to one of the specific heads of power given to it under the Constitution. It is not possible therefore for Parliament to give to a corporation the power to do anything which *seems to the corporation* to be necessary for carrying out an activity, if legislative power with respect to that activity is circumscribed by the Constitution. As Parliament cannot conclusively determine the limits of its own power, it cannot give such authority to the Government or to an administrative body.

If Parliament purported to give the corporation powers beyond those possessed by the Parliament the Act would be declared invalid or else the High Court would under section 15A of the Acts Interpretation Act 1901–66 "read down" the statute so that the corporation would only have the power which Parliament could confer upon it.

For example, the Commonwealth has power over trade and commerce with other countries or among the States. It has no general power over the internal trade of a State. The Commonwealth therefore does not have authority to empower an airline corporation to conduct airline services between places in the same State unless it is incidental to an inter-State journey.[23]

Section 19 of the Australian National Airlines Act 1945–66, therefore, limits the functions and duties of the Commission to operating airline services between any place in a State and any place in another State (under the commerce power) or between places within a Territory or between a place in a

22. *Ante*, p. 12.
23. Under s. 51 (xxxvii) of the Constitution matters may be referred to the Parliament of the Commonwealth by the Parliaments of the States and under s. 19A of the Australian National Airlines Act 1945–66 the Commission may establish intra-State airline services where a State has referred the matter to the Commonwealth.

Territory and another part of the Commonwealth (under the territories power), or for the transport of mails by air between any places in Australia (under the postal power). The need for the Commonwealth to so limit the operations of a statutory corporation gives more opportunity for judicial intervention.

Where the function given is clearly within constitutional power, however, the statutory corporation is usually given power to "do all that is necessary or convenient to be done for, or as incidental to, in relation to, or in connexion with," the particular function. This language is very broad and gives little opportunity for the courts to supervise the activities of a corporation where they are not beyond constitutional power. Nevertheless, challenges to actions of statutory corporations are made and those actions are sometimes declared *ultra vires*. A recent example is *Helicopter Utilities Pty. Ltd.* v. *Australian National Airlines Commission*.[24] In that case the Airlines Commission and the Commonwealth entered into a contract for the hire by the Commonwealth of helicopters over an extended period for use on an Antarctic expedition. The New South Wales Supreme Court held that the Commission had no power under the Act to enter into the contract. The Court held that while the defendant might operate helicopters as an incident to its regular airline services and make use of them in other ways to avoid waste, the use of helicopters in the instant case was not incidental to the operation of an airline service. There is little doubt that the Commonwealth Parliament could if it wished have given the Commission power to enter into the contract. The case therefore rested upon lack of statutory power rather than absence of constitutional power in the Parliament.

One of the major problems in relation to the challenging of actions of statutory corporations is the question of *locus standi*. Recently in *Logan Downs Pty. Ltd.* v. *Federal Commissioner of Taxation*[25] the High Court held that a mere taxpayer did not have standing to seek a declaration that certain powers to be exercised by the Wool Board were invalid.

The existence of a federal system in Australia provides another means of challenging the powers of statutory corporations if they go beyond constitutional power. The High Court recognised from an early date that the Attorney-General of a State was competent to sue for a declaration and injunction in relation to invalid Commonwealth legislation. In *Attorney-General* v. *The Commonwealth*[26] the High Court allowed a suit brought by the Attorney-General for the State of Victoria at the relation of the Victorian Chamber of Manufactures against the Commonwealth claiming a declaration that the carrying on of the business of making non-military uniforms at the

24. (1961) 80 W.N. (N.S.W.) 48. The application for an interlocutory injunction was refused because of doubts whether the plaintiff, as a competitor of the defendant, had standing to maintain the suit.
25. [1965] A.L.R. 954.
26. (1935) 52 C.L.R. 533.

Commonwealth clothing factory was beyond the powers of the Commonwealth.[27]

Generally, however, while the corporations can be prevented from acting *ultra vires*, it is difficult to ensure by judicial remedies that the corporation will provide the services that it is required to provide under the Act. Although the corporations are usually placed under a duty to perform certain functions, the duty is expressed in very general terms so that the only appropriate remedy—mandamus—could rarely be used to enforce the duty. It would be very difficult for example to obtain a writ to compel the Airlines Commission to fulfil its duty to "exercise the powers conferred by the last preceding subsection, as fully and adequately as may be necessary to satisfy the need for the services specified in that subsection, and to carry out the purposes of this Act."[28]

THE USE BY GOVERNMENT OF PUBLIC COMPANIES

On occasions, Australian Governments, instead of setting up statutory corporations, have used the device of incorporation, under the Companies Act of a State, for the purpose of pursuing some public objective. In Australia, the two best known are Qantas Airways Ltd. and Commonwealth Hostels Ltd. Both of these are companies registered under the Companies Act of a State. Qantas Airways Ltd. is Australia's international airline and it is fully-owned and controlled by the Commonwealth Government. Commonwealth Hostels Ltd. manages most of the Commonwealth-owned hostels for migrants and for public servants.

The public company is of course particularly useful in the case of what are called "mixed undertakings" where Governmental and private interests provide the capital of an undertaking and both share in its direction. Some years ago this form of undertaking operated in the case of Amalgamated Wireless (Australia) Ltd. and Commonwealth Oil Refineries Ltd. When the Liberal-Country Party Government came into power, however, they sold the Governmental shares in each of those companies and they are now purely private enterprise. In the case of Qantas, this company started off as purely private enterprise but its shares were acquired by the Commonwealth Government.

As a matter of policy the use of public companies by Governments should be avoided. The registration of a company provides far less chance of debate than in the case of a statutory corporation, where the terms of the Bill are

27. In *The Commonwealth* v. *Australian Commonwealth Shipping Board* (1926) 39 C.L.R. 1, a suit was brought successfully by the Commonwealth Attorney-General on the relation of the Secretary to the New South Wales Chamber of Manufactures against the Australian Commonwealth Shipping Board, a statutory corporation, for a declaration that the Board had no power to enter into an agreement with a municipal council to supply, deliver and erect on municipal land fifteen turbo-alternator sets.
28. Section 19 (2) of the Australian National Airlines Act 1945–66.

subject to Parliamentary scrutiny and discussion. None of these "democratic" advantages of a statutory corporation is offset by any greater efficiency. The form of the public company, from this point of view, seems to have no advantages at all over that of the statutory corporation.

In Australia, however, it does not seem that the commercial corporation whose shares are all State-owned gives rise to any special problem of control so far as the Government is concerned. In the case of Commonwealth Hostels Ltd. for example, the memorandum and articles of association provide for appointment of directors by the Minister and that a director is to cease to hold office upon being required in writing by the Minister to resign. The accounts of the company are audited by the Auditor-General. A contract between the company and the Commonwealth provides that the company comply with any directions of the Minister as to "the policy to be adopted by the company in carrying out its undertaking as to the management and control of the hostels."[29]

DEFINITION OF A PUBLIC CORPORATION

Professor Garner has tentatively defined a public corporation as "a legal entity established normally by Parliament and always under legal authority, usually in the form of a special statute, charged with the duty of carrying out specified Governmental functions in the national interest, those functions being confined to a comparatively restricted field, and subjected to some degree of control by the executive, while the corporation remains juristically an independent entity not directly responsible to Parliament."[30] In one respect, I think this definition is open to criticism. It seems to me that the element in the definition stating that the functions of a public corporation are "governmental" introduces an unnecessary degree of vagueness. Australian judges and lawyers have in recent years criticised or at any rate played down the dichotomy between functions that are "inalienable functions of Government" and those that are not.[31] What functions are regarded as "Governmental" clearly depends on the traditions of the country or the political philosophy of the individual making the distinction. For example, the function of providing railway services in Australia has, for over a century, been regarded as truly Governmental in character. If the test were whether the service conducted was analogous to other services provided by private enterprise then a conclusion might be drawn that running a railway was not a Governmental function. If on the other hand, the test is whether the particular service could, from a practical point of view, have been conducted by

29. The above facts regarding this company are obtained from the High Court's judgment in *The Commonwealth* v. *Bogle* (1952–53) 89 C.L.R. 229.
30. Garner, *ante*, p. 4
31. For example, the High Court judgment in the *Professional Engineers' Case* (1959) 107 C.L.R. 208.

private enterprise than it is clear that in Australia the railway system belongs to the category of "Governmental functions."[32]

In any case it would seem that bodies such as the Australian Broadcasting Control Board and other regulatory corporations and the Repatriation Commission and similar bodies concerned with hearing cases relating to the payment of pensions and other social services would, on any test, be considered "Governmental."

THE ADVANTAGES OF THE PUBLIC CORPORATION

The question whether there should be some degree of independence from Ministerial control is not necessarily the same problem as whether there should be a corporation. As Professor Sawer has pointed out[33] the tendency in Australia has been to create a corporation where a degree of independence from Government control is required. The question whether there should be independence and, if so, to what degree, is however the more important one. Whether a corporate form is desirable gives rise to less serious matters of policy. *Assuming there is to be a degree of independence,* whether a corporation should be created will depend largely on the functions that it is intended to confer. In the case of a commercial undertaking for example, the corporate form is obviously as convenient in a public enterprise as it is in a private enterprise. On the other hand, many of the regulatory agencies could probably carry on their functions just as well without being created a corporation, that is by the Commonwealth simply creating a board and giving it independent powers.

The corporate form will usually be more convenient where the agency is in the possession of a considerable amount of property or is engaged in commercial transactions.

But what are the reasons for placing an agency—corporate or otherwise—outside the normal civil service system and free to some degree from Governmental control?

The very nature of the institution set up may require freedom from Government control. The Australian National University, although a statutory corporation, could hardly be termed a "university" if it was generally subject to Government control. However, even in the case of a university, some controls might be appropriate. In the case of the Australian National University the council cannot, except with the approval of the Governor-

32. In *The Federated Amalgamated Government Railway and Tramway Service Association* v. *The New South Wales Railway Traffic Employes Association* (1906) 4 C.L.R. 488, the High Court said in reply to an argument that the business of common carriers was not a part of any recognised branch of government, legislative, judicial and executive, that "in the year 1900, when the Constitution was adopted, the construction and maintenance of railways was in fact generally regarded as a governmental function in all the Australian colonies . . . " (p. 539).
33. W. Friedmann, *The Public Corporation*, p. 42.

General, alienate, mortgage, charge or demise any lands of the University except by way of lease for any term not exceeding twenty-one years. The statutes of the University are required to be approved by the Governor-General. The council of the University is required to transmit to the Governor-General each year a report of the proceedings of the University containing a true and detailed account of the income and expenditure of the University during the year, audited in such manner as the Treasurer directs. A copy of each such report is laid before both Houses of Parliament.

A corporation or other independent body may also be useful in two opposing situations: first, where it is desired that representatives of sectional interests should manage the enterprise and, secondly, where it is desired to ensure that a particular institution should not fall prey to sectional interests.

In Australia, the "representative principle" is adopted in the case of marketing boards. To some extent it may also be seen to operate in the case of the Repatriation Commission. The major function of this Commission is to deal with claims for war pensions. Although the members of the Commission are appointed by the Governor-General, provision is made to ensure that one of the Commissioners is to be appointed from a list submitted by the Returned Servicemen's League.

The second situation is involved where freedom of speech and information require that those managing any medium such as a newspaper or broadcasting or television service should be free from political control. The most obvious example in Australia is of course the Australian Broadcasting Commission. The reliance of the Commission on annual appropriations however suggests opportunities for indirect control. Nevertheless, the Act makes a separation between matters of control over staffing, contracts, finance and so on and control over the programmes of the Commission.[34]

In a Federation such as Australia, the statutory corporation is the most appropriate vehicle for joint Commonwealth/State activities. The Aluminium Commission referred to above was of this nature. The River Murray Commission and the Joint Coal Board also come within this category. The departmental structure and ordinary principles of responsible governments cannot be easily fitted into a state of affairs where two different Governments and the laws of at least two different parliaments are necessary to give effective powers. The independent statutory corporation is an ideal instrument for receiving a variety of powers and functions from different sources. The danger of this form of "co-operative federalism" is that the political controls of the corporations are *of necessity* weaker than where the existence and functions of the body are entirely the creation of one Government and Parliament.

34. There are provisions for the Minister to require broadcasting and television stations by notice in writing to refrain from broadcasting any material and also provisions for enabling the Government to take control over matters to be broadcast in cases of an emergency. But these provisions apply to both the Commission and commercial broadcasting interests.

I understand that similar fears regarding the absence of political control have from time to time been expressed in relation to some of the institutions of the European Economic Community.

In the case of tribunals whose duty it is to assess facts or to give decisions or advice based on objective principles, it is in many cases obviously desirable that the body be free from Ministerial control so far as its main function is concerned. But it is not always necessary that the tribunal be made a corporation. In Australia the tendency has been to incorporate these bodies as in the case of the Tariff Board, the Repatriation Commission and the Stevedoring Industry Authority. On the other hand, the Commissioner of Trade Practices[35] is not incorporated.

In the case of commercial enterprises, much of the discussion in Britain has revolved around the question of nationalised industries. The most famous exposition of the need for statutory corporations in these cases is that of Herbert Morrison in his book *Government and Parliament*: "[I]f we establish the public corporation, it must be for certain reasons. What are they? They are that we seek to combine the principle of public ownership, of a broad but not too detailed public accountability, of a consciousness on the part of the undertaking that it is working for the nation and not for sectional interests, with the liveliness, initiative, and a considerable degree of the freedom of a quick-moving and progressive business enterprise."[36]

His view has since been questioned.[37] It is by no means obvious that an independent corporation will necessarily be more efficient than a Government department. The power of the Minister directly to control or indirectly to influence many of the corporations mentioned above is very great. Much depends on the character of the Ministers and the members appointed and their tenure of office. Some Government departments, for example, have high morale and enthusiastic officers; some public corporations are quite inefficient.

However, in Australia there are no corporations which run a nationalised industry in the sense that is referred to in Britain. Railways, postal and telephone services have traditionally been run by State monopolies. The postal and telephone services are administered by a Commonwealth department, while the railways are managed by Australia's oldest statutory corporations. These corporations are however not typical from the point of view of direction or control, staffing or financial methods. As one writer has stated: "The railways never quite escaped from the web of departmental tradition, even though they pointed the way for other public enterprises."[38]

Two major attempts to effect nationalisation in Australia were defeated as

35. Trade Practices Act 1965–69.
36. Oxford University Press 1954, pp. 282–283.
37. L. Webb, "Freedom and the Public Corporation" (1954) 13 *Public Administration* 101 (Sydney).
38. R. L. Wettenhall, *Railway Management and Politics in Victoria 1856–1906*, RIPA (ACT Group), May 1961, p. 90.

I

a result of the courts declaring them unconstitutional. The first attempt was in respect of inter-State airlines, the second in respect of banking.[39] So far as the "commercial" federal public corporations are concerned, they all compete with private enterprise, for example, the Commonwealth Trading Bank, the Australian National Airlines Commission and the Australian Coastal Shipping Commission. In the Australian States there are public corporations competing with private enterprise in diverse fields ranging from banking and insurance to brickfields, sawmills and engineering works. As many of these activities in both the public and private spheres are regulated by Government departments or agencies it is desirable that the public enterprises be separate from the ordinary departmental structure.

CONCLUSION

There is little doubt that, generally speaking, Governmental control over statutory corporations in Australia is in many respects greater than was the case say thirty years ago. The motive behind this is doubtless that referred to by A. H. Hanson,[40] namely that Governments are committed to economic planning. Open competition between public corporations and Governments or among public corporations for finance and, in a full employment economy, for staff is inconsistent with this general Government responsibility. Nevertheless the degree of independence to be given to a public corporation is the greatest problem of all. It is difficult to generalise having regard to the manifold purposes for which such corporations are used. So far as Commonwealth public corporations are concerned there seems to be little consistent principle or policy regarding the questions:

(a) whether there should be an independent body,
(b) whether that body should have corporate personality, and
(c) what forms of control should be exercised over the body.

One thing however does emerge from the Australian experience and that is that the statute setting up the corporation should define as precisely as possible the fields of control so that the respective responsibilities of the Government, the Minister and the corporation are not confused. Such confusion can only lead to inefficiency, the avoidance of which is supposed to be one of the reasons for establishing a corporation in the first place. Dr. Wettenhall has summed up the Australian experience as follows: "Not only in the Victorian Railways has the attempt to provide conditions of managerial freedom for public enterprises operating within a democratic governmental system produced new important problems quite apart from the old ones it was

39. *Australian National Airways Pty Ltd* v. *The Commonwealth* (1945) 71 C.L.R. 29; *Bank of New South Wales* v. *The Commonwealth* (1948) 76 C.L.R. 1 (High Court), (1949) 79 C.L.R. 497 (P.C.).
40. *Public Enterprise and Economic Development* (London) (1959).

intended to solve. The very nature of administration assumes that there will always be problems to solve, but difficulties are exacerbated when ill-defined or poorly understood limits of authority bring out jealousies and conflicts, and confuse the location of responsibility. The public corporation form is more prone to these faults than the department, whatever its other virtues. Some of the greatest upheavals in Australian public administration have been provided by crises affecting public corporations and their relations with the central Governments. . . . "41

41. *Railway Management and Politics in Victoria 1856–1906*, RIPA (ACT) p. 87.

CHAPTER 14

THE PUBLIC CORPORATION IN ISRAEL*

WITH one exception[1] public corporations began to develop in Israel only since the establishment of the State.[2] Within the twenty years, however, which have since passed, this modern combination of Government and business has developed considerably and now occupies an important place in the country's administration and economy. Such quick development in a State so young and so little developed as Israel tends to prove how vital and useful this form of organisation is for a modern welfare State. If the years past may be an indication for those to come, a further increase in the importance of the public corporation may safely be predicted.

1. CHARACTERISTICS OF A PUBLIC CORPORATION

Without venturing on any definition, I shall try to state the main features which seem to make up what is called a public corporation. Against this general description the particular picture of the Israeli scene may then be drawn.

"All public corporations have a dual nature; they are instruments of national policy, but they are autonomous units with legal independence and certain aspects of commercial undertakings."[3] As their very name indicates, they are, on the one hand, *corporations* and on the other hand *public bodies*.

As a corporation, *i.e.* a separate legal entity, the public corporation is distinct from the State and to be distinguished from a Government department. It has a name of its own under which it carries on its activities. "It has . . . defined powers which it cannot exceed, and is directed by a group of men whose duty it is to see that those powers are properly used."[4] Its property is not part of the State assets. Its budget is separate from that of the State. Its liabilities are not charged on the General Revenue. Its funds are raised and administered on its own responsibility. It is, unless a statute specifically provides otherwise, subject to the general law of the land, may be prosecuted for criminal offences, and lacks the privileges or immunities enjoyed by the Government or its departments. Its managers and employees are not civil servants; their terms of employment are not those of the Civil Service.

What makes the public corporation a public body is its dependence from,

* By Dr. U. Yadin, The Hebrew University, Jerusalem.
1. The Citrus Control Board, operating since 1940.
2. In 1948.
3. W. Friedmann, *Law and Social Change in Contemporary Britain*, 1951, at p. 191.
4. *Per* Denning L.J. in *Tamlin* v. *Hannaford* [1950] 1 K.B. 18, at p. 23.

and its responsibility to the central authorities of the State. A public corporation is not created voluntarily by individuals. Rather is it established and organised, and its powers and purposes are defined by action of the State—legislative or executive—and the State retains full power to modify its organisation and functions, or to abolish it altogether. Moreover, a public corporation has no corporators or members who would decide on its policy, appoint and remove its directors, resolve on the distribution or otherwise of its profits, and eventually receive its dividends and, on liquidation, its surplus assets. The members of its management are appointed, removed and replaced, their tenure and terms of office are fixed, and general directions are given to them, by the Government or one of its Ministers. Its activities are under the immediate supervision of the Government and the more general control of Parliament. "Any surplus will normally be plowed back into the business."[5] The disposal of surplus assets, if not laid down by Parliament, is left to the decision of the Government. Budgets and accounts are submitted to and discussed by Parliament or one of its committees.

2. THE GENERAL ISRAELI BACKGROUND

Turning now to Israel, some facts should first be set out in order properly to evaluate the present position relating to public corporations.

Until 1948 the territory of Israel was part of British Mandated Palestine. There was no Parliament, no responsible or elected Government. The Administration was headed by a Commissioner, appointed by the Government of Great Britain, in whose hands all authority, both legislative and executive, was concentrated. All Government activities were carried out directly by the several Government departments.[6]

The country was run on the usual lines of British colonial administration. Roads, ports and airports were constructed. Concessions were granted for the supply of electricity, the construction of pipe lines and refineries, and the extraction of minerals from the Dead Sea. In such important fields, however, as the development of water and other natural sources, agriculture, housing, credit facilities, shipping or air transportation, the Government's activities were either non-existent or confined to supervisory measures.

However, where the Mandatory failed, Jewish organisations came in. There were certain institutions which—although not clothed with executive power in the ordinary sense—assumed for the Jewish population of Palestine the character of semi-authoritative or quasi-governmental bodies. First in rank was the Jewish Agency for Palestine, dealing with immigration, colonisation and development in general, and also with internal defence. Next stood the

5. W. Robson, "The Public Corporation in Britain Today" (1950) 63 Harv. L. R. 1321, at p. 1330.
6. None of which had any measure of independence or separateness.

Jewish National Fund (*Keren Kayemet*) for the acquisition, holding and development of land, and the Jewish Foundation Fund (*Keren Hayessod*) whose main purpose was the financial maintenance of new agricultural settlements. The Palestine Jewish Colonisation Association (Edmond de Rothschild Foundation), known as PICA, and the Palestine Land Development Company Ltd. (PLDC), both engaged in what their names indicate, should also be mentioned here. These institutions were much more than public utility corporations. Indeed they were very much like public corporations, although perhaps in a somewhat unorthodox fashion.

With the establishment of the State of Israel, most if not all of this underwent fundamental changes. The status of mandated territory gave way to that of a sovereign State. The colonial administration was replaced by democratic State organs: the Parliament (called *Knesset*) elected by universal, direct, proportional suffrage; the President elected by the Knesset; the Government responsible to Parliament (much on the English pattern); and the State Comptroller appointed by the President and responsible to the Knesset. These authorities, although preoccupied by problems of defence and finance, at once tackled the great objects of the new State: immigration and development. The results, as far as our review is concerned, were twofold.

One result was that the above semi-official Jewish institutions were affected. Their position *vis-à-vis* the Jewish State was, of necessity, different from what it had been *vis-à-vis* the Mandatory Government. Many of their activities were taken over by the new Ministries. Some of their objects became obsolete. The body in which these changes were most spectacular was the Jewish Agency for Palestine. While its aims and objects were newly formulated by its central organ in accordance with its own constitution,[7] it was, by an enactment of the Knesset, given a new constitutional and legal status, much at variance with that which it had during the Mandate.[8]

7. The purposes and basic policy of the Jewish Agency for Palestine are laid down by the Congress of the World Zionist Organisation. The first Congress of that Organisation, held in August 1897 at Basle, Switzerland, had declared: "The aim of Zionism is to create for the Jewish people a home in Palestine secured by public law." By the 23rd Congress, held in August 1951 at Jerusalem, this was replaced by the following declaration: "The aim of Zionism is to strengthen the State of Israel, to ingather the dispersed into Palestine and to secure the unity of the Jewish people."
8. The Mandate for Palestine, approved by the Council of the League of Nations in 1922, provided in Art. 4: "An appropriate Jewish agency shall be recognised as a public body for the purpose of . . . co-operating with the Administration of Palestine in such . . . matters as may effect the establishment of the Jewish national home . . . The Zionist organisation . . . shall be recognised as such agency." For a concise description of the organisation of the Jewish Agency and its operation under the Mandate, see Report of the Palestine Royal Commission (Peel Commission) 1937, Cmd. 5479, pp. 172–174. Now, by s. 4 of the Status of the World Zionist Organisation, the Jewish Agency for Palestine Law, 5712–1952, it is provided that "the State of Israel recognises the World Zionist Organisation as the competent agency which will continue to operate in the State of Israel for the development and colonisation of the country . . . " Further sections of the law deal with the legal status of the Jewish Agency and the ways and means of its "co-operation with the Government."
Somewhat similar enactments were passed in 1953 and 1956 with regard to the above-mentioned *Keren Kayemet* and *Keren Hayessod* respectively.

The second result was that, in addition to the expansion of direct Government activities, a great number of new agencies were created for the implementation of a variety of tasks. First in time was the Development Authority established in 1950. Other bodies set up by or on behalf of the State include, under the heading of:

(a) Development and Natural Resources: Dead Sea Works Ltd. 1952[9]; Natural and Regional Water Authorities (1959); Israel Lands Administration (1960).

(b) Agriculture: Citrus Control Board (1940); The National Plantations Ltd. (1952); Boards for the Production and Marketing of Ground-Nuts (1959), Vegetables (1959) and Egg and Poultry Products (1963).

(c) Industry: Chemical Products and Phosphates Ltd. (1946); Haifa Refineries Ltd. (1959).

(d) Banking and Finance: Israel Bank for Agriculture (1957); Bank of Israel (1954); Bank for Industrial Development Ltd. (1957); Lotteries Board (1967); Securities Authority (1968).

(e) Transport and Tourism: Zim, Israel Shipping Company Ltd. (1945); El-Al, Israel Airlines Ltd. (1949); Government Tourist Corporation (1955); Dan Hotels Company Ltd. (1961).

(f) Housing: Amidar, Israel National Housing Ltd. (1949); Israel Housing and Development Ltd. (1961).

(g) Services: Red Shield of David (the Israel counterpart of the Red Cross) (1950); National Insurance Institute (1953); Employment Service (1959); Ports Authority (1961); Broadcasting Authority (1965).

(h) Culture and Education: Board of Higher Education (1958); Israel Centre for the Advancement of Human Culture (1958); Israel National Academy of Sciences (1961).

(i) Local Administration: Association of Towns (since 1955); National Parks Authority and Nature Reserves Authority (1963); Streams and Springs Authorities (1965); Building and Clearance of Resettlement Areas Authority (1965).

(j) Professions: Council of Auditors (1955); Bar Council (1961); Council of Land Valuers (1962).

3. DETAILS OF SOME PUBLIC CORPORATIONS

After this general survey, a more detailed description is now required of bodies having the qualities of public corporations. Neither the list of bodies, nor the particulars given in respect of any one of them are exhaustive. The following is a selection of typical forms and characteristic provisions.

The Citrus Control Board, the "oldest" body of this kind in the country,

9. The numbers in brackets indicate the year in which the respective body was set up.

was constituted by the Citrus Control Ordinance 1940. It now consists of three Ministers or their representatives and of eight representatives of the organised citrus growers, appointed by the Minister of Agriculture. It is a body corporate, appoints its own employees and fixes their salaries. Its accounts are "subject to audit in the same manner as if the moneys of the Board were public moneys. . . . "[10] Once a year it has to submit a detailed estimate of its expenditure to the Minister of Agriculture for his approval. The Board may conclude contracts for the shipping of citrus fruit, advertise citrus fruit and undertake research in by-products and foreign markets. With the approval of the Minister of Agriculture it may make rules regulating the area of citrus cultivation and for the control of picking, storage, transportation, trading, packing and export of fruit. It may collect a levy on citrus fruit to be applied for its purposes.

The Board for the Production and Marketing of Vegetables, established by a Law of 1959,[11] consists of not less than twenty members of whom not more than one quarter are Government representatives and at least one a representative of the Jewish Agency. The Law contains elaborate provisions on the appointment and terms of office of the Board's members and for the setting up of a managing committee of ten and a Committee of Control. Vegetables may be marketed only through marketing agents approved by the Board. The Board's functions correspond to those of the Citrus Control Board, but in addition include the power to regulate production quotas, minimum prices and subsidies to producers. The Board is a body corporate. Its budget is subject to approval by the Minister of Agriculture and the Minister of Commerce and Industry. The Law is silent as to the Boards employees and its duty to report to the Government or the Knesset.[12]

The Employment Service was set up in 1959[13] mainly for the purpose of operating labour exchanges on behalf of the State instead of the private labour exchanges previously operated by trade unions. The law declares the Service to be a corporation, subject to the inspection of the State Comptroller and "under the general supervision of the Minister of Labour" who may perform any act which the Service is bound to, but omits to perform.[14] The "supreme authority" of the Service is the Employment Service Board, appointed by the Minister of Labour and consisting, in addition to Government representatives, of an equal number of representatives of employees and employers. The "directive and executive authority" of the Service is the management con-

10. Citrus Control Ordinance 1940, s. 14.
11. The Vegetable Production and Marketing Board Law, 5719–1959, Laws of the State of Israel (hereafter LSI), vol. 13, p. 245.
12. The Egg and Poultry Board, established by the Egg and Poultry Board (Production and Marketing) Law, 5724–1963, LSI, vol. 18, p. 10, is similarly organised. In addition to powers corresponding to those of the Vegetables Board it may, through a Fines Committee, impose fines up to LI. 1000 (about 280 dollars) on breeders or dealers for contravention of its regulations and rules.
13. By the Employment Service Law, 5719–1959, LSI, vol. 13, p. 29.
14. ss. 3–6 of the Law.

sisting of the director, his deputy and the holders of certain designated managerial posts in the Service, all of them appointed by the Minister after consultation with the board.[15] The other employees of the Service are appointed by the management "in accordance with the rules for the appointment of State employees"; their terms of employment are the same as those of State employees "with such modifications as the management may, with the approval of the Minister, determine."[16] The management prepares the annual budget which the board submits to the Minister who in turn presents it to the Knesset for approval. "The expenditure of the Service under the approved budget shall be covered from Treasury funds."[17]

It might be interesting to give some detailed illustrations also from among the limited companies mentioned above. The framework of this survey, however, does not allow to go into such details. Suffice it to indicate that in some of those companies, such as El-Al Ltd. or Dead Sea Works Ltd., State holdings amount to 99 per cent. or even 100 per cent., while in Amidar Ltd., Zim Ltd. and others they stand at 75 per cent. to 80 per cent. In certain cases, such as the Bank for Industrial Development Ltd., the State holds only 25 per cent. of the equity capital. Where undertakings of this kind are carried on by the State in partnership with others, the partners are sometimes private commercial undertakings; more often they are themselves public corporations, such as the Jewish Agency or the Development Authority.

4. LEGAL CLASSIFICATION

These various institutions are readily divided into two main groups: statutory bodies and commercial companies. Each of the first group derives its existence from a special enactment[18]; its "charter" is subject to amendment by means of a Law of the Knesset, and only in this way.

Those of the second group have all been constituted under, and are governed by, the provisions of the general statute relating to companies, the Companies Ordinance of 1929.[19] They have their memorandum and articles of association, need their certificate of incorporation and, except for private companies as some of them are, their certificate to commence business; they have to register their debentures and charges with the Registrar of Companies and to

15. ss. 8–16 of the Law.
16. ss. 17, 18 of the Law.
17. ss. 70–72 of the Law.
18. Mostly a Law of the Knesset, in some isolated cases an Ordinance from the Mandatory period.
19. Although there have been recommendations of committees of experts and a comprehensive Draft for modification or replacing of this Ordinance, it has undergone only minor amendments within the last 20 years. Originally derived from the English Companies Act of 1929 it is, accordingly, much nearer to that Act than to the English Acts of 1948 or 1967. The only major reform was brought about by the Securities Law, 5728–1968 (not yet published in LSI), which effected important changes in the law relating to prospectuses, current reporting and the regulation of the Tel-Aviv Stock Exchange.

file with him their annual return[20]; they are liable to be wound up by the court on the petition of their creditors; in short: they are in all matters of formal organisation on the same footing as ordinary, non-public trading corporations.[21]

Some institutions occupy an intermediate position between these two main groups, being companies to which, under a special statute for each case, the provisions of the Companies Ordinance apply with certain modifications. They also enjoy, under their respective statutes, certain privileges with regard to other enactments.[22] A further small category is formed by bodies which, although set up by statute, have not been endowed with distinct legal personality. Although in terms of substance and constitutional policy they are not basically different from full-fledged statutory entities (and, on principle, could as well have been organised as such), they are not included in this survey.[23]

On first view it seems as if the division into bodies set up by special statute and those set up under the Companies Ordinance were decisive: the former are public corporations, the latter are not. On closer examination, however, it appears that this distinction does not serve as a dividing line of any real value. The true picture is rather that of a continuous line leading from bodies that have all or most features of a public corporation through various shades and grades down to those which have only few of its characteristics. Along this line the distinction between statutory and non-statutory bodies is haphazard. And some of the Government corporations organised as private companies, *i.e.* in a form nearest to that of a partnership between small artisans, seem to be closer to the full-fledged public corporation than many others.

Instead of arranging the institutions listed and described above in "order of precedence" according to the degree of resemblance to the "ideal type" of

20. In this latter respect additional requirements are now contained in the Securities Law mentioned *supra*, note 19.

21. It is to be noted that so far nothing has been done in order to adapt the provisions of the Companies Ordinance to the particular needs of these modern mixed bodies, nor has there been a statute conferring on them any special status or exemption from the general rules of company or other law. Everything required for achieving particular arrangements and combinations has therefore to be done by skilful use of the existing legal framework.

22. To this group belong the *Keren Kayemet* and the *Keren Hayessod*, which had been organised as companies in England and were nostrified by the Keren Kayemet Le-Israel Law, 5714–1953 (LSI, vol 8, p. 35) and the Keren Hayessod Law, 5716–1956 (LSI, vol. 11, p. 24). Water authorities under the Water Law, 5719–1959, LSI, vol. 13, p. 173, also are companies on which special status and powers are conferred under the Law.

23. This category includes the Israel Lands Administration set up by the Government by virtue of the Israel Lands Administration Law, 5720–1960 (LSI, vol. 14, p. 50), the Council for Higher Education established by the Council for Higher Education Law, 5718–1958 (LSI, vol. 12, p. 217) and certain professional councils such as the Auditors' Council established by the Auditors Law, 5715–1955 (LSI, vol. 9, p. 27) or the Valuers' Council established by the Minister of Justice by virtue of the Land Valuers Law, 5722–1962 (LSI, vol. 16, p. 61). Sometimes it is doubtful whether or not an institution is a body corporate, see the provisions of the Postal Bank Law, 5711–1951, (LSI, vol. 5, p. 138) regarding the Postal Bank.

a public corporation, the elaboration of some common features will help to
clarify their character.

5. LEGAL STATUS AND POWERS

All institutions under review, whether of the statutory or the company group,
are *separate legal entities*. As such they are different not only from the Government, its Ministries or departments, but also from pseudo-separate Government agencies "which are auxiliary to and almost integrated in the great
departments of State, created to undertake specialised tasks,"[24] such as the
Railways Administration,[25] the Administrator-General[26] or the various
Custodians (of Enemy Property,[27] of Absentees' Property,[28] of Germans'
Property.[29] It is true that some of these organs have the status and style of
corporations sole; others enjoy other forms of perpetual succession; others,
again, have a budget forming a self-contained unit within the general Government budget. These features of partial separateness, however, are not sufficient to bring them within the category of public corporations. They are no
more than what Scott L. J. in *London County Territorial Association* v. *Nichols*
called "direct emanations of the Crown."[30]

The second common feature of the several bodies is the *specific determination of their powers*. They are not "multi-purpose authorities," such as the
State, the municipalities and other bodies of local government,[31] but "functional organisations created for specific purposes."[32] This goes without saying where organisation under the Companies Ordinance was chosen. That
Ordinance expressly requires the memorandum of association to lay down the
company's objects[33] and the various Government companies did of course
comply with this requirement. The same, however, also applies to the statutory bodies, although here the legislator was free to adopt whatever other
arrangement he had preferred. As it happens, not only Red Shield of David[34]
and the Ports Authority[35] were given clear and narrowly defined objects, but
even the law creating the Development Authority[36] contains an elaborate

24. Robson, *op. cit., supra*, note 5, at p. 1321.
25. Under the Government Railways Ordinance 1936.
26. Under the Administrator General Ordinance 1944.
27. *Cf.* Trading with the Enemy Ordinance 1939.
28. *Cf.* Absentees' Property Law, 5711–1951, LSI, vol. 5, p. 63.
29. *Cf.* German Property Law, 5710–1950, LSI, vol. 4, p. 142.
30. [1949] 1 K.B. 35.
31. It should, however, be observed that among the public corporations there are
some which serve certain, specified activities of local authorities: Associations of Towns
under the Associations of Towns Law, 5715–1955, LSI, vol. 9, p. 54, belong to this
group.
32. *Cf.* Friedmann, *op. cit. supra*, note 3, p. 190.
33. s. 5 (1) (b).
34. Under the Red Shield of David Law, 5710–1950, LSI, vol. 4, p. 127.
35. Under the Ports Authority Law, 5721–1961, LSI, vol. 15, p. 152.
36. Development Authority (Transfer of Property) Law, 5710–1950, LSI, vol. 4,
p. 151.

enumeration of objects, surprisingly similar to that commonly found in the memorandum of association of a trading company.[37]

As separate entities both kinds of bodies have *property rights and liabilities* of their own. With regard to the statutory bodies, the power to acquire, hold and dispose of property was either given to them expressly or is implied in the section conferring upon them corporate status.[38] On companies such powers are conferred either by their memorandum of association or by virtue of the Second Schedule to the Companies Ordinance.[39] In both cases, such property as the corporation acquires is not State property. The restrictions and formalities imposed by the State Property Law, 5711–1951,[40] on the disposition of State property are, therefore, on principle not applicable to the disposition of property held by these bodies. But in the case of National Plantations Ltd. a certain provision of the State Property Law has been incorporated, by reference, in the memorandum of association of the company; and under the statute creating the Development Authority any transfer of immovable property by that Authority is subject to Government approval.[41]

It is by reason of their separate personalities, assets and liabilities that contractual and other legal relationships may exist between the State and a public corporation. Thus, under laws of 1950 and 1951,[42] loans were granted by the Government to the Citrus Marketing Board for the purpose of lending certain amounts to citrus growers on the security of their groves and crops, and the claims of the Board against its borrowers served in turn as security for its debt to the Government. Again, under the Development Authority (Transfer of Property) Law this body is empowered to sell property to the State, to buy property from the State and to carry on activities "together or in partnership with State institutions."[43] Moreover, the State's investments in Government companies is effected by way of loans granted to them and of subscribing to their shares.[44]

37. In the case of associations of towns (see *supra*, note 31) the objects of any given association are determined by the Minister of the Interior on the setting up of the association, the statute being an enabling one and not directly operative. With regard to all other statutory bodies the objects are laid down by the statute itself.

38. Earlier statutes creating such bodies specify—following English drafting practice—their power to "enter into contracts, acquire, hold and transfer property and be a party to any legal or other proceedings." Since about 1959 a more concise wording has been employed, namely that the respective institution "shall be a body corporate, capable of rights, duties and legal acts".

39. Which contains a long list of supplementary powers of companies incorporated under that statute.

40. LSI, vol. 5, p. 45.

41. Development Authority (Transfer of Property) Law, 5710–1950 (LSI, vol. 4, p. 151), s. 3 (4) (*d*).

42. Citrus Growers Law (American Credit) Law, 5710–1950, LSI, vol. 4, p. 134 and Citrus Growers Loan (Development) Law, 5711–1951, LSI, vol. 5, p. 24.

43. ss. 3 (4), (10) and 6 of the Law.

44. According to the report of the Government Companies Authority (a nonstatutory unit of the Treasury) for 1967–68, Government's investment in loans to 137 companies amounted on March 31, 1968, to about LI. 3,255,000,000, while its shareholding in those companies amounted to about LI. 1,097,000,000.

6. FINANCIAL STATUS AND CONTROL

Being the property of separate bodies, the assets of the corporations here reviewed are not liable for debts charged on the General Revenue. On the other hand, the General Revenue is, unless specifically charged, not responsible for their debts or liabilities. The Postal Bank Law, 5711–1951, contains a provision proclaiming the liability of the State for the debts of the Bank.[45] State liability for certain debts of company-type corporations arises, in each case, by way of a special guarantee.[46]

As to the budget of statutory bodies, sometimes prior approval by the Knesset or its Finance Committee is required,[47] more often the budget is subject to approval by the Minister or Ministers charged with the implementation of the law by which the body was created.[48] Other statutes are silent on this point. Almost invariably the financial activities of these institutions are under the (*ex post*) supervision of the State Comptroller.[49] Corporations organised as companies are their own masters as far as periods of planning and estimates of income and expenditure are concerned. Their own management is alone responsible for keeping their activities within those estimates. Even with regard to the moneys invested by the Government in their undertakings[50] any control exercised by Governmental organs or representatives for ensuring that such moneys are actually applied according to their destination does not amount to anything similar to budgetary control of Parliament or Government. Since about 1958 efforts have been made to remedy this situation by imposing on Government corporations the duty to submit their estimates in advance to the Minister concerned and to report to him on the financial results of their activities. It seems, however, doubtful how far this administrative arrangement—unenforced as it is by statutory provisions—has been implemented in practice. On the other hand the supervisory function of the State Comptroller extends also to this kind of bodies, at least in so far as they are "undertakings . . . in whose management the Government participates."[51]

45. s. 15 of the Law (*supra* note 23). For those who would deny to the Postal Bank the status of public corporation and consider it as integrated in the Ministry of Postal Service (*cf. supra*, note 23), this provision is mere surplusage.
46. Under the State Guarantees Law, 5718–1958, LSI, vol. 12, p. 163. On March 31, 1968, such guarantees stood at a total of about LI. 1,000,000,000, according to the report mentioned *supra*, note 44.
47. This is the case with regard to the Development Authority, the Employment Service and the Securities Authority.
48. The Agricultural Boards, the Drainage Authority and the National Insurance Institute are examples for this type of arrangement.
49. Under the State Comptroller Law (Consolidated Version) 1719–1959, LSI, vol. 12, p. 107, in conjunction with express provisions of the various enactments. Several of the annual reports of the State Comptroller (which are published also in English) contain valuable information and comments on public corporations.
50. *Cf. supra*, notes 44 and 46.
51. State Comptroller Law (*supra*, note 50), s. 9 (5). Companies are, in addition, subject to ordinary commercial accounting.

7. GOVERNMENT CONTROL

The measure of Government control apart from budgetary control varies from case to case even more than does budgetary control. There are bodies which have been put under "the general control of the Minister" concerned.[52] There are many cases in which the Government is entitled to appoint all or at least some part of the members of the governing organ. There are a variety of provisions by which certain resolutions or transactions—whether of a financial or operational character—are subject to Government approval or may be disallowed by the Government.

Here again statutory authorities and private corporations rank side by side. With regard to the former, matters are regulated in most cases by the statute itself, sometimes by regulations made under the statute. With regard to the latter, provisions are contained in their memorandum or articles of association and, in addition, Government is maintaining its control by resolutions and directions which are binding on its representatives on the board of directors and in the general meetings of those companies. The great elasticity which the Companies Ordinance allows for the division of share capital into different classes of shares and for the formulation of the rights of shares is being put to use for this purpose.

It is this direct Government control, more than any other single factor, which distinguishes the companies here analysed from ordinary commercial companies, including those in which the State is financially interested as holder of shares or debentures. It is submitted that a public corporation does not lose its character as such by the mere fact of being organised in the form of a company under the Companies Ordinance, as long as those who hold its decisive shares, appoint its management and are in a position to lay down its policy are the State, the Government or other public corporations.[53] On the other hand, the mere fact that the State or any of its agencies have some—or even a substantial—shareholding in a company without enjoying this specific measure of control over it, does not transform that company into a public corporation.

8. STATUS OF EMPLOYEES

A further item among the significant features is concerned with the employees of the several bodies here under review. "Public corporations are not under the Treasury as far as personnel matters go; they recruit their own personnel and may have salary scales, varying from those of the Civil Service."[54]

52. The Employment Service is an example in point, cf. Employment Service Law 5719–1959, LSI, vol. 13, p. 29.
53. In the organisation of Government controlled companies the form of subsidiary companies has been frequently employed.
54. Ogg and Zink, *Modern Foreign Governments*, 1950, p. 166.

This is true of the statutory type of corporations as well as of the companies type. It does not, of course, apply to non-independent Government agencies such as the Custodian of Absentees' Property[55] or the Postal Bank.

The several statutes establishing public corporations show a considerable variety of provisions in this regard. Sometimes the statute is silent.[56] Sometimes it simply empowers the statutory body "to engage agents, employees and other servants and to fix the terms of their service."[57] More often the conditions of appointment and terms of service are assimilated to those of civil servants, either absolutely[58] or with such modifications as may be laid down by the corporation with the approval of the Minister concerned[59] or the Government.[60] "Terms of service" generally include salaries. More detailed provisions are contained in more recent statutes.[61] An unusual provision occurs in the Ports Authority Law, 5721–1961[62]; it lays down that terms of employment and salaries "shall be fixed by agreement between the Authority and the organisation representing the greatest number of the Authority's employees."[63]

The question whether or not the employees of an institution are civil servants is important for the application to them of certain statutes dealing with the status, rights, duties, privileges and disabilities of civil servants, such as the State Service (Appointment) Law, 5719–1959,[64] the State Service (Restriction on Party-Political Activity and Fund-Raising) Law, 5719–1959,[65] the State Service (Discipline) Law, 5723–1963,[66] certain provisions of the Evidence Ordinance and the Penal Law Revision (Public Servants) Law, 5717–1957.[67] Employees of independent public corporations *not* being State employees, those statutes do not apply to them automatically. They can apply

55. The Absentees' Property Law, 5710–1950, s. 3 (c) provides that the Custodian may appoint his employees, but emphasises that "their status shall be that of any other civil servants."

56. Such is the case with regard to Drainage Authorities, Agricultural Boards, the Bar Council, Associations of Towns. Statutes conferring special status on privately organised companies, such as the Keren Kayemet and Keren Hayessod and the statute regulating the water authorities also pass in silence over this subject.

57. The citation is from s. 3 (8) of the Development Authority (Transfer of Property) Law, 5710–1950. The provisions concerning the national parks and nature reserves authorities are similar.

58. As in the case of the Securities Authority and the National Insurance Institute (s. 82).

59. *Cf.* Employment Service Law, 5719–1959, ss. 17, 18.

60. *Cf.* Ports Authority Law, 5721–1961, LSI, vol. 15, p. 152, s. 18 (a).

61. Such as the Broadcasting Authority Law, 5725–1965, LSI, vol. 19, p. 103, ss. 24, 25.

62. LSI, vol. 15, p. 152, s. 18 (b).

63. It may be noted that labour disputes seem to be more frequent in the ports of the Authority than in the undertakings of any other public corporation. There is, however, no clear evidence of causal connection between the type of arrangement and the number of labour disputes.

64. LSI, vol. 13, p. 87, which, *inter alia*, requires civil servants to be Israeli citizens.

65. LSI, vol. 13, p. 203.

66. LSI, vol. 17, p. 58.

67. LSI, vol. 11, p. 89. The Law relates primarily to offences of bribery.

only by virtue of special provisions to that effect, and some provisions of this kind do, indeed, exist.[68]

No statutory regulation applies to the employees of companies, including Government companies which are public corporations. Such tendencies as may exist for assimilating their selection, appointment and terms of employment to those of the Civil Service are implemented by means of Government directives, or by specific directions issued by Ministers to their representatives on the directorate or in the general meeting of the companies.

9. Public Corporations as a Category: Some Legal Problems

Although most of the institutions reviewed here have certain characteristic features it must be realised that until now neither statutes nor—with one exception—judicial decisions have used the generic term of "public corporation" *as a technical term*.[69] Instead, a number of closely related conceptions and terms are used here and there. Whether in a given issue one of these terms does or does not apply to any of the said institutions depends not on whether that institution is a public corporation but whether it has such features as are envisaged by that particular term.

Under this aspect the term "public corporation" and the classification for which it stands lose much of their practical value. Instead of subjecting a number of institutions to a general definition and dividing them into those which are, and those which are not, within the category of public corporations—however this category be defined—the relevant task seems rather to be one of determining for each and every purpose, on the strength of the several attributes of a given institution, whether a certain legal consequence does or does not follow.[70]

The following are a few illustrations of the way in which this line of approach may become relevant. On each item only the problem can be indicated. Answers, even tentative ones, are in general beyond the scope of this paper.

The Supreme Court of Israel sitting as a High Court of Justice may "order State authorities and their officials . . . to do or refrain from doing any act in the lawful exercise of their functions. . . . "[71] Which of the bodies here re-

---

68. On the one hand, the Penal Law Revision (Public Servants) Law, 5717-1957, declares that the employees of the National Insurance Institute, the Bank of Israel, the Jewish Agency, Keren Kayemet, Keren Hayessod and the General Labour Exchange (now the Employment Service) are "public servants" for the purpose of that enactment, alongside with State employees. On the other hand, the Broadcasting Authority Law, 5725-1965, provides, in s. 40, that for the purpose of several of the said enactments "the employees of the Authority shall be deemed to be State employees."
69. The only Supreme Court judgment forming an exception to this statement is referred to *infra*.
70. The words of Devlin J. in *Bank voor Handel* v. *Slatford* [1952] 1 All E.R. 314 at p. 320, with regard to the term "servants or agents of the Crown" are very much in point.
71. Courts Law, 5717-1957, LSI, vol. 11, p. 157, s. 7 (*b*) (2).

viewed are "State authorities" within the meaning of this provision so as to make them amenable to the writ of mandamus? Which of their officers are "officials of State authorities"? And if there are among them such authorities or officials, which of their acts are done "in exercise of their functions"?

Under section 6 of the Law and Administration Ordinance, 5708–1948,[72] no Government tax or other "obligatory payment to Government" may be imposed or increased except by virtue of a Law of the Knesset. Can the levy provided for by the Citrus Control Ordinance 1940 in favour of the Citrus Control Board be increased by the Minister of Agriculture who is charged with the implementation of that enactment, or does such an increase require a Law of the Knesset?

Are rent restriction statutes to be applied to premises owned by public corporations? Here, again, no general classification is of decisive value. Each body has its own merits. In England the so-called territorial associations have been held to be exempt from the restrictions imposed on a landlord by the said statutes,[73] while the British Transport Commission was held to be subject to them.[74] What would be the position if the Development Authority or any other of the above bodies should claim eviction from their property?

This last question is part of a larger problem: is any of the above bodies, though endowed with a certain measure of separateness, "a sufficiently intimate emanation of the Crown to attract the contagion of Crown status"? True, in the Republic of Israel there is no "Crown" in the English sense. There is, however, still in force the following provision contained in an Ordinance of 1945: "Save as may be otherwise expressly provided, no enactment shall affect any right of or impose any obligation upon the State."[75]

It is submitted that none of the corporations with which we are here concerned may rely on this provision. They are all so separate from the State as not to enjoy any automatic exemption, immunity or privilege. It would have to be "otherwise expressly provided" not in order to deprive them of any inherent immunity, but only if it was desired to confer upon any of them any privileged status.

Although in Israel there is very little legal authority on problems connected with public corporations, there is one case in which the above proposition as to immunity has amply been confirmed. When the Development Authority was fined[76] for not having provided a shelter in one of its buildings, its counsel pleaded exemption from the duty to do so by virtue of the above section 42 of the Interpretation Ordinance. Rejecting this contention, Justice Landau,

---

72. LSI, vol. 1, p. 7, s. 6.
73. *Territorial Forces Association* v. *Philpot* [1947] 2 All E.R. 376; *London County Territorial Association* v. *Nichols* [1949] 1 K.B. 35.
74. *Tamlin* v. *Hannaford* [1950] 1 K.B. 18.
75. The citation is from the Interpretation Ordinance in its revised version of 1954 in which "State" was substituted for "the Crown or His Majesty's Government in the United Kingdom or the Government (of Palestine)."
76. Under the Civil Defence Law, 5711–1951, LSI, vol. 5, p. 72.

speaking for the Supreme Court, pointed out that "a public body existing separately from the ordinary government administration is not within the term 'State' for the purpose of section 42."[77] He emphasised that the decisive consideration was "not the nature of the functions of the body but rather its organisational structure" and that the question of Government control was of little or no weight.[78]

10. GENERAL CONCLUSIONS

"In our times the legislator employs this instrument of the public corporation whenever he considers it advisable to take the implementation of a certain governmental task out of the framework of the ordinary government apparatus and to entrust it to an autonomous juristic person specially created for the implementation of that task. . . . By means of this separation from the ordinary government apparatus the legislator achieves a great measure of flexibility, as he is at liberty to design the legal structure of each public corporation according to his needs and the nature of the task which the corporation is destined to fulfil."

These words of Justice Landau[79] aptly describe the policy reasons for the setting up of public corporations and the possibilities implied in this form of organisation. The Government of Israel has made ample use of these possibilities. The number of public corporations—whether of the statutory or the companies type—is already considerable and may safely be expected to rise even more in the future. Some of the bodies now existing are functionally not very different from Government departments, although legally they form separate entities. Others, however, such as the Ports Authority, the Broadcasting Authority or El-Al, are full-fledged public corporations in the modern sense of the term, comparable to those created in England by the Nationalisation Acts or the authority which was so successful in the Tennessee Valley.[80]

In England, although some undertakings such as broadcasting or air transportation have from the outset been organised as public enterprises, the most important public corporations now operating are those of certain industries which had been built up and run by private or local initiative and capital and were later taken over by the State (Bank of England, electricity, coal, gas, road transport). In Israel the trend seems to be in the opposite direction. While some of the public corporations, like the Keren Kayemet, the Israel Standard Institute, the Red Shield of David, the Labour Service and certain water authorities, have replaced organisations which had previously existed in some

77. Cr A134/58, *Development Authority* v. *Att.-Gen.*, 13 P.D. 722 at p. 726 (Hebrew).
78. It may be noted that the Israeli court referred to, and partly relied upon, the leading English cases of *Tamlin* v. *Hannaford*, and *Bank voor Handel, etc.* v. *Slatford*, *supra*.
79. In the *Development Authority* case, see note 77.
80. The comparison disregards, of course, the difference in dimensions.

other form, most of them are original creations of the central Government, set up for purposes and engaging in activities for which private or other non-Governmental initiative and capital are, for the time being, not available.

In certain fields—mainly, of course, those of a commercial character—there is a certain tendency of co-operation with private or semi-private interests. The Bank for Industrial Development Ltd., one of the biggest financial institutions of the country, is here in point.[81] This is only one example of the numerous undertakings in which State funds are invested side by side with private—local or foreign—capital. To the extent, however, that State participation and control in these mixed bodies decreases, they gradually pass from the sphere of public to that of private enterprise.

81. The State holds about 54 per cent. of the total share capital of this company and about 27 per cent. of its voting power. The rest is held by a variety of commercial undertakings. Lately there have also been cases in which wholly-owned Government companies or Government holdings in mixed companies have been sold to private trading firms.

Chapter 15

PUBLIC CORPORATIONS IN EAST AFRICA*

1. Introduction

AN account of the development of public corporations in Tanzania, Kenya and Uganda since these countries became independent in 1961, 1962 and 1963 respectively[1] must necessarily be preceded by some general comments on the public law and economic background against which that development must be seen, for there are fundamental differences between these countries and the others discussed in this book. In the field of public law, whereas these other countries are concerned to fit public corporations into a well-established and accepted framework of government, operating within a relatively stable polity, in East African countries the major problem is what sort of framework of government to have and upon what principles it should be based in order to achieve a measure of lasting political stability. Since independence, there have been constant and major changes in the Constitutions of all three countries, by means both of law and of revolution, and these show no signs of abating. In part these changes are due to factors external to the law, but in part they reflect the ambivalent nature of the public law itself, and attitudes of political leaders towards it.

At independence the rulers of these countries were given a liberal constitution, and inherited an authoritarian administrative structure. The former presumed an open society, with political dissent permitted, an executive responsive to a legislature which in turn was enabled to perform its checking role on the Executive; the latter presumed a closed society with political dissent carefully contained, and an administration not open to effective control either politically via the legislature, or legally via the courts. The intention of the departing colonial power was no doubt that the liberal constitution should gradually prevail over the authoritarian administration, and it may well be that this ideal was shared by some of the new rulers, but the practice has tended to be the reverse. Neither the nature of the constitutional changes nor the speed with which they have been brought about have been similar in all three countries, but their direction has been.[2] Furthermore, although these

* By Professor A. W. Bradley, University of Edinburgh and J. P. W. B. McAuslan, University of Warwick.

1. Tanzania comprises Tanganyika which became independent in 1961, and Zanzibar which became independent in 1963. The two countries joined together to form the United Republic of Tanzania in 1964.

2. All three countries are republics with executive presidencies. However, Tanzania is a one-party State with the President not a member of the legislature, and Uganda arrived at republican status via a government *coup d'état* in 1966. Kenya has evolved into a parliamentary presidency through constitutional means.

changes have not gone unchallenged both in and out of the three legislatures, and there have been genuine attempts to redefine the boundaries of legitimate executive power[3] and the mode of its control, the sum total of all these efforts is that at the end of the 1960's there is still a lack of congruence between constitutional and administrative law, both in letter and spirit. This hinders the emergence of a stable constitutional order. The growth, and constant inquiries into the workings, of public corporations which have been such a feature of this branch of public law must be seen in the context of a continuing preoccupation with all the institutions of government.

Since independence, all three countries have established several new, and reorganised several old, public corporations, in order to further the implementation of economic development plans. Any evaluation of the public corporation must accordingly be seen equally in the context of the general strategies of economic development in the three countries—strategies which comprehend both political and economic objectives.[4]

In a broad sense the general strategies of development are the same for all East African countries. It is when one moves away from generalisations that important differences appear. The broad common general strategy is that the development of the economy will be brought about through the development of its agricultural sector. Apart from that overriding purpose agricultural development is seen to have two secondary purposes. First, as agriculture is the sector in which most Africans are employed, to develop this sector is the most obvious way to increase African incomes and African participation in the economy generally. Secondly, by expanding and diversifying the agricultural sector, the economy will be less dependent on one or two crops only for its foreign exchange and more foreign exchange will be available to finance industrial development and the social services. Industrial development is important as it is regarded as the key to structural changes in the economy, emphasised especially in Uganda, with largely untapped hydro-electric potential, and Tanzania, the least industrialised of the three States.

The policies designed to carry through this strategy bring out the differences between the three countries. Tanzania is placing great emphasis on self-reliance as opposed to reliance on foreign aid, a radical increase in the economic role of the State, directed towards a basically public-sector economy, and the attainment of national control over economic policy decisions as opposed to that exercised in the past by foreign investors and aid donors. The

3. Particularly in Tanzania. See the Report of the Presidential Commission on the Establishment of a Democratic One Party State (Dar es Salaam 1965), the Permanent Commission of Enquiry Act 1966 (the Tanzanian Ombudsman) and the First Annual Report of the Permanent Commission (Dar es Salaam 1968).
4. Tanganyika Five-Year Plan for Economic and Social Development 1964–69; Development Plan of the Republic of Kenya 1966–70; Work for Progress: Uganda's Second Five-Year Plan 1966–71. See, too, Green, "Four African Development Plans: Ghana, Kenya, Nigeria and Tanzania" (1965) 3, *Journal of Modern African Studies* 249; and "Cautious Growth Promotion and Cautious Structuralism: The Kenya and Uganda Development Plans", (1966) E.A. Econ. Rev., 19.

most dramatic expression of this policy was the publication in 1967 of the Arusha Declaration[5] and the nationalisation of banks, insurance, trading and industrial companies which followed it. Kenya intends to maintain the present shape of the economy but with increasing African participation, and is relying on large-scale private investments, both internal and foreign, for expansion. Public activity will concentrate on identifying development opportunities, but the actual development will be undertaken mainly by private enterprise. Public enterprise will come in where private enterprise either cannot, will not, or should not develop some activity. The policy represents Kenya's version of African Socialism, first set out in the well-known Sessional Paper No. 10 of 1965.[6] While Uganda hopes to achieve structural change in the economy as in Tanzania, she is adopting more the Kenya approach to the task. The existing mixed economy is to continue, but with a key part to be played in development by the para-Statal bodies, as public corporations are called in Uganda's Second Five-Year Plan, "Work for Progress." There is, however, no intention that the economy is to become primarily a public sector one.

The functions of the public corporations created or reorganised since independence go some way towards showing how these policies have been implemented in law and administration.[7] In Tanzania, after the creation and

5. A statement of policy issued by the National Executive Committee, a key policy-making body of the ruling party, the Tanganyika African National Union (TANU).

6. "African Socialism and its Application to Planning in Kenya," a statement of the political philosophy of the Government of Kenya and described as an extension in detail of the 1963 Election Manifesto of the Kenya African National Union and the Constitution of Kenya.

7. The range and extent of public corporations in East Africa are shown by these figures, based on legislative information available in August 1968.

1. Agriculture (commodity and marketing boards): Kenya 19 (e.g. Coffee Marketing Board, Maize and Produce Board), Tanzania 13 (including National Agricultural Products Board), Uganda 7.

2. Investment and development agencies: Kenya 4 (including Agricultural Development Corporation and Industrial and Commercial Development Corporation), Tanzania 3 (including National Development Corporation), Uganda 2 (including Uganda Development Corporation).

3. Industry, trade and public utilities: Kenya 6 (including Tourist Development Corporation, National Irrigation Board), Tanzania 7 (including Tanganyika Electricity Supply Co. Ltd., National Insurance Corporation), Uganda 6 (including Uganda Electricity Board).

4. Finance and banking: Kenya 4 (including Land and Agricultural Bank of Kenya, Agricultural Finance Corporation, Central Bank of Kenya), Tanzania 6 (including Bank of Tanzania, National Bank of Commerce and Tanzania Audit Corporation), Uganda 2 (including Bank of Uganda).

5. Social Service, educational, cultural and welfare: Kenya 13 (including National Library Service Board and National Housing Corporation), Tanzania 15 (including National Swahili Council and governing boards of four colleges), Uganda 10 (including Public Libraries Board, National Housing Corporation and five public trusts).

Not included are (a) the many subsidiary and associated companies of the development corporations, (b) the five East African corporations (Airways, Development Bank, Harbours, Post and Telecommunication, Railways), (c) the public enterprises in Zanzibar (which include State trading, motor trade, transport, rice mills, building, fuel and power).

expansion in 1962–64 of the National Development Corporation and the National Agricultural Products Board, which is concerned with the marketing of food crops, and the programme of nationalisation in early 1967, public corporations are now actively involved in many industrial, commercial and agricultural enterprises formerly carried on in the private sector. They have been established not so much to get Africans into the economy, though that is important, as to ensure that the State, politically independent since 1961, can become economically independent by being able to make or influence the major economic decisions in the country.

Kenya presents a complete contrast. There, new public corporations have been established for three purposes. First, to continue the old lending role of public corporations in Kenya—this applies to the Agricultural Finance Corporation, the reorganised Industrial and Commercial Development Corporation, and to some extent the Agricultural Development Corporation. Secondly, to provide the institutional framework for joint ventures with overseas capital—this applies to the Development Authorities established by the Minister of Agriculture under the authority of the Agriculture Act, to the National Irrigation Board and to the Agricultural Development Corporation. All these corporations are, however, empowered to act alone, and the two last have taken over and are running purely Government enterprises, demonstration farms and irrigation schemes in particular. Thirdly, to assist Africans to participate as private traders in the commerce and trade of the country—this applies to the National Trading Corporation and the National Property Company, whose functions are to re-orient wholesale trade from Asian into African hands, and to buy up suitable sites in good shopping areas and lease them to Africans. These last two corporations illustrate the Government's seeming reluctance to be too directly involved in the establishment of important public enterprises for they were created by the Industrial and Commercial Development Corporation as wholly-owned subsidiaries acting under powers contained in the Companies Act which has been applied to it by the Minister of Commerce and Industry.

The functions of Uganda's public corporations fall mid-way between those of Tanzania and Kenya. The Uganda Development Corporation and the Uganda Electricity Board are both to play major direct roles in the industrial development programme, while the statutory commodity boards and the National Trading Corporation are designed to obtain some of the import–export trade and wholesale–retail trade for Africans and to stimulate agricultural sales, so reducing the subsistence element of the economy. The State's role is emphasised in industrial development, the private individual's in commercial and agricultural development.

The purposes for which public corporations have been established indicate that they are envisaged as having both economic and political uses. Indeed it is difficult to disentangle economic from political uses in such aims as

redirecting trade into African hands, whether State or private, increasing the
African stake in the economy, stimulating investments and enabling the
Government to have a larger, or the major, say in economic decision-making
in the country, all of which aims emerge from the three development plans.
But to state that the existing corporations appear from the development plans
and their constituent statutes to have been allocated the foregoing functions
explains neither why so much use has been made of the public corporation,
as opposed to other administrative devices, particularly the Government department, nor whether the law and practice of the established corporations
is likely to assist them to carry out their planned functions. It is to these
matters that we now turn.

The following may be advanced as reasons why East African Governments
have established public corporations rather than entrusting new public undertakings to Government departments. First, where an enterprise is of a commercial character and is revenue-producing, its performance may be assessed
by the simple yardstick of profitability, and it will be more efficient if administered as a business. In its simplest form, this argument applies only to
a few public corporations in East Africa—the insurance corporations, the new
commercial banks, the Apolo Hotel Corporation in Uganda, and possibly
TANESCO. Where, as in the Tanzanian nationalisations of 1967, the reason
for nationalisation is the political argument for public ownership rather than
overt dissatisfaction with the performance of the business nationalised, it is
quite feasible to expect the new corporations to conform with purely commercial standards.[8]

Yet many public corporations, in East Africa as elsewhere, have undefined
social service and public utility objectives; conversely, Government departments frequently provide services with a commercial flavour. The urban
dweller in Dar es Salaam pays water rates to a Government department and
his electricity bill to a public corporation. The new trading corporations in
each country,[9] designed to extend African participation in trade, have to
balance purely commercial considerations against wider factors of public
interest. The marketing policies of the commodity boards have wide fiscal
and economic implications. So do the investment decisions of the development corporations, especially in their effect on regional development within
a country[10]; by contrast, management of individual subsidiaries of the development corporation is more clearly a commercial matter, though pricing policies

8. The National Bank of Commerce is required "to provide in accordance with the
conditions appropriate in the normal and proper conduct of banking business, adequate
and proper banking services and facilities" (s. 4 (1) (a), Act No. 1 of 1967). The State
Trading Corporation is required "to conduct its business in an efficient manner and
in accordance with the best mercantile traditions" (s. 4 (1) (b), Act No. 2 of 1967).
9. Tanzania—State Trading Corporation. Kenya—National Trading Corporation.
Uganda—National Trading Corporation.
10. e.g. see the debates in the Uganda Parliament on the Annual Reports of the
Uganda Development Corporation on July 19, 1961, and November 15, 1962.

and labour relations are of wide political interest. The line between Government and business is also blurred when a new corporation is given such wide terms of reference that it may develop its activities either as a business or as a regulatory agency.[11]

Secondly, public corporations are believed to be inherently more efficient than a Government department, and to be particularly useful when a branch of the central Government is not functioning well. This was suggested in Uganda as a reason for setting up the National Housing Corporation[12] and in Kenya for setting up the National Irrigation Board.[13] There is both some pessimism about improving civil service efficiency and also an optimistic belief in the public corporation as a panacea for difficult administrative problems. Another important factor is the relative weakness of local government which explains the use of national corporations for such purposes as housing and libraries.

But, in East Africa as elsewhere, public corporations are not always more enterprising and more efficient than their Government equivalents. In the case of the Industrial and Commercial Development Corporation of Kenya, in 1967 the Minister's powers were extended to enable him to *initiate* schemes of development for implementation by the Corporation,[14] and the Uganda Development Corporation was in 1967 criticised for sluggishness and lack of drive.[15] Where administrative procedures are already inclined to be slow, the creation of public corporations may not so much simplify administration as complicate it. In 1965 in Kenya, the criticism was made that the Minister of Agriculture had to spend his time going round from board to board for advice before any decisions could be made.[16]

Whether or not the public corporation is more expensive in overheads and staff costs than departmental administration, many M.P.s believe that it is. Certainly, most public corporations in East Africa are free to pay better salaries than are paid to the Civil Service. It clearly involves unnecessary expense if, when a new corporation is established, higher salaries are paid to former civil servants performing the same work as before, as happened with the National Housing Corporation in Uganda.[17] Against this is the argument favoured by the General Manager of the Tanzanian NDC in 1967 that business

11. *e.g.* the National Dairy Board of Tanzania, set up by the Dairy Industry Act, No. 32 of 1965.
12. Debate on the Uganda National Housing Corporation Bill, Second Reading, June 1964.
13. Irrigation Act, No. 13 of 1966.
14. Debate on the Kenya Industrial Development (Amendment) Bill 1967, Second Reading, May 22, 1967.
15. *Uganda Argus*, April 29, 1967, p. 3, reporting speech by the Minister of Commerce and Industry.
16. House of Representatives debate on Second Reading, Agricultural Development Corporation Bill, March 23, 1965, speech by Mr. Ngala-Abok M.P.
17. See debate on the Uganda National Housing Corporation Bill Second Reading in June 1964, and also report of Uganda Auditor-General on the Appropriation Accounts for 1964–65, p. 23.

is essentially different from Government, that payment by results is justified, and that salary scales must attract the able and ambitious.[18] But there are stronger institutional safeguards against nepotism and other abuses in the Civil Service than in the public corporations and more than one proposal has been made for a commission to regulate para-Statal staff conditions on the lines of the Public Service Commissions.[19]

Thirdly, the creation of some corporations meets the wishes of foreign sources of capital, technical assistance and trade. These sources may wish their grants, loans or investments to be handled directly by a corporation, on which they can be represented, rather than by a Government department. Foreign governments, particularly those with centrally planned economies, prefer making trade agreements with State boards. Yet in so far as these Governments are concerned with the efficient administration of their loans and trade agreements, the proliferation of public corporations detracts from rather than adds to administrative efficiency.

Fourthly, an expatriate may be appointed as chief executive officer of a public corporation whereas today no expatriate could hold office as principal secretary in a department. Similarly, the management of a corporation may be contracted out to a foreign company. This has been done in Tanzania both for the leading industrial firms in which the Government compulsorily acquired a majority shareholding[20] and also for the State Trading Corporation and the Tanzania Audit Corporation.

Whether or not the public corporation is a more effective means of administration than an efficient Government department, the three Governments have preferred to create corporations rather than adjust departmental techniques to the conduct of economic activities. But there seems little justification in East African conditions for talking of the autonomous public corporation. A UN Seminar on the organisation of public enterprises has emphasised that autonomy has to be earned, rather than prescribed by law, decree or convention.[21] Even in the case of the joint business venture, it is more apt to talk in terms of partnership between Government and the private investor rather than autonomy. In the field of broadcasting, autonomous services were abolished in Kenya and Tanzania and broadcasting is now a direct responsibility of the central Government in each country. A question discussed in all three countries has been the possibility of using co-operative

18. Interview with A. W. Bradley at Dar es Salaam, May 5, 1967.
19. A Tanzanian government committee was appointed in May 1967 to inquire into the relationship between civil service salaries and salaries in the para-Statal organisations, headed by the then head of the Civil Service. In a debate on the Uganda National Trading Corporation Bill on July 4, 1966, Mr. Mayanja M.P. called for the standardisation of salaries paid by the para-Statals. In Kenya, a working party on statutory boards and corporations has considered this matter, but no report was published.
20. Industrial Shares (Acquisition) Act, No. 5/1967, and see Bradley, "Legal Aspects of the Nationalisations in Tanzania" (1967) 3 E.A.L.J. 149, 173, note 105.
21. Report of UN Seminar on Organisation and Administration of Public Enterprises, UN 1966, ST/TAO/M/35, p. 9.

institutions rather than public boards for such purposes as commodity marketing. The general attitude of the Governments is that co-operative unions are not yet strong enough to discharge such burdens[22] but the Government departments concerned probably favour the closer control which they may exercise over the public corporations. There is little to suggest that Governments have been unable to control corporations whenever politically they have wished to do so.

2. Ministerial Powers over Public Corporations

One of the most important aspects of public corporation law in East Africa, directly concerning the extent of corporate autonomy, is that dealing with relations between corporations and Ministers. This may be looked at under several heads.

(1) Appointment and dismissal of members and staff

Whatever may have been the position in colonial times, where, particularly in Kenya, producer-representation on marketing boards was provided for by a system of election of producers by producers, the general rule now is that, whatever the type of corporation, the Minister under whose portfolio a public corporation falls appoints a majority of the members of the corporation and often appoints the whole board. Are there any statutory limitations on the Minister's exercise of power, and what are the terms and conditions on which appointments are made?

In some cases there are no limitations, the Minister having unfettered power to appoint whom he will. Thus, orders establishing commodity boards under the Tanzania Agricultural Products (Control and Marketing) Act merely provide that the boards shall consist of between ten and twenty people appointed by the Minister. More usually, some limitations are provided in the constituent statute or order, though often of a vague and subjective variety. A common form requires the Minister to appoint only those persons who have had experience of, and/or shown capacity in, such fields as industry, commerce, finance, administration, or the organisation of workers. This provision or a variant of it appears in the nationalisation legislation of Tanzania which established the National Bank of Commerce and the State Trading Corporation, and the legislation establishing the Industrial and Commercial Development Corporation of Kenya, and the Uganda Development Corporation and National Trading Corporation.

The above-mentioned statutes all impose this limitation in such a form that there is no need for the Minister to specify, when appointing, which appointee

22. For Kenya, see speech by Mr. Mboya, Minister for Economic Planning and Development to the Kenya Parliament on July 29, 1966. For Tanzania, see the Government Observations on the Report of the Presidential Committee of Inquiry into the Co-operatives and Marketing Boards.

is meant to have what experience. Nor is there any need for him to appoint a balanced membership; a civil servant and six trade unionists would comply with the statute. A more effective limitation, in theory at least, appears in the Agricultural Development Corporation Act of Kenya; there the Minister appoints the chairman and eight members of the corporation but of the eight members, at least one must be an accountant, one have knowledge of international finance and one have knowledge of the marketing of agricultural produce.

Another common limitation is provided by the policy of continuing producer-representation on the statutory commodity boards. With two exceptions—the Kenya Tea Development Authority and the Coffee Board of Kenya—election of producers has been replaced by the appointment of producers by the Minister. The simplest form may be illustrated by the Lint and Seed Marketing Board of Tanzania. Of its sixteen members, all appointed by the Minister, ten must represent the cotton industry, of whom five must represent growers. In the case of the Lint Marketing Board of Uganda, the Minister appoints six out of nine members of the Board, to represent growers and co-operative societies.

Two variations of this simple form may be mentioned. First, the Minister may be required to appoint producers from a panel or from nominations put forward by producers. Thus, the Sisal Board of Kenya consists of eleven persons, of whom the Minister appoints three smallholder growers from a panel of five put forward by the Central Agricultural Board, and three plantation growers from a panel of five nominated by the Sisal Growers Association. The second variation, less used, is a mere requirement of consultation prior to the appointment of producer-representatives—thus before appointing five producer-representatives to the twelve member Cotton Lint and Seed Marketing Board of Kenya, the Minister must consult with the Central Agricultural Board.

Finally, the presence of ex-officio members on boards and corporations may be regarded as a limitation in so far as it operates to prevent the Minister from appointing all the members. Such ex-officio members are of two kinds—Ministers and civil servants. Tanzania has established two public corporations, the National Development Corporation and the National Water Resources Council, the majority of whose members are Ministers with particular portfolios, the rest being appointed by the President at his discretion.

With few exceptions, civil servant ex-officio membership never amounts to more than two or three persons per corporation, always a minority. Most frequently, particularly in Kenya, the Director of Agriculture or his representative is required to serve on the commodity boards and other agricultural corporations. In all three countries the Ministry of Finance is represented on many corporations, particularly those concerned with lending and spending.

With regard to terms of service and dismissal, limitations on the Minister's power are fewer than in relation to appointment. With very few exceptions, members, other than ex-officio ones, are appointed on such terms and conditions as the Minister thinks fit; unless otherwise stated on appointment, members are appointed for two or three year terms which are renewable, and members may be removed from office at any time without cause shown by the Minister. Where the legislation provides for removal for some general cause, no provision is made for any inquiry or hearing prior to removal, nor might it always be possible to bring an action in the courts alleging wrongful dismissal; to win it would be more difficult still. The Bank of Tanzania Act empowers the President to remove a director only for inability to perform his duties or for misbehaviour, and broadly similar provisions exist in the Central Bank legislation of the other countries. If an action for wrongful dismissal were commenced, the courts would, in the absence of clear evidence to the contrary, be almost bound to accept the Minister's or the President's word that there was sufficient cause for removal. Only where removal is permitted for failure to attend a certain number of meetings of the corporation, could actions for wrongful dismissal be hopefully prosecuted, but since the power to remove without cause is in addition to that power, a Minister has a ready defence to such an action.

Far more so than the unfettered powers of appointment, these powers place corporation members firmly under the control of the relevant Minister and deny the corporations that feeling of independence usually regarded as necessary for the successful performance of their functions. Practice indicates that Ministers in all three countries are prepared to use, and use frequently, their powers, especially in the interests of politics. All Governments, but particularly Kenya's (though this may be an impression caused by the fact that that Government is more open about the matter), regard membership of corporations as an opportunity to exercise political patronage. Ex-Ministers, M.P.s and long-standing party members are put on the corporations, often as chairmen, and if they fall out of favour, they tend to be replaced by other persons who need to be rewarded or placated by office. The legislation does not prevent this use of Ministerial powers, but while it continues, the board members will be more beholden to their Ministers than even the legislation suggests would be the case. Such patronage does not apply to all corporations—for instance the membership of the Central Banks is carefully selected for its expertise in public finance and allied fields—nor to all appointees, but it is sufficiently pervasive to be a crucial factor in assessing the effectiveness of the corporations. More broadly, patronage may be justifiable in that all Governments must, to some extent, reward their supporters. This is particularly important in a new nation whose political stability may be upset by a few disgruntled politicians, in which there are few private directorships and no peerages to compensate for loss of office, and in which the available talent for board posts is spread rather thinly. But to use public corporations for this purpose is not wholly compatible with using them as the spearhead or the pump-primer of economic development.

The same general comments may be made about Ministerial power to appoint staff. Many statutes, particularly in Tanzania, empower the Minister to appoint the chief executive officer of the corporation, or allow the corporation to do so subject to the approval of the Minister, which usually comes to the same thing. The terms and conditions of service for such an appointment are provided for in similar fashion. More rarely, and more questionably, Ministers are given powers relating to the appointment of other members of the staff of corporations. Thus, in Uganda, Ministers may issue directives to the Link Marketing Board and the Coffee Board requiring them to obtain Ministerial approval before specified servants or classes of servants are appointed. Committees inquiring into the industries in which these boards operate have criticised the adverse effect on staffing and morale that indiscriminate use of these powers has had.[23]

Two general questions arise from the existence and exercise of these powers. First, the matter of Africanisation is often uppermost in Ministerial minds when these powers are provided for and used. Public corporations may have been created so as to employ expatriates in important positions without attracting too much political attention as would be the case if they were still employed as civil servants, but matters have not always worked out as hoped for. The Tanzanian Presidential Committee on Co-operatives and Statutory Boards[24] drew attention to unsatisfactory relationships between the boards and the producers, and amongst the staff of the boards because of the presence of "unsympathetic" expatriates on the staff, and recommended that the Central Establishment Division of the President's Office "address itself to the problem of the Africanisation of the boards, in consultation with the board members, most of whom are Africans."[25] In the next breath the Commission highlighted the problem which this tends to bring in its train, and which the Uganda committees have found to exist, when it stated that it was not suggesting "the premature promotion of unqualified men, or the employment of Africans who are not fit material."[26] The fact remains that Africanisation, though necessary, means that chances must be taken, and this is bound to affect the work of the corporations.

Secondly, a point previously mentioned, the absence of uniform terms and conditions of service of corporation staff is a problem for each country. Competition amongst the corporations for scarce managerial skills drives up salaries, drains talent from other necessary jobs, and increases administrative

23. Cotton Industry Report, 1966, pp. 50–52, paras. 174–179. Coffee Industry Report 1967, pp. 70–72, paras. 5.18–5.21.
24. Report of the Presidential Special Committee of Inquiry into Co-operative Movement and Marketing Boards 1966, p. 48, paras. 265–269.
25. Para. 267.
26. Para. 268.

costs. Standard terms of service, or amalgamation of boards to reduce costs as has been proposed in Tanzania and Uganda, would further cut into corporations' autonomy but would help to spread available talent more evenly, and to keep high salaries in the public sector from rising further.

(2) Rule-making powers

All statutes empower the Minister to make rules and regulations relating to various aspects of the corporations' work, sometimes including regulations on matters of internal organisation and management, *e.g.* frequency of meetings, voting and the keeping of minutes. But few statutes provide for the Minister to consult with or seek approval from the corporation before making these rules. A common Tanzanian provision empowers the Minister to "make regulations prescribing all matters which are by this Act required or permitted to be prescribed, or for carrying out or giving effect to the purposes and provisions of this Act. . . . "[27] An unfettered Ministerial power in Uganda is illustrated by the Produce Marketing Board Act which empowers the Minister to make statutory instruments for the proper performance by the Board of its functions.

Examples of consultations may be found in all countries but, particularly in Tanzania, these are exceptional, and there is nothing which readily explains why some corporations are specially treated. Thus in Uganda the Minister may make regulations about the dairy industry but only after consultation with the Dairy Corporation, whose functions *inter alia* are to develop and control all aspects of the industry, but consultation is not required with the Uganda Tea Growers Corporation, a body with broadly the same functions, before the Minister makes regulations about the tea industry. In Tanzania, the Minister must consult the Coffee Board before prescribing grading areas, but need not consult the National Agricultural Products Board before prescribing a crop as one to be controlled by the Board. In practice no consultation appears to take place, for one of the major criticisms of the Tanzanian Presidential Commission on Co-operatives and Marketing Boards was that the Government decided policy and pursued the administration of agriculture without consulting boards on any matter.[28] In Kenya the Minister must consult with the Agricultural Development Corporation before making rules on a wide variety of matters but not with the Industrial and Commercial Development Corporation before exercising similar powers.

The same lack of clear policy pervades the rule-making powers of corporations, though in general these are much narrower than the comparable powers of Ministers. Many corporations are not expressly empowered to make rules, though some could doubtless achieve some of the purposes for which rules are

27. National Bank of Commerce (Establishment and Vesting of Assets and Liabilities) Act, No. 1 of 1967, s. 17.
28. Report cit. p. 44, para. 242, p. 47, para. 260.

useful in other ways. For instance the State Trading Corporation of Tanzania is not empowered to make by-laws (unlike the National Trading Corporation of Uganda), but since the former corporation may enter into "any transaction which in its opinion is calculated to facilitate the proper and efficient carrying on of its activities ... "[29] it could, by using standard-form contracts, and through its monopoly position in the import/export trade for general merchandise, lay down what would be in effect a set of rules for that trade.

Not all corporations could thus overcome a lack of rule-making powers, and amending legislation could usefully rationalise the position. Probably too little consideration has been given to a proper division of rule-making powers between Minister and corporation, and draftsmen have had to include wide general powers for one or both of the parties. Given that both parties are to have rule-making powers it might be better if specific powers are given to each with a general residual power to the Minister. As matters stand, the provisions described illustrate the reluctance of the three Governments to give the corporations a free hand in their ordinary administration of policy.

(3) Consents with particular reference to financial powers

The same theme runs even more clearly through the question of consents. To what extent may corporations act, particularly in financial matters, without first obtaining Ministerial approval? In all countries the answer is in practice less and less, but the division of responsibilities in law may tell us much about relationships between corporation and Minister. First we may consider non-financial matters. A distinction must here be made between statutory commodity boards and other corporations. There is a very close administrative relationship between the commodity boards and the relevant Ministry, usually the Ministry of Agriculture. Indeed in some respects the corporate personality of the boards has masked the fact that in the last few years they have become little more than specialist departments of the Ministry, with the key members of the board being the chairman, usually a political colleague of the Minister's, and the ex-officio members from the Ministry. All reports on the performance of these boards in the three countries have stressed both the important role they play in crop control and marketing and the overriding Governmental concern in their operations. The legislation has tended to emphasise Governmental concern and the consequent need for supervision; there is at best a co-operative approach to the administration of agricultural marketing with the boards acting as junior partners. So much is this the position that the *raison d'être* of the commodity boards is difficult to see. Indeed the Tanzanian Presidential Commission recommended the abolition of several, the amalgamation of others, and a change in their position so that they became the agents of the co-operatives, and envisaged a future when their functions would be

29. State Trading Corporation (Establishment and Vesting of Interests) Act, No. 2 of 1967, s. 4 (2) (*d*).

taken over entirely by the co-operatives.[30] Not all these recommendations were accepted by the Government. Nothing so drastic has been proposed in Kenya despite several similar inquiries, which leads one to suspect that these boards survive, just because they exist, and have existed for some time—most boards in Kenya have a longer history than those in Tanzania—and are as much a part of the machinery of Government as are Ministries and the Civil Service, which may be reformed but hardly abolished.

A consideration of Ministerial power in relation to public corporations other than the commodity boards must include financial matters, for these other corporations are, with one or two exceptions, spending and lending corporations. All corporations with borrowing powers may exercise them only with the prior approval of the Minister and, sometimes in addition, of the Minister of Finance. Some statutes—for instance, the National Development Corporation Act of Tanzania—impose an upper limit on a corporation's borrowing powers though this may be raised by a resolution of the National Assembly. In the case of a development corporation whose business it is to initiate industrial or agricultural enterprises, Ministerial control over borrowing powers is tantamount to Ministerial control over all the functions of the corporation, at least in its early years until it has built up substantial reserves of its own and can finance development from its own resources. This is perhaps unavoidable since Governments guarantee loans from funds such as the World Bank and the Commonwealth Development Corporation, and must ensure that loans are used on worthwhile development.

In addition to this general control over borrowing, several statutes provide for more specific financial controls. Thus, without the prior authority of the Minister, the Uganda Development Corporation may not establish new undertakings, acquire any interest in any undertaking or increase its capital in any undertaking. The Uganda Electricity Board must act in accord with a general programme settled from time to time with the Minister in carrying out any developments involving a large capital outlay, or any reorganisation. The Land and Agricultural Bank of Kenya is required to obtain the consent of the Minister before lending money on a mortgage for more than 80 per cent. of the value of agricultural land. Both the Lint Marketing and the Coffee Boards of Uganda must submit annual estimates of capital and recurrent expenditure to the Minister for his approval. Finally, commodity boards often have power to impose a levy on the produce which they are controlling, but only with the approval of the Minister. In some cases the Minister is empowered not merely to approve the exercise of the power but to confer the power on the board in the first place, a control which itself represents a derogation from the principle that only the legislature should authorise taxation.

All countries then have a reasonably clear policy that public corporations, of whatever kind, must be subject to strict control in the way they raise their

30. Report cit. p. 41, paras. 223–224, pp. 43–44, paras. 237–242.

K

money and, as to major expenditure, in the way they spend it. It is a reasonable assumption that this policy is largely dictated by the fact that in the final analysis few if any of the corporations can be regarded as completely financially secure, and if they make a loss or collapse, the Government will have to bail them out, and repay loans whether to local or overseas lenders. It is in a sense, therefore, the precarious financial position of the Governments, so much at the mercy of the terms of international trade, and with a very small tax-base, that forces them to deny the corporations greater financial freedom. The evidence from the longest-standing development corporation, the UDC, suggests that within the limits of the law, a corporation with a determined and experienced chairman can achieve sufficient financial freedom to operate in a commercial manner. But such chairmen either do not exist, or are not now appointed. A more significant indication of current practice is that the chairman of the Agricultural Development Corporation in Kenya is the Minister of Agriculture, and the National Development Corporation in Tanzania has six Ministers amongst its ten members. In addition to the Government's position as financial guarantors of the corporations, the disciplines of the Development Plan increase the centralising tendencies which all three Governments have displayed since independence. An administrative climate of centralisation and tight financial control runs directly contrary to the principle of autonomy of public corporations.

(4) Directives

No final conclusion can be reached on the relationship in practice between corporations and Government until we have examined the power of Ministers to issue binding directives to the corporations and the use made of this power. In some respects this is the most important aspect of the relationship, for if given in wide terms, and used often and in virtual disregard of the division of responsibilities set out in the constituent statute, much of that statute and the preceding discussion are rendered otiose.

Yet this is one Ministerial power which has consciously been increased by amending legislation in the last six years. Where before the power was non-existent, it now exists, and where it was exercisable only subject to safeguards, the safeguards have been eliminated. With the exception of the three Central Banks, and the Tanzania Audit Corporation, which is however subject to directions from the Controller and Auditor-General, no statute establishing a public corporation in any country since its independence has been without a provision empowering the Minister to give directives to the corporation. The provisions differ from each other, however, and some incorporate safeguards against abuse.

A typical, unlimited general power is found in the Lint Marketing Board Act of Uganda: the Minister "may at any time and on any matter . . . give directions to the Board as to the exercise of its powers or the carrying out of its duties or functions and the Board shall give effect to any such directions."[31] Similar provisions exist in many statutes in Kenya and Tanzania, though in the latter country the Minister's power is in theory cut down when, as with the State Trading Corporation, he may only give directions of a general character in relation to matters appearing to him to affect the national interest. Some statutes enable the Minister to give directions on specific matters; thus the Electricity Act of Uganda empowers the Minister to give directions to the Uganda Electricity Board as to the disposal of its assets, and the Coffee Act of Tanzania empowers the Minister to give the Tanganyika Coffee Board directions on the export and sale of coffee and the transport of coffee through Tanzania.

Less common than the power is the existence of safeguards on it. Two types may be mentioned. The first is consultation. In Uganda the Uganda Electricity Board must be consulted by the Minister before he issues directives to it; in Tanzania, the Minister must consult the Governor of the Bank of Tanzania before giving directions of a general character to the National Bank of Commerce. But how effective as a safeguard is such consultation? The main benefit from the corporation's point of view is to receive some advance warning of an impending directive, rather than that the corporation should hope to alter a proposed directive very much. Consultation with an outside body, on the other hand, may be more effective, depending on the status of the body concerned.

A more important limitation is the second type which permits a corporation to decline to comply with a directive until certain conditions are met. Thus, the Kenyan Minister of Agriculture may after consultation with the Minister of Finance instruct the Agricultural Development Corporation to initiate or assist in the initiation of an enterprise. If, however, the Corporation considers the enterprise economically or otherwise unsound it shall not be required to proceed with the work until the Government has undertaken to reimburse it for any losses which it thereby incurs. In assessing the value of this provision in strengthening the Corporation *vis-à-vis* the Government, account must be taken of the Minister of Agriculture's position as chairman of the Corporation and the Ministerial power of appointment to, and dismissal from, the Corporation. These inevitably detract from the members' willingness to make use of their legal powers and raise a doubt as to whether such restraints on Ministerial power are of any value.

This doubt receives support from the considerable documentation that exists of the use to which Ministers have put their power to give directions and the ill effects of this on the corporations. Committees and commissions of inquiry usually state the dilemma without being able to offer a solution, and proposals which they make for ameliorating the situation are usually ignored by Governments. The dilemma is that the public corporations occupy

31. Cap. 234, s. 4 (3).

an increasingly important position in the country's economy. A Government geared to planning, and responsive to the electorate, must be able to ensure that the corporations comply with the plan, both in general, and if necessary in detail, for they are, in many respects, the major administrative tool for plan implementation. Yet the conferring of wide powers of direction on a Minister opens the way for abuse, and for the corporations' initiative and commercial sense to be weakened.

Some evidence as to the existence of this dilemma may be mentioned. The Committee of Inquiry into the Cotton Industry in Uganda in 1966 gave a classic example of a Ministerial directive which cut across the commercial judgment of the Lint Marketing Board.[32] The Minister directed the Board to investigate the possibility of changing its marketing policy from using private firms of exporters to a direct sales policy. Before the Board had completed its study of the problem it received another Ministerial directive to make the change, the purpose being to cut out non-African middlemen. The Board was equipped neither administratively nor in experience to carry out the new policy and was forced to engage one of the non-African firms as its agent to market the cotton. The sole result of the Ministerial directive therefore was to destroy the Board's freedom to encourage competition amongst private firms of exporters, and to make it possible for the one firm that was the Board's agent to exploit the Board and hence the producers. The Committee recommended that the Minister's power should be confined to issuing directives of a general character, and then only after consultation with the Board, but the wide powers quoted above still apply to this Board, and have been incorporated into laws establishing other corporations since the Committee reported.

The Tanzanian Presidential Commission on the Co-operatives and Marketing Boards noted that Ministerial pressure on the Development and Credit Banks had resulted in those bodies making some loans of doubtful soundness; it recommended that the Government should revert to its original and statutory role in relation to the banks of vetoing proposals only.[33] Finally, a committee in Kenya on statutory bodies found that there was too much Ministerial interference and control (in 1963 the law relating to nearly all statutory commodity boards had been altered to allow for Ministerial directives[34]) and suggested that administrative machinery was needed to moderate control and prevent it being too much at a Minister's personal discretion.

More than anything else hitherto discussed in this section, these exercises of Ministerial power indicate that no East African Government considers that it is possible to grant the corporation much freedom of action, despite the deleterious effects on some of the corporations that failure to do so has had.

32. Report cit. pp. 44–50, paras. 152–173.
33. Report cit. p. 51, para. 276.
34. Statutory Marketing Boards (Amendment of Laws) Act, No. 45 of 1963.

The law, whether on directives, financial control or appointments of members and staff, is shown, usually by official reports written with commendable frankness, to be just the starting point for a wide-ranging Ministerial control of corporations rather than an attempt to divide responsibilities between corporations and Ministers. This would be understandable and to some extent justifiable if the control was directed towards some definite planned objective, but too often the motive for control is one of politics or patronage. The official reports say this should stop, but it goes on. Why is this?

To some extent, the East African Governments are merely experiencing the same difficulties that other Governments with more developed administrations have experienced in fitting public corporations into their traditional notions of responsible government, control of the bureaucracy, and accountability to the legislature. The problem is compounded in East Africa by the different forms that government is taking and by the fact that while the political wing of the Executive is always developing and changing, the administrative wing remains rather traditional and stationary. Again the existence of the Development Plans requires, or is thought to require, constant Ministerial control, whatever inquiries and commentators might say.

But this is not the whole answer. The important point is that the evidence suggests that the amount of Ministerial control is constantly increasing, and that its nature is political rather than economic. The reason for this may lie in what political scientists have called the practice or phenomenon of associational integration[35]; the desire of the ruling party in a new and politically unstable State to bring all possible rival power centres under its control, so as to minimise the possibility of opposition to its rule. Investigations of this phenomenon have hitherto concentrated on such institutions as opposition parties, the Civil Service, the police and armed forces, and the universities, but the same need to control may explain the trends in public corporation law and practice, and why political factors are regarded as more important than economic ones when control is exercised. On this analysis, changes in the formal wording of the law to limit the Minister's power, or calls for a restrained, more objective exercise of the power, or a reversion to the degree of control exercised in the past, all of which have been suggested by various inquiries, may be irrelevant, and are unlikely to be heeded. Nor are present limitations on the Minister's power very significant when set against both the totality of the Minister's legal powers and the political need to exercise them. Any alteration in the law to limit Ministerial powers, to increase the publicity attendant upon their exercise, to confer greater security of tenure on corporation members, etc., however desirable it may be, must be preceded by a

35. Coleman and Rosberg: *Political Parties and National Integration in Tropical Africa* (University of California Press) (1964) pp. 664–665.

change in the practice if it is not to be ignored. This in turn is dependent upon wider political factors, a discussion of which is outside our scope but which may be summarised as being the development of feelings of security, confidence and success on the part of the political élites of the East African countries.

3. PARLIAMENTARY CONTROL OF THE PUBLIC CORPORATIONS

Many Westminster parliamentary procedures have been inherited by the unicameral national assemblies at Kampala, Nairobi and Dar es Salaam. Question time, adjournment debates, debates on legislation and on the estimates, debates on the speech by the Head of State at the opening of a new session and Public Accounts Committees are all to be found. Even in Tanzania where the Constitution provides for a presidential form of government, Ministers are members of the National Assembly and the formal practices of Ministerial responsibility are observed. But superficial resemblances as regards parliamentary control of the Executive should not conceal the very real differences in political organisation which exist both between the East African countries and more developed countries and also *inter se*. East African Parliaments sit for much shorter periods than other Parliaments and cannot be regarded as being in constant session. Few M.P.s have experience of the professions, business and commerce. In each country most M.P.s will be doing their parliamentary work in their second or even third language. Little use is made of committees with the result that there tend to be few opportunities for detailed scrutiny of the work of the Executive. In Tanzania, the one-party Constitution precludes the existence of an opposition in the National Assembly; in Kenya and Uganda, although a small minority of M.P.s form an opposition, the national assemblies do not now function in a way which observes the rights of the opposition.

It is against this background that we must consider the extent to which Parliaments in East Africa effectively control the activities of public corporations and of Ministers in relation to public corporations. Except as regards the Uganda Development Corporation and the Uganda Electricity Board, which to a varying degree since independence have officially been regarded as autonomous, there are few examples in parliamentary debates of a Government expressly disclaiming responsibility for the corporations. In particular, the three National Assemblies have not experienced the difficulties of the British House of Commons concerning the questioning of Ministers about the corporations. Ministers are usually prepared to supply M.P.s with information and to defend a corporation's policy where necessary. One recent study of the work of the Tanzanian National Assembly since the general election in October 1965 suggests that it was mainly parliamentary pressure, manifested partly in the questioning of Ministers, that led to the setting up of the Presidential Committee on Co-operatives and Marketing Boards.[36] As the line between departmental activities and the public corporations is often indistinct, the performance and policies of the public corporations are commonly raised during general discussion of Governmental activity. Thus the rather shapeless debates in Kenya and Uganda on the presidential speech at the opening of Parliament range over the whole field of public activities without distinguishing between departments and corporations. At the annual estimates meeting, the boards linked with a particular Ministry are discussed while the estimates for that Ministry are being considered. A third such opportunity occurs when Parliament is debating a new development plan. In so far as matters raised during these debates are replied to by the Government, criticism of the corporations, or of Government policy towards the corporations, is met by the Minister responsible, but from the nature of the occasion, criticism is unlikely to be penetrating.

Some examples of this kind of parliamentary discussion may be given.[37] In the debate on the second Ugandan Five Year Development Plan held in July 1966, one M.P. raised the issue of the structure of the public corporations, the future developments in the UDC "empire," the degree of Ugandanisation in UDC enterprises, and the need for State subsidies to the UEB to enable supplies of electricity to be extended as a social service.[38] In the same debate another M.P. raised the question of the difficulty which board members experienced in criticising the actions of a chairman who was also the chief executive officer.[39] In a debate on the Presidential address, another Ugandan M.P. criticised the National Trading Corporation for its lack of progress, referred to the need for the National Housing Corporation to co-ordinate its plans with the Ministry of Housing and city councils, and expressed the view that politicians of the calibre of Ministers were needed on the boards of corporations and not civil servants.[40]

More detailed discussion of public corporations is likely in the following circumstances: (a) on the consideration of Bills which propose to set up new corporations or seek to amend the law relating to existing corporations; (b) on occasions when specific approval is needed from the national assembly for

36. *One Party Democracy*, ed. L. Cliffe, East Africa Publishing House, 1967, pp. 344–345. Cliffe also gives the following analysis of questions asked in the first five meetings of the 1965 National Assembly: agriculture and water 159 (15·7 per cent.), marketing and co-operatives 65 (6·4 per cent.), commerce and industry 97 (9·6 per cent.), social services and housing 148 (14·6 per cent.).

37. Because debates in the Tanzanian National Assembly are conducted almost entirely in the Swahili language, illustrations will be drawn mainly from debates in Kenya and Uganda. The interest of the Tanzanian National Assembly in the financing of Government enterprises was shown in September 1966, when the Assembly rejected a supplementary estimate providing for a loan to the insolvent Tanganyika National Transport Co-operative Society Ltd.

38. Uganda Parliamentary Debates (cited as U.P.D.), July 12 and 13, 1966, pp. 703–722, Mr. Mayanja.

39. U.P.D., July 22, 1966, p. 1005, Mr. Omadi.

40. U.P.D., June 12, 1967, Mr. Mugeni.

financial transactions involving the corporations, *e.g.* the approval of supplementary estimates required for a grant or subsidy to a corporation, or the approval of Government guarantees needed in connection with foreign loans to the public corporations[41]; (*c*) during discussion of a corporation's report and accounts which have been laid before Parliament.

(1) Legislative debates

A good example of a second reading debate occurred on March 23, 1965, on the Kenya Agricultural Development Corporation Bill. In moving the second reading, the Assistant Minister for Agriculture explained the procedure by which projects of agricultural development could be approved for inclusion within the Development Plan and for support by the ADC. "Let it not be forgotten that this corporation is virtually going to be a Government owned and Government operated body, because of the powers of direction from the Cabinet and the Minister." A dozen M.P.s spoke in the debate, dealing (*inter alia*) with the need for this new corporation and their anxiety about the confusing multiplicity of agricultural boards; the composition of the board and the relative suitability for membership of politicians and civil servants; the need to utilise M.P.s in the activities of the board; and regional balance in the board's membership. Several members referred to the Minister's power to appoint to the board: one asked for a right of appeal against removal from the board by the Minister; another referred to what he called the notorious conduct of the Minister of Co-operatives in making appointments which, he said, had recently been improved because of parliamentary criticism. In replying to the debate, the Government spokesman met the request for the appointment of politicians to the board by invoking the powers and responsibility of the Cabinet: major policy decisions would be settled by the Cabinet Development Committee. The House would have the usual control over the operations of the corporation, "just as they have over any other corporation," and the annual report would be laid in Parliament and subject to questioning. Nevertheless the Government agreed that the membership of the board would be increased to enable at least one M.P. to be appointed. Subsequently, the Government appears to have provided no specific occasions for debating the affairs of the ADC, nor have individual M.P.s initiated such debates.

The issues which interest M.P.s in Uganda may be illustrated from the second reading debate on a Bill to create the Uganda Tea Growers Corporation.[42] In opening the debate, the Minister of Agriculture stressed the help that the Government would give to the corporation by seconding staff and providing roads in tea growing areas. Amongst the points raised in debate

---

41. See, *e.g.* debates relating to guarantees for the Uganda Electricity Board on February 8, 1967, and the Uganda Lint and Coffee Marketing Boards on February 17, May 17, and June 29, 1966.

42. U.P.D., January 31, February 1, 1966.

were—the methods of recruitment to the corporation's staff and the need for objective grounds of appointment; the danger of employing too many top executives, in particular a full-time chairman as well as a full-time executive officer; the danger of the board becoming a rubber stamp for the Minister's policy in view of his power to dismiss members of the board; the need for standardisation of salaries paid by para-Statal organisations; the danger of civil servants in the Ministry vetoing commercial decisions of the corporation; and the need for public audit and for the laying of reports and subsidiary legislation by the board before Parliament.

Several themes recur in these Ugandan debates. The danger of political bias in board appointments was raised on both the National Trading Corporation Bill[43] and the Dairy Industry Bill.[44] The standardisation of salaries is raised more than once: as one M.P. explained, "the para-Statals are now going to employ more people than the Government."[45] An M.P. who suggested that civil servants seconded to the service of the National Dairy Corporation might find themselves in an uncertain position received the reply from the Minister that there was no fear of double loyalty, "as both the Corporation and the seconded staff come under my Ministry."[46] Inevitably some loose ends are left by the debates. An example of inconclusive discussion occurred in the case of the National Trading Corporation debate,[47] when the Minister failed to clarify the twofold aim of the corporation, which was intended to assist African traders in business and also to begin trading on its own account. Moreover in all the instances given, parliamentary discussion is confined to speculation as to the success of a proposed corporation and is not a method of controlling existing corporations.

Legislative debates with a greater claim to be regarded as a means of control occur on Bills which seek to amend existing legislation, such as the Bills which have sought to increase government powers over the corporations or, more recently, to permit civil servants to become chairmen of the public corporations.[48] Before agreeing to pass proposed amendments of this kind, Ugandan M.P.s have discussed more aspects of corporation affairs than would strictly be justified by reference to the nature of the amendments and the Speaker's exhortation to limit discussion has not always been heeded. Thus in a debate on a Bill to enable the National Housing Corporation to form a company to promote housebuilding by Ugandans, M.P.s used the opportunity to voice their dissatisfaction with the whole work of the NHC.[49]

These debates characteristically consist of a series of sometimes unrelated points made by individual M.P.s and not of sustained arguments for or against

43. U.P.D., June 30, 1966.
44. U.P.D., April 20 and 21, 1967.
45. Debate on National Trading Corporation Bill 1966, U.P.D., July 4, 1966.
46. Debate on Dairy Industry Bill 1967, U.P.D., April 21, 1967.
47. U.P.D., June 30, 1966.
48. *e.g.* National Insurance Corporation (Amendment) Act, Act No. 8 of 1968.
49. U.P.D., May 3, 1967.

a Bill as a whole. However valid the points themselves, the Uganda and Kenya Governments seem rarely to accept the advice given.

(2) Discussion of reports and accounts

The parent Acts of public corporations generally require that a report and accounts be presented annually to the relevant Minister and laid before the National Assembly. This of course assumes that there is a parent Act: TANESCO and the National Insurance Corporation in Tanzania are two Government-owned companies with no statutory constitution which were, until the Tanzania Audit Corporation Act 1968, free from any requirement to lay reports and accounts in Parliament. Where the report and accounts must be laid in Parliament, a time limit is frequently provided for this to be done. Although the legislation is reasonably uniform in these respects, the practice is much less uniform, and particularly in Kenya and Tanzania delays in the preparation and laying of reports are not uncommon. In an extreme case it was reported that accounts of the Tanzanian National Housing Corporation had not been laid for 1963–65, in breach of a statutory requirement that a resolution of the Assembly be obtained if laying was delayed for more than six months after the end of the financial year.[50] Also in Tanzania, the National Agricultural Products Board, which has wide responsibilities for marketing many agricultural products, was by 1967 seriously behind in publishing its accounts.[51]

To judge from the parliamentary record, the Ugandan Administration has the best performance in this respect. Accounts for the major corporations are regularly laid before the Assembly, usually between six and twelve months after the ending of the financial year concerned. What is no less important from the point of view of parliamentary control, the Government generally tables a motion to receive the accounts so enabling M.P.s to discuss the progress of the corporation. The debate is generally opened and replied to by the Minister responsible for the corporation but M.P.s who hold a directorship in the corporation may take part to explain the corporation's policies. In recent years, the Government has invariably arranged for the reports of the UDC and the UEB to be discussed each year, but not all reports are discussed in this way. In 1961 the reports of the Coffee and Lint Marketing Boards for the financial year 1959–60 were each debated but in 1963 it emerged that Government practice had changed: in future it would be for individual M.P.s to table a motion on the reports if they felt so inclined.[52] The effect of this change is that the reports of these two boards are no longer debated. More recently, the report and accounts of the National Insurance Corporation were discussed and this will probably also be done in the case of the newer National

50. Report of Controller and Auditor-General for 1964–65, p. xxiv.
51. Report of Controller and Auditor-General for 1965–66, p. xxxv.
52. Debate on Lint Marketing Board (Amendment) Bill, U.P.D., October 1, 1963.

Trading Corporation. The conclusion is that, as in the case of subsidiary legislation which has to be laid before Parliament, individual M.P.s are unlikely of their own initiative to make full use of opportunities for parliamentary discussion of executive conduct. Much depends on how far a Government encourages parliamentary discussion by providing specific occasions for it.

(3) Parliamentary discussion of the Uganda Development Corporation 1961–66

The UDC was established by the Protectorate Government in 1952 as a means of promoting industrial and manufacturing development in Uganda. By the 1960s, it had come to control a wide variety of rapidly developing enterprises ranging from the manufacture of shirts, tea-pots and fertilisers to the control of Uganda Hotels. On July 19, 1961, in proposing that the reports and accounts for 1960 be adopted, the Minister for Commerce and Industry attributed the success of the UDC to its autonomy; the chairman of the UDC would always welcome ideas about future projects from M.P.s, but "industry generally goes to the place where it is likely to be most successful"; Government's prime duty was to create conditions which were vital for stimulating commercial and industrial development and not to participate directly in this development. The tone of the debate was generally respectful of this cautious policy. M.P.s urged that industrial development should be spread more evenly between regions, that UDC products should be cheaper and that the rate of Africanisation should be faster. Only one M.P. suggested that it was not sufficient for the Government merely to provide facilities for the private sector to prosper; he criticised statutory restrictions which inhibited the UDC from entering more lucrative activities available to private enterprise and suggested that although the Minister might not have power to dictate to the UDC, his advice would be heeded.[53]

A year later, the feeling of many M.P.s had changed. Not only the increasing speed of the progress towards independence but also a change of government led to a debate in September 1962 of a motion that the chairmanship of the UDC should not be held by any person who was a member of the Cabinet. Mr. J. T. Simpson, who had been chairman and managing director of the UDC since its inception and was an elected M.P. had accepted office as Minister of Economic Affairs, in which capacity he was the Minister responsible for UDC matters. The Opposition objected to this plurality primarily because it brought party politics into the UDC: how could the chairman of the UDC disagree with a Government measure when he himself shared the collective responsibility of the Cabinet? The Government reply referred to the size of the Government's investment in the UDC, to the fact that major UDC decisions were subject to Cabinet approval and to the need

53. U.P.D., July 20, 1961, Mr. Babiiha, pp. 1391 et seq.

for closer co-operation between UDC and Government.[54] Although arguments such as these were directly contrary to those put forward in the previous year, they prevailed for the time being. But the National Assembly was still restive when two months later the UDC's report for 1961 was debated, and adoption of the report was moved by Simpson as Minister for Economic Affairs. He emphasised Government responsibility for the UDC—and relied on a favourable report on the UDC which a World Bank mission had made in 1961.[55] But M.P.s were not satisfied and attacked the personal empire which the chairman had built up which, they alleged, was lagging behind in Africanisation and had distributed industrial development unfairly through Uganda. Replying to the debate, Mr. Simpson began with a brave but impossible attempt to salvage the concept of autonomy: but he undertook to refer to the board the suggestions made.[56] A week later the Assembly passed a motion urging the Government to hold an inquiry into allegations of racial discrimination at Kilembe Mines, in which the UDC had a minority holding, after a heated debate in which more personal attacks on the chairman were made.[57]

By July 1963, the chairman of the UDC had resigned from the Government although not from Parliament, and the Government proposed amendments to the UDC Act to remove statutory restrictions on the scope of the UDC's activities and to authorise the appointment of a joint chairman. The Government spokesman emphasised that the UDC could not be run as a Government department and that it did not become a political organ through the chairman having a seat in Parliament.[58]

The UDC's report for 1962 was debated in November 1963. The Minister took pains to re-assert the concept of UDC autonomy: the Government were not concerned with the daily operations of the UDC but only with overall policy aspects. Notwithstanding this, M.P.s made detailed criticims of UDC affairs as well as the more basic point that Parliament should not always consider how much profit the UDC had made, but also how much it had contributed to the economic and social development of Uganda.[59] The reply to the debate was given, not by the chairman of the UDC, but by the Minister who "generously" agreed to reply to detailed points raised by the Opposition.

In September 1964, when the accounts for 1963 were debated,[60] the Minister of Housing and Labour reported further progress, especially in Ugandanisation; Mr. Simpson, who had already retired as an M.P., was about to retire as UDC chairman and would be succeeded by a Ugandan. Although

54. U.P.D., September 17, 1962.
55. U.P.D., November 15, 1962, pp. 374 *et seq.*
56. U.P.D., December 14 and 17, 1962.
57. U.P.D., December 22, 1962.
58. U.P.D., July 4, 1963, pp. 788 *et seq.*
59. U.P.D., November 21, 1963, Mr. Arain.
60. U.P.D., September 29, 1964, pp. 3126 *et seq.*

not all M.P.s were satisfied by this and there was one allegation that Ugandanisation had been achieved at the expense of introducing tribalism, most points raised were trivial in comparison with the debate of the previous year (*e.g.* why did ties have to be worn in Uganda Hotels?). The spokesman for the trade union movement urged that as the UDC was a semi-Government organisation, the Government should see that minimum wages for workers in UDC enterprises were increased.

By February 1966, when the accounts for 1964 were debated, the feeling of the National Assembly towards the UDC had evidently become much more favourable.[61] M.P.s referred to the UDC's "most successful year," extended their congratulations to the chairman of the UDC and (the wheel of history having turned) spoke affably of "Jimmy" Simpson. Of the five M.P.s who spoke in the debate, one was a director of the UDC, three between them held six directorships in UDC companies, and only one had no direct interest in UDC activities. Under these circumstances, it becomes less easy to classify parliamentary discussion as a means of external control.

In opening this debate, the Minister of Commerce and Industries, Mr. Lubowa, had spoken from the traditional text, namely that the subject of the debate was general policy and not day-to-day administration. By December 1966, when the report for 1965 was discussed,[62] Mr. Lubowa had given way to Mr. Obwangor, whose approach was noticeably tougher. Mr. Obwangor stressed the Government's responsibility for seeing that the UDC was efficient. The UDC was intended to be a commercial, profit-making body within the Government's broad economic policy. No part of Uganda should be starved of development. He criticised the UDC for maintaining three property firms in view of the shortage of Ugandan managers. Backbench M.P.s were also more critical than in the previous year: many UDC projects had been started under the British and were still only partly owned by the UDC; too great a burden was laid on the chairman of the UDC; the report was late and uninformative; and one UDC company had made a loss for two consecutive years. These criticisms were replied to by an M.P. who was a UDC director and by the Minister, who met criticism of the failure of UDC to carry out decisions which had been made by assuring the House that he had directed that every minute of the UDC should be sent to him and that he would see that the necessary action was taken. He also answered a renewed complaint about cassava prices by stating that he would soon be ordering the UDC through its subsidiary to pay at least 10 cents per pound for cassava, an extreme example of Ministerial intervention in a commercial decision.

Following these indications of direct Ministerial involvement in UDC affairs, it is not surprising that the Minister summoned a meeting of the

61. U.P.D., February 2 and 3, 1966, pp. 931 *et seq.*
62. U.P.D., December 19 and 20, 1966, pp. 1533 *et seq.*

UDC board in April 1967, when he informed them of the Government's serious dissatisfaction at the "colossal losses" being made by most of the subsidiary companies; streamlining and reform of the UDC administration were urgent.[63] It remains to be seen whether the UDC has been prodded into efficiency by these Ministerial exhortations and, more significantly, whether this vigorous intervention has led to increasing Ministerial control of the UDC's commercial policies and corresponding inroads into the earlier concept of autonomy.

(4) Participation of M.P.s in boards of public corporations

The participation of M.P.s and other politicians in the work of the public corporations has already been considered in the context of Ministerial powers of appointment to the public corporations.[64] But it also must be considered in relation to parliamentary control. There is no general exclusion of M.P.s from serving on the boards of public corporations in East Africa. Only rarely is a legal disqualification of M.P.s found: thus Tanzanian and Ugandan M.P.s are disqualified from appointment to the boards of the Banks of Tanzania and Uganda,[65] along with directors of other banks, public officers and so on. Contrary to the views of the various committees of inquiry mentioned earlier which recommended less use of politicians,[66] M.P.s frequently suggest that politicians are needed as members or chairmen of the boards and in a debate on the National Insurance Corporation of Uganda one M.P. criticised the inadequacy of its board which did not contain a single M.P.[67] The impression is given that some M.P.s would welcome more opportunities of holding such appointments. Since the number of educated and experienced citizens in public life is limited and the work of an M.P. as such is not full time, there is a case for permitting some M.P.s to hold office in the corporations. In the absence of parliamentary committees to scrutinise the corporations, service on a board may be almost the only way an M.P. can inform himself about its work.

But this work of M.P.s raises a number of problems. Is the M.P. responsible to Parliament for his work as board member or only to the Government? This problem is more acute where an M.P. is chairman of a board. How far should M.P.s' criticism and requests for information on the affairs of a board be directed to the Minister or to the M.P./chairman? A Tanzanian M.P. raised this question in June 1963 in relation to the National Agricultural Products Board whose chairman was then an M.P. The official answer, given in the National Assembly by the chairman of the NAPB and not by the

63. *Uganda Argus*, Kampala, April 29, 1967.
64. Above, pp. 271–275.
65. Bank of Tanzania Act No. 12 of 1966; Central Bank of Kenya Act, cap. 491. For an analysis of the central bank legislation in the three countries, see Newland, *Finance for Development* (East African Publishing House) (1968) pp. 25–30.
66. Above, p. 274.
67. U.P.D., December 19, 1966, pp. 1520 *et seq.*

Minister of Agriculture, was that where the chairman was in the Assembly
he was responsible to the Assembly to explain whatever he was doing on the
board. Shortly afterwards the Minister of Agriculture himself became chairman of the NAPB so the constitutional difficulty was resolved by merger.[68]
But would a regular practice have developed of including the M.P./chairman
along with Ministers as an addressee of M.P.s' questions? In Uganda,
M.P./directors have frequently taken part in debates on the corporations,
sometimes defending the corporations against M.P.s' charges, but the major
responsibility for replying to debates has rested with the Minister. In Kenya,
during the Agricultural Development Bill debate, the Government stated
that M.P.s appointed to the board would be directly responsible to the
Minister.[69]

Clearly widespread membership of public corporations by M.P.s would
affect the role of Parliament in calling the public corporations to account.
So long as civil servants are excluded from membership of the National
Assembly (as they are in Kenya and Uganda—in Tanzania they are excluded
from elected membership) there will be a constitutional reason for distinguishing between the public corporations and the Civil Service. Yet the tendency
is to assimilate the public corporations to Government departments, at least
from the point of view of Ministry control. Where a Minister directly ad-
ministers a corporation, this could well emasculate the independent contribution of an M.P./board member to Parliamentary debate. But so far as corporations retain some autonomy, and until the East African Parliaments
develop new techniques of calling corporations to account, the position of
the M.P./board member is potentially valuable as a link between Parliament,
the corporations and the public.

4. FINANCIAL ACCOUNTABILITY

The variety of national public corporations is so great that no single pattern
of financial performance could be imposed as has been attempted in respect
of the supra-national East African corporations.[70] But whatever kind of economic achievement may be expected of a corporation, there is an evident
public interest in requiring it to observe satisfactory standards of accounting.
Financial accountability is one field in which there should be no gap between
law and practice. Nearly all corporations are expressly required by statute to
maintain accounts. Normally the parent legislation deals with the preparation,
audit and publication of accounts and the presentation of audited accounts to
the Minister for laying before Parliament. Often the audited accounts have
to be accompanied by an annual report on the corporation's activities. We

68. Tanganyika Parliamentary Debates, vol. 7, cols. 360 and 1030.
69. See also Kenya Parliamentary Debates, House of Representatives, March 23,
1965, for an incident involving an M.P./board member.
70. Art. 72, Treaty for East African Co-operation.

will consider here the various audit requirements which exist and the Tanzanian solution to the problem of auditing corporation accounts.

As with other aspects of the legislation, there is a notable lack of uniformity in detail. Thus the form of accounts is variously required to conform to the best commercial standards, or to the standards imposed by company law, or to Minister's regulations (if any) or it may well be subject to no detailed provision. As regards the form of audit, the following are some of the variants found in Uganda: audit by a person approved by the Minister (Coffee Marketing Board, Lint Marketing Board); audit on the Companies Act basis by an auditor appointed annually by the board and approved by the Minister (Uganda Electricity Board, Uganda Development Corporation); audit by an auditor appointed by the board of the corporation (Uganda Credit and Savings Bank, and Uganda Commercial Bank—though in the latter case the Minister may order the Auditor-General or any other person to make an interim audit); audit by the Auditor-General (Uganda Planning Commission); audit on the Companies Act basis by the Auditor-General or an auditor approved by him, with the Auditor-General having the right to draw the Minister's attention to any particular matters arising from the audit (National Housing Corporation, National Insurance Corporation); and audit by the Auditor-General or such other auditor as the Auditor-General may appoint with the prior approval of the Minister, with the Auditor-General having power at any time to examine the books on the request of the Minister (Bank of Uganda). In Kenya, similar variants may be found, but it is only necessary to mention the Agricultural Finance Corporation, where audit is by the Auditor-General or such other person as the *Minister* may appoint—a provision which seems undesirable in principle—and the Wheat Board of Kenya, where there is no provision for accounting.

Notwithstanding such variations in the law, the Auditor-General in each country has been able to help to maintain adequate accounting arrangements, largely because of the direct impact of many of the corporations' financial transactions on central government accounts.

Thus in his report on the 1961–62 Appropriation Accounts, the Kenya Controller and Auditor-General commented on the state of Government negotiations with the Maize Marketing Board over payment for maize imported for famine relief and on the unsatisfactory handover from the Kenya Broadcasting Corporation to the Government radio service. The Tanzanian Auditor-General in his report on the 1964–65 Accounts drew attention to the losses incurred by the National Development Credit Agency; to the dissatisfaction of professional auditors with the accounts of COSATA, a Government sponsored venture in retail and wholesale trading; and to the fact that the National Housing Corporation accounts for the two previous years had not even been made available to the Minister for Housing. In his report on the 1965–66 accounts, the Tanzanian Auditor-General commented on the fact that the accounts of the Rural Settlement Commission (which subsequently was dissolved) laid before the National Assembly did not give a true and fair view of the Commission's affairs; on the lack of a time-limit for the production of the accounts of the National Agricultural Products Board and the fact that the Board's accounting was defective and in arrears; on the draft accounts of the National Co-operative Bank for 1965–66, which cast doubt on whether its financial affairs were being managed in a prudent and business-like manner as required by law[71]; and on the fact that the accounts of the National Housing Corporation for 1963–1965, belatedly laid in the National Assembly, did not give a true and fair view of the Corporation's affairs.

In recent reports the Uganda Auditor-General has drawn attention to unconstitutional financial dealings between the Government and the Coffee Marketing Board, inadequate accounting by the National Council of Sports, the unauthorised use of Government grants paid to various public corporations, the payment of substantial additional allowances to civil servants seconded to the National Housing Corporation, and to high expenditure incurred by the National Insurance Corporation as its first action in buying a house and a car for its chairman. He has also commented on the rapidly increasing number of public corporations for whose accounts he has become statutorily responsible, whereas the older public corporations remain subject to other audit arrangements.

The effectiveness of these reports depends on the seriousness with which they are taken by the Government and Parliament. Clearly they cover only part of the problem of auditing the public corporations. Would it be desirable, as recent legislative trends in Uganda suggest, for all public corporations to come under the Auditor-General? Would an Auditor-General be more concerned with matters of legality and order than with the special demands of commercial accounting? Are existing audit departments in East Africa strong enough to deal with a wider range and volume of work?

A novel answer to these problems is provided by the Tanzania Audit Corporation Act[72] which created a new corporation with the duty of providing auditing, accounting and advisory services for a lengthy list of named statutory bodies and other prescribed bodies. Audit by the new corporation was substituted for the audit provisions of twenty-six statutes and future legislation creating new corporations will presumably follow this pattern.[73] The Minister of Finance may require the Tanzania Audit Corporation to audit the accounts of twenty-one named companies within the public sector. The

71. The Auditor-General reported that the Bank "had felt compelled to grant loans which would not be considered on a purely commercial basis"; in future, where there were other over-riding considerations, the matter would be referred to the Minister for Finance.

72. Act No. 1 of 1968.

73. *e.g.* National Scientific Research Council Act, 1968, s. 10: "Subject to any direction to the contrary given by the President, the accounts of the Council shall be audited by the Tanzania Audit Corporation."

Corporation may by agreement provide auditing services for any other person. The statutory auditing is to conform to the best professional standards and is generally to be carried out within fifteen months from the end of the financial year concerned. Subject to the Auditor-General's power, after consultation with the Board of the Audit Corporation, to give the Board directions as to the exercise of the functions of the Corporation, the Corporation is not subject to the direction or control of any other person or authority. Reasonable audit fees are to be charged and the Corporation is so to conduct its business that its revenue is not less than sufficient for meeting the charges properly chargeable to revenue, taking one year with another. The accounts of the Corporation itself will be audited by the Auditor-General and, with an annual report, will be sent to the President and laid before the National Assembly.

This new scheme adds considerably to the powers and functions of the Controller and Auditor-General. In particular, if the President fails to lay the annual report and accounts of the Audit Corporation before the National Assembly within the prescribed time, the Auditor-General must submit them himself to the Speaker who in turn must lay them before the Assembly.[74] Although a private accountant in Tanzania would regard this measure of public enterprise in his profession as a threat to the auditor's independence, the legislative safeguards and the constitutional position of the Auditor-General should help to prevent political interference with the new Corporation's work. For an initial period, management of the Corporation has been entrusted to a Danish firm of Government auditors, who will train future Tanzanian accountants.

The twin origins of the Tanzania Audit Corporation lie in the 1967 nationalisations (which magnified an already existing audit problem) and in the prevailing political ethos in Tanzania which is rigorously opposed to waste and corruption in public life. The effectiveness of the new audit arrangements, which are more rational and comprehensive than the statutory hotch-potch which they replace, will depend on continuing political support. Significantly, amongst recent audit reports in East Africa it is only the Tanzanian Auditor-General who pays tribute to the work of the Public Accounts Committee of the National Assembly to which he reports.[75]

5. The Kenya Maize Commission of Inquiry

The reports of official committees of inquiry are a valuable source of information on the operation of the corporations. Appointed by the Executive, often in response to parliamentary pressure or public unrest, these committees have

74. Tanzania Audit Corporation Act, s. 9 (4).
75. Report of the Controller and Auditor-General on the Accounts for 1965–66, p. x. In Kenya, the leader of the Opposition is the chairman of the Public Accounts Committee, which may formally be correct but probably leads to the Government taking little notice of its reports.

exposed weaknesses in administration and have suggested ways in which public economic activity may become more efficient. The Maize Commission of Inquiry in Kenya, the most elaborate of the post-independence inquiries, is the one most closely directed to the affairs of a particular public corporation. It was established under the Commissions of Inquiry Act,[76] the Kenya equivalent of the U.K. Tribunals of Inquiry (Evidence) Act 1921. The occasion for the inquiry was a national food crisis caused by a severe maize shortage during 1964–65, coupled with serious allegations in press and Parliament of corruption and unfairness in the distribution of such maize as was available. These allegations were primarily against the Minister of Marketing and Co-operatives, Mr. Paul Ngei, M.P., and the Maize Marketing Board. The chairman of the Commission was a High Court Judge and its two members were a Minister of State and an M.P. The Commission were required to examine the causes and extent of the maize shortage, to consider arrangements for the distribution and marketing of maize and to investigate the allegations of corruption and unfairness. The Commission took evidence on thirty-seven days from 144 witnesses, including Ministers, civil servants, members and staff of the Maize Board, politicians, business men and members of the public. State Counsel acted for the Commission, and interested parties were legally represented.

The 200-page report[77] revealed a variety of distinct but interlocking administrative problems. Neither the Maize Board nor the Ministry of Agriculture had kept adequate statistics of maize production, without which accurate decisions about prices and production trends were impossible. Although improvements in the price structure for maize were recommended, the Commission accepted that there should be no return to the free marketing of maize and that the Board's monopoly of marketing should remain, at least until such time as the co-operative movement had fully developed. Steps taken to deal with the maize shortage had been inadequate. In particular, there had been many unfortunate delays in obtaining shipments from U.S.A., for which responsibility was attributed to a number of Government departments (including the Minister of External Affairs and the Kenyan Embassy at Washington) as well as to the Maize Board, which had failed until too late to appreciate the urgency of the shortages. During the shortages, improvised distribution arrangements involving the provincial administration had been introduced alongside the Maize Board's usual methods of supply and this had been widely misunderstood. "Grey-market" activities had occurred, and undue profits had probably been made by traders and millers. M.P.s and Ministers had intervened during the shortage to obtain supplies of maize for individuals or localities. In particular, the Minister for Marketing and Co-operatives, who at the height of the shortages was responsible for the Maize

76. Cap. 102.
77. Published by the Kenya Government Printer in June 1966, price 6s.

Board, and who had been successively member and chairman of the Board, had used his official position to obtain financial advantages for himself, his wife and other close relations.

For the future, the Commission recommended that politicians should not be appointed to marketing boards. The executive responsibilities of the general manager should be increased and Government representation on the boards should be strengthened, while the Minister responsible for the Board should confine himself to issuing general policy directives. The accountancy procedures of the Maize Board should be improved. In times of extreme shortage, stringent price control should be introduced, and supplies should be distributed solely by the provincial administration. The rules regarding the business interests of Ministers and their close relations should be enforced more rigorously.

What relevant conclusions can be drawn from this report? First, that even though the form of public corporation is used for operating the marketing scheme, the responsibilities involved are Governmental. Maize, the staple food of most Kenyans, "is a national issue because lack of maize means famine and famine means political unrest which the Government would do everything to avoid."[78] The Board's statutory duties included importing and exporting maize to meet the needs of both consumers and producers in Kenya.[79] Whatever the statutory position might be, the Board had always obtained Ministry consent before importing maize. When by a combination of circumstances, a prolonged shortage developed, the division of responsibility between the Maize Board, the Ministry of Agriculture, a new Ministry of Marketing and Co-operatives actually created during the period of shortage, and the provincial administration, led to administrative weakness, especially in the lengthy saga of the American shipments. Although the Commission of Inquiry recommended against converting the Maize Board into a smaller, advisory body concerned only with maize policy, leaving marketing to be carried out by national agents acting for the Ministry of Agriculture, it is not clear from the report what the advantages of an executive board are, as opposed to having a marketing division of the Ministry of Agriculture. What does emerge is that in its administrative relationships with other Government departments, a board without the full and energetic support of its Minister will be in a position of weakness.[80] Situations in which a corporation appears ineffective may, because of the close link with Government, be explained by general administrative shortcomings rather than by failures of the corporation.

78. Report, para. 241.
79. Maize Marketing Act, cap. 338, s. 13 (1).
80. See, *e.g.* para. 247 of the Report quoting the following Maize Board minute: " . . . *it was agreed* to advise Government that the Board cannot continue to operate effectively unless Government deals promptly with the Board's requests and shows confidence in the decisions made by the Board."

Secondly, concerning the role of politicians as members and chairmen of public boards, it is true that most instances given in the report concerned one particular Minister. Thus it is recorded that, amongst other things, soon after his appointment as chairman of the Board, Mr. Ngei arranged for his second wife to be employed by the Board as his personal secretary; that he personally arranged for the granting of licences and permits to businesses of which his wife was the main proprietor; that while Minister, he appointed as sole broker for the Kenya Agricultural Produce Marketing Board a newly formed company, knowing that its directors included his brother, the brother of a fellow Minister and the wife of the chairman of the Marketing Board (the three persons concerned being unaware that they had been appointed directors); and again that as Minister he had delayed ordering an impartial investigation into the affairs of the West Kenya Marketing Board, since he had "for some unknown reason, a soft corner for the general manager."[81] But it is doubtful whether this kind of conduct is sufficiently disapproved of in Kenyan public life, since within a few months of his resignation as Minister of Marketing and Co-operatives Mr. Ngei was re-appointed to a different Cabinet post, even before the Commission of Inquiry had reported. Participation by politicians in the corporation probably increases rather than diminishes the risk of occurrences like those recorded. The reliance within Government departments on standard procedures and public auditing provides greater safeguards than exist in many corporations, and at the risk of detracting from the commercial initiative of corporations, should be extended to them if, as has occurred, politicians continue to be appointed to the corporations despite the recommendations of the Commission to the contrary.

What have been the consequences of the Maize Report? Notwithstanding demands from a few M.P.s that the Report be debated, no debate was arranged by the Government. Indeed, the Government took the evasive course of issuing its statement on the Report in the form of a paper laid before the National Assembly, a procedure which took M.P.s—and the Speaker— unawares and deprived M.P.s of the opportunity of questioning the Government.[82] The statement itself hardly deals adequately with the many issues raised by the Commission's Report. Probably domestic political developments in Kenya during the first six months of 1966 explain why more rigorous action was not taken by the Government and why Mr. Ngei had been readmitted to the Cabinet. Although the Government's decision to establish a new Maize and Produce Board was administratively carried into effect during 1966, the new Board was not retrospectively legalised until nine months later.

81. Chap. 12 of the Report, para. 505.
82. The brief, general statement issued by the Office of the President on July 14, 1966, was given no press publicity. It mentioned various recommendations about the structure of marketing of maize which had been or were being implemented or considered. In regard to the instances of corruption and abuse of official position, etc., it was stated: "The Commission's findings on various allegations are accepted and the remedial measures are being taken to prevent a recurrence."

On this occasion,[83] several M.P.s criticised the Government for abolishing the Maize Marketing Board without lawful authority, but clearly the time for effective discussion of the Maize Report had passed.

It must not be assumed from this affair that the relevant political and administrative factors are uniform throughout East Africa. For example, a Tanzanian "maize affair" would probably not have ended as it did in Kenya, primarily because of the different political ethos of the Nyerere administration. In comparison with some of the spectacular failures of public corporations in West Africa, the weaknesses revealed by the Maize Report are all of a kind curable with increasing administrative experience—provided that the problems are recognised and not conveniently forgotten.

6. Conclusions

So diverse are the public corporations of East Africa that no single conclusion can be drawn from the above discussion. But there are several unresolved issues which should be emphasised. First, the increasing number of corporations in each country contributes to a serious problem of an over-elaborate administration which is inadequately staffed and controlled. It is not conducive to efficiency that so many public bodies exist often to do very similar work, that personnel are constantly shifted to new jobs or given increased responsibilities as new corporations are established, and that fewer and fewer M.P.s exist who are not drawn into the administration through membership of corporations or similar bodies. Despite reports which recommend rationalisations and mergers, few take place as vested interests become established. This might not be so serious were there adequate co-ordination between corporations *inter se* and between them and Governments but all reports indicate that co-ordination is nowhere fully effective. Without a co-ordinated and efficient administration the Development Plans of the three countries will have little chance of success. Failure here will have far-reaching political effects.

Secondly, just as the framework of institutions within which the corporations are placed differs from that in a developed country, so the position of the law is not the same. In many developing countries there is a gap between the form and the effectiveness of law. Importance is attached to the technical processes of law, the use of law as a means of establishing administrative institutions with wide powers and the coercive effect of law to punish those who disobey official orders. But there is little understanding of the role of law as a means of regulating the complex relationships which arise between a multitude of different corporations and the Government on the one hand, and the legislature and the public on the other. While a constituent statute of a corporation in East Africa bears many recognisable features of, for example, such a statute in the UK, it would be wrong to conclude that the body which

83. Kenya Parliamentary Debates, March 22, 23 and 28, 1967.

is established is the same institution as a UK corporation. The crucial part of an East African statute is that which confers powers on the Minister. It is probably more accurate to recognise a corporation as a corporate part of a Ministry, with its members and senior staff largely being Government party supporters or civil servants as in a Ministry, than to apply the concept of the autonomous public corporation. This may most clearly be seen with the agricultural marketing boards, but there are signs of the same phenomenon appearing in the development corporations.

Thirdly, the disparities between the constituent statutes of the corporations, even within each country, make more difficult the task of those trying to keep within the law in running the corporations and more easy the abuse of power by those minded so to do. The remedy might be to enact a Public Corporations Act, an equivalent in the public sphere of the Companies Act of each country—Zanzibar already has a Decree on these lines—which would set out the manner in which corporations might be created, a detailed list of matters which the constituent instrument must contain, and certain general principles of operation, e.g. conduct of members and staff, financial rules, internal *modus operandi*, which would be deemed to apply to all corporations, present and to come. Some uniformity and publicity would thus be introduced into an area which at the moment lacks the former, and only obtains the latter spasmodically when a committee of inquiry reports.[84]

Fourthly, there is a potential conflict between the use of the public corporation as a tool of national economic policy, and the international economic co-operation enjoined by the Treaty for East African Co-operation, which came into effect in 1967. Competing national industrial development, conflicting agricultural marketing prices and practices, divergent banking and credit policies may all result from decisions of public corporations taken in the best interests of the State and in pursuance of the Development Plan, yet cutting across the spirit of the Treaty. Public corporations are a major tool for an autarchic economic policy while the Treaty presupposes that Governments will follow an integrationist economic policy.

There is no simple solution to these and other problems which have been discussed any more than there are simple solutions to the wider problems of constitutional and administrative development of which they form a part. Politicians and civil servants will continue to have to experiment to find the best form of administration for implementing their ambitious plans of economic and social development. But they would do well to pause before creating yet more public corporations, and increasing their control over those that exist, for it is by no means certain that a large, over-centralised and under-controlled administrative machine is conducive either to economic development or political stability. They should pay more attention to those

84. *Cf.* (Ghana) Statutory Corporations Act 1964, Act 232, and State Enterprises Secretariat L.I. 457/65 (which established a general supervisory secretariat).

reports of official inquiries which advise a reduction in numbers and
Ministerial control, greater co-ordination of those that remain, and a clearer
indication of their powers and functions. Such a reversal of present trends
might result in better use being made of scarce managerial and administrative
talent, more funds being devoted to development rather than its administration, and a greater possibility of meaningful parliamentary and financial
accountability.

Part IV
Conclusions

CHAPTER 16

GOVERNMENT ENTERPRISE:
A COMPARATIVE ANALYSIS*

THE countries represented in this volume differ widely from each other in their geographical location, in the degree of their industrial development, in the philosophy and organisation of their government, and in many other respects. But they have all found it necessary, especially since the end of the First World War, to develop public enterprises which would fulfil some of the many complex new tasks of government in forms other than those of departmental administration. The development of a more or less autonomous form of public enterprise has in very few cases been the result of a deliberate and systematic set of legislative and administrative measures. The post-war nationalisations of Great Britain and France, and the Soviet-type organisation of State industries, are probably the only examples of the creation of a series of public corporations based on a definite political and legal theory. In the great majority of cases, the various forms of public enterprise have developed as empirical responses to specific needs, without any preconceived theory, and without much uniformity. Yet, out of the very diversity of these developments certain broad conclusions of great theoretical and practical significances seem to emerge.

MOTIVES AND PURPOSES OF THE ESTABLISHMENT OF GOVERNMENT ENTERPRISE

The Economist observed some years ago, in a criticism of the policy of British Labour, that "the most likely field for State enterprise in an expanding economy is where private enterprise is undeveloped: in new industries and new products where the risks are great and the private *entrepreneur*—in an age of capital scarcity and high taxation of profits—may well hang back."[1]

This passage indicates one, but only one, of the two major motives for the establishment of public corporations and other forms of Government enterprise in so many countries, and in so many different fields. One of these motives is practical necessity, the indispensable need, in undeveloped countries—usually those of vast areas and relatively scarce populations as well as insufficient resources—to intervene, in the interest of the general development of the country, in ventures which private capital is either not willing or not able to launch. It is not, therefore, surprising that railways and other basic

---

* By Professor W. Friedmann.
1. June 20, 1953.

utilities, such as electric power or irrigation, constitute a favourite field of public enterprise, as the contributions on Australia, Canada, Germany, Italy and East Africa, among others, clearly show.

The need to spur economic development, in the light of national priorities, and in the absence of sufficient responsible private capital, accounts for the great importance of State enterprise in the developing countries. Government development corporations in Latin America, such as the Corporacion de Fomento de Chile, or the National Financiera de Mexico, have long played a major part in the economic development of these countries. In India one of the two national development corporations is State-owned, the other—with important financial support from the World Bank—is private. The article by Professor Bradley and Mr. McAuslan shows the role played by development corporations in East Africa—although they have not all been equally successful and, as in other developing countries, are often in danger of becoming tools of political power-play and manipulations. This, of course, destroys one of the main purposes of public corporations: the relative detachment of business operations of national concern from direct political control, through autonomy of management and accounting.

These cases of State intervention and development have often been supplemented by defence and strategic considerations. Defence needs have been paramount in the creation of publicly controlled and directed atomic commissions, characteristically one of the few recent examples of Government federal enterprise in the United States. Most of the present Canadian Government corporations are creations of the last war. A further stimulus for the creation of separate public authorities has come from the demand for Government intervention in times of severe economic depression. In Britain, the great depression of the early thirties resulted in the establishment of a series of agricultural marketing boards, and for this there are parallels in most of the other countries of the British Commonwealth. In the United States the great depression mainly produced new supervisory agencies, although the Tennessee Valley Authority is also to a large extent an outcome of the depression.

Beyond the demands caused by defence needs and severe economic crisis, the sphere of legitimate Government intervention remains controversial. In many continental countries as well as in Great Britain and the Dominions, the public operation of such public utilities as the supply of electricity, gas and water has long been recognised as a legitimate public activity which in Germany is predominantly operated by local or regional authorities or special *Öffentliche Anstalten*, and in the British Commonwealth generally by State or provincial authorities. In Britain many of them have now been transferred from local to central government responsibility. But in the United States the question how far electric power should be developed by public authority or private enterprise is still controversial, and the battle between public and private power continues unabated.

The other main inspiration is political philosophy. Earlier socialist theory was not much concerned with the technicalities and instrumentalities of socialisation as compared with its principles. Moreover it was developed at a time when the complexity of economic, technical and other managerial functions did not compare with contemporary conditions. Modern moderate socialist theory has, therefore, used the public corporation as a compromise between the older ideas of socialism and the newer necessities of economic management. The series of nationalisation laws which after the last war socialised, in Britain, the basic industries of coal, transport, electricity and gas, and, in France, coal, electricity, gas and press enterprises, were the expression of a political philosophy which demanded the public control of these basic industries as well as certain other enterprises. They also represented a new conception of the practical managerial tasks facing the State in the operation and administration of such giant industries. But even in these cases it is easy to over-emphasise the political element. The nationalisation of the coal industry had been advocated in Great Britain for several decades, mainly because of the vast differences in efficiency between the many private coal mines, and the impossibility of modernising the coal industry on the existing legal and economic basis. Electricity had already been in public hands, albeit in those of the local authorities, to the extent of nearly 50 per cent. and there was a national grid system directed by a public corporation, the Central Electricity Board. The railways had for years been operated by four large companies whose rates were fixed by a public tribunal, and which were predominantly non-competitive with each other.

In the great majority of cases a blend of political and practical factors has been the determining motive for the constitution of public corporations. A maximum of practical considerations, and a minimum of socialist or even semi-socialist philosophy, may be said to have prevailed in such countries as Canada where socialism is generally weak. But a mixture of practical and political considerations has determined developments in such countries as Australia, Israel or India, and to some extent also the acquisition of State interests in private undertakings in Germany and Italy after the First World War. In Australia, State initiative in the development of railways, power, forests and other utilities was a practical necessity. But it was supported by a philosophy and tradition of State intervention which has been a characteristic feature of Australian development. In Israel, the socialist philosophy predominating in this new country has certainly played a part in the vast, and— as Dr. Yadin's articles shows—still expanding share of the State in the development of Israel's economic resources; but the sheer practical inevitability of State initiative in the development of a poor country, under conditions of exceptional stress and emergency and scarcity of private capital, has certainly played at least an equal part. Again, in India, political and technical considerations may be said to have combined in the nationalisation of air transport and insurance, and the predominance of State ownership in the newly developed steel industry.

The first important conclusion which emerges from a comparison of the contributions on this point is that the public enterprise as a whole should not be judged predominantly by ideological preconceptions. In most cases public corporations have been established in response to practical needs, and they have often been successful in ideologically uncongenial surroundings. One of the most successful public enterprises is the Ontario Hydro-Electric Commission, created in 1907 in the most conservative of Canada's provinces, and a model for many others. And, at least outside the United States the Tennessee Valley Authority has been accepted as an outstanding example of successful public enterprise in a definitely non-socialist country. As Professor Abel observes, with some restraint "Technical disputes as to how much credit is due the TVA must be resolved by those with greater technical qualifications than mine, although it is clear that for some reason or another the region where it operates has advanced industrially and economically, relatively faster than the country as a whole." On the other hand, Sweden, which has had a social-democratic Government for many years and is regarded as one of the main practical pioneers of democratic socialism, has operated with a minimum of nationalisation and public enterprise. As Professor Strömberg points out, the natural resources and the heavy industries of Sweden are still predominantly in private hands, and socialist policy operates mainly through the instrumentality of taxes, subsidies and certain supervisory regulations. Where public control was required, Sweden used to be content to operate through State controlled monopolies constituted as private companies. But in recent years, the Government has become the major shareholder in the companies controlling broadcasting, liquor and tobacco. Few people would think of Italy as a pioneer of socialism, but as Professor Treves observes, a major part of all productive enterprise in Italy is now controlled, directly or indirectly, by the Government. Nor is this merely a matter of scattered and unconnected holdings. Through its participations in private industries and the complete control of certain other companies, the State in Italy exercises a decisive influence on the country's economic life, including such vital industries as shipping, iron and steel, electric power, and the exploitation of minerals and fuels. In Great Britain, the conduct of certain basic industries through giant public corporations is now generally accepted as a permanent fact of public life. But, while few people contend seriously that the nationalisation of these industries has been a national, political or economic disaster, there are not many more who would assert that it has brought the millennium, or that it has finally solved production or labour problems.

A comparison of the contributions made to this volume should show clearly that the establishment of public enterprises of a more or less autonomous character has become a general feature of modern public life and that it should be judged on its merits, as a legitimate instrument of modern government. At the one end, even the most "free enterprise" minded Governments are faced with a multitude of responsibilities which they cannot discharge by traditional means. At the other end, the Soviet Union has been compelled by sheer economic and managerial necessities to decentralise the administration of the socialised industries in the form of relatively autonomous public corporations.

PRINCIPAL FORMS OF PUBLIC ENTERPRISE

The variety of forms in which the various States have, at different times, proceeded to establish public enterprises is almost infinite, but three main types emerge to which almost every public enterprise approximates: (1) departmental administration; (2) the joint stock company controlled completely or partly by public authority; and finally (3) the public corporation proper, as a distinct type of corporation different from the private law company. Each of these three types will be briefly analysed in a comparative perspective.

As the tasks of Government multiplied, as a result of defence needs, postwar crises, economic depressions and new social demands, the framework of civil service administration became increasingly insufficient for the handling of the new tasks which were often of a specialised and highly technical character. At the same time, "bureaucracy" came under a cloud. In Great Britain the late Lord Hewart had written of "the new despotism," and Dr. C. K. Allen of "bureaucracy triumphant." In France the *Conféderation Générale du Travail* (CGT) had stated in its Programme in 1920 that "We do not wish to increase the functions of the State itself nor strengthen a system which would subject the basic industry to a civil service régime, with all its lack of responsibility and its basic defects, a process which would subject the forces of production to a fiscal monopoly. . . . " This distrust of government by civil service, justified or not, was a powerful factor in the development of a policy of public administration through separate corporations which would operate largely according to business principles and be separately accountable. In the common law countries, where the Government still enjoys considerable immunities and privileges in the fields of legal responsibility, taxation, or the binding force of statutes, other considerations played their part. It seemed necessary to create bodies which, if they were to compete on fair terms in the economic field, had to be separated and distinct from the Government as regards immunities and privileges.[2]

DEPARTMENTAL GOVERNMENT ENTERPRISE

Mr. Drake has given a survey of the main features of the "Morrisonian" concept of public enterprise, which has played a decisive part in the British

2. As will be shown below, this problem has by no means been satisfactorily solved in all the common law jurisdictions.

development: "the vesting of nationally owned industrial enterprises in purpose-built corporate bodies with a large measure of independence, but with statutory general duties to provide services...." The form of the nationalisation of British and French industries in 1945–46 was undoubtedly to a large extent due to the public distrust of a civil service régime. It is, therefore, all the more interesting to note that in some countries there has been a backward swing of the pendulum. In the United States the Government Corporation Control Act of 1945 indicates a definite tendency to revert from the semi-autonomous public corporation to departmental administration, although this appears to be largely due to the elimination of all the advantages of management by public corporations by a hostile Congress.

A mixture of many different reasons, some of a purely temporary or regional character, appears to determine the specific form in which public enterprise is conducted.

Administration of vast and complex enterprises by Government departments is still frequent, especially in the case of railways, posts and forests. But their autonomy differs only in degree from that of separately constituted corporations. Swedish railways, New Zealand forests or British, French and German postal services have, for many years, been operated on the basis of a separate financial administration and a largely specialised management, although they may come under a Ministerial budget and rank for legal and constitutional purposes as Government enterprises.[3] As Professor Drago points out, the French régies operating the alcohol and postal services have long enjoyed financial autonomy. The recent transformation of the British postal services into a public corporation proper indicates that the latter is regarded as a more suitable legal form for the operation of a complex and revenue-producing service. Similar proposals have been made in the United States where the postal services, under a junior member of the Cabinet, the Postmaster-General, are still run as a departmental service and, therefore, subject to interference by the Congress. The service is inefficient and in constant deficit, largely because various lobbies, through Congress, obtain outrageous mailing privileges for bulky advertising matter, and the appointments of local postmasters are a treasured patronage of Congress. This makes the conversion of the postal service into a business-like corporation an unlikely prospect. There are many gradations between the Government department proper and the public corporation. If in Great Britain and in France the recent tendency has been to constitute public administrations in the form of separate corporations there is, in both countries, a definite distinction between the social service and the commercial corporation. The former is usually under closer Ministerial control and generally more directly linked with

3. The German *Bundespost* is, under the Act of 1953, halfway between a government department and a public corporation. See above, p. 156.

Government than the latter. It constitutes, in many ways, an intermediate form between the purely departmental administration and the separate and autonomous public corporation. It is also interesting to note that the official Canadian classification[4] establishes four categories of Governmental enterprises. In the first are Government departments proper, in the second are the so-called "departmental corporations," in the third, the "agency" corporations, and in the fourth "proprietary" corporations. Generally speaking, the departmental corporations would correspond to the administrative or social service corporations of the British and French pattern. Most of the commercial and industrial corporations would correspond to either the "agency" corporations or, more frequently, the "proprietary" corporations. As Professor Hodgetts points out, "the departmental corporations are closely akin to an ordinary department and are financed by appropriations." Through the variety of terminologies, classifications and analyses we see something of a common pattern. Any Governmental enterprise of some administrative, managerial and financial complexity requires a considerable degree of autonomous administration. But the administrative and social services, which are generally non-profit making, must be under closer supervision of the competent Ministry because they depend on appropriations of a non-commercial character. On the other hand, a great many Governmental enterprises are as capable as the corresponding type of private enterprise—which they either replace or with which they may compete—of earning a profit, and whether they do so or not, it is essential that their operations should be conducted and scrutinised on a self-contained basis. Hence their greater independence and, in some cases as in Great Britain, the distinction between commercial auditing in the case of the commercial corporations and public auditing by the Comptroller and Auditor-General in the case of the social services corporations. Between these various types there are different degrees of legal and managerial independence, whether they are described as Government departments, departmental corporations or public corporations proper. The German position shows perhaps most clearly that we should not become the slaves of terms and classifications. The two giant State enterprises—the railway and postal services—which for generations have been conducted by the State, have, in the post-war period, been reconstructed, not with full legal personality but with most of the essential attributes of public corporations. Yet, according to a long German tradition, the permanent senior employees not only of the post but of the more autonomous railways have civil service status. They are *"Beamte."* In this case the distinction between "civil service administration" and "business administration" loses its distinguishing mark. Railway and post officials are civil servants of a special functional and technical character, but they are equal to their Ministerial colleagues in status and emoluments.

4. Financial Administration Act 1951, Pt. VIII.

L

This study might then provide a valuable corrective, from the experience of many countries, to an exaggerated phobia about management by bureaucracy. No public corporation or Government enterprise is completely autonomous. No Government department administering a service of some magnitude can be managed without a considerable amount of independence. It is a matter of degree, of shades which vary according to political considerations, the traditions of the country concerned, the efficiency of the civil service and a good many other factors.

GOVERNMENT ENTERPRISE THROUGH JOINT STOCK COMPANIES

Many countries have adopted the form of a commercial company, both in cases where the State joins private enterprise in the conduct of certain commercial corporations, and also in other cases where the State alone acquires the control of a commercial undertaking or newly establishes an entirely Government-controlled corporation. The deliberate choice of the company form, side by side with the form of the public corporation proper, is clearly seen in the case of France. As Professor Drago shows, France has established some nationalised industries in the form of public corporations proper (*établissements publics*), but the company form has been retained first for existing commercial companies in which the State has become the sole shareholder, as in the case of the Banque de France and the nationalised insurance societies; and, second, where the State has acquired a controlling interest in commercial undertakings without altogether displacing private shareholders. Prominent examples of this latter type are the *Companie Nationale du Rhône*, most important of the hydro-power undertakings of France, and the *Société Nationale des Chemins de Fer* (SNCF), as well as the air transport company "Air France" which corresponds to the public air transport corporations in Britain, Australia, Canada, New Zealand and India.

Where the State acquires a minority or a majority interest in an existing undertaking, the preservation of the form of the joint stock company is understandable enough. The State appears as a new partner and usually wishes to upset the existing pattern as little as possible. Its role in this case is legally not different from that of the acquisition of a controlling share packet by private interests. The fact that this form occurs so frequently on the Continent is mainly explained by the aftermath of the First World War, when such countries as France, Germany and Italy found themselves left with industrial State interests of varying significance and magnitude scattered throughout the economy. Germany in 1923, and Italy in 1933, proceeded to co-ordinate their Government holdings in giant holding companies (VIAG in Germany, IRI in Italy). In both countries, as the respective chapters show, these holding companies control a great variety of interests including many companies in which the State either has controlling or minority shares, but in Germany the tendency has been towards reduction of the role of the State[5] while Italian developments have been in the opposite direction. The IRI, the ENI and, most recently the ENE (National Electricity Board) in Italy have become major instruments of State policy. Their main interests include the merchant navy, iron and steel, telephones, electricity, oil, natural gas and other minerals. No doubt the differences in the state of industrial development reached by these two countries play a part in the different attitudes. In Italy—a country poor in natural resources and, until recently, relatively backward in industrial development—the help of the State has been more essential for the further development of the nation's economy than in highly industrialised Germany.

There is only a difference in degree between an entirely State-owned company, and one in which the Government holds only a controlling or even a strong minority interest. It is, however, very interesting to note that in a number of countries the form of the joint stock company has been chosen for the organisation of new enterprises, controlled by the Government and deliberately designed to carry out a public service. In all these cases the pattern of the commercial company has been adopted only to be profoundly modified, in some cases, so as to make the choice of the form a rather meaningless fiction. In Canada, for example, there is little if any mixed economic enterprise. Most of the public enterprises are of recent origin and were deliberately established by the Crown for specific purposes, some in connection with the war effort. A number, but by no means all of them, have been established as limited companies under the Dominion Companies Act. Shares have been issued as a matter of form rather than of substance, for the shares were duly issued to directors appointed by the Minister. As Professor Hodgetts further points out, these shares were endorsed over by the owners to the Minister so that the Government was thus assured of complete control. These companies were normally created through orders-in-council but a number of other Crown corporations were established by statute and approximate more closely to the British type of public corporation. Broadly, the difference between the two is confined to matters of form and registration. Similarly, the German railways in the inter-war period were constituted as a *Gesellschaft* with a share capital entirely held by the Reich. In all these cases the company form serves merely as a convenient cloak. However, in a number of other cases there has been a more genuine use of the company form for the purposes of Government undertakings. In Israel, for example, which has experimented with all forms of public enterprise, one of the mining concerns has been incorporated by Ordinance with a capital consisting of ordinary shares only, all but one of which were subscribed and held by the Development Authority. Its memorandum and articles of association contain provisions prohibiting the distribution of profits to the shareholders and reserving

5. In recent years the Federal Government has sold portions of its shares in Volkswagen, Preussag and Veba to the public, while retaining minority holdings.

to the Government certain powers of winding up. Other companies, however, have been established with different capital shares. In Sweden too, the stock company is the predominant pattern of public enterprise. The Tobacco Monopoly, for example, has a share capital of 120 million crowns, 119 millions of which are owned by the State, with 1 million held by Government nominees. Further restrictions upon freedom of movement of this company follow from a special contract between the Government and the private shareholders by which the latter cannot, on the one hand, freely transfer their shares, while, on the other hand, they must sell them to the Government on demand.

In Italy, not only is a great proportion of public economic interests organised in commercial holding companies and other participations, but the organisation of the new public corporations has been modelled on that of the joint-stock company. But in the process the substance has disappeared and only the form remains. The shareholders' meeting either does not exist or has only very limited functions. The Government appoints all or most of the directors and often decides how to distribute any profits. In most cases, the company is merely a form by which the State or the public authority exercises its control. In those cases a type of organisation deliberately designed as an instrument of public management and control would seem to be preferable to the adoption of the shadow rather than the substance of the company form.

Until a few years ago, the use of the commercial company, either for State enterprises or for mixed public–private undertakings, was almost unknown in Britain, although not in other common law countries, such as Australia and Canada. As Mr. Daintith describes in detail, the last few years have brought a dramatic change. The Labour Government has proclaimed public participation in selected private enterprises as a "signpost for the Sixties." In pursuit of this policy, the Government took a 50 per cent. participation in the ailing Fairfield Shipyard, and later a $17\frac{1}{2}$ per cent. interest in a new amalgamated group, Upper Clyde Shipbuilders. The Industrial Expansion Act 1968 includes Government acquisition of equity shares, mainly through the new Industrial Organisation Corporation, as one means of industrial investment expansion and rationalisation. The mixed company has thus become a respectable and deliberate instrument of State economic involvement in Britain—as it has long been in many other countries.

THE PUBLIC CORPORATION PROPER

None of the many countries which have developed new autonomous forms of public enterprise have attempted a general theoretical definition of the "public corporation." It is still very much an institution and a concept in a state of flux and constant development.

However, one of the purposes of this comparative study is to find out how far, across the diversity of origins, purposes, legal systems, and economic ideas, the comparable institutions created by the different countries treated here may have developed certain common features. For the purposes of such an analysis it may be convenient to take the characteristic features of the modern British public corporation as a starting point. A comparison of the main features of the British public corporation with those of the corresponding institutions of other countries may lead us some way towards a generally valid definition.

The characteristic features of the British corporation are summarised in Professor Garner's chapter. His threefold classification of commercial undertakings, managerial bodies, and regulatory and advisory bodies, corresponds broadly to the distinction between commercial, social service and supervisory public corporations made by the present writer some years ago.[6]

The commercial and industrial corporations are financed not by parliamentary appropriations but by revenue-earning permanent assets. They are directed to balance revenue and expenditure (over a period of years), and any profits generally have to be ploughed back into the development of the enterprise. They are commercially audited. The social service corporations operate under a Ministerial budget. Although they have, in many cases, vast managerial and financial responsibilities, they are not revenue-earning, and they are audited by the Comptroller and Auditor-General. The commercial and industrial public corporations do not participate in any of the legal privileges and immunities of Government. The social service corporations possibly do in some cases. Generally, the public corporations have altogether a dual nature. In their commercial and managerial aspects they resemble commercial companies and they have essentially private law status. But in so far as they fulfil public tasks on behalf of Government and Parliament they are public authorities, and, as such, subject to control of the Government, within the limits defined by statute and as developed by practice and defined—on rare occasions—by the courts.

These characteristic features will form the basis of our comparative observations.

(1) Creation of the public corporation

It appears to be a universal practice that public corporations are created either by special statute or by a Government ordinance. Unlike the commercial company they do not automatically come into existence by fulfilling certain statutory requirements. The creation of a public undertaking by special statute serves to distinguish the public corporation proper from the public undertaking which is established under the company law though the State provides the entire capital and holds all or virtually all the shares,

6. *The New Public Corporation* (1947); "The Legal Status and Organization of the Public Corporation," p. 16 *Law and Contemporary Problems*, 576 (1951). The distinction has been adopted, *e.g.* in *Tamlin* v. *Hannaford* [1950] K.B.18.

directly or through one of its own undertakings. From the point of view of function and purpose the distinction is certainly often an artificial one. Thus, in Israel, which experiments with both types of public enterprise, those which are established as share companies are registered under the Companies Ordinance, whereas others like the Development Authority are created as statutory bodies. It is, of course, a different question how far the statute or the ordinance which establishes a public corporation refers for its constitution to specific articles of the Company Law. This is incorporation by reference.

(2) Legal personality

Separate legal personality is an almost indispensable aspect of the public corporation. In order to operate with the necessary degree of independence it needs the attributes which go with legal personality. The great majority of public corporations are specifically and expressly equipped with such personality in all the countries under study. However, there are exceptions and qualifications. The South Australian Dried Fruits Board has for many years been an active public corporation, carrying out a multitude of transactions which presuppose legal personality, although it has not been equipped with such personality by any legislative or administrative document.[7] On the other hand, Germany provides us with the not very convincing construction of a "*Sondervermögen*," a separate fund without legal personality, in the case of both the Federal Railways and the Federal Post. The practical consequences of this theoretical denial are largely mitigated if not wiped out by the capacity of the railways to sue and be sued, to make contracts and engage in any other transactions which normally go with legal personality. Again, it is not quite certain whether the Soviet State corporations are independent legal personalities or, being part of the State, are only treated as such. In practice, at any rate, they have all the attributes of such legal personality. On the other hand, government departments, naturally, have no specific separate legal personality, but even where railways or postal services or forestry commissions are operated as government departments and not equipped with separate legal personality, they must, in fact, be treated very largely as separate units for purposes of administration, budgeting and transactions. Thus, as Professor Strömberg points out, the Swedish Railways have long enjoyed a *de facto* operational and financial autonomy which gives them greater independence than that enjoyed by some public corporations proper. In the common law jurisdictions, the main legal difference between a Government department and a public corporation may well be that the former partake of such Government privileges and immunities as remain whereas the latter do so either not at all or only to a limited extent. The Canadian classification of Government enterprises in the Finance Administration Act of 1951 realistically appreciates the relativity of the differences between the various shades of Government

7. See G. Sawer, in Friedmann (ed.) *The Public Corporation*, at pp. 21 *et seq.*

enterprises by classifying Government departments and departmental corporations together with agency corporations and proprietary corporations as public corporations in the wider sense, while limiting most of its provisions on auditing and financial management to the latter two groups.

In practice it is clear that any enterprise falling under the general description of a public corporation must have the essential requirements of legal personality: it must be capable of suing and being sued, of concluding contracts; it must be liable in torts, hold and dispose of property; it must have a separate name and a separate administration; its assets and liabilities must be kept distinct from those of the Government in general, whether or not it legally forms part of it. Given these essential features we need not unduly worry about the theoretical requirements which make it desirable for some legislators to deny the full status of legal personality to some of the enterprises analysed here. Students of jurisprudence have long been aware of the relativity of legal personality and it is no longer heretical to assert that there are various shades and degrees of legal personality.[8]

(3) Administration by an independent board

As regards the administration of the corporation, there is again a remarkable uniformity of practice in the different countries. Overwhelmingly the administration is in the hands of a governing board appointed by the Minister, the Cabinet or—what amounts to the same thing in the British Commonwealth—by the Governor-General-in-Council or the Governor-in-Council.

The alternative, a body of Appointing Trustees, which was attempted in the case of the now defunct London Passenger Transport Board, and which has been abandoned for the newer British public corporations, does not seem to find favour in other countries either. The most significant exceptions from the system of appointing an independent board are the French public corporations resulting from the nationalisation of certain industries. Here the governing boards are based on a tripartite principle; they are composed of representatives of Government, trade unions and consumers' organisations. Both Professor Drago[9] and Professor Robson, in a comparative analysis of the British and French public corporations,[10] have strongly criticised this system, which appears to have resulted in a constant tug-of-war between the different representatives and interests instead of providing a balanced administration in the public interest. The recent authoritative *Rapport sur les Entreprises Publiques*,[11] has added the criticism that the Government which does and should exercise supervisory functions is also represented through the tripartite

8. On this point see, among others, Paton, *Jurisprudence* (2nd ed., Chap. XVI); Friedmann, *Legal Theory* (5th ed., Chap. 34).
9. "The Public Corporation in France," in Friedmann (ed.) *The Public Corporation* (1954) at p. 120.
10. In *Problems of Nationalised Industry* (ed. Robson), Chap. XIV.
11. Groupe de travail du Comité Interministériel des Entreprises Publiques, 1967 (Nora Report).

Conseil d'Administration in the management of the enterprise. There seems little doubt that the solution now universally adopted in Britain and the Commonwealth and in most of the other countries, of an independent, though widely based, governing board responsible to the Government and to nobody else, is the preferable system. In Great Britain this has sometimes been balanced by the establishment of advisory Consumers' Councils in the case of the industrial public corporations. There has been much discussion on the effectiveness of these Consumers' Councils which even on the most favourable estimate has been modest.[12] Advisory Councils have also been established for the recently constituted Indian Air Corporations.

A certain blend between the two systems is attempted in the re-organisation of the German Federal Railways. The actual direction and management is in the hands of a board of four who are appointed by the Minister or, in case of difficulties, by the Cabinet after certain consultations. But besides the *Vorstand,* there is, in accordance with a general pattern of German company administration, a *Verwaltungsrat* which is composed of members nominated by four different groups of the community. A similar pattern has been chosen for the Federal Post except that the Minister himself there takes the place of the board. And Professor Drago notes a comparable evolution in the newest of French public enterprises, the *Entreprise Minière et Chemique* (EMC). This has a managing board and a supervisory *Conseil*—corresponding somewhat to the distinction between *Vorstand* and *Aufsichtsrat* in German company law.

An important question is whether the supervising Minister or his representative should himself be part of the management of the corporation. Generally, the answer to this question is in the negative. On this point, countries whose legal and political systems are otherwise as divergent as those of Britain, Germany, France, the USSR, the United States, India, Italy and Australia are unanimous. It is significant that in Germany, where formerly the General Manager of the railways was also Minister of Transport, there is now a clear separation. The Minister of Transport has considerable powers of supervision, but he is emphatically not a part of the management. The postal services, on the other hand, have remained under the direction of a Minister.

The most significant and somewhat surprising exception is provided by Canada. Despite earlier Government protestations to the contrary, the practice of having a Ministerial representative as a member of the boards of the public corporations is now fairly universal. This is criticised by Professor Hodgetts with strong arguments. In mixed undertakings of the joint-stock company pattern the representation of the State by civil servants, or in some cases Ministers, is inevitable. But if the public corporation proper is to have the maximum of autonomy and independence in its management, as distinct from its general responsibility to the public, the blurring of managerial and

12. See Professor Garner's account in Chap. 1, *ante*, p. 21.

supervisory functions is most undesirable. It is, of course, possible that a
Minister, by constant interference from above, might restrict the autonomy
and independence of management of a public corporation even more than by
being directly, or through a member of his Ministry, represented on the
board. In either case, the idea of the public corporation is falsified. But
where a Ministerial representative sits on the board it seems almost impossible
to attain the necessary independence whereas a moderate and restrained use of
the directing power on the part of the Minister does make such autonomy
possible, as the example of the British public corporations administering the
nationalised industries has shown.

One final point for comparative consideration under this heading is that, in
Britain at least and probably in the other Commonwealth jurisdictions, the
trade unions appear to have come to prefer the independently appointed
board to one on which they are directly represented. This is contrary to
certain earlier attitudes, particularly the demands of the coal miners which
reflected syndicalist ideas. By being unrepresented as such on the board, the
unions retain greater liberty in the negotiation of collective agreements with
the board as employer, and although the British trade unions—and the corresponding workers' organisations in other countries—have generally supported
the nationalisation of basic industries, they appear to prefer the solid reality
of independent bargaining power to the less certain benefit and enhanced
status which direct participation in the administration of such industries may
bring. The difficulties resulting from direct representation are illustrated by
the French experience.

(4) Status of employees of public corporations

The public corporations in the common law jurisdictions have entirely followed the rule that their employees should not have the status of civil servants.
This is an outcome of the conception that the corporations should, as far as
possible, approximate to the ideas of business management and not be tied
too closely to the Civil Service. One consequence of this freedom has been
the possibility of paying somewhat higher salaries to the leading executives
of the corporations, a situation which is not altogether to be welcomed, for it
means that very often the executive of a public corporation will receive a
higher salary than the most senior member of the Ministry which supervises
it and whose responsibilities are scarcely inferior to those of the top personnel
of the corporation. But, there seems no present intention of changing this
status. Nevertheless, service in the public corporations is not the same as
service in a commercial company. It is a form of public service and requires,
as the late deputy chairman of the National Coal Board has pointed out,[13]
that the staff of the public corporations must be imbued with the ideal of
public service. If and when a special type of training for this specialised form

13. Sir Arthur Street in *British Government Since 1918* (1950), pp. 188–190.

of public service will be developed, the status of the personnel of the public corporations may more and more closely approximate to that of the Civil Service without being formally part of it.

In the Commonwealth, the situation is similar. For example, the Crown Corporations in Canada have pension plans, some of which are similar to those of private concerns, others to civil service regulations; others, again, have their own pension schemes established by statute or order-in-council. Collective bargaining has recently been extended to the Civil Service proper.

There remains the question of status. In that respect there may well be a substantial difference of outlook between the common law countries and the continental countries. The status of a *Beamter* in Germany and some other countries on the Continent carries a prestige which is not readily understood in the Anglo-American countries, although in Britain, and at least parts of the Commonwealth, the Civil Service enjoys far greater prestige than it does in the United States. But it certainly does not go to the length of a permanent employee of the nationalised railways or of a nationalised aviation company considering himself a better man if he has the status of a civil servant instead of being a mere employee on contract. In Germany, however, to take the most prominent example, the permanent employees of the railways and the postal services have always been civil servants and no change has been made in this respect, despite the recent strengthening of the autonomy in the administration of these services. It is a matter partly of tradition and sentiment, partly of economic considerations. On the other hand, this means that the salaries of the employees of such services are mostly in accordance with the corresponding rates of the Civil Service in the Government departments.

In both France and Italy the situation appears to be rather confused. In France the status of employees of public enterprises is generally governed by private law. But the status and conditions of the employees of the nationalised gas and electricity industries closely approximate to those of the Civil Service. In Italy, civil and administrative courts compete strongly, in an unresolved controversy, for jurisdiction over the employees of the public corporation whose status appears to hover uneasily between private and public law.

To what extent the employees of the public corporations should be civil servants or not, is obviously a matter which is strongly influenced by traditions, by the status of the Civil Service, by the desire for security and by other considerations which vary considerably from country to country. But again, the differences should probably not be exaggerated. In the first place, the technical public services such as railways, posts, electricity and gas corporations on the Continent employ a large proportion of technical and other employees who are not civil servants. In the second place, many of their employees who have the status of civil servants, constitute in fact a highly specialised technical category within the Civil Service subject to special training and constituting a special career largely separate from that of the general

Civil Service. In some cases, statutes even provide for the possibility of higher emoluments for "special services."[14]

On the other hand, it has often been pointed out that the methods and conditions of large scale private enterprise, including the status of their employees, approximate more and more closely to that of similar public enterprises. There is still a considerable difference as regards freedom of collective bargaining. But in an increasing number of countries—Great Britain and France are prominent examples—the civil servants now possess highly developed organisations which negotiate with the Government on quasi-union lines. And Canada, in 1967, introduced collective bargaining methods into the Civil Service. The increase of large scale collective bargaining more and more limits the freedom of private enterprise in the regulation of the status of its employees, except perhaps at the very highest levels. The philosophy of social security, and the demands of the modern managerial society, appear to bring the public and the private sectors closer together by making private industry more "public" and public services more "private" in their methods. Finally, if the public corporations become, as they appear to do in a number of countries, a permanent and respected part of the fabric of the community, there will probably develop a spirit of continuity in public service which will bring their employees closer to the ideas and status of the Civil Service, whether or not they theoretically form part of it. The great question is whether ideals and status of public service can develop without the widespread civil service habit of "playing safe," of taking no more action than is required. The public corporations, faced with immense practical tasks, must preserve and develop a sense of enterprise and urgency.

(5) Provision of finance

The financial foundation of the public corporation is obviously a factor of particular importance. It is generally true in this sphere, as in others, that he who pays the piper calls the tune. There are, in the practice of nations, two main methods of financing the public corporations: periodical appropriation from the national budget, and the provision of permanent capital assets. None of the British corporations have shares. But while the social service corporations are normally financed through Ministerial appropriations, which are charges on the national budget, the commercial and industrial corporations own revenue bearing assets, on which they can borrow from the Government or the public, and they are generally independent of recurrent appropriations, except for certain statutory possibilities of Exchequer grants.[15]

14. *e.g.* the *Bundespostgesetz* of 1953.
15. A notable exception is the Commonwealth Development Corporation which invests through loans and equity participations in public and private enterprises throughout the Commonwealth. Despite many years of successful operation, the CDC still depends for its capital on funds borrowed from the Treasury at commercial rates of interest, and on borrowing powers, as determined from time to time by the Government.

Apart from the United States and the Soviet Union, this practice appears to be fairly universal. But, as has been pointed out before, many countries prefer to finance the public enterprises of a commercial or industrial character not through the vesting of assets by statute but through the formation of State controlled joint-stock companies to which the State or another public authority, or both together, and in some cases a minority of private capital, subscribe the shares. Italy, Sweden, Israel, South Africa and Pakistan provide examples of this method of financing which does, however, share with the public corporation proper—of the commercial, not of the social service type—the feature that assets are provided once and for all, and not subject to annual debate on the budget estimates. In Israel, for example, most of the commercial public undertakings appear to be financed in this way while one of the few public corporations proper, the Development Authority, is financed through annual appropriations under strict government control. In Great Britain, this applies only to social service corporations, such as the Regional Hospital Boards, which are not expected to be self-supporting.

The practice of annual or periodic appropriations and strict control by the Bureau of Budgets prevails in the United States, at least on the federal level. The main reason appears to be the all-pervading influence of politics and parliamentary pressure groups which do not look kindly upon any even relative autonomy conferred by independent finance or management on a public authority. It took the Tennessee Valley Authority about ten years before it emerged from the annual battles for appropriations in the different committees of both Houses of Congress to a position of relative safety, due, in large part, to the sheer magnitude of its achievement. In the Soviet Union, on the other hand, the closeness of the control exercised by the planning authorities for economic and political reasons alike does not permit any true financial autonomy, although the Statute on the Socialist State Economy of October 4, 1965, has considerably increased the freedom of State enterprises in the handling of their circulating assets. Politics, therefore, intrude into the administration of the corporations in both countries, though in a different manner and for very different reasons. There is little doubt that any genuine freedom of management and initiative requires that the public corporations, at least those of a revenue-earning character, should have permanent assets freely at their disposal and not be dependent on periodical political battles in Parliament or other instruments of Government. However, it is equally clear from the studies presented in this volume that nowhere is the public corporation completely independent in its financial status and operation. Nor indeed could it be as long as it forms in some respects a part of Governmental responsibilities. A frequent blend between the two main methods of financing mentioned above is the provision of State grants from the national budget. In Great Britain this is provided for only in the case of the air corporations, which required support in the post-war era of reconstruction. In France, subsidies are more frequent and have tended to threaten the autonomy of the corporations. Indeed, a large number of substantial *ad hoc* State grants is worse than annual appropriations which are at least a subject of regular debate.[16] As many public corporations are established for the very reason that they cannot be operated by private enterprise, either because long-term development is required or because they have to be rescued from an extraordinary crisis and emergency,[17] it is obvious that, in a number of important cases, there must be provisions for either non-recurrent or periodical State grants. It is, however, important that this method of interference should be reduced to a minimum and that it should be strictly circumscribed by statute. Certainly, the main purpose of the commercial and industrial public corporation can be fulfilled only if in the long run it stands financially on its own feet. To finance major capital expenditures, public corporations are often empowered to issue bonds whose interest usually has treasury guarantee (*e.g.* in Great Britain and Italy). It is beyond the province of this volume to discuss the question of economic policy, whether and to what extent public corporations should be profit-earning or simply attempt to balance revenue and expenditure.[18] Suffice it to point out that in Britain some of the nationalised industries have had continuous deficits (such as British Railways) while others normally show profits (such as British European Airways) and a third group (*e.g.* the National Coal Board and the BOAC) fluctuate between profits and deficits. The reasons for this are complex. The nature of the enterprise, the quality of the management, the degree of monopoly enjoyed and, not infrequently, political demands or concessions imposed by the Government, are all contributory factors. The question of disposal of profits is obviously another important aspect of financial policy. There is a great variety of provisions in this respect, but in most cases the statute provides that the profits must be ploughed back into the development of the enterprise (as in Great Britain) or the State, as sole or principal shareholder, decides their distribution. In other words, where the public corporations are not directed by statute to apply profits to the development of the enterprise, they go to the State, either at the disposal of the competent Minister or automatically. In some cases only—of which the nationalised banks in Italy are an example—profits go to the shareholders of whom the State or a State-controlled company is one. It is difficult to see any alternative to these solutions.

16. The *Fonds pour le Développement Economique et Social* (*FDES*) has in theory the task of co-ordinating financial priorities and investments in the public sector. But, according to the *Rapport sur les Entreprises Publiques* (at p. 87) its competence extends only to 50 per cent. of the investments in Energy and Transport, much the most important fields of public enterprise.

17. Examples of the former are the railways in the British Commonwealth; an example of the latter, the German railways after the last world war.

18. For a discussion of this complex question concerning the British corporations, see the articles of Professors Lewis, Sargent Florence and Gilbert Walker in *Problems of Nationalised Industry* (ed. Robson), Chaps. X and XI.

PUBLIC AND PRIVATE LAW ASPECTS OF THE PUBLIC CORPORATION

The position of the public corporations between private and public law is, perhaps, the most complex of the many problems which this new institution, deliberately blended of public and private law elements, presents to the comparative lawyer. Moreover, this is one of the matters where the often exaggerated differences between continental and Anglo-American jurisprudence really do matter. It is true that all the countries represented in this volume struggle with the problem of how to fit the public corporation into the existing legal system, considering that they engage on the one hand in activities traditionally reserved to private enterprise and controlled by private law while, on the other hand, they are public authorities responsible to the organs of government. The technical aspect of the problem, however, differs considerably as between the common law jurisdictions and the civil law systems. The continental countries represented in this volume—France, Germany and Italy—all have had, for many decades, a well-established distinction between private law and public law and a generally parallel separation of civil and administrative tribunals. This, as common law jurists have come to recognise more and more since the days of Dicey, is a great advantage. The existence of a complete and integrated system of administrative law, with the jurisdiction of administrative courts behind them, has made it easier for the growth of public functions in the Welfare State to be fitted into the categories of law. In the common law jurisdictions on the other hand, the traditional aversion to any dualism of the legal system has led to the haphazard growth of a multitude of administrative functions and specialised administrative tribunals which still lack proper co-ordination—although the British Tribunals and Inquiries Act of 1958 indicates some acceptance of the idea of administrative justice. Therefore, no adequate remedy is available to a citizen against a public authority. However, when it comes to the assimilation and legal treatment of a new pragmatic institution like the public corporation—which blends elements of different branches of law—the clear-cut, systematic distinctions, of the Continental systems have their disadvantages. The Continental doctrine—especially in France and Italy—is greatly worried by the question of allocation of the various aspects of the public corporation to the private or public law sphere, and to the respective jurisdictions. It feels constrained to extract from the rather protean character of the public corporations certain theoretical elements traditionally associated with the distinctions of public and private law, elements such as the fulfilment of public functions or the legal source of their existence. Such an approach is bound to be artificial because, in the continental and in the Anglo-American jurisdictions alike, legal categories framed under completely different economic and social conditions do not take account of the tremendous growth of State functions which have occurred during the last century. The difficulties are further increased by the fact that a large proportion of the new public enterprises are clothed in the form of commercial companies, whereas others take the form of statutory corporations. To make the test of public or private law character simply depend on the more or less formalistic accident whether an enterprise has been constituted as a commercial company, shares of which are held by the State, or as a statutory corporation, is obviously unsatisfactory. As Dr. Yadin observes, the distinction does not serve as a dividing line of any real value. In the Continental systems, the classification of an institution as one of public law has far-reaching consequences. Not only does it mean that its actions are generally judged by administrative rather than civil courts, but it also means that it must be fitted into the hierarchy of public authorities and is subject to certain principles of Government supervision. Thus, the Continental courts and jurists are largely unable to develop the legal aspects of the public corporation unhindered by concepts and distinctions which scarcely apply in their traditional neatness to a new institution that blends the attributes of both. However, Professor Drago notes an important though still uncompleted evolution in France. The key concept is that of a *"concessionaire de service public."* Regardless of their legal form, the *concessionaires*—which include the basic utilities, electricity, gas and transport—are, for most purposes subject to public law. The other public enterprises which include coal mines, oil enterprises, manufacturing and banking are subject to private law. However, even the *concessionaires* may conclude transactions in the forms of private law (*gestion privée*). The *Rapport sur les Entreprises Publiques* (Nora Report) supports this distinction on the ground that it reflects the difference between basic public services and competitive activities. Not everybody will agree with the soundness of this criterion which puts, for example, coal mining in one category and electricity in another.

As regards the industrial and commercial Government enterprises the presumption is that they are also liable to pay taxes and other public charges in the same manner as commercial companies of private law. This presumption does not apply to the "*établissements administratifs*", which correspond to the social service corporations of English law. By means of this distinction a certain flexibility has been established for the public corporations of a commercial character, but it does not affect their public law responsibilities in the administrative sphere, and their subjection to permanent and far-reaching government control about which something more will be said later.

The more empirical approach of the common law, and the absence of a clear concept and institutions of administrative law, has made the treatment of the public corporations in the common law sphere somewhat easier. For one thing, the common law systems do not have to distinguish between legal persons of public and of private law, nor are they hampered by any compulsion of categorising an institution as being either one of public or of private law and, therefore, of necessity, subject to certain principles of the one or the other type. But the common law systems, too, have been troubled by the difficulty of squaring concepts and legal rules of earlier times with institutions and conditions to which they scarcely apply. It has taken English and American courts many years to concede that the exercise of an industrial or commercial activity on behalf of the State does not deprive such activity of its "Governmental" character.[19] But a great many anomalies in the common law remain, in particular as regards the immunities and privileges of the Crown in such matters as immunity from the binding force of statute, debt priority, freedom from taxes and other public charges. And common law courts have—quite unnecessarily—struggled with the further problem of whether public corporations should be protected by the "shield of the Crown." Professor Sawyer[20] has rightly criticised the use of this concept, which may strike the Continental lawyer as no less artificial and unreal than the prolonged theoretical disputations over the distinctions between public and private law status, in Continental jurisprudence, may strike the common law lawyer. Although the recent statutes which, in Great Britain and most of the Dominions, make the Crown actionable before the ordinary courts in most cases, greatly reduce the scope of its former privileges, enough remain, especially in the field of statutory duties, liability to taxes and debt priority to make the problem an important one. In Britain the new public corporations have been clearly detached from the remaining privileges by being made specifically liable to be sued, and for rates, taxes and other public charges like private individuals. This corresponds to the solution reached in French and other Continental legal systems through the notion of *"gestion privée."* But it is still controversial whether the administrative or social service corporations do or do not partake of the privileges of the Crown. The recent English cases appear, at long last, to move towards the abandonment, not only of totally antiquated notions of "proper" functions of Government, but also of the concept of "shield" or "emanation" of the Crown.[21] It may be hoped that eventually the British courts will extend this insight to international law, where they still not only maintain the doctrine of absolute immunity, but apply it to Government corporations.[22] In the days of the National Health Service, provision of drugs for hospital services has been held to be a "service of the Crown," and the BBC has been held not to be entitled to the Crown's

19. *Cf.* for the United States the 1945 decisions of the Supreme Court in *United States* v. *New York*, as quoted by Professor Abel. For England see the decision of the Court of Appeal of 1950 in *Tamlin* v. *Hannaford* [1950] 1 K.B. 18, at pp. 36 *et seq.* For Australia see the decision of the High Court in the *Professional Engineers* case [1959] 107 C.L.R. 208, and the observations by Professor Zines, above, p. 239. On the whole problem see the present author's *Law and Social Change* (1951), pp. 210 *et seq.*, 310 *et seq.*; Denning, *The Changing Law* (1953), pp. 25 *et seq.*

20. *The Public Corporation*, note 7, *supra.*

21. See Drake, *supra*, p. 44.

22. *e.g., Baccus SRL* v. *Servicio Nacional* [1957] 1 Q.B. 438.

immunity from taxation.[23] The crux of the matter is that the public corporation is a new type of institution which has sprung from new social and economic situations and changing functions of Government, and that it therefore does not neatly fit into old legal categories. Instead of forcing it into them the latter should be adapted to the needs of changing times and conditions.

It should now be clear why extraordinary complexities beset the question of the extent of public responsibility of the public corporation in nearly all the countries dealt with in this volume.

PUBLIC CONTROLS OVER GOVERNMENT ENTERPRISE

The manner and extent of public controls over Government enterprise is the most important and delicate aspect of the whole problem of balancing commercial and managerial autonomy against the minimum of supervision demanded by the public character and purpose of government enterprise. French and Italian doctrine have elaborated certain distinctions, referred to by Professors Lévy and Treves, between *a priori* and *a posteriori* controls. The former called "*tutelle*" (*tutela*) express the power of the State to approve or disapprove certain actions of the enterprises, as a condition of their legal validity. The latter (*contrôle, vigilanza*) indicate the power of the State to annul or correct certain transactions. But Professor Lévy points out that *tutelle* and *contrôle* are, in France becoming increasingly intertwined.

Another division is functional, determined by the type of public authority concerned. To the three types of control analysed in Mr. Drake's paper—which represent the administrative, legislative and judicial branches of Government—we might add a fourth: audit control.

(1) Ministerial control

The extent of Ministerial and other executive direction over the activities of the public corporations is perhaps the most crucial but also the most elusive of all the problems which this new form of enterprise creates.

As we have seen, some countries prefer to make the Minister or his representative a member of the board itself. Others tend to reduce the status of an independent corporation to that of a Government department whenever the wish prevails that the executive and the Government should have a direct controlling influence over its management. In all these cases (such as a number of Canadian corporations) the position is relatively clear. There is no attempt to disguise the directive influence of the Government on the management of the corporation although, of course, in practice such direction may be more or less pronounced according to the personality of the Minister, the status of the corporation, the strength of its permanent personnel and other variable factors. The real problem arises in the great majority of cases where the corporation is supposed to be autonomous in its management but subject

23. See Diplock L.J. in *BBC* v. *Johns* [1965] Ch. 32.

M

to general direction from the Government. There is not a single country represented in this volume which denies the right of Ministerial direction altogether. Indeed, the very idea of the public corporation would make such a position impossible. But there is almost infinite variety as to the extent of the directive and controlling powers of the Government. The most usual form of control is the requirement of Ministerial approval for certain transactions. This is a general feature in countries where public corporations are part of the structure of administrative law and thus under the control of their administrative superiors. In France, the *Conseil d'État* has expressly affirmed the right of Government supervision over the activities of public corporations, including the power of approval for important decisions and the budgets of the corporations. In the common law countries, the principle of autonomy is more strongly developed. In Britain, only a limited range of decisions and transactions of the corporations require Ministerial approval. However, it is almost impossible to assess accurately the real, as distinct from the theoretical, extent of the powers because relations between the corporation and the competent Minister are inevitably close and continuous; in many cases it may be that Ministerial direction is not exercised openly, but behind closed doors, that it does not take the form of a directive but of mutual consultation or other informal contacts. Professor Robson[24] has criticised the Ministerial tendency in Britain of "talking things over with the chairman at lunch, in the club, in the House of Commons, in the department, without disclosing either to the public or to Parliament the real extent of their intervention." In a country like the Soviet Union, any autonomy of an economic or indeed any other organisations can only be relative. Political and planning authorities cannot recognise any legally binding limits, which would prevent them from interfering with management when they consider intervention necessary in the interests of the national plan or political conformity, or for other reasons of which the executive itself is the sole judge. But Professor Abel shows that in the United States too—at least in the federal sphere—the Ramspeck Act of 1940 and the Government Corporation Control Act of 1945 between them have gone far to destroy the usefulness of the Government corporation as a relatively independent organ of public enterprise. Traditional distrust and hostility toward the idea of public undertakings seem to have combined in this case. The Ramspeck Act authorised the application of civil service laws to employees of federally-owned and controlled corporations (with the exception of the Tennessee Valley Authority), at the discretion of the President, who has made much use of this authority. More serious, however, was the Government Corporation Control Act of 1945 which subjects Government corporations to ordinary budgetary and auditing requirements, and also authorises the Director of the Budget to recommend their treatment as standard Government agencies. This must be taken together with the fact

24. *Nationalised Industry and Public Ownership* (1960), at p. 162.

that the "Comptroller-General and the General Accounting Office have never confined themselves to standard auditing operations . . . " and that "the tradition as developed by them has been not that of verifying but approving accounts, of reviewing expenditures or commitments to determine whether they are authorised in the light of the interpretation of the statutes deemed proper by the Comptroller-General." As in addition all the Government corporations are financed by annual or bi-annual Congressional appropriations, it may not be unfair to conclude that the public corporations—at least on the federal level—no longer enjoy much autonomy in the United States.[25]

On the other hand, in the countries with public law systems and ideas of the continental type, we have already seen that the classification of a public corporation as a public authority inexorably subjects it to Government control over its policy, its finance and its management. This seems to leave the major countries of the British Commonwealth, as those in which the most serious effort at blending autonomy and policy direction has been made. In Australia, one of the pioneer countries of the public corporation, the degree of Ministerial direction varies greatly, as is shown by Professor Zines' detailed survey of the various statutes. What he observes of the Australian situation is surely of general application.

In the case "of many . . . corporations, the power of the Minister or the Government to control the corporation has been limited by statute to . . . express matters. . . . Of course, by virtue of control over these matters, it may be possible for the Minister to indirectly control the policy of the corporation, especially where the corporation is dependent for the major part of its funds on annual appropriations by the Parliament." Recent statutes, a detailed opinion of the Solicitor-General, and an inquiry of the Joint Parliamentary Committee of Public Accounts all agree on the principle that Ministerial control should be confined to matters of policy, as distinct from day-to-day management. But this may, as Professor Zines observes, be an empty distinction unless statutory or administrative guidelines spell out the distinction.

Similar problems emerge from the now massive legislation and considerable practical experience of the numerous British public corporations. For Canada, Professor Hodgetts indicates a tendency in recent statutes to introduce the Ministerial power of issuing directives. Moreover, as we have seen, the Canadian practice favours the inclusion of a member of the staff of a Ministry on the governing board itself, which tends to reduce its autonomy.

The general pattern adopted in virtually all the British statutes, regulating the recently nationalised industries, is a Ministerial power to give "directions of a general character as to the exercise and performance by that corporation of their functions in relation to matters appearing to the Minister to affect the national interest." In addition to these powers there are certain specific

25. State Corporations—e.g. those of New York State—are, in autonomy of management and finance, much closer to the British type of public corporation.

powers of approval where a major outlay of capital for development is involved, with regard to certain appointments and, in a number of other cases.[26] The term "national interest" has been criticised in Parliament and elsewhere, and it may be that "national security" would have limited the power of interference. Generally, the power of issuing directions has been used with restraint. During the first decade of operations only a few directions were given: the former Iron and Steel Corporation was restrained from altering the structure of the industry, pending its denationalisation; a decision by the Transport Commission to increase London passenger tariffs was vetoed. On a later occasion, a Labour Minister interfered with the fixing of steel prices by the then nationalised Iron and Steel Corporation—an action which led to the resignation of the chairman. A much publicised and debated Ministerial interference was the direction given by the Minister of Aviation a few years ago to the BOAC to purchase a number of British-made VC-10 aircraft, well in excess of the number deemed desirable by the board. The direction was later modified. Far more influence than would appear in official directives can be exercised behind the scenes; in particular, as a single Government authority, the Minister for Fuel and Power, is responsible for four of the major corporations concerned: The National Coal Board (as well as the Area Electricity and Gas Boards), The Gas Council, the British Electricity Authority and the Atomic Energy Authority. This position underlines the point made by Professors Hodgetts and Robson: if the power of issuing directives is to become the general pattern, then it is particularly important that formal Ministerial or Cabinet directives should be fully publicised so that Parliament can know who has made the final decisions. Without such requirements parliamentary control is likely to become increasingly fictitious; but no theoretical provision can solve what is essentially a permanent and inevitable tension to be reduced by practice, custom and enlightened administration. The most important factor reducing undue Ministerial or political interference in the management of the corporations will be their efficiency and their success. The experience of the Tennessee Valley Authority, the Canadian and Australian Government airlines, the Ontario Hydro-Electric, and of some, at least, of the British nationalised industries, shows that after a certain time a well-managed public corporation can establish a status and a respect which will prevent undue interference. In regard to day-to-day management, British practice appears already to be settled. The Ministers will not normally answer questions in Parliament relating to day-to-day management and the current conduct of business operations.

(2) The co-ordination of Government control

Only a few countries have made attempts to create special Government organs for the co-ordination of controls over government enterprises. The most im-

26. They are discussed in detail in Mr. Drake's paper, see above pp. 33 *et seq.*.

portant is the Ministry for State Participations, set up in Italy in 1956. As Professor Treves points out, the Minister, through his power to issue general directives to the Government-controlled enterprises, exercises considerable influence, though he does not supersede the control exercised by the Ministers functionally concerned with the different enterprises. The Minister for State Participation must submit an annual report to Parliament. Another model which requires careful study is the institution of the State Comptroller created in 1949 in Israel. The statute provides that this office is established "for maintaining control over the financial activities, the economic enterprises and the property of the State." As Dr. Yadin reports, his supervisory functions comprise Government departments, State undertakings or institutions and any other undertakings, institutions, funds or bodies in whose management the Government participates. The office of the State Comptroller is linked with parliamentary control as the Comptroller must submit yearly reports to the *Knesset*, the Parliament of Israel.

But elsewhere, Governmental controls remain apportioned among various departments and authorities, without overall co-ordination. In Great Britain there is still no institutional co-ordination between the administrative policies concerning the different public corporations. It is, to some extent, an accident that one Minister, the Minister for Fuel and Power, has supervisory authority over four of the industrial corporations, which are in sharp competition with each other, as they supply competing forms of energy. Although some co-ordination is achieved by consultation between the different Ministers, this co-ordination is likely to be occasional and secret. Other countries would do well to study the Saskatchewan example where the Government Finance Office "is not only a central financial agency through which the legislature and the Treasury Department are able to operate, . . . but also an agency for co-ordinating and reviewing policies pursued by particular corporations." This co-ordination includes personnel policy, salary questions, accounting methods and expansion programmes.[27]

On the whole, efforts to co-ordinate policies and administrative practices of the different public corporations and other State enterprises are still exceptional, but it is a safe prediction that the demand for such co-ordination will become steadily more urgent.[28]

(3) Parliamentary control

The question of the extent to which Parliament does and should control the operations of the public corporations is an exceedingly difficult one, as it goes to the root of modern democracy. Almost all the countries dealt with in this volume have provided for some form of parliamentary control. The usual

27. See Blakeney in Friedmann, *op. cit. supra*, note 7, at p. 102.
28. The French *Rapport sur les Entreprises Publiques* (1967) is sceptical of Government co-ordination of public enterprises, because of the differences in their functions and needs; but it recommends a "Holding Centrale" for all State participations.

practice is that of submitting regular accounts through the competent Minister to Parliament. In Great Britain, where the question of parliamentary debate on the activities of the public corporation has been the subject of extensive discussion,[29] the affairs of the public corporations are usually discussed through parliamentary questions or through debates which may take place under several different procedures.[30] Some agreement has been reached on the borderline between interference with day-by-day management and debates on general policy questions. In the field of parliamentary control, Britain has pioneered, through the institution of the Select Committee on Nationalised Industries of 1956. There is general agreement that this Committee has, through a number of careful and searching reports, greatly helped in the understanding of the problems of Government enterprises. While the reports have often been critical, they have also provided valuable links between Parliament and the boards of the enterprises. There is a parallel institution in the Canadian Province of Saskatchewan which has provided a Select Parliamentary Committee on Crown Corporations. Other parliamentary committees, such as public accounts committees, or select committees on expenditure can, of course, to some extent, discuss the affairs of the corporations with the assistance of the Comptroller and Auditor-General. But, with the exception of the institutions just mentioned, parliamentary controls over public enterprises are diffuse and haphazard.

Professor Robson has recommended an efficiency audit commission.[31] A similar recommendation was made by the British Select Committee on Nationalised Industries some years ago. But, as Mr. Drake points out, the Select Committee still lacks an officer of the status of the Comptroller and Auditor-General, or one with high administrative experience, or a professional accountant. There appear to be many obvious advantages in a specialised public authority of this kind. Above all, this control extends to public enterprises whatever their specific form. As we have seen, many public enterprises are constituted in the form of joint-stock companies, and the difference between these and public corporations proper is often a matter of pure form or accident, and not one which should justify different treatment; certainly not where the State is the predominant or sole shareholder. Perhaps only an independent public administrative authority which is staffed with expert officials, can, in due course, acquire the necessary comprehensive judgment on the activities of public enterprises and their significance in the national economic life, on the efficiency of their management, on their actual or potential profitability, on their relations to private enterprise and other important aspects. Comprehensive information, filtered and analysed through

29. See the article by E. Davies M.P. in *Problems of Nationalised Industry* (ed. Robson), Chap. V.

30. They are enumerated in the Report of the Select Committee on Nationalised Industries (London, HMSO, 1953), p. 111.

31. In *Problems of Nationalised Industry*, at pp. 322 *et. seq.*

such an office, will probably make parliamentary control more effective than any other device.

(4) Audit control

It is, of course, generally accepted that the public corporation and similar public enterprises must be audited by independent experts. There is, however, a considerable variety of practice as to the question whether the Comptroller and Auditor-General, or private auditors should audit these corporations. In Britain the Labour Government, despite considerable objections in Parliament and elsewhere, insisted that the commercial character of the operations of the newly nationalised industries made it imperative that only commercial auditors should audit their affairs. A comparison shows that this is not the universal practice. In Australia, the audit is generally made by the Comptroller-General. The nationalised India Air Corporation, though otherwise closely modelled on the corresponding British Act, provides for audit by the Comptroller and Auditor-General. In Israel, the office of the State Comptroller combines general efficiency and policy control with auditing functions. In Canada, the industrial corporations are generally audited privately but recent statutes provide that the Auditor-General is eligible for this audit. In 1967, the Public Accounts Committee of the Canadian Parliament reported in favour of auditing of all public corporations by the Auditor-General. In the United States, as has already been mentioned, auditing is carried out by the Comptroller-General who is not only an auditor, but a critic of policy.

In the systems which have the Continental type of administrative law, the public audit control follows as a matter of course from the public law status of the public corporations. In France, the *Cour de Cassation* decided as early as 1856 that all public bodies whose funds form part of the public domain are subject to public accounting procedures. Their expenditure is now subject, it appears, to the dual control of *"controleûrs d'état"* established by laws of 1935 and 1944, and of the *"Cour des Comptes"* which is an independent administrative tribunal specifically concerned with the review of the financial management of Government departments and public enterprises. The nationalised industries are, in addition, subject to the control of a special Audit Commission (*Commission de Vérification des Comptes des Entreprises Publiques*) established in 1948 which has been described by Professor Drago[32] as "juridical" but which appears to exercise on behalf of Parliament functions not unlike those of the State Comptroller of Israel, or the Select Committee on Crown Corporations of Saskatchewan, as it "annually examines the accounts in general, the balance sheets and the profit and loss accounts of the nationalised enterprises, and draws from this examination its conclusions on their financial results." In Italy there are no fewer than three audits over public enterprises: the corporation's own boards of auditors, the Treasury

32. See Friedmann, *op. cit.* at p. 136.

and—since 1958— the *Corte di Conti*; these various auditing functions should, in Professor Treves' judgment, be both simplified and better co-ordinated. The *Corte di Conti* has functions similar to those of the French *Cour des Comptes* and the German *Rechnungshof*. The German railways under the new law are also subject to a dual control, first by a special Audit Office established within the organisation itself, and second, in their capacity as a public authority, by the Federal Audit Court (*Bundesrechnungshof*) which is entitled to demand any information that it deems proper.

On the whole, it is clear that most countries are still experimenting with the most appropriate form of audit control and the blending of commercial and public accountancy principles. There appears to be, however, an increasing tendency to create at least one organ which could specialise in the auditing and the general financial conduct of the public economic enterprises.

(5) Judicial control

Two forms of judicial control must be distinguished: on the one hand there is the general legal responsibility for breach of contract, tort or other actions which lead to legal sanctions. In the common law jurisdictions all the public corporations—not only those constituted in the form of commercial companies—appear now to be subject to the jurisdiction of the ordinary courts. In some cases, the statute has specifically declared them liable before the courts. Thus, the British Regional Hospital Boards, despite their expressed character as Crown servants, are expressly made legally liable before the courts. In other cases the legal liability follows from the constitution of the enterprise as a separate legal entity and from incidental provisions. In the Continental systems, the legal responsibility of the public enterprises is determined by their public law status. According to the doctrine and practice which, with some variations, has established itself in Germany, France and Italy alike, the public corporations, insofar as they are public authorities, are normally suable before the administrative courts. In that case they are treated according to the principles of administrative law which do, indeed, admit compensation for injuries done to third parties, but take into account the discretion claimed for the proper exercise of administrative functions. On the other hand, authorities exercising economic and commercial functions may choose to conclude their transactions in the form of private law and in that case are liable before the ordinary civil courts. For the third party, the jurisdiction of the administrative instead of the civil courts is not necessarily a disadvantage.[33]

Another aspect is the special control exercised over the public authorities restraining the abuse and the extension of statutory power conferred upon

33. As shown by the doctrine of *imprévision* developed by the *Conseil d'Etat*, which allows the private party to a Government contract a revision of terms when unforeseen circumstances have greatly upset the equilibrium, whereas the civil courts have constantly rejected such adjustments.

them. In the Continental jurisdictions this judicial supervision is exercised through the administrative courts, most of which have worked out tests based on the French concepts of "*excés de pouvoir*" and "*détournement de pouvoir*." These broadly correspond to the concept of abuse of power which has been developed in English law.[34] The powers of the public corporations, especially where they administer a public monopoly, are usually so widely framed that their actions cannot easily be invalidated.[35] In the Continental jurisdictions, where the practice of the courts has had time to establish itself over a very long period, the possibilities of judicial interference probably go somewhat further but there are now well-established principles which allow a fair measure of predictability comparable to the position in private law. It should, however, be pointed out that in Italy at least, side by side with this power of judicial invalidation which is controlled by established doctrine and precedent, a purely administrative invalidation of transactions by the public corporation is effected by exercise of the so-called *tutela*, and that for administrative as well as legal reasons. Such a state of affairs is apt to jeopardise the management of the corporations and the rights of third parties, who enter into transactions with the corporations.

On the whole, *ultra vires* supervision over public corporations, or the corresponding judicial control by administrative courts on the Continent is limited in scope. It is all the more important that they should, more explicitly and unambiguously than at present, be liable for their ordinary legal transactions in the same manner as another legal person.

SOME GENERAL CONCLUSIONS

This symposium shows that countries widely divergent in their social philosophy, their tradition, background and legal systems, have adopted some form of semi-autonomous public enterprise for certain tasks, because in every country which has reached a fairly advanced stage of industrial and social development, one or several of the three following factors exist: first, the necessity of certain long-term development schemes, especially in the field of public utilities, which none but the State is prepared to undertake, if necessary, at the risk of a permanent financial subsidy. Secondly, social and political ideas sufficiently widely accepted to demand that the State should take over responsibility for certain activities of economic and social life from private enterprise or develop new services (*e.g.* soil conservation or unemployment assistance). Thirdly, the growing technical complexity of social and economic managerial functions which make a more or less pronounced administrative independence for some public activities and services indispensable. In addition, public enterprise, largely in the form of development corporations, has

34. See *The Public Corporation*, pp. 123 *et seq.*, 182 *et seq.*, 222 *et seq.*, See also the discussion in Brown and Garner, *French Administrative Law*, *passim* and p. 123.

35. See for an example, the English case of *Smith* v. *London Transport Executive* [1951] A.C. 555.

become an essential instrument of economic development in the economically backward countries which have insufficient private venture capital to develop the utilities and industries which are given priority in the national development plan. Not infrequently, these public development corporations—such as the Uganda Development Corporation—directly or through subsidiaries, enter into partnerships with national or foreign private enterprises, or they offer shares to the public.

Certain common features of the public corporation emerge from the various experiments carried out in the different countries. These common features are: first, separate identity whether or not fully expressed in theoretical legal personality; secondly, separate management by an independent board of experts which is responsible for general policy to the executive, and in a more general way to the legislature; thirdly, a separate fund, whether it be provided by shares, by permanent capital assets or by recurrent appropriations; fourthly, public accountability through examination of the annual reports of the corporation by Parliament, and independent auditing, whether by commercial or public auditors, by administrative or quasi-judicial organs; fifthly, the approximation, as far as possible, of the legal status and responsibilities of these enterprises to those of private legal persons, without prejudice to their public responsibilities, which usually will characterise them as public authorities for purposes of Government and judicial supervision.

Beyond this, it would be difficult to discern common international features of the public corporation. As we have seen, many public enterprises take the form of joint-stock companies, usually because the State has acquired shares in these enterprises, often reluctantly and without any wish to upset the existing organisational and legal structure. But in these cases the deviations from the administration of the genuine joint-stock company are generally so considerable as to make this a highly questionable form of public economic activity. Where, as in most cases, State controlled joint-stock companies and public corporations exist side by side, it is most essential that, as in the case of the Israel State Comptroller or the Italian Ministry for State Participations, public enterprises of *all* types should be co-ordinated for purposes of administrative, political and audit control. The share company with public participation is, however, a useful and flexible instrument in certain circumstances: it is appropriate to genuine mixed enterprise where public and private capital together participate in a common venture with due distribution of risks and rights. Thus, the giant Italian State Corporations—notably the IRI—have established a network of subsidiaries constituted as commercial companies in which private capital participates to a considerable extent.

The commercial company form also commends itself where a public enterprise—such as a Governmental development corporation—engages in a joint venture with national or foreign private investors, and the respective degrees of financial interest and control must be expressed in percentages of shares.

Finally, the commercial company is a convenient vehicle for the full or partial privatisation of an originally wholly Government-owned enterprise.

The most important of the many problems with which every country under study struggles, mostly with indifferent success, is that of the proper balance of managerial autonomy and political responsibility, which latter involves a measure of public direction. Ultimately this is a matter of political practice and tradition which no written law can satisfactorily solve; but at least certain general principles seem to emerge from this comparative study: First, Ministerial control over Government enterprises should be confined to matters of general policy, and not extend to managerial detail, and the distinctions between policy and management matters should, as far as possible, be spelled out. Secondly, direction should, as far as possible, be open, not disguised, so as to enable the public and Parliament to assess the proper extent of autonomy and the policy problems involved. Thirdly, the control should be made more constructive and effective by a co-ordinating agency—such as the Israel State Comptroller or the Italian Ministry for State Participations, on the executive side—and a representative standing parliamentary committee on the legislative side, such as the British Select Committee on Nationalised Industries or the *Commission de Vérification des Comptes* on the Accounting side. These Committees should be provided with a professional staff. Fourthly, the Government enterprise, in its various forms, should be regarded as a new species of public authority which, in many ways, has a dual character. It should be detached far more than has been the case up to the present from the legal and administrative structure of the general public authority. This applies with particular force to the Continental systems where the theoretical preoccupation with classification has, especially in France and Italy, led to an excessive degree of public control, incompatible with the idea of a public corporation. Since, on the Continent as elsewhere, public corporations are usually created by special statute or decree, it appears perfectly possible to regulate their status separately as has been done in some cases. For example, special rules have been laid down on the status of employees, on the degree of Ministerial supervision, and other matters. A good example of special regulations for this type of enterprise is the German legislation on railways and postal services. Fifthly, it should be far more clearly than hitherto recognised that the functions of State and Government have widened and changed to the extent where they demand institutions with new features. Commercial, industrial and other managerial functions are today proper Government functions, but they require, in many ways, a special type of legal organisation. Where the Continental countries struggle against the fetters of their theory of administrative law, the common law countries are still obstructed by remnants of feudal theory which has provided the Government—Crown or Republic—with certain immunities and privileges. How far these privileges as such should still remain is a separate question. In so far as they do remain—and they are still considerable—they should not extend to any of the public corporations, either as regards legal liability and legal rights, or as exemption from taxes and charges, priority or privileges in debt collection, etc. The combination of public law controls, on the one hand, and private law personality, on the other hand, may still be a difficult matter to accept for the legal purist, but it is absolutely essential.

Compared with these fundamental matters, such questions as whether the employees of a public corporation should be civil servants or not, whether auditing should be by commercial or public auditors, an audit court or a combination of all these institutions, or even whether the administrative courts (where they exist) rather than the ordinary courts should have jurisdiction over public corporations and other enterprises are of relatively subordinate importance.

The organisation and co-ordination of a form of government enterprise that blends managerial autonomy and flexibility with public policy controls is a task of increasing urgency. The sphere of government responsibility will have to be vastly increased, as a result of the belated recognition that drastic control over economic development, over the balance of town and country, and, above all, over the uses of water, earth and air—on an international as well as a national scale—are nothing less than a condition of civilised survival. These are, of necessity, public responsibilities. In a growing number of cases, public, or joint public-private enterprises will have to carry out these functions. It is the lawyer's task and opportunity to improve and sharpen the legal tools.

APPENDIX

APPENDIX

THE GOVERNMENT'S REPLY TO THE
REPORT OF THE SELECT COMMITTEE *

In Chapter 4 is to be found a highly critical account of the report of the Select Committee on Nationalised Industries on Ministerial Control of those industries.

The Government have now issued their reply to the report.[1] It begins with a welcome to "this valuable and comprehensive Report" and then proceeds to reject or sidestep its principal recommendations.

The Committee's most important proposal regarding organisation was the creation of a Ministry of Nationalised Industries to be responsible for their efficiency. The Government reject this major change in the machinery of government on four grounds: (1) It would be a mistake to separate responsibility for efficiency from responsibility for the wider public interest, which would remain with other Ministries, because the two aspects are inextricably linked. (2) The sector Ministries are concerned with the economic health of private as well as public enterprise (the interest of the Minister of Power in the privately owned oil industry is an example), and it would be wrong to separate them. (3) The separation of responsibility for efficiency and for the public interest in respect of each nationalised industry would involve more work and increased staff both for the Government and the public corporations. Conflicts between "efficiency" and the public interest would be harder to resolve if each were handled by a separate department and the chairmen of the nationalised industries could be faced with very embarrassing situations. (4) The Government do not share the Select Committee's belief that the creation of a Ministry responsible only for the efficiency of nationalised industries would reduce Ministerial intervention, since the supervision of efficiency could cover not only existing statutory controls but many others as well.

The most important economic recommendation of the Select Committee was a fervent belief in the virtues of marginal cost pricing which they insisted should be the standard policy for the nationalised industries. The Government's reply is a superb example of diplomatic evasion. It merely states that the Government "welcome the Committee's general endorsement of the policy for pricing set out in Cmnd. 3437" [the White Paper on Economic and Financial Objectives]. The Committee suggested that this policy had not been laid down with sufficient clarity to be an unambiguous guide to the indus-

---

* Postscript to Chap. 4 by Professor W. A. Robson. Reprinted by kind permission from *Political Quarterly*, Vol 40, at p. 494.
[1] Cmnd. 4027/1969, H.M.S.O.

tries making individual pricing decisions. The Government point out that the White Paper was intended "only as a statement of general principles, in which it was necessary to set out a series of possible qualifications of the marginal costing principles" (para. 20). The Government declare their intention of elaborating these principles and qualifications in working out pricing policies with the industries.

As I point out in Chapter 4 the Treasury White Paper expressed a very far-sighted and balanced view about pricing policy which the Select Committee transformed into a series of dogmatic statements of an unrealistic and exaggerated kind. The Government reply does not advance one inch beyond its previous attitude—it merely ignores the steamed up views of the Select Committee.

The Government is conciliatory in accepting proposals by the Select Committee for further discussions about this and that while not conceding any firm commitment for change. Thus, they accept the recommendation that discussions should take place between the Treasury, D.E.A. and the departments to clarify their respective roles in the control of investment; that sponsoring departments should take the initiative in bringing together the nationalised industries to discuss common problems; that the public corporations should have opportunities to meet the Treasury and explain their investment programmes and other matters. The Government promises to bear in mind the recommendation that Ministers should publish periodic White Papers about the performance and prospects of the industries. They accept that periodic reviews of the test discount rate for investment decisions should be made, based on the evidence available from the private sector. They are willing to discuss with the industries the problem of devising a capital-rationing system for use when cuts in investment are necessary. They will re-examine, as the Committee urged, the case for repealing the existing Ministerial controls over the research and training programmes of the nationalised industries.

On the other hand, the Government are unwilling to introduce legislative sanctions for Ministerial control over pricing policies. They are unwilling to promise that Ministers will refrain from examining and deciding on individual investment projects. They do not agree that Ministers' powers should be extended so as to have a statutory right to issue formal directives on any matter which appears to them to be in the national interest. The reply states that possession of such wide general powers would in the Government's view lead to increased pressure on Ministers to interfere with the management of the industries. This in turn would require additional staff to be employed in the whole field in which such powers could be exercised. The Government prefer the existing Ministerial relationships with the industries which they regard as broadly satisfactory. "Within this framework practical conventions and usage have evolved which preserve an acceptable degree of autonomy for the industries while at the same time providing the necessary degree of accountability to Parliament" (para. 17).

It would hardly be possible to make a statement which more strongly contradicts the whole tenor and the main arguments of the Select Committee's report, with its explicit denunciation of the motives which underlie Ministerial action, its frequently reiterated allegation that Ministers are suffering from confused ideas in their relations with the public corporations, its censorious attitude towards almost every aspect of the Minister–Board relationship, and its general tone of superiority and condescension towards departments in their dealings with the public corporations.

The Government have indeed thought not twice but several times about adopting the panaceas for public enterprise contained in the Mikardo report. It is to be hoped that the Conservative Party will be equally level headed in its response.

INDEX